WHAT THE CHURCH IS ALL ABOUT

A Biblical and Historical Study

By

EARL D. RADMACHER

MOODY PRESS
CHICAGO

To
my wife, Ruth,
who has been a constant
source of help and strength
as my co-heir (1 Pet 3:7)

Moody Press Edition, 1978

Original Title:
THE NATURE OF THE CHURCH

The use of selected references from various versions of the Bible in this publication does not necessarily imply publisher endorsement of the versions in their entirety.

Library of Congress Cataloging in Publication Data

Radmacher, Earl D
What the church is all about.
First published under title: The nature of the church.
Bibliography: p. 394.
Includes indexes.
1. Church. I. Title.

BV600.2.R29 1978 262'.7 78-16993

ISBN 0-8024-9407-2

Printed in the United States of America

CONTENTS

PREFACE TO THE REVISED EDITION

Before we can talk about what the church ought to *do,* we must understand what the church *is.* Understanding the nature of the church is basic and foundational to the programming of its activities. If, for example, the church rather than the world is the "field," with an admixture of "wheat and tares" (re Augustine) in Christ's parable of Matthew 13, then its mission will be quite different from its mission if it is composed of only the regenerate. The purpose, the mission, and the organization of the church are all based on its nature.

This question of the nature of the church was basic in 1948 in Amsterdam when the World Council of Churches began, and it is still basic today. Names have changed, but the trends are the same. The trend toward the external, visible union of the church continues to progress. In 1960 it was Pope John XXIII and the Archbishop of Canterbury, Dr. Geoffrey Francis Fisher. Today it is Pope Paul VI and the present Archbishop of Canterbury, Donald Coggan. The goal is still the same: one world church. The latest development, presented by the twenty-one-member Anglican-Catholic International Commission, is a forty-four hundred word product of eight years of study called "The Authority of the Church." This proposal, which would link 580 million Roman Catholics and 60 million Anglicans, states that Rome should have authority over the union.

Other conferences on union are mounting as well. The year 1978 promises to be the time when Lutheran and Roman Catholic theologians will culminate a series of sessions with a joint statement on papal infallibility. An unprecedented conference is represented by the National Council of Churches' Christian-Moslem Task Force. Members of seven denominations are co-operating in the program, which is seeking reconciliation and understanding between Christians and Moslems.

While these efforts at union are interpreted positively by some, even among evangelicals, many others see them as dark, foreboding clouds of the apostate church of the end times.

At the same time, however, there are promising developments taking place within some churches. In contrast to the tongue-lashing the church was receiving in the 50s and 60s, especially by parachurch movements, the 70s have witnessed a growing respect for the centrality of the church in the program of Christ on earth and a growing understanding of the church's nature. One of the books that may yet prove to have been a landmark or a turning point in this new respect for the church is Findley Edge's *The Greening of the Church*. Undoubtedly many factors were involved in the change of attitude toward the church, but there has been a definite move from preaching "What Is Wrong with the Church?" toward preaching "What Is Right with the Church?" Furthermore, parachurch ministries have recognized this change in attitude and have thus felt it necessary to justify their existence by claiming to be an "arm of the church."

Not only has there been a growing respect for churches that are founded on the Word of God and are committed to the Christ of the Word, but there has been a clearer understanding of their nature, organization, and mission. Books such as *Body Life* by Ray Stedman, *The Community of the Spirit* by Norman Kraus, and *God's Forgetful Pilgrims* by Michael Griffiths have driven home the idea of the church as community and the importance of "one-to-another" in Scripture. Instead of seeing the church as simply a congregation of independent believer-priests who gather from time to time to receive cognitive input and then go their separate ways, believers began to recognize their role as dependent sheep who need to recognize their need for each other and their responsibility to demonstrate submission to Christ by being in submission to the leadership as well as the membership of the flock, the church of God.

As I look to the future, I believe that the churches that are true to the Word of God are in for some of their most glorious days as they meet the challenges of balancing evangelization and education, discerning the work of the church gathered and the work of the church scattered, mobilizing the church through the discovery and development of spiritual gifts, and clarifying the role of a shared, multiple leadership.

Should our Lord choose to tarry in His return for His church, I anticipate the years ahead with great excitement.

EARL D. RADMACHER

1

THE INTRODUCTION

I. The Importance of the Subject

In August 1948, Christian leaders came to Amsterdam from all parts of the world to participate in the historic assembly that brought the World Council of Churches into being. Behind all the theological discussion, the most urgent question that faced them was, What is the church? "The first fact to face," said the moderator, "is that there is no agreed Christian interpretation of the doctrine of the Church."[1] This initial impetus set in motion an unending stream of ecclesiological discussion and definition. Theological liberalism, becoming increasingly convinced that society and man cannot be remade simply by education and science, claims to have "rediscovered" the church. An eminent spokesman, J. Robert Nelson, states:

> The recovery and elaboration of the doctrine of the nature of the Church is one of the chief aspects of Protestant theology in this century. It was preceded by a long period of unrestrained individualism, which regarded the Church as being extraneous to the Christian faith and a strictly human, mundane organization. For this important change there are at least three reasons: the wide consensus of biblical scholars that the Church belongs to the saving work of Jesus Christ; the struggles of Christians during the two world wars and under tyrannical persecution and their need to distinguish the Church from the rest of mankind; the encounters of the divided denom-

1. The World Council of Churches, *Man's Disorder and God's Design,* 1:17.

> inations in mission fields and in the ecumenical movement. This recovered doctrine has to do not merely with what the Church *does* in the world, but with what it *is*.[2]

Evidencing a certain anxiety, Brunner asks:

> What is the church? This question poses the unsolved problem of Protestantism. From the days of the Reformation to our own time, it has never been clear how the church, in the sense of spiritual life and faith—the fellowship of Jesus Christ—is related to the institutions conventionally called churches.[3]

Thus, scarcely any concept of Christian doctrine of the present time stands so greatly in need of clarification from the ground up as that of the church.

ECCLESIASTICAL ECUMENICITY

Among the several attempts to answer this question have been the proposed solutions of the ecumenical movement. This movement has perhaps gained its greatest momentum in the recent pronouncement by Eugene Carson Blake, moderator of the United Presbyterian Church:

> I propose to the Protestant Episcopal Church that it together with the United Presbyterian Church in the United States of America invite the Methodist Church and the United Church of Christ to form with us a plan of Church Union.[4]

This proposal given in San Francisco in December 1960 for merger of four church bodies bringing together nearly twenty million communicants is not important because of its uniqueness, for merger talk is scarcely novel in the current theological debate concerning the nature of the church. The suggestion is extremely significant, however, because of the excited reaction

2. J. Robert Nelson, "Church," in *A Handbook of Christian Theology*, ed. Marvin Halverson and Arthur A. Cohen, p. 53.
3. Emil Brunner, *The Misunderstanding of the Church*, p. 5.
4. Eugene Carson Blake, "A Proposal Toward the Reunion of Christ's Church," *Christian Century* 77:1508.

that it evoked. Television cameras, radio microphones, and a crowd of reporters and photographers were on the spot to capture the pulse of the people—and it was high. Never before has the mood for merger been so intense. Episcopal Bishop Pike called the idea as important in church history "as the Reformation itself."[5]

This rapidly advancing trend toward ecclesiastical ecumenicity is not simply the ill-begotten religious fervor of some small segment of Christendom. Rather, it includes, to a greater or lesser extent, all major religious bodies. Thus, ecumenicity is one phase of the current theological debate on the nature of the church. It is having an airing in Roman Catholic, liberal, and orthodox circles.

Roman Catholic ecumenicity

For the first time in more than three hundred years the Roman Catholic Church is now making gestures of friendly feeling toward the other branches of Christendom. The first of such gestures was proffered to Dr. Geoffrey Francis Fisher, Archbishop of Canterbury, when he had an audience with Pope John XXIII on December 2, 1960. Fisher said that the Pope expressed "his great desire—as he did on many other occasions—to increase brotherly feelings among all men."[6] Further ecumenical discussions are in the offing according to the new Greek Orthodox Metropolitan of Canada, Bishop Athenagoras of Toronto. The summit meeting for which tentative plans have been arranged would include Pope John XXIII, the Archbishop of Canterbury, and Ecumenical Patriarch Athenagoras of Istanbul. As an effective bulwark against Communism, the bishop suggests a federation that would give equal status to the Orthodox, Roman Catholic, and Anglican communities.

It is evident then that Rome is making renewed and intensive effort to realize her concept of the church, a universal visible

5. "Merger," *Christian Herald* 84:6.
6. "Homage and Courtesy," *Christianity Today* 5:247.

institution under the autocratic headship of one man who is supposed to be the vicar of Christ. Young observes:

> The Roman Catholic church has never joined with other religious bodies unless she was completely in control of the situation. Couple with this the fact the spirit in the non-Roman Catholic world today is that of uniting churches at any price, doctrinally speaking. Put these two things together and it is not difficult to imagine organized Christianity in rapport and under the domination of Rome once again.[7]

Liberal Protestant ecumenicity

Liberalism finds the epitome of its expression in the proposals of the National Council of Churches. The council, too, feels that the petition of Christ for unity in John 17 cannot possibly be realized until there is one world church. The now immortal proposal by the noted champion of ecumenicity, Eugene Carson Blake of the United Presbyterian Church in the U.S.A., seems to imply that the secret of the success of the church can be found in bigness. The advocate of the big church feels that society would be better off—it could even be saved—if only church institutions could be bigger. He has found that a loosely knit federation on a cooperative basis has not accomplished his desire of a world church. The cry now is to "shed the blood of our denominational separateness." It seems that Charles Clayton Morrison spoke prophetically when he stated many years ago exactly what Blake and others declare today:

> It is this amorphous character of the Church of Christ, its formlessness, its intangibleness, its invisibility and its empirical impotence that the ecumenical movement is out to overcome. In a word, the whole aspiration and purpose of this world-wide movement among Christians is to bring the Church of Christ into an empirical existence so that we *can* see it, *can* lay hold of it and so that it *can* lay hold of us and draw us into itself. The goal of the ecumenical movement cannot be envisaged in

7. G. Douglas Young, *The Bride and the Wife*, p. 70.

> any terms short of the actual embodiment of the now unembodied Church of Christ.[8]

More recently, to a plenary session of the assembly, James I. McCord, President of Princeton Seminary stated: "Cooperation is not enough. . . . It is a luxury now that we can no longer afford. . . . We must take a radical step forward in our quest for visible, corporate unity."[9]

As a practical way to begin implementing the desired unity at the local level, Bishop Pike suggested that denominations begin establishing new churches on a cooperative basis, in a sort of "federated" operation within local congregations. In other words, a single congregation might well be fully a part of several denominations. This arrangement could include multiple ordinations if necessary. Pike stated: "I envision a single congregation with multi-denominational connections as a practical step preliminary to church union."[10]

This, then, is the liberal answer to the question of the nature of the church. The goal is nothing less than a one world superchurch. It is most interesting to note, however, that there is not unanimity of endorsement of this program by liberals. Rather sarcastically Bishop Gerald Kennedy recently quipped: "Any man who raises a question about the desirability of church union is regarded suspiciously as if he had spoken against prayer or virtue."[11] Because of the incisiveness of his thinking on this subject, portions of the remainder of his article are now quoted at length.

> Now we are being told that we must all move into one organic union just as fast as we can. People get all excited by the suggestion that there are three churches where there ought to be one. No one asks whether this is the way forward and no

8. Charles Clayton Morrison, *The Unfinished Reformation*, p. 54.
9. "News," *Christianity Today* 5:245.
10. Ibid.
11. Gerald Kennedy, "The Church and Unity," *Christian Century* 78:170.

one raises the possibility that we might find more questions than answers on this route. . . .

We thought at one time that a smaller world would mean more peace and goodwill among men. Recent events have not substantiated this theory. Relatives who get along fine when they come together at Christmas often have a bad time of it when they all move into the same house. Some of the worst in-fighting that I have observed was not between leaders of different denominations but between the leaders of the same denomination. Brethren, what little I know about human nature leads me to suspect that bringing 18 million church members into one organization will not necessarily produce either better or more effective Christians. . . .

One of the main problems of any church is its machinery. We must have organization to make a church function and the bigger the church the more machinery. This is something that is always overlooked by the "ecumaniacs." It all sounds so spiritual and satisfying until a skeptic begins to think of all the administration involved. Then my feet get chilled. Let us face it: the only way an ecclesiastical institution the size of the Roman Catholic Church can function effectively is to be authoritarian. Is this our goal? . . .

I am of the opinion that, generally speaking, Protestantism has been less effective in its organic unions than in its separateness and unity through councils and cooperation. I am not willing to cast aside what has proved to be effective in spite of many obvious weaknesses for a theory which has proved to be short on results where it has been tested. . . . Organic union is neither an ultimate aim nor a desirable one. . . . I believe that we can have unity in the best sense without an organic union of the Protestant churches.[12]

The foregoing quotations set forth the opposing forces within liberal Protestant ecumenicity. On the one hand are those who are making an almost hysterical plea for organizational unity; they make it appear that the church depends upon a human

12. Ibid., pp. 170-71.

institution for life and influence. They would destroy denominational seminaries, minimize theology and distinctive doctrines, and assimilate all denominations into one visible, organized church. The other ecumenical force would limit its activities to fostering good relations among existing Christian churches, manifesting their fundamental agreement, and stressing their spiritual unity.

It is most significant to note that in all of the liberal ecumenical dialogue there is no attempt to set forth what the authoritative Word of God says concerning the nature of the church. Invariably their goals are pragmatic. The emphasis is upon building a bigger and better corporate institution so that they can control the unruly forces in society and thus control history. The biblical "Thus saith the Lord" is conspicuous by its absence. Thus, the liberal stress on ecumenicity demands a thorough biblical investigation of the nature of the church. There remains yet one further ecumenical emphasis.

Orthodox Protestant ecumenicity

The spokesmen for this group call their attitude neoevangelicalism, indicating thereby that there is something new that should claim the attention of Christians today. Among their contentions is the charge that fundamentalists have "neglected the doctrine of the Church."[13] Another attack has come from the pen of Edward J. Carnell:

> I concluded that fundamentalism had formulated its view of the church with an eye to the interests of the cult. Fundamentalists believe they are superior because they have withdrawn from the historic denominations; they imagine that they alone glorify the gospel. Since the fundamentalist is deprived of the happy security which comes from communion with the church universal, he must devise substitute securities all his own.[14]

13. Carl F. H. Henry, *Evangelical Responsibility in Contemporary Theology*, p. 46.
14. Edward John Carnell, "How My Mind Has Changed," *Christian Century* 77: 378.

While there are those in the orthodox camp contending for a more ecumenical outlook concerning the nature of the church, there are also equally outspoken men of orthodoxy who oppose the endeavors of neoevangelicalism. Edwin J. Young, professor of Old Testament at Westminster Theological Seminary, states:

> Perhaps it is not incorrect to say that the New Evangelicalism would like to build up the church without any reference to the church. It stresses evangelism, and does not always show itself discriminate with respect to those whom it invites to support it. It stresses scholarship and education. In fact, it stresses just about everything except the all-important doctrine of the church, and the need for vigorous contending for the Faith. . . . Is then the New Evangelicalism the answer to the present-day situation? For our part we say no, and we say no emphatically. Here is a temporary phenomenon, and the sooner it passes, the better for the church. . . . There is much in Fundamentalism that is admirable, and if we were compelled to choose between Fundamentalism and New Evangelicalism, we should choose Fundamentalism without any hesitation.[15]

Thus, within the ranks of those calling themselves orthodox is a wide divergence of opinion concerning the nature of the church. This very disagreement demands a thorough investigation of the doctrine of the church. John Sanderson sounds an appeal:

> A crying need today is a study of the doctrine of the Church against the background of today's needs and opportunities. Such a study would neither emphasize one aspect of ecclesiology at the expense of the other nor view the two aspects of the Church as totally distinct. . . .
>
> A greater appreciation then of the doctrine of the Church can serve to correct false tendencies and perhaps to hold errant

15. Edward J. Young, "Where Are We Going?," *The Presbyterian Guardian* 28:154.

> emotions in check as wild charges are brought to the judgment of a full-orbed Scripture doctrine. When this is done, purity and unity will be seen in their true light, and neither will be sacrificed for the other.[16]

There is the call from both sides, then, for a deeper understanding of the doctrine of the church. The neoevangelical charges that the fundamentalist has forgotten the unity of believers, while the fundamentalist charges that all too frequently church membership is meaningless.

It has been seen, then, that the prominence of the church in contemporary theological debate demands an investigation of its very essence and nature in order to determine its God-appointed place in the world today. There is yet another factor, however, that points up the importance of this investigation. It may be termed theological reactionism.

THEOLOGICAL REACTIONISM

Someone has said, "The pendulum of the clock does not stop in the middle but swings from one extreme to the other." Such is also often the case in theological formulations. It is usually difficult for a person to maintain a balance of expression when he is particularly zealous to strike a note that has long been missing. G. C. Berkouwer has very adequately expressed the problem:

> Reaction is a phenomenon in Christian thought that has played a large role in the history of the Church and its theology. Reaction from some unbiblically one-sided proposition has often landed theology in another unbiblically one-sided proposition. Theologians attacking a caricatured theology have often created their own caricature of Christian thought. Observing that a given aspect of faith was neglected, Christians have often proceeded to accentuate that aspect so much that it

16. John W. Sanderson, *Fundamentalism and Its Critics*, pp. 38-39.

> became the be-all of the faith, with a resulting neglect of other aspects.[17]

Although Berkouwer applies this to the doctrine of election, the words are also apropos for ecclesiology. On the one hand, in some cases there has been an emphasis on the universal church to the practical elimination of any place for the local church. On the other hand, theological reactionism has produced such an emphasis on the local church in some quarters that it has resulted in the denial of the universal church.

Emphasis on the universal church

One of the finest treatments of systematic theology in print is that written by Lewis Sperry Chafer. Areas of theology that are often neglected by other authors are given adequate biblical treatment in these volumes. Ecclesiology is one of those areas that had previously suffered from neglect and inadequate treatment. After outlining the three major divisions of ecclesiology (i.e., the organism that is the body of Christ, the organization that is the visible, local expression of the body of Christ, and the walk and service of those who are saved), he points out a serious weakness:

> Though of tremendous importance, the first and third of these divisions are practically never treated in works of Systematic Theology, while the second, if mentioned at all, is usually restricted to peculiar features of some sect or branch of the visible church with specific reference to organization and ordinances.[18]

Later Chafer expresses the reason for this neglect:

> The all but universal disregard on the part of theologians for the Pauline revelation respecting the Church has wrought confusion and damage to an immeasurable degree. Two fac-

17. G. C. Berkouwer, "Election and Doctrinal Reaction," *Christianity Today* 5:586.
18. Lewis Sperry Chafer, *Systematic Theology*, 4:29.

> tors serve as paramount causes of this deplorable neglect, namely, (a) the Reformation did not recover this truth as formerly it was held by the early church, and (b) the attitude of the theologians, being bound and confined within the limitations of Reformation truth, has been that of avoiding what to them seems new.[19]

Chafer feels that it was not until the middle of the last century that this extensive and important body of teaching was set forth into a doctrinal declaration, and that by J. N. Darby, from whom sprang the Brethren movement.[20] Concerning this movement, Chafer states:

> These highly trained men have produced an expository literature covering the entire Sacred Text which is not only orthodox and free from misconceptions and disproportionate emphasis, but essays to interpret faithfully the entire field of Biblical doctrine—that which theology confined to the Reformation failed to do.[21]

Many will agree that Darby and his followers made valuable and helpful contributions as genuine students of the Bible. At the same time, however, others will declare that in certain areas of ecclesiology Darby was deficient. Speaking of Darby's first ecclesiological pamphlet, "Considerations of the Nature and Unity of the Church of Christ," Goddard states:

> The indefiniteness and lack of perspicuity which characterize this article—his first ecclesiological paper—may be said to characterize almost all of his ecclesiological writings. . . . Certainly everyone who has read Darby's replies to Rochat and Olivier must agree with Neathy that they are "bewildering" and that "he says almost nothing explicitly, and we are left to catch glimpses of his meaning as we proceed."[22]

19. Ibid., 4:36-37.
20. Ibid., 4:37.
21. Ibid.
22. John Howard Goddard, "The Contribution of John Nelson Darby to Soteriology, and Eschatology," p. 160.

It should be remembered, however, that Darby lived in a day of much confusion concerning the church. The failure to distinguish between the church as the body of Christ composed only of living members and the church as the house of God—an external system in which there are tares—was, according to him, the root of many and serious errors. He writes:

> The thought that admission into the house conferred the privileges of the body has been the root of the systematic corruption of Christianity, which has acquired the reverence of ages, was not shaken off at the Reformation, and is now corrupting the Protestant systems, which were thought to have freed themselves from its fetters.[23]

Although there was evident justification for alarm, it seems that in his reactionism against apostasy in the organized churches he went to the other extreme and developed a system that minimized the organization. He declares:

> I fully recognize that there was an organization in apostolic and scriptural times, but affirm that what now exists is not the scriptural organization at all, but mere human invention, each sect arranging itself according to its own convenience, so that as an external body, the Church is ruined; and though much may be enjoyed of what belongs to the Church, I believe from Scripture that the ruin is without remedy.[24]

This emphasis had its effect indirectly on later Bible scholars who also reacted against the apostasy of the professing church and the unbiblical identification of the true church with the professing church. In some cases this led to a minimizing of the importance and function of the local church. One could gain such an impression from the following statement by Scofield.

> Much is said concerning the "mission of the church." The "church which is his body" has for its mission to build itself up

23. John Nelson Darby, *The Collected Writings of J. N. Darby*, ed. William Kelly, 14:23.
24. Ibid., 14:517.

> until the body is complete (Eph. 4:11; Col. 2:19), but the visible church, *as such,* is charged with no mission. The commission to evangelize the world is personal, and not corporate (Matt. 28:16-20; Mark 16:14-16; Luke 24:47, 48; Acts 1:8). So far as the Scripture story goes, the work of evangelization was done by individuals called directly of the Spirit to that work (Acts 8:5, 26, 27, 39; 13:2, etc.).[25]

Although these men themselves had a healthy respect for the local church and its responsibilities, their emphasis tended to cause some to neglect the local church. All too frequently it is said that "we want *Christ*ianity, not *church*ianity." The truth in the statement is that loyalty to a temporal organization can never replace, or even vie with, loyalty to our Saviour. But there is error in the statement. A true loyalty to Christ involves a love for, and a loyalty to, the church. A true doctrine of the church forbids setting the church over against Christ.

This reactionism that fails to give proper place to the local church demands further investigation of the doctrine of the church. There remains, however, one further element of reaction to be noted.

Emphasis on the local church

One person, disillusioned by the imperfections of the local church, finds his satisfaction in assurance that he belongs to the invisible church; another, appalled by the neglect of the local church, denies that there is any other. This latter emphasis seems to deny the universal church in order to exalt the local assembly. B. H. Carroll writes:

> All teaching in the direction that there now exists a general assembly which is invisible, without ordinances, and which is entered by faith alone, will likely tend to discredit the particular assembly, which does now really exist and which is the pillar and ground of the truth.

25. C. I. Scofield, *The Scofield Bible Correspondence School,* 3:431.

> More than once when I have inquired of a man, are you a member of the church? the reply has been, I am a member of the invisible, universal, spiritual church.[26]

Another educator writes in the same vein:

> If one is a member of the invisible church which is always considered the greater by those who believe in such an idea they are often satisfied to neglect the local church. Their attending, giving, and working in it is neglected to some extent usually because they really don't believe it is important.[27]

Others would deny, however, that the solution to the indifference of some toward the local church will be found in the abandonment of belief in the universal, invisible church. Van Gilder writes:

> However much we may deplore the tendency in some quarters to undervalue the local church, the corrective for over-emphasis in one direction is not over-emphasis in another; the corrective for one error is not the cultivation of another error.[28]

Having now examined the extremities of the contemporary debate concerning the nature of the church, one is able to realize more clearly the importance of a lucid, biblical investigation. What really is the body of Christ? Is it a visible, universal institution with a visible head such as the Roman Catholic Church has and such as the World Council of Churches seems to be striving for? Is it an invisible society of believers who are united by the new birth and have no responsibility to any earthly, visible institution? Is it simply the local assembly of believers who have separated themselves from fellowship with all others? What exactly is the nature of the church, the body of Christ?

26. B. H. Carroll, *Baptists and Their Doctrines*, p. 48.
27. Edward H. Overby, *The Meaning of Ecclesia in the New Testament*, p. 27.
28. H. O. Van Gilder, *The Church Which Is His Body*, pp. 29-30.

II. THE STATEMENT OF PURPOSE

Anyone who endeavors to engage in the explanation and elucidation of theological statement is confronted with several knotty problems. The first and probably most common of these is the problem of communication. The art of communication simply involves "the way we express ourselves." Each person has a certain grid through which he sees things, and he expresses himself in the light of this viewpoint. Other persons often have difficulty understanding because they see truth through a different grid. When one comes to the study of the church, he finds that Christians do not always mean the same thing when they speak of "the church." Thus, it is the purpose of this writer to be definitive enough and complete enough so as to eliminate many of the problems of communication.

A second problem that is often encountered is the failure of certain works to present a complete and thorough discussion. Especially is this true when dealing with the doctrine of the nature of the church. Often writers are concerned about selling the reader on their particular viewpoint. The result has been a disproportionate emphasis, for example, between the universal and local aspects of the church. The only solution to such a problem is to present an unabridged treatment of the biblical information on the subject of the nature of the church. Thus, it is the purpose of this book to endeavor to eliminate the disproportionate emphasis between the universal and local aspects of the church.

Finally, it is always difficult not to be subjectively conditioned by one's family tradition, educational background, and denominational affiliation. Van Gilder writes:

> It is never easy, particularly in one's own interpretation of Scripture, to tell to what extent subjective attitudes—prejudices, predilections, and preconceptions—have influenced one's judgment. It is, for example, a standing jest that the pastor with the program of a local church to promote believes

> in "store-house tithing," while the Bible teacher with a radio program or a school to promote, does not.[29]

Being aware of these tendencies, it is the purpose of this writer to combine the objective values and contributions of background and training with a fresh and objective study of the words of biblical revelation.

III. THE METHOD OF PROCEDURE

The lessons of history are invaluable guides in the forging of doctrine; thus, first a careful survey of the history of the doctrine of the church will be made. Then, in the following chapter, the contemporary ecclesiological discussion will be investigated in an attempt to set forth the numerous explanations of the church. With this background of historical and contemporary discussion, a definition of the church will be set forth on the basis of a careful and thorough study of the usage of *ekklesia** in nonbiblical and biblical sources. Growing out of this study of *ekklesia* is the recognition of the dual aspect of the church, universal and local; thus, the remainder of the book will be devoted to a study of the universal church, the local church, and the relation of the one to the other.

The most extensive chapter of this work will be that which treats the universal church. Of necessity, it must deal with the unfavorable extremes as well as the unacceptable presentations of the universal church. Also included will be a treatment of the historical beginning of the church and an explanation of the biblical figures expressive of the nature of the church.

The chapter on the local church is meant to explore the mission and purpose of that organization together with the responsibility of each individual believer to that organization. The final chapter, then, is intended to show the very intimate relationship of the local church to the universal church, the latter being the pattern of the former.

29. Ibid., p. 28.
*English transliterations of Hebrew and Greek words will frequently be used in this book.

2

THE HISTORY OF THE DOCTRINE

I. The Introduction

Value of the historical study

"If the doctrine is ancient, it is correct." Although no one would blatantly espouse such a premise, yet, practically speaking, it would seem that many contemporary writers are governed by it in their conclusions. If a doctrine has been comparatively late in development, it is considered unworthy of acceptation. Attitudes of this nature caused Charles Spurgeon to remark one time that it was about time to stop quoting the church Fathers and begin listening to what the grandfathers have to say, meaning, of course, the apostles. One is reminded of the words of Luther:

> I ask for the Scriptures and Eck offers me the Fathers. I ask for the sun, and he shows me his lanterns. I ask where is your Scripture proof? and he adduces Ambrose and Cyril. . . . With all due respect to the Fathers I prefer the authority of the Scriptures.[1]

Having noted the aforementioned caution, let the reader be aware, on the other hand, that there is a very definite value in a well-balanced study of the historical development of doctrine. Church history has great value as an explanation of the present.

1. Frederick W. Farrar, *The History of Interpretation,* p. 327.

It is much easier to understand the present if one has some knowledge of its roots in the past. The explanation for the presence of more than two hundred fifty religious groups is to be found in church history. Cairns states:

> Present-day problems of the Church are often illuminated by study of the past. The refusal of most modern dictatorial rulers to permit their people to have any private interests separate from their public life in the state is more easily understood if one remembers that the Roman emperors did not think that one could have a private religion without endangering the existence of the state. The relationship between the Church and state has again become a real problem in Russia, China, and the Russian satellite states, and it is to be expected that these states will persecute Christianity just as Decius and Diocletian did in their day. The danger inherent in the union of the Church and state through the state support of parochial schools and through the sending of envoys to the Vatican is illuminated by the interference with the Church by the temporal power beginning with the control of the Council of Nicaea by Constantine in 325.[2]

Not only will church history serve to explain the present, but the lessons of the past should help present and future generations to avoid the errors and pitfalls of former generations. Such is certainly Paul's meaning when he says in 1 Corinthians 10:11: "Now all these things happened unto them for ensamples: and they are written for our admonition, upon whom the ends of the world are come." It is usually true that the new heresies are merely old heresies in a new guise.

COMPARATIVE LATENESS OF THE DEVELOPMENT OF THE DOCTRINE

The early church was without any exact definitions concerning the nature of the church. In fact, the church did not present itself as a problem until comparatively late in church history.

2. Earle E. Cairns, *Christianity Through the Centuries*, pp. 18-19.

But the neglect was not due to a lack of church consciousness among Christians of the earlier church. MacGregor explains:

> Early Christian consciousness of the Church was, however, akin to the consciousness that a healthy man has of his enjoyment of energy and life. Such a man does not give much thought to the workings of his digestive system; he is not likely to inquire about his metabolism or to ascertain whether there is too much cholesterol in his blood. So when St Paul rejoices at being "in Christ" he is at the same time expressing his joy as a member of "the Body of Christ."[3]

Rise of heresies

Some have objected to relatively recent developments in the doctrine of the nature of the church because these formulations did not have the testimony of antiquity on their side. It should be noted, however, that the necessity for making distinctions was not at once apparent to the early church. Van Gilder states:

> Any student of the history of Doctrine knows that doctrinal formulations were the outgrowth of controversies. So long as New Testament teachings were unchallenged, there was no need for definitive statements.[4]

With the rise of heresies, then, it became imperative to name some characteristics by which the true church could be known.

Logical order of dependence

There is yet a further factor that explains the late development of this doctrine. Dogma is a development in time—a work of the human spirit operating on the matter furnished to faith in divine revelation. Furthermore, this development has not been simply a spasmodic growth without rhyme or reason; contrariwise, the development exhibits a specific and purposeful order. A clue to this orderly development is seen in the

3. Geddes MacGregor, *Corpus Christi: The Nature of the Church According to the Reformed Tradition*, pp. 3-4.
4. H. O. Van Gilder, *The Church Which Is His Body*, p. 27.

parallelism that exists between the theological system and the historical development of dogma. The noted authority in this area, James Orr, writes:

> Has it ever struck you, then . . . what a singular *parallel* there is between the historical course of dogma on the one hand, and the scientific order of the textbooks on systematic theology on the other? The history of dogma, as you speedily discover, is simply the system of theology spread out through the centuries . . . and this not only as regards its general subject-matter, but even as respects the definite succession of its parts. The temporal and the logical order correspond.[5]

Not only is it true that this specific order does exist, but it is to be noted further that there is a recognizable law that underlies the development; that is, there is a logical principle that determines it. Orr explains:

> The method, briefly stated, is simply to take the doctrines in the order of their logical dependence; in which one forms the presupposition of the other. The doctrine of redemption, *e.g.*, presupposes that of the Person of the Redeemer, and, prior to that, the doctrine of sin; the doctrine of sin, again, throws us back on the general doctrine of man, and also on the character, law, and moral administration of God; the doctrine of God, on the other hand, underlies everything—the doctrine of man, of sin, of Christ, of salvation, of the purpose of the world, of human destiny.[6]

Thus, this law of the logical order of dependence has resulted in the postponement of the development of the doctrine of the church to the present era. It is interesting to note that even Orr in his development of dogma does not include a section on ecclesiology. In his day, the discussion of eschatology was just coming to the fore. He explains that "there has never been an epoch for eschatology as for other doctrines,"[7] and again, "the

5. James Orr, *The Progress of Dogma*, p. 21.
6. Ibid., p. 23.
7. Ibid., p. 345.

modern mind has given itself with special earnestness to eschatology questions."[8] Since the latter part of the nineteenth century, when Orr wrote, the doctrine of the church has become one of the major subjects of theological discussion.

Likewise, most of the major theological works written in former generations do not give special attention to the doctrine of the church. Berkhof notes:

> It seems rather peculiar that practically all the outstanding Presbyterian dogmaticians of our country, such as the two Hodges, H. B. Smith, Shedd, and Dabney, have no separate locus on the Church in their dogmatical works and, in fact, devote very little attention to it.[9]

It has been seen, then, that the doctrine of the church has only recently become the subject of extended discussion. Thus it is the purpose of this chapter to seek out the ideas of the church that have prevailed in history. The investigation begins with the patristic period, thus passing over the apostolic period.

II. THE PATRISTIC PERIOD

Although there are no exact definitions of the church in the patristic period, some of the roots of the doctrine are found in the earliest literature of the Christian era. As one approaches this literature, he finds that, since the beginning of the post-apostolic period, there have been two specific trends that have manifested themselves in the development of the doctrine of the church. On the one hand there has been the trend toward external unity, and, on the other hand, there has been the trend toward internal purity.

THE TREND TOWARD EXTERNAL UNITY

The evidence of this trend toward external unity is most easily seen by noting men rather than movements. This research

8. Ibid., p. 29.
9. Louis Berkhof, *Systematic Theology*, p. 553.

is not meant to be exhaustive but to present a cross section of the early tendencies and development of the doctrine.

Clement of Rome

The first document of interest, written approximately contemporaneously with the book of Revelation, comes from the pen of Clement, a leader in the church at Rome. This document, which was an epistle of the church at Rome to the church at Corinth, makes no effort to define in detail ecclesiological truths, but it does present some obvious implications. On the basis of the four usages of *ekklesia* in the epistle, it is interesting to note the dogmatic but contradictory statements of various historical studies. Williams declares:

> Clement was the first among the Fathers to stress the distinction between the visible and the invisible Church, between the mystical Body of Christ and the actual fellowship on earth.[10]

Dana uses the same writing of Clement, however, to prove a totally different viewpoint. He states: "The word *ekklesia* occurs only four times in the entire epistle, but each time it is used in an undeniably local sense."[11] Again Fish states in regard to certain quotes from Clement:

> Now, these forms of statement are sufficient to show that the church from which, as also that to which, Clement wrote were independent local bodies governing themselves, and not any indefinite fractional part of some great body which bore that name.[12]

The lack of objectivity is immediately apparent in these contradictory statements. A consideration of all that Clement said reveals that he had a strong concern for the unity of local

10. Robert R. Williams, *A Guide to the Teachings of the Early Church Fathers*, p. 133.
11. H. E. Dana, *A Manual of Ecclesiology*, p. 99.
12. E. J. Fish, *Ecclesiology: A Fresh Inquiry as to the Fundamental Idea and Constitution of the New Testament Church*, p. 107.

churches, in which are the elect of God. When Clement speaks of the local church, he always qualifies the use of *ekklesia* with a descriptive adjective or phrase. In the salutation of his letter to the Corinthians he says: "The church of God living in exile in Rome, to the church of God exiled in Corinth."[13] Again he speaks of them as "the solid and ancient Corinthian Church."[14] The local church is also spoken of as "Christ's flock."[15]

The only other mention of the *ekklesia* clearly refers to a universal body that includes all the elect of God. He declares: "By reason of rivalry and envy the greatest and most righteous pillars [of the Church] were persecuted, and battled to the death."[16] It is clear that this reference goes beyond the local church, because he refers to Peter and Paul and other martyrs as being among those "righteous pillars."

Clement's use of "the body" gives evidence that he sees the body of Christ as a group much larger than the local church, because, although he is writing to the *ekklesia* at Corinth, he includes himself and everyone else in the body. Using the physical body as an example, he says:

> The head cannot get along without the feet. Nor, similarly, can the feet get along without the head. "The tiniest parts of our body are essential to it," and are valuable to the total body. Yes, they all act in concord, and are united in a single obedience to preserve the whole body.
>
> Following this out, we must preserve *our* [italics not in the original] Christian body too in its entirety. Each must be subject to his neighbor, according to his special gifts.[17]

Clement further informs the Corinthians that the strife in their local church has repercussions beyond that local body.

13. Clement *The Letter of the Church of Rome to the Church of Corinth, Commonly Called Clement's First Letter* Salutation.
14. Ibid., 47.
15. Ibid., 57.
16. Ibid., 5.
17. Ibid., 37-38.

> Why is it that you harbor strife, bad temper, dissension, schism, and quarreling? Do we not [all] have one God, one Christ, one Spirit of grace which was poured out on us? And is there not one calling in Christ? Why do we rend and tear asunder Christ's members and raise a revolt against our own body? Why do we reach such a pitch of insanity that we are oblivious of the fact we are members of each other?[18]

Finally, Clement declares that the first church, the spiritual church, was created before the sun and moon.[19]

Thus, a study of Clement's works reveals that he had a high regard for the unity of the visible church as expressed in the obedience to the local church officers. He also sees an invisible or spiritual church, however, which includes all believers, even those who have died. His intense desire for the unity of the visible church contains the seeds for the future development of the episcopacy.

Ignatius

When beginning a study of the second century, one comes first upon the writings of Ignatius and Polycarp. Both of these men were contemporaries of the apostle John; thus, their writings are very pertinent. Ignatius suffered martyrdom about A.D. 115, but during the last days of his life, after he had been condemned to be cast to the beasts in the Roman amphitheater, he wrote seven epistles, which are still extant in reliable form. A study of these epistles reveals that Ignatius used the word *ekklesia* thirty-nine times. It is quite evident that he had a healthy regard for the importance of the local *ekklesia.* Dana speaks to this point:

> At least thirty times the word is used in unquestionably local significance. Of the remaining nine occurrences of the term, five are used in the generic sense, while three present a univer-

18. Ibid., 46.
19. Clement *An Anonymous Sermon, Commonly Called Clement's Second Letter to the Corinthians* 14.1.

> sal significance. One reference is of doubtful meaning, but it is probably universal (Philad. 3:2). So seventy-seven percent of the usage of the term in Ignatius is local, illustrated in such expressions as "the church in Syria" (Mag. 14:1), "the other churches" (Rom. 9:3), etc. This indicates that primary in the thinking of Ignatius was the notion of the church as a local assembly.[20]

Although the local *ekklesia* was paramount in Ignatius's thinking, it is not correct to say, as some have, that this was his only usage of *ekklesia*. For example, after using a few "local" examples, Fish says of Ignatius: "He knew then, not a universal church, whether visible or invisible, but churches local and multiplied."[21] This is plainly wrong in the light of the evidence. Ignatius thought of the church not only as a local congregation, but also as a universal institution extending throughout the whole world. He writes:

> Since, also, there is but one unbegotten Being, God, even the Father; and one only-begotten Son, God, the Word and man; and one Comforter, the Spirit of truth; and also one preaching, and one faith, and one baptism; *and one Church which the holy apostles established from one end of the earth to the other by the blood of Christ* [italics not in the original], and by their own sweat and toil; it behoves you also, therefore, as "a peculiar people, and a holy nation," to perform all things with harmony in Christ.[22]

To the Smyrnaeans he wrote:

> From whom we also derive our being, from His divinely-blessed passion, that He might set up a standard for the ages, through His resurrection, to all His holy and faithful [followers], whether among Jews or Gentiles, *in the one body of His Church* [italics not in the original].[23]

20. Dana, pp. 101-2.
21. Fish, p. 110.
22. Ignatius *The Epistle of Ignatius to the Philadelphians* 4 (longer version).
23. Ignatius *The Epistle of Ignatius to the Smyrnaeans* 1 (longer version).

Finally, and most conclusively, Ignatius is remembered for being the first one to use the phrase *he katholike ekklesia,* the catholic or universal church. "Wherever the bishop shall appear, there let the multitude [of the people] also be; even as, wherever Jesus Christ is, there is the Catholic Church."[24]

Thus, it is evident that Ignatius used *ekklesia* both in a local and a universal sense. Although he placed great emphasis upon subjection to the bishop as the way to achieve unity and avoid the growth of heresy, he never exalted the bishop of Rome as superior to other bishops. Any hierarchal development was limited strictly to the local church. Ignatius states his hierarchy of authority as follows:

> Let all things therefore be done by you with good order in Christ. Let the laity be subject to the deacons; the deacons to the presbyters; the presbyters to the bishop; the bishop to Christ, even as He is to the Father.[25]

It is evident, then, "that by this time one of the elders in each church had become a monarchal bishop to whom fellow elders were obedient."[26] But each local church was directly related to Christ and not to some hierarchal institution as was to be the case later in the Roman church. As Neve succinctly states it: "The episcopate was still congregational, and not diocesan."[27] The individual congregation, subject to the bishop and the presbytery, is a copy of the church universal, which is led by Christ and the apostles. Christ and the preaching of the apostles, therefore—not the episcopacy—condition the unity of the church universal. Dana concludes:

> Though Ignatius knew the church chiefly as a local and self-governing body, yet he exhibits foregleams of those very developments which found their consummate fruition in Roman Catholicism.[28]

24. Ibid., 8 (shorter version).
25. Ibid., (longer version).
26. Cairns, p. 79.
27. J. L. Neve, *A History of Christian Thought,* 1:40.
28. Dana, p. 102.

Polycarp

This apostolic Father was at Smyrna, a short distance from Ephesus, where dwelt the apostle John, and was probably much under the personal influence of John. Only one of his epistles has been preserved, that to the Philippians, and *ekklesia* occurs only twice in this epistle. In both instances it is used in a local sense.

Although Polycarp's idea of the church seems to be characterized by apostolic simplicity, there is indirect evidence that before the close of his life he had accepted the universal view of the church. The evidence consists of a general epistle of the church at Smyrna, where Polycarp had ministered, describing his martyrdom to the other churches. Both the local and universal concepts are joined in the salutation.

> The church of God that sojourns at Smyrna to the church of God that sojourns at Philomelium, and to all those of the holy and Catholic Church who sojourn in every place.[29]

Again toward the close of the epistle, it is written of Polycarp:

> By his patient endurance he overcame the wicked magistrate and so received the crown of immortality; and he rejoices with the apostles and all the righteous to glorify God the Father Almighty and to bless our Lord Jesus Christ, the Saviour of our souls and Helmsman of our bodies and *Shepherd of the Catholic Church throughout the world* [italics not in the original].[30]

Finally, the epistle teaches that the individual congregation is but a local representative of the great universal church.

> And the whole crowd marveled that there should be such a difference between the unbelievers and the elect. And certainly the most admirable Polycarp was one of these [elect]; in whose times among us he showed himself an apostolic and prophetic teacher and bishop of the Catholic Church in Smyrna.[31]

29. *The Martyrdom of Polycarp, Bishop of Smyrna, as Told in the Letter of the Church of Smyrna to the Church of Philomelium* Salutation.
30. Ibid., 19.
31. Ibid., 16.

Irenaeus

By the close of the second century, the concept of the universal church was taking very definite shape. Perhaps the greatest promoter of the idea of the organic unity of the church was Irenaeus, and his most important work comes under the title *Against Heresies.* An examination of the usage of the word *church* in this writing reveals a significant change from the apostolic age. After investigation, Dana writes:

> In it [i.e., *Against Heresies*] the word *church* occurs one hundred and thirty-three times. Five of these are in quotations from the New Testament and two in summaries of the views of heretics, so do not represent in any way the views of Irenaeus. In one instance the word is used as descriptive of the Old and New Dispensations. We have to consider then one hundred and twenty-five instances which may be regarded as indicating what Irenaeus believed about the church. One of these is probably what we have described as the generic use of the term (III, 4, 3). The word is used twenty-one times in a local sense, and one hundred and three occurrences are universal in meaning. That is, eight-three percent of Irenaeus' usage of the term is universal. *Note the* complete reversal of the New Testament force of *ekklesia.*[32]

The earlier emphasis was upon the local *ekklesia,* which was directly related to Christ, the head of the spiritual *ekklesia;* the emphasis by the time of Irenaeus, however, was upon the organic unity of the visible, universal church. This becomes very apparent by noticing a few statements from *Against Heresies.* Speaking of the unity of the faith of the church, he says: "The Church, though dispersed throughout the whole world, even to the ends of the earth, has received from the apostles and their disciples this faith."[33] Herein, Irenaeus stresses not only the universality of the church, but also that it is the divine custodian

32. Dana, pp. 107-8.
33. Irenaeus *Against Heresies* 1. 10. 1.

and dispenser of the truth. Speaking to this same point again, he says:

> As I have already observed, the Church, having received this preaching and this faith, although scattered throughout the whole world, yet, as if occupying but one house, carefully preserves it. She also believes these points [of doctrine] just as if she had but one soul, and one and the same heart, and she proclaims them, and teaches them, and hands them down, with perfect harmony, as if she possessed only one mouth. For, although the languages of the world are dissimilar, yet the import of the tradition is one and the same. For the Churches which have been planted in Germany do not believe or hand down anything different, nor do those in Spain, nor those in Gaul, nor those in the East, nor those in Egypt, nor those in Libya, nor those which have been established in the central regions of the world.[34]

In his attempt to establish the organic unity of the visible church, Irenaeus went a step further than his predecessors by setting forth a perpetual succession of bishops from Christ.

> We are in a position to reckon up those who were by the apostles instituted bishops in the Churches, and [to demonstrate] the succession of these men to our own times. . . .
>
> Since, however, it would be very tedious, in such a volume as this, to reckon up the successions of all the Churches, we do put to confusion all those who, in whatever manner, whether by an evil self-pleasing, by vainglory, or by blindness and perverse opinion, assemble in unauthorized meetings; [we do this, I say,] by indicating that tradition derived from the apostles, of the very great, the very ancient, and universally known Church founded and organized at Rome by the two most glorious apostles, Peter and Paul; as also [by pointing out] the faith preached to men, which comes down to our time by means of the successions of the bishops. For it is a matter of necessity that every Church should agree with this Church, on account

34. Ibid., 1. 10. 2.

> of its preeminent authority, that is, the faithful everywhere, inasmuch as the apostolic tradition has been preserved continuously by those [faithful men] who exist everywhere.[35]

With Irenaeus, then, the lines are drawn tighter. As yet there was no suggestion of one bishop for the whole church, but the seed was sown. In his endeavor to preserve the pure doctrine from heretical admixture, he makes this universal church the divine custodian and dispenser of truth. Furthermore, he limits salvation to those who are within the bounds of this catholic church.

This development in the dogma of the church is not without a reasonable logic. Scripture repeatedly affirms that believers are members of one body in this age, and that that body is the church. What is more reasonable, then, than that unity should be recognized as one of the distinguishing characteristics of the church, and that, in due time, organic unity, unity of the church viewed as an organism, should find expression in political unity, unity of the church viewed as an organization? If the church is one, why should it not be organized as one? While this type of reasoning is quite plausible, its natural outcome is deplorable. Its fruit is the medieval church with its almost unlimited power, and its correspondingly great corruption.

Reasonableness was not the only factor underlying this development. Two other motives served as guiding factors. Neve states them cogently:

> *First,* there was the interest in the *purity or apostolicity of the Church's teaching.* This interest led to a recognition of the bishop for the purpose of safeguarding the truth. . . . It led first to a recognition of the bishop-presbyters as over against the Pneumatics; next, to a recognition of one bishop in each congregation; then to a special recognition of the bishops located in places where the Apostles had labored; after that, to the recognition of a college of bishops; and finally, to the rec-

35. Ibid., 3. 3. 1-2.

> ognition of a monarchical episcopate at Rome. *Second,* there was the interest in the *holiness of the Church,* or the purity of the Church's life, or let us say, the interest in repentance as an institution of the Church. These questions—purity of teaching and purity of life—have been the two outstanding motives for developing the Church and its institutions.[36]

Unfortunately, the desire to stem the rise of heresies resulted in a unity that veered away from the biblical doctrine of the church—an external unity that was later to prove devastating to true soteriology as well as ecclesiology.

Cyprian

Before Cyprian, very little was done to formulate a doctrine of the church, but the seriousness of the circumstances that surrounded him conspired to make him a zealous defender of ecclesiastical prerogatives. The church was threatened without by persecution and within by schism, and such conditions were calculated to create in Cyprian some very definite opinions about ecclesiastical authority. He has the distinction of being the first to develop fully the doctrine of the episcopal church. His two chief points of contention are the unity of the catholic church, and the authority of the bishop. These are largely developed in his most important treatise, *On the Unity of the Church.* That Cyprian gives unmistakable expression to his belief in the unity and universality of the church is evidenced by his repeated usage of the expression "The Catholic Church." Further, he declares that "God is one, Christ is one, His Church is one."[37] The real crux of the Cyprianic conception of the unity of the church, however, is found in his defense of the unbroken chain of episcopal succession beginning with Peter.

> The Lord says to Peter: "I say unto thee that thou art Peter, and upon this rock I will build my Church; and the gates of

36. Neve, 1:70.
37. Cyprian *The Epistles of S. Cyprian, Bishop of Carthage and Martyr, with the Council of Carthage on the Baptism of Heretics* 39. 5.

> hell shall not prevail against it. I will give unto thee the keys of the kingdom of heaven: and whatsoever thou shalt bind on earth shall be bound in heaven; and whatsoever thou shalt loose on earth shall be loosed also in heaven." He builds the Church upon one man. True, after the resurrection he assigned the like power to all the apostles, saying: "As the Father hath sent me, even so send I you. Receive ye the Holy Ghost: whose soever sins ye remit, they shall be remitted unto him; whose soever ye retain, they shall be retained." *Despite that, in order to make unity manifest, he arranged by his own authority that this unity should, from the start, take its beginning from one man* [italics not in the original]. Certainly the rest of the apostles were exactly what Peter was; they were endowed with an equal share of office and power. But there was unity at the beginning before any development, to demonstrate that the Church of Christ is one.[38]

With such a concept of succession, Cyprian and others could challenge the heretics: "Produce the origin of your churches; display the order of your bishops, running through succession from the beginning in such a way that the first bishop had as his teacher and predecessor some one of the apostles."

If there was a direct succession of bishops from Peter, then the next obvious step was the development of the episcopate for the whole church. Previously there was a bishop at the head of each local church, with no mention of one bishop for the church at large. With Cyprian, however, the bishops constitute an organism that represents the whole church. He writes:

> It is particularly incumbent upon those of us who preside over the Church as bishops to uphold this unity firmly and to be its champions, so that we may prove the episcopate also to be itself one and undivided. . . . The episcopate is a single whole, in which each bishop's share gives him a right to, and a responsibility for, the whole.[39]

38. Cyprian *The Unity of the Catholic Church* 4.
39. Ibid., 5.

Again, his formula is stated succinctly:

> Whence you ought to know that the bishop is in the Church, and the Church is in the bishop; and if any one be not with the bishop, that he is not in the Church. . . . The Church, which is Catholic and one, is not cut or divided, but is indeed connected and bound together by the cement of priests who cohere with one another.[40]

In such a close-knit system it is not difficult to see why Cyprian taught that there could be no salvation for anyone outside the bounds of the church. He writes:

> If you abandon the Church and join yourself to an adulteress, you are cut off from the promises of the Church. If you leave the Church of Christ you will not come to Christ's rewards, you will be an alien, an outcast, an enemy. You cannot have God for your father unless you have the Church for your mother.[41]

Within this universal episcopacy, outside of which there is no possibility of being saved, there were bound to be those churches that were highly regarded—churches where the martyred apostles or their co-laborers had taught. These "mother-churches" had guarded the pure doctrine with extraordinary care and thus were entitled to special respect. It was natural that of these "mother-churches" Rome should receive a position of primacy. Neve summarizes Cyprian's view:

> Cyprian shared the general belief that Rome was the Church where Peter had been bishop. His view was as follows: Rome represents (*monstretur*), so to speak, the unity of the Church Universal, as Peter represented that unity among the Apostles; the Church of Rome is the representation of the great idea of the Church's unity. Cyprian therefore directed the Church of his day to the See of Rome "where priestly unity had taken its beginning."[42]

40. Cyprian *The Epistles of S. Cyprian* 68. 8.
41. Cyprian *The Unity of the Catholic Church* 6.
42. Neve, 1:75.

Although Cyprian himself refused to recognize any special authority of the Roman bishop over the other bishops, his followers took his statements to their logical conclusion. His concepts simply contributed to the progress of error and corruption in the church. Neve concludes:

> But Cyprian's peculiar conception was too speculative and too idealistic to maintain itself in the praxis of church-life; the tendency of the age was in the direction of a powerful authority concentrated in a hierarchy. . . .
>
> The Cyprian theory of safeguarding the unity of the Church was soon overtaken by the actual development which established the bishop of Rome as the visible head of the Church.[43]

Augustine

Undoubtedly it is true that between Paul and Luther there was no man of the church of greater significance than Augustine. As James Orr has said: "No grander figure, despite his undeniable limitations, has ever risen in the Christian Church than Augustine."[44] Unfortunately, however, he was an ardent exponent of absolute and unbending ecclesiastical authority. Dana states:

> If Cyprian laid the foundation for Romanism, Augustine erected the papal throne, and blazed the way for the colossal tyranny of the Roman Catholic hierarchy, which cast its blighting shadow upon the succeeding centuries, and was a potent factor in determining medieval history as the "Dark Ages." But these consequences were, of course, never anticipated by Augustine, even though they were the logical outgrowth of his theory of the church.[45]

As was so often the case, *controversy* became the occasion of developing further the popular ideas about the church. From the Augustinian conflict with Donatism came his development

43. Ibid., 1:75, 77.
44. Orr, p. 26.
45. Dana, p. 116.

of ecclesiology, and his view of the nature of the church should be considered in the framework of that controversy. During the Diocletian persecution, many had been unfaithful and denied the faith. After the persecution the question arose as to the readmission of the lapsed into the church. The state church, under Constantine, favored readmission, but the Donatists took the position that the church must be a communion of real saints. The election of a bishop proved to be the spark that set off the conflagration. Gunnar Westin writes:

> Belief among various church groups that the bishop recently elected in Carthage had been consecrated by one who had failed to maintain a stedfast faith during the Diocletian persecution resulted in refusal to recognize the new bishop. Dissenters elected a bishop of their choice to take his place. A deep cleavage in the North African churches resulted. At first appearance the parties seemed to be uniformly strong. In fact, in some places the schismatic group was stronger. From then on the movement was known as Donatism after Donatus the Great, who for a generation was the powerful leader of this new fellowship.[46]

After Augustine returned to Africa as bishop of Hippo Regius, it became his task for two decades to win these heretics back to the catholic church. When theological argument proved to be of no effect, he instructed that they must be resisted and overcome by means of force. Out of this controversy, then, came Augustine's somewhat confusing and contradictory doctrine of the church. Before examining the works of Augustine, perhaps it would be well to note Berkhof's summary of this contradiction between his concept of the church and his doctrine of sin and grace.

> On the one hand he is the predestinarian who conceives of the Church as the company of the elect, the *communio sanctorum,* who have the Spirit of God and are characterized by

46. Gunnar Westin, *The Free Church Through the Ages,* pp. 17-18.

> true love. The really important thing is to belong to the Church so conceived, and not to be in the Church in a merely outward sense and to partake of the sacraments. . . . The real unity of the saints and therefore of the Church is an invisible one. At the same time it exists only within the catholic church, for it is there only that the Spirit works and that true love dwells.
>
> On the other hand he is the Church-man, who holds to the Cyprianic idea of the Church, at least in its general aspects. The true Church is the catholic Church, in which the apostolic authority is continued by episcopal succession. It is spread throughout the world, and outside of it there is no salvation, for it is only within its pale that one is filled with love and receives the Holy Spirit. Its sacraments are not merely symbols, but are also accompanied with an actual exertion of divine energy. God really forgives sins in baptism, and in the Lord's Supper actually gives spiritual refreshment to the soul. For the present this Church is a mixed body, in which good and evil members are present, but it is destined for perfect purity in the future.[47]

It remains then to examine in detail the doctrine of the nature of the church as found in Augustine. With simply a cursory reading of his works, it becomes immediately apparent that the word *church* in its local use is a rarity and overwhelming emphasis is given to the one, most holy, catholic church. This concept of the unity and universality of the church was adopted from Cyprian, from whom Augustine quotes very extensively. But the Donatist schismatics forced Augustine to point out more specifically that there is no possibility of being saved without being baptized into the visible organization. Augustine warns the Donatists:

> And so there is one Church which alone is called Catholic; and whenever it has anything of its own in these communions of different bodies which are separate from itself, it is most

47. Louis Berkhof, *The History of Christian Doctrines*, pp. 235-36.

> certainly in virtue of this which is its own in each of them that it, not they, has the power of generation. For neither is it their separation that generates, but what they have retained of the essence of the Church; and if they were to go on to abandon this, they would lose the power of generation. The generation then in each case proceeds from the Church.[48]

On another occasion, to the catechumens, he writes succinctly: "But ye begin to have him [God] for your father, when ye have been born by the church as your Mother."[49]

This same fact is repeatedly given in his sermons by reminding the hearer that only those in the church have the Holy Spirit. He writes: "And thus sins, because they are not forgiven out of the Church, must be forgiven by that Spirit, by whom the Church is gathered together into one."[50] And again: "remission of sins, seeing it is not given but by the Holy Spirit, can only be given in that Church which hath the Holy Spirit."[51]

The Donatists reminded Augustine of a weak point in his theory of salvation by baptism into the catholic church. How could he account for those who were baptized and yet were obviously not Christians? This forced Augustine to make a distinction between the visible church and the invisible church. The latter is found within the catholic church and its members are holy. His main illustration of this mixture of good and evil in the church is the parable of the wheat and tares in Matthew 13.*

> Now the Lord Jesus Christ explained this parable also; and said that He was the sower of the good seed, and He showed how that the enemy who sowed the tares was the devil; the time of harvest, the end of the world; His field, the whole world. And what saith He? "In the time of harvest I will say

48. Augustine *On Baptism, Against the Donatists* 1. 12. 14.
49. Augustine *On the Creed: A Sermon to the Catechumens* 1.
50. Augustine *Sermons on Selected Lessons of the New Testament* 21. 33.
51. Ibid.

*It should be noted at this point that Augustine equates the church with the kingdom of heaven. Cf. *Of Holy Virginity* 24.

> to the reapers, Gather ye together first the tares, to burn them, but gather the wheat into My barn." Why are ye so hasty, He says, ye servants full of zeal? Ye see tares among the wheat, ye see evil Christians among the good; and ye wish to root up the evil ones; be quiet, it is not the time of the harvest. That time will come, may it only find you wheat! Why do ye vex yourselves? Why bear impatiently the mixture of the evil with the good? In the field they may be with you, but they will not be so in the barn.[52]

Apparently the inconsistency of saying the church is the kingdom of heaven and is also the world in the same parable did not present a problem to him.

Elsewhere he speaks more plainly of the "party of the devil"[53] within the church. The devil has children inside, but God has no children outside of it. These wicked ones are among the clergy as well as laity.

> I tell you of a truth, my Beloved, even in these high seats there is both wheat, and tares, and among the laity there is wheat, and tares. Let the good tolerate the bad; let the bad change themselves and imitate the good.[54]

Although it is not the purpose of this book to answer the problems of soteriology created by Augustine's ecclesiology, yet his solution to the presence of wicked ones in the church, the body of Christ, should be noted. Briefly stated it is as follows. Not all those in the church are of the elect. Thus, not all are predestinated to eternal salvation, but only those who have been given the gift of perseverance. These are those who are members of the invisible church within the visible church.[55]

It is doubtful that a consistent theory of the church can be forged from the mass of materials Augustine has given. By way of conclusion to this study of his views, let the reader note the

52. Augustine *Sermons on Selected Lessons of the New Testament* 23. 1.
53. Augustine *On Baptism, Against the Donatists* 4. 10. 15.
54. Augustine *Sermons on Selected Lessons of the New Testament* 23. 4.
55. Augustine *On Rebuke and Grace* 20-22.

lack of synthesis as developed in the following questions by Berkhof:

> Which is the true Church, the external communion of the baptized or the spiritual communion of the elect and the saints, or both, since there is no salvation outside of either? Moreover, how is the Church, as constituted of the number of the elect, related to the Church as the communion of the faithful? They are clearly not identical, for some may be of the faithful who are not of the elect and are finally lost. And when Augustine says that no one has God for a Father, who does not have the Church, that is the one visible catholic Church, for a mother, the question naturally arises, What about the elect who never join the Church? Again, if the one visible catholic Church is, as he maintains, the true body of Christ, does not this prove the contention of the Donatists that wicked persons and heretics cannot be tolerated in it? Once more, if the Church is founded on the predestinating grace of God, how is it possible that they who have once received the grace of regeneration and the forgiveness of sins in baptism, should lose this again and thus forfeit salvation? And, finally, if God is the only absolute source of all grace and dispenses it in a sovereign way, can it be considered proper to ascribe this power to the visible Church with its sacraments, and to make salvation dependent on membership in that organization?[56]

Summary

It has been seen that during the first four centuries there gradually developed a trend toward external unity. The motivation for such an emphasis was perfectly natural. Ancient Christianity faced the confusion of views in interpreting its fundamental facts. There needed to be a common faith. This sense of need of a common faith was steadily productive of a catholic consciousness, an instinct for unity of all Christian forces. And unity always raises a demand for centralization. As early Christians drifted more and more away from an appre-

56. Berkhof, *The History of Christian Doctrines*, pp. 237-38.

ciation of the spiritual values of their religion and toward tangible expression and externalism, they came more to gravitate around an earthly center of control.

Although the stages cannot be sharply defined, for they blend into one another, there seem to be about three stages of development of ecclesiasticism. First, was the appearance of the monarchal bishop to whom fellow elders were obedient. Difference of opinion on questions of doctrine and consequent confusion resulted in turning to the dominant person among the elders for a final verdict. Thus, the bishop came to be regarded as the custodian of the faith. Unity in the local congregation was to be preserved by submission to the bishop.

Secondly, there was the development of the ecumenical domination. It was inevitable that the bishops of the great cities should gain pre-eminence in influence and prestige. The churches in smaller towns and villages turned to them for advice. Thus developed the metropolitan bishop. Again, it was inevitable that bishops from the greatest and most ancient churches would have influence over the others. Thus, the pattern of an episcopacy for the whole church was being developed. Hand in hand with this growth of the episcopacy was the blossoming of the universal consciousness and practical disappearance of the concept of the local congregation as related to Christ.

The final step, then, was the development of Roman supremacy. The concept of a universal church, which began to find expression in Ignatius and was definitely advocated by Irenaeus, demanded a centralizing of authority and control. What more obvious place could be chosen than Rome, the capital of the empire, the chief city in all the theological contests of the early Christian centuries, but most important, the church that they claimed to be established by Peter, the head of the church. Thus, it was not difficult for Cyprian to convince the catholic church at large of the primacy of the Roman see. It remained for Augustine to develop the system of Cyprian and lay the foundations of papal supremacy. His battle with the Donatists forced him to develop an ecclesiology that could explain the presence of wicked men in the church, which is the body of Christ. Using the parable of the tares and wheat, he developed the idea that the church is a *corpus mixtum*. Both good and evil men are within the church until the time of the harvest, which is the end of the world. Thus, he became the first to distinguish an invisible church within the one, holy, visible, catholic church, outside of which is neither possibility of salvation nor knowledge of the truth. The local churches were no longer conceived of as separate units, but as part of the universal church. They were only regarded as true churches as long as they were loyal to the catholic church as a whole. Thus, four centuries produced a complete reversal of emphasis as to the local church.

THE TREND TOWARD INTERNAL PURITY

The development of the sacramental, authoritarian church with its emphasis on externalism in religion did not develop without definite opposition movements. These heretical movements (so called because of their opposition to the visible universal church) considered the holiness of its members as the real mark of the true church. The groups grew out of a reaction against the gradual secularization and the increasing worldliness and corruption of the church. Only in recent years has any concerted effort been given to the study of these movements.

Out of the study has grown the concept of the free church through the ages. Gunnar Westin, a noted authority in the study of the free church movement, defines the movement.

> These congregations may be defined, therefore, as free churches because they won adherents and members who, when they freely accepted the word, turned away from the life of sin and voluntarily were baptized. . . .
>
> Again it can be established that the primitive Christian assembly was a free church in that it had no relationship, sub-

> ordinate or coordinate, with any constituted authority or the state. For these churches there was a clear line of demarcation between the church and the "world."[57]

Among these groups it was not possible to discover any centralized church authority, for the local churches were independent, yet with a real sense of relationship one to another.

Unfortunately, information about the opposition movements is scarce and what is available is not always reliable. The historical material documenting these groups was often destroyed because these groups were heretics. Also, in most cases research on the free church movement must be based on the reports of the antagonists or the one-sided material obtained from the law courts.[58] These factors should definitely be kept in mind as one studies the free church movement. The movements cannot be whitewashed of their errors, but they should be credited with whatever contribution they did make.

Marcionism

One of the first groups to register a reaction against the development of a sacramental, authoritarian church during the latter portion of the second century was headed by Marcion, a prosperous shipowner from Asia Minor. When Marcion separated from the church, probably about A.D. 140, a large number of people followed him to establish a separate church. So rapid was the spread of the movement, Justin Martyr was able to write a few years later that it had spread among all nations of mankind.[59] Blackman writes: "No other single man had called forth such a volume of anxious apologetic from the Church."[60] It is felt that there may have been a few years when the Marcionite church threatened to win more adherents than the remainder of the Christian church could then boast. Relatively

57. Westin, pp. 1-2.
58. Ibid., p. 25.
59. Justin Martyr *The First Apology of Justin Martyr* 1. 26.
60. Edwin Cyril Blackman, *Marcion and His Influence*, p. ix.

little is known, however, about this most vigorous heretical movement, for it was destroyed, its records were lost, and knowledge of it is only found in the profuse writings of its enemies.[61]

It is apparent, however, from what information is extant that the most significant of Marcion's teachings was repudiation of the close tie the church had with the Old Testament, especially its sacerdotal system. Westin writes:

> The imitation of Judaistic practices in the Church was regarded by many as a departure from both the example and teaching of Jesus as well as from the Pauline concept of the gospel as free to all. Marcion and his followers rejected the allegorical method of interpretation, which made it possible to apply the Old Testament practices to the congregation's way of life.[62]

Thus, the Marcionite movement was a reaction against the Judaistic infiltration of the institutionalized church. Being a major competitor to the primitive catholic church, it was regarded as a peril. Thus, by means of severe imperial edicts, many of the Marcionites were martyred and many were driven into hiding. But this movement against Judaism and ecclesiasticism in the church was to break forth again under the leadership of Montanus.

Montanism

Another opposition movement against ecclesiasticism in the institutionalized church during the patristic period was Montanism. Cairns says of this movement: "It represented the perennial protest that occurs in the Church when there is overelaboration of machinery and lack of dependence on the Spirit of God."[63] Here was an autonomous movement that opposed the centralization of power and the rise to prominence of the bishop

61. John Knox, *Marcion and the New Testament*, p. 1.
62. Westin, p. 10.
63. Cairns, p. 111.

in the local church, and that stressed the priesthood of the individual believer. It endeavored to combat the formalism of the externally organized church. Noting that it was an ecclesiastical reaction as well as a reform movement, Neve writes: "It protested against the incipient secularization of the Church and sought to restore the Church to its original status."[64]

Unfortunately, as so often happens in such movements, Montanism swung to the opposite extreme and developed some fanatical misinterpretations of Scripture. Although it was discredited because of its misinterpretations of Scripture, this powerful movement paved the way for a series of movements that has continued down through the entire history of Christianity—movements that refused to be swallowed up by the incipient centralization and secularization of the institutional church.

Donatism

As was noted previously, the Donatistic controversy became the occasion of Augustine's development of his ecclesiology. In contradistinction to Augustine's declaration that the true church was the visible catholic church with its admixture of both good and evil, the Donatists insisted that the true church was a fellowship of real saints only. Therefore, they endeavored to purge the church of the unholy element. She must not have bishops who betrayed the truth in times of persecution.

A second element that characterized the Donatists as a free church movement was their refusal to allow the state to interfere in the affairs of the church. When the emperor sought to win the Donatist adherents through gifts of money, Donatus responded: "What does the emperor have to do with the church?"

> With these words, Donatus gave the free church movement for all time a slogan, a slogan that has often been repeated.

64. Neve, 1:59.

> The persecution during the time around 340 could not make the Donatists give up their convictions. Donatism was now clearly a free church movement from this point of view: it stood adamantly opposed to any intermingling of state power with the organization of the church.[65]

Although the Donatistic movement itself was wiped out about two hundred years later by the Mohammedan invasion, its free church principles were perpetuated in such groups as the Paulicans, Cathari, Waldensians, Lollards, Hussites, and Anabaptists.

By way of summary, it has been seen that while the major trend in the development of ecclesiasticism was toward an external centralization and control of the church, yet there was also an opposing movement that laid stress on the internal purity of the church. As opposed to the Augustinian admixture of good and evil, they considered the true church to be composed only of real saints. The local representation of the true church had autonomous characteristics and emphasized that the laity are also priests before God under the guidance of the Holy Spirit.

III. THE MIDDLE AGES

The doctrine of the church as developed by Cyprian and Augustine was quite complete; thus, the Scholastics have very little to say about it. Otten, a Roman Catholic historian, says:

> This system was taken over by the Scholastics of the Middle Ages, and then was handed down by them, practically in the same condition in which they had received it, to their successors who came after the Council of Trent.[66]

Strangely enough, however, although there was relatively no development in the doctrine of the church, yet the church itself "actually developed into a close-knit, compactly organized, and

65. Westin, p. 20.
66. Bernard John Otten, *Manual of the History of Dogmas*, 2:214.

absolute hierarchy."[67] Because the purpose of this chapter is primarily to recognize the development of the doctrine of the nature of the church in history, it will not be necessary to examine original sources at length from this period of relatively no development.

GREGORY

Dogmatic thought in the church for the last half of the first millennium of Christian history was ruled by Gregory the Great, the first man to be elected to the papal chair. Neve summarizes the hierarchal development as seen in Gregory:

> The *Church* properly speaking was held, at least theoretically, by Gregory to belong to the saints of all ages. But in the concrete the Church was to him as to Rome today a *civitas Dei,* a temporal state with the pope at its head, therefore a *corpus mixtum* comprising naturally the good and the bad.[68]

Thus, Gregory gave full emphasis to one side of Augustine's doctrine—the visible organization; but he disregarded the Augustinian development of the invisible church—the communion of real saints within the visible church.

AQUINAS

The perfection of Scholasticism was reached in Thomas Aquinas in the thirteenth century. He gave theology a modern reworking but added nothing of new content to the doctrine of the church. MacGregor notes:

> It is noteworthy that St. Thomas, who neglected little that pertained to sacred doctrine, devotes less space to the doctrine of the Church, in the course of all his vast theological writings, than almost any modern theologian would give this subject within the compass of a single book covering major theological issues of the day.[69]

67. Berkhof, *The History of Christian Doctrines,* p. 238.
68. Neve, 1:174.
69. MacGregor, p. 28.

He goes on to summarize what Aquinas does have to say:

> Approaching ecclesiological questions only in the most general, not to say superficial, manner, he is content to describe the Church as a *corpus mysticum* having Christ as its Head, and to liken the Holy Spirit to the heart of the Church, invisibly quickening and unifying it. . . . But the predominant thought of St. Thomas on the nature of the Church is that it is a mystical body, comprising both the faithful on earth, who as the *ecclesia secundum statum viae* constitute the *congregatio fidelium,* and the beatified in heaven, the *ecclesia secundum status patriae,* which he calls the *congregatic comprehendentium.*[70]

It becomes evident, then, that even apart from the paucity of his references to the subject, he made no considerable advance on the ecclesiology of Augustine. It is true, however, that he did give great impetus to the already developed doctrine of papal supremacy wherein the external head of the church became an absolute monarch. He assigned the pope a place in dogmatics in which he set forth the infallibility and unrestricted sovereignty of the pope over the church and state.[71]

Thus, the development of the doctrine of the church remained static until the later Middle Ages, when the forerunners of the Reformation began to express dissatisfaction with the church.

WYCLIFFE

The movement for which Wycliffe was responsible—Lollardism—was another in the line of free church movements. Repudiating the authoritarian position of the church and believing in the priesthood of all believers, the Lollards set out with the primary task of studying and declaring the Word of God.

Wycliffe's views on the nature of the church are found in his

70. Ibid., pp. 28-30.
71. Thomas Aquinas *The Summa Theologica of Saint Thomas Aquinas* 2. 2. 1. 10.

work *De Ecclesia*;† however, his ecclesiology is not as complete as one might desire. The concept of the invisible church of all the elect, which is present in Augustine, is habitually employed by Wycliffe. He speaks of this invisible body as the *corpus mysticum*. The Church has, indeed, a visible manifestation in the world; but its origin and its home is in an invisible world. MacGregor says of Wycliffe's doctrine:

> He never really departs, in principle, from what he says in the opening chapters of the *De Ecclesia,* to the effect that the Church, though a reality that can be known by those who belong to it, is essentially spiritual in nature. He did adopt, it is true, a distinction that Augustine had made in controversy with the Donatists, the distinction between the true Body of Christ and the simulated (*permixtum, simulatum*) Body. The wheat and the chaff are mixed on the threshingfloor. . . . But he does not work out ecclesiologically how the *corpus mysticum* is related to the *corpus permixtum,* which is almost the first question a modern theologian would be likely to ask.[72]

Thus, Wycliffe was still Augustinian in his doctrine of the nature of the church, but he was one of the first men in the Roman church to rebel against the hierarchical, visible, universal church. He emphasized the priesthood of all believers as members of the mystical body of Christ. Unfortunately, he did not make any attempt to relate this body to the local *ekklesia.* In his development, then, the church was considered on its invisible side. Wycliffe defined it as the whole body of God's elect, passing over the Roman idea of a visible, outward organization.

By way of summary, it has been seen from a representative sampling of the leading theologians of the Middle Ages that no new content was added to the doctrine of the church; however, the church itself was more and more solidified into a thoroughly

†This work later came to have tremendous significance with Huss and the Hussites in Bohemia.
72. MacGregor, pp. 35-36.

organized and absolute hierarchy. Toward the end of the Middle Ages, winds of dissension were stirring and precursors of the Reformation emerged in such men as Wycliffe.

IV. THE REFORMATION

The Reformation was not one movement but four, although the four were vitally related. In addition to the Lutheran and Calvinist movements, there was, in England, the Anglican movement. In addition, there was the Anabaptist movement, now more generally and more accurately referred to as the left wing of the Reformation; this Anabaptist movement is now being widely reassessed and better understood.[73]

LUTHERAN

The Leipzig Disputation in which Luther countered Eck was the immediate cause of the rapid development by Luther of his teaching on the nature of the church. "The Papacy at Rome: An Answer to the Celebrated Romanist at Leipzig" was a counterattack in which Luther unfolded the teachings he had maintained at the Leipzig Disputation.

It was natural that Luther should speak out against the widespread Roman demand that Christianity must get together into one worldwide visible ecclesiastical order, for in Luther's mind the one true church was already a spiritual community composed of all living believers in Christ. Writing against the Roman external conception, he says:

> The Scriptures speak of the Church quite simply, and use the term in only one sense. . . . [It] is called the assembly of all the believers in Christ upon earth. . . . This community or assembly consists of all those who live in true faith, hope and love; so that the essence, life and nature of the Church is not a bodily assembly, but an assembly of hearts in one faith. . . . Thus, though they be a thousand miles apart in body, yet they

73. Westin, pp. 39-45. Cf. also Franklin Hamlin Littell, *The Anabaptist View of the Church: A Study in the Origins of Sectarian Protestantism*, pp. xiii-xiv.

> are called an assembly in spirit because each one preaches, believes, hopes, loves, and lives like the other. . . . And this unity is of itself sufficient to make a Church, and without it no unity, be it of place, of time, of person, of work, or of whatever else, makes a Church.[74]

As scriptural proof of this spiritual nature, he quotes John 18:36: "My kingdom is not of this world" and Luke 17:20-21: "The kingdom of God cometh not with observation: neither shall they say, Lo, here, or lo, there! for behold, the kingdom of God is within you."‡ He continues: "the true, real, right, essential Church is a spiritual thing, and not anything external or outward, by whatever name it may be called."[75]

Although Luther spoke so vehemently against the use of the term *church* to designate the external organization, yet he never repudiated his doctrine of a local, restricted assembly. He explains:

> For the sake of brevity and a better understanding, we shall call the two churches by different names. The first, which is the natural, essential, real and true one, let us call a spiritual, inner Christendom. The other, which is man-made and external, let us call a bodily, external Christendom: not as if we would part them asunder, but just as when I speak of a man, and call him, according to the soul, a spiritual, according to the body, a physical man; or as the Apostle is wont to speak of the inner and of the outward man. Thus, also the Christian assembly, according to the soul, is a communion of one accord in one faith, although according to the body it cannot be assembled at one place, and yet every group is assembled in its own place.[76]

The question then arises as to how one can recognize the true church in its assembled form on earth. Luther responds:

74. Martin Luther, "The Papacy at Rome," in *Works of Martin Luther,* 1:349.

‡Notice that Luther equates the church and the kingdom in true Augustinian tradition.

75. Luther, 1:353-54.

76. Ibid., 1:355.

> The external marks, whereby one can perceive where this Church is on earth, are baptism, the Sacrament, and the Gospel; and not Rome, or this place, or that. For where baptism and the Gospel are, no one may doubt that there are saints, even if it were only the babes in their cradles.[77]

That there were both saints and hypocrites in these assemblies was readily admitted by Luther.[78] He does not seem overly concerned, however, for he readily falls back on the invisible concept. In fact, Luther gave very little, if any, serious attention to the New Testament pattern of the local church. In Schaff's list of creeds of the Lutheran church, the only statement on the nature of the church is the following weakly supported statement from the Augsburg Confession of 1530.

> Though the Church be properly the congregation of saints and true believers, yet seeing that in this life many hypocrites and evil persons are mingled with it, it is lawful to use the Sacraments administered by evil men, according to the voice of Christ (Matt. xxiii. 2): 'The Scribes and the Pharisees sit in Moses' seat,' and the words following. And the Sacraments and the Word are effectual, by reason of the institution and commandment of Christ, though they be delivered by evil men.[79]

This is as close as these documents come to making any statement on the nature of the local church, and certainly it must be agreed that this is a weak attempt at it. MacGregor observes: "Questions of ecclesiastical order are regarded as external and incidental; they are concerned only with the 'clothes' of the Church, not with its fundamental nature."[80]

It seems that the doctrine of the invisible church was used to serve an unscriptural purpose. It allowed them to give only

77. Ibid., 1:361.
78. Ibid., 1:362.
79. Philip Schaff, *The Creeds of Christendom, With a History and Critical Notes,* 3:12.
80. MacGregor, p. 8.

scant attention to the New Testament pattern of the local church. Yoder indicts them:

> The Reformers formed a persecuting state church; but at the same time they were protected themselves against any criticism which might have objected that their church was not what a church should be by the fact that their church, being visible, could never be the true church anyway. Since our church is not the true church, they said in effect, the state is free to organize and administer it as it seems best. This concession to Hellenism, the admission that the invisible and timeless is more real than the visible and historical, has avenged itself a hundred fold in occidental piety, ethics, and social responsibility.[81]

Perhaps Yoder is too severe in impugning their motives, but the fact is nevertheless true that as a result of Luther's teaching, the state gained control of the church.

CALVINISM

In contrast to the vagueness of Luther, Calvin appears to have developed a definite theory on the relation of the invisible church to the external ecclesiastical institution. Calvin uses the term *church* in a threefold sense. In agreement with Augustine, Wycliffe, and Luther, he sees the invisible church as consisting of all of the elect.

> Sometimes by the term "church" it means that which is actually in God's presence, into which no persons are received but those who are children of God by grace of adoption and true members of Christ by sanctification of the Holy Spirit. Then, indeed, the church includes not only the saints presently living on earth, but all the elect from the beginning of the world.[82]

This church is invisible, Calvin affirms, in the sense that it is

81. John H. Yoder, "The Prophetic Dissent of the Anabaptists," in *The Recovery of the Anabaptist Vision,* ed. Guy Frankin Hershberger, pp. 98-99.
82. John Calvin *Institutes of the Christian Religion* 4. 1. 7.

spiritual, but also in the sense that it is able at times to survive only in a hidden state.

> But because a small and contemptible number are hidden in a huge multitude and a few grains of wheat are covered by a pile of chaff, we must leave to God alone the knowledge of his church, whose foundation is his secret election.[83]

His second usage of the term *church* was with respect to the universal church.

> Often, however, the name "church" designates the whole multitude of men spread over the earth who profess to worship one God and Christ. . . . In this church are mingled many hypocrites who have nothing of Christ but the name and outward appearance. There are very many ambitious, greedy, envious persons, evil speakers, and some of quite unclean life. Such are tolerated for a time either because they cannot be convicted by a competent tribunal or because a vigorous discipline does not always flourish as it ought.
>
> Just as we must believe, therefore, that the former church, invisible to us, is visible to the eyes of God alone, so we are commanded to revere and keep communion with the latter, which is called "church" in respect to men.[84]

In defense of this universal church, he exclaims: "The church is called "catholic," or "universal," because there could not be two or three churches unless Christ be torn asunder [cf. I Cor. 1:13]—which cannot happen!"[85] Thus, at heart Calvin was a true ecumenicist. He cherished the hope that, if only the forces of reform could be well organized, the unity of the visible church, for long obscured, would be seen clearly again by the light of purified doctrine and practice. MacGregor says of Calvin's doctrine:

> From this insistence on the unity of the church as visible,

83. Ibid., 4. 1. 2.
84. Ibid., 4. 1. 7.
85. Ibid., 4. 1. 2.

> together with his recognition elsewhere that even under the tyranny of Rome the visibility of the True Church had not been entirely destroyed, it is plain that from the time of his earliest formulation of an ecclesiology, Calvin never thought of the organization of the Reformed Church as involving a separation from the medieval institution; it was, rather, a vivification of the Body of Christ that had become oppressed and encumbered by a diabolical cancer that sought to destroy it.[86]

So in his fully developed doctrine of the church, he follows and restates the fundamental Cyprianic doctrine that outside the church there is no salvation. Like Cyprian, he teaches that he cannot have God for his Father who has not the church for his Mother.

> But because it is now our intention to discuss the visible church, let us learn even from the simple title "mother" how useful, indeed how necessary, it is that we should know her. For there is no other way to enter into life unless this mother conceive us in her womb, give us birth, nourish us at her breast, and lastly, unless she keep us under her care and guidance, putting off mortal flesh, we become like the angels. . . Furthermore, away from her bosom one cannot hope for any forgiveness of sins or any salvation.[87]

In Calvin's revision of his *Institutes* in 1539, he developed a further breakdown of the idea of the church.

> The church universal is a multitude gathered from all nations; it is divided and dispersed in separate places, but agrees on the one truth of divine doctrine. . . . Under it are thus included individual churches, disposed in towns and villages according to human need, so that each rightly has the name and authority of the church.[88]

Thus, in Calvin's mind, the universal church is simply an aggre-

86. MacGregor, p. 47.
87. Calvin, 4. 1. 4.
88. Ibid., 4. 1. 9.

gation of all of the local churches on earth. It remains to be seen in further chapters, if this adequately represents the New Testament pattern.

Because membership in this church was essential to salvation, Calvin was careful to set forth the marks whereby the true church could be distinguished.

> Wherever we see the Word of God purely preached and heard, and the sacraments administered according to Christ's institution, there, it is not to be doubted, a church of God exists.[89]

It seems, then, that Calvin never really achieved a severance of alliance between soteriology and ecclesiology. In his concept of the universal church, he merely took a half step from organizational unity to sacramental unity. The functions of preaching of the Word and administration of the sacraments, he felt, constituted the essential elements in the identification of the church.

Finally, Calvin perpetuated the church-and-state amalgamation that characterized the Roman church. He gave explicit instructions concerning the duties of civil government.

> Yet civil government has as its appointed end, so long as we live among men, to cherish and protect the outward worship of God, to defend sound doctrine of piety and the position of the church, to adjust our life to the society of men, to form our social behavior to civil righteousness, to reconcile us with one another, and to promote general peace and tranquillity. . . . It . . . also prevents idolatry, sacrilege against God's name, blasphemies against his truth, and other public offenses against religion from arising and spreading among the people.[90]

In evaluating the Reformer's position of binding the church to the state, Perry Miller writes:

89. Ibid.
90. Ibid., 4. 20. 2-3.

> The Deity Himself had commanded that all men's thoughts be turned toward redemption, and had prescribed certain ways and means. The Church could not accomplish this unaided by civil authority. The reformers envisaged a simple and plausible arrangement wherein they, the professional experts in Biblical knowledge, should teach the state its duties, and the State should silence contradiciton. The highest function of the State, therefore, was the loving care of the Church, the maintenance of its eternal being in uniformity throughout the kingdom, and the physical support of its censures.[91]

This Genevan development became the characteristic Protestant theory of state and church.

The teachings of Calvin on the church became incorporated, for the most part, into the Westminster Confession of Faith, 1647, and accepted by the Reformed churches.[92]

ANABAPTISTS

The great German church historian Ernst Troeltsch has pointed out that in the history of the church two major sociological types had developed. On the one hand was the free church movement, to which he gave the name "sectarian." The other type Troeltsch termed as the "institutional" or "established" church. Between these two types there had been an unbalanced struggle from the second century until the Reformation. In his use of the term "sect" he sought to designate a special sociological type that, through perpetual reference to primitive Christianity and the Bible, sought to apply and carry out the principles of the gospel.[93] Westin highlights the essence of this institutional-sectarian contrast:

> The priestly hierarchy claimed to have apostolic tradition, sacramental grace, and the jurisdiction of the Church. The free churches, on the other hand, stressed voluntary fellowship

91. Perry Miller, *Orthodoxy in Massachusetts, 1630-1650,* p. 7.
92. Cf. Schaff, 3:657-59.
93. Ernst Troeltsch, *The Social Teaching of the Christian Churches,* 2:461.

> patterned after the practice of the early church, the demand for holy living, and the absolute authority of the Bible.
>
> The sects maintained that these ideas and principles of primitive Christianity were not simply starting points for the historical development of Christ's church but that they were ideals and patterns for all generations.[94]

These so-called sects were summarily considered as satanic heresies by the established church. The Winn Professor of Ecclesiastical History at Harvard Divinity School, George Huntston Williams, states:

> The Radical Reformation . . . was ruthlessly suppressed alike by Protestant and Catholic magistrates. It is an anomaly of Western history in modern times that the lands in which dissent first found heroic expression muzzled it so swiftly and brutally that only its echo was to be heard thereafter in the interiorized and socially often quite conservative form of Pietism.
>
> . . . The major Protestant Reformers and their associates were the bitterest foes and persecutors of the Anabaptists; and Protestant scholars and polemicists, beginning with Martin Luther, Ulrich Zwingli, Philip Melancthon, John Calvin, and Henry Bullinger, drew and redrew a composite portrait of them as fanatics and revolutionaries.[95]

Because of this malignant prejudice, the historians of the day dismissed these groups without attempting to gain a documentary understanding or an objective judgment. This pre-judging and condemnation of the free church movement has been carried on even in later times, a truth illustrated by subsequent Protestant historical accounts of the Anabaptists in the time of the Reformation. Only in recent years has a serious research attempt been made among historians to reconstruct a true picture of the Anabaptist movement.[96]

94. Westin, p. 40.
95. George Huntston Williams, *Spiritual and Anabaptist Writers,* pp. 24, 26.
96. Ibid., pp. 40-45.

The word *Anabaptist* is a Latin derivative of the Greek original, *anabaptismos* (rebaptism). Actually, the name was applied by Lutherans and Zwinglians to those who separated themselves from the main body of the state churches. The radicals themselves rejected the name. Evans says:

> They repudiated the name, insisting that infant baptism did not constitute true baptism and that they were not in reality re-baptizers. Their argument was of no avail. The name was so conveniently elastic that it came to be applied to all those who stood out against authoritative state religion.[97]

Littell has pointed out why their enemies insisted on the use of the term.

> "Anabaptist" was a popular term with the authorities because it afforded them an excuse for forcefully suppressing the radicals. The enemies of the movement were insistent on the use of the term "Wiedertäufer" or "Anabaptistici" because the radical groups thereby became subject to the death penalty. Under the ancient Roman law against the rebaptizers (Donatists), those called "Anabaptist" could be suppressed by the sword.[98]

Thus, historically the term *Anabaptist* became a slippery epithet that was flung about contemptuously. In the perspective of this book, however, a study of the Anabaptist church view is a study in the origins of sectarian Protestantism.

A brief consideration of this movement is essential at this point in order to have a complete picture of the ecclesiological situation in the time of the Reformation, for right at the heart of the Anabaptist interpretation of Christianity is the Anabaptist view of the church. The Anabaptists were primarily interested in a restitution of the "true church" gathered and disciplined upon the apostolic pattern as they understood it.[99]

97. Austin P. Evans, *An Episode in the Struggle for Religious Freedom: The Sectaries of Nuremburg, 1524-1528*, pp. 14-15.
98. Littell, p. xv.
99. Ibid., p. xvii.

The great Reformers—Luther, Zwingli, Calvin—had tremendous regard for the living tradition of the historic church. They moved cautiously, for they had no urge to unchurch themselves. They hesitated to abandon the principle of the territorial church —parish or national. As they saw it, the existing church was indeed the true church, but it had fallen on evil days and into unworthy hands. Therefore, they sought to bring about a spiritual renewal from within. The Anabaptists, however, set out to discard the territorial church pattern and replace it with the pattern they saw in the New Testament. Their objective was not to introduce something new but to restore something old. "Restitution" was their slogan, a restitution of the early church. From the Anabaptist point of view, the difference between the Reformers and themselves was the difference between reform and restitution. Price writes:

> As the Anabaptists saw it, the task for the sixteenth century Christians was nothing else than the reconstitution of the true church itself, restoring that which had lapsed rather than reforming that which had erred. . . . Only the restoration of a church which had, in reality, long since ceased to exist was adequate to God's demand and the need of the times. The Church of Rome—and the church of the Reformation, insofar as it remained a territorial or parish church—could not vindicate its place in history or be usable in God's scheme.[100]

Thus, there was a basic difference between the Reformers' and the Restorers' view of the church. The real problem between them was not the act of baptism but the mutually exclusive concepts of the church. The difference in the interpretation of the *subject* of baptism only served to highlight the irreconcilability of the two views of the church.

Basic to an understanding of the Anabaptist viewpoint is the understanding of the terms *fall* and *restitution* as applied to the church. The whole idea of the recovery of New Testament

100. Theron D. Price, "The Anabaptist View of the Church," in *What Is the Church?*, ed. Duke McCall, p. 101.

Christianity was tied up with the thought that at some point in Christian history the pattern was lost. The church experienced a fall from the golden age when martyr-heroes followed Christ to death. The restitution party, in the main, dated the fall from Constantine. Littell explains:

> We must remember that they counted the fallen condition of the church *from the days of Constantine until the beginning of their own movement. The Reformers also belonged to the period of the Fall.* The Anabaptists said that the revival began with Luther and Zwingli, but when the Reformers clung to the old idea of Christendom, the radicals counted them out. The criticisms directed against the imperial Roman religion are the criticisms directed against the Reformers: church and state were amalgamated, empty formalism and spiritual slackness prevailed, infants were baptized into Christianity before their understanding could give the membership any content.[101]

The basic factor in the fall, then, was the union of the church and state. The means by which this illicit union was perpetuated was the rite of infant baptism. Price writes:

> It was by flooding the church with hordes of nominal Christians that the "fall' was introduced. Then by including children en masse in baptism, rather than one at a time by conversion of life, the "fall" was perpetuated.[102]

In contrast to these evidences of a fallen condition, the Anabaptists set forth the evidences of a truly restored church.

> Restitution was considered to have been accomplished wherever churches were gathered on the principle of responsible faith and regenerate life (of which believer's baptism is the sign but not the cause); whenever congregations were spiritually governed and cohered on the principle of mutual nurture and mutual rebuke; whenever the terms of communion were essentially moral and ethical rather than sacramental

101. Littell, pp. 64-65.
102. Price, p. 105.

> (with the sacraments being primarily symbols of a communion between the church and God, and between believer and believers).[103]

Garrett has put it succinctly as "a restored, gathered congregation or brotherhood of baptized believers under discipline and separated from the world and from the state."[104] This, to them, was evidence of a true church. This view was quite different from the views of the great Reformers of the sixteenth century who saw the church and state as practically coextensive and held that all citizens of a territory, except those excommunicate, were held to be members of the established church.

By 1535, there were many Dutch Anabaptists living in England, and thereafter their numbers increased steadily. The proportion who were Anabaptists is unknown, but in 1562 Dutch people in England numbered thirty thousand.[105] It is not unreasonable to conclude that they had a definite influence on the movement of Separatism in England. In fact, study of the matter shows that England followed only Germany and the Netherlands in interest in Anabaptist teaching.

ANGLICANISM

Of the four major movements in the Reformation, the fourth, and, for America, one of the most important, was the Anglican Reformation in England. It differed from the others in that it had no dominant ecclesiastical leader, such as Luther or Calvin, but was dominated by the ruler who became head of the national church. Actually, the Anglican Reformation began as a political move on the part of Henry VIII. In order to get a divorce from Catherine of Aragon, and the right to marry Anne Boleyn, he had to bring the Roman church in England under his control. Cairns observes that "it began as a political movement, continued as a religious movement, and concluded with

103. Ibid., p. 106.
104. James Leo Garrett, *The Nature of the Church According to the Radical Continental Reformation,* p. 11.
105. Williston Walker, *The Creeds and Platforms of Congregationalism,* p. 6.

the Elizabethan settlement in the middle of the sixteenth century."[106] The most important step in the separation of the church in England from the papacy was taken in the Act of Supremacy in 1534. The Act declared that the king was "the only supreme head in earth of the Church of England."[107] In theology, however, the Church of England remained true to Rome. The Six Articles passed by Parliament in 1539 reaffirmed transubstantiation, communion in one kind, celibacy, and auricular confession.[108] Thus, at the death of Henry VIII, the English church was a national church with the ruler at its head, but it was still Roman Catholic in doctrine.

Protestantism suffered several reversals during the Roman Catholic reaction under Mary Tudor, but her successor, Edward VI, carried out the religious phase of the English Reformation that Henry had begun as an ecclesiastical movement. Not until the reign of Elizabeth, however, was a final doctrinal statement adopted by the church. The Thirty-nine Articles were accepted by Parliament in 1563 as the creed to which all pastors of the Anglican church must subscribe. This creed, with slight modifications in 1571, has been the creed of the Anglican church since that time.

This creed seems very limited in its statement concerning the church. Article XIX, speaking of the church, says:

> The visible Church of Christ is a congregation of faithful men, in the which the pure Word of God is preached, and the Sacraments be duly ministered according to Christ's ordinance in all those things that of necessity are requisite to the same.[109]

One readily notices that there is no explicit mention of the invisible church. Some may say that the use of the words "visible"

106. Cairns, p. 354.
107. Henry Bettenson, *Documents of the Christian Church,* pp. 321-23.
108. Ibid., p. 331.
109. In Leonard Hodgson, "The Doctrine of the Church as Held and Taught in the Church of England," in *The Nature of the Church,* ed. R. Newton Flew, p. 123.

and "faithful" implies that the article takes for granted the doctrine of the invisible church. However, Hodgson writes:

> The significant thing about the article, when compared with contemporary Reformation literature, is its omission of any reference to the invisible Church. The opening words, when taken in conjunction with the title, imply that there is only one Church, the visible. Moreover, Article XXVI (7) shows that "faithful" must mean professed believers, not those whose faith is known to God alone.[110]

Writing on the Anglican church, Leicester C. Lewis says:

> Among Anglicans the term Invisible Church seems quite meaningless. They do not see how the New Testament attitude of "telling it" to the Church could be rational if the Church were invisible and, equally, would they find it difficult to "hear" an invisible Church. It cannot be too strongly emphasized that for Anglicans the Church is the society of people, primarily here on earth. When Anglicans use the term Invisible Church they mean by it that larger part of the visible Church which has passed from this life to the life beyond.[111]

It is not difficult to understand why the Anglican church should be one of the foremost promoters in the ecumenical movement if one knows the Anglicans' historically strong emphasis on the unity of the visible church on earth. Furthermore, the Anglicans were content to be very moderate in their doctrinal statements. MacGregor observes:

> The English Reformation, though it had both Lutheran and Calvinistic elements in it, sought to preserve as much of the old structure of the medieval Church as seemed to be compatible with the elimination of medieval abuses. . . . English churchmen were on the whole less inclined to vigorous theological formulation than to a moderate pruning, in the light of

110. Ibid., p. 133.
111. Leicester C. Lewis, "The Anglican Church," in *The Nature of the Church*, ed. R. Newton Flew, p. 309.

the new learning, of the theological tradition they felt they already had.[112]

There were those within the Anglican church, however, who were not satisfied with halfhearted attempts at reform. They contended that too many "rags of popery" were still in the Anglican church, and they wanted to purify the Anglican church in accordance with the Bible. These Puritans, as they were nicknamed,§ threatened to change the Episcopal state church into a Presbyterian or Congregational state church. Miller writes:

> They might disguise their ultimate objective under occasional programs of lesser reforms in ceremony and ritual, but as long as the Biblical warrant for church polity remained their basic assumption nothing short of a Presbyterianized Church could really content them.[113]

At the beginning, the Puritan party remained amorphous in ecclesiology. It was not clearly Presbyterian or Congregational. Not until the Presbyterians came into combat with the Separatists did Presbyterian and Congregational distinctives become an issue among the Puritans.

At the heart of Congregational polity were two essential features: namely, the restriction of church membership to the proved elect and the autonomy of particular congregations. Thus, Henry Jacob, a regular Puritan turned Congregationalist, defined a church, in 1605, as

> a particular Congregation being a spirituall perfect Corporation of Believers, & having power in it selfe immediately from

112. MacGregor, p. 11.

§In its strict use the word *Puritan* signified that group of men who wished to replace the hierarchy with another ecclesiastical system, most specifically Presbyterianism. It was used more loosely, however, and any conspicuously pious person was apt to be dubbed Puritan by his more liberal contemporaries. Cf. Miller, p. 22.

113. Miller, p. 25.

> Christ to administer all Religious meanes of faith to members thereof.[114]

After 1604 he constantly attacked Presbyterianism: "I affirme that No Synod vnder ye Gospell hath power by Gods ordinance to prescribe & rule Ecclesiastically sundry whole Churches if they consent not to."[115] Bradsaw declares the latter point even more specifically:

> We confine and bound all Ecclesiastical power within the limits onely of one particular Congregation, holding that the greatest Ecclesiastical power ought not to stretch beyond the same.[116]

It must be remembered, however, that the Puritans, whether Presbyterian or Congregationalist, were not dissenters but a party within the Anglican church. Some Puritans, as in the case of Thomas Cartwright and his followers, wanted a Presbyterian state church; other Puritans, like Henry Jacob and his followers, wanted a Congregational state church. The latter group included both independents and Separatists. The independents must be distinguished from the Separatists, who wanted (a) separation of the church and state, and (b) congregational government of the church. Speaking of the independents, Miller observes:

> During the reign of James we suddenly encounter a small group of men who were to all intents and purposes Puritans, who were insistently anti-Separatists, but who had, nevertheless, quietly accepted the Separatists' discipline.[117]

This was the glaring inconsistency of non-Separatist congregationalists. While they were defending congregational polity, they were at the same time justifying their remaining in the

114. Champlin Burrage, *Early English Dissenters in the Light of Recent Research,* 2:157.
115. Ibid., 2:165.
116. William Bradshaw, *A Protestation of the Kings Supreamacie, Made by the Nonconforming Ministers, Which Were Suspended or Deprived,* pp. 91-92.
117. Miller, p. 75.

hierarchical Anglican state church. John Paget, a Presbyterian, had the acumen to see that the anti-Separatist congregationalists' polity was the same as that of the Separatists,[118] and yet, Henry Jacob maintained, "I never was, nor am, separated from all public communion with the congregations of England."[119] Thus, they protested that they never intended separation from the Church of England. Miller summarizes the labyrinthine process of their reasoning:

> Thanks to their deft stratagems they were always prepared to protest that they were not Separatists, even at the very moment when they were erecting independent churches in England or gathering them on foreign shores. They were trying to show that men who wished simply to realize potentialities already inherent in the Church were far different from men who wish to destroy it and begin anew. Those who never questioned that they should be coerced into conformity, even when a temporarily misguided monarch was coercing them in the wrong direction, might reasonably be considered loyal Englishmen. . . . They denied that any *ecclesiastical* authority had a right to expel ministers from particular churches; but just so soon as the King himself authorized the expulsion, though it remained intrinsically an unjust act, still, as it was the act of a *magistrate,* they did not rebel. . . . *The peculiar twist of their philosophy enabled them to look upon these depravations with equanimity, even while they continued to declare that the act had not affected the essential character of the true churches* [italics not in the original].[120]

Unlike the independent or non-Separatist congregationalists, the Separatists would have nothing to do with the state church. The first man to set forth forcefully the Congregational prin-

118. John Paget, *A Defence of Church Government Exercised in Presbyteriall, Classical, and Synodall Assemblies; According to the Reformed Churches,* p. 30.
119. John Paget, "A Declaration and Plainer Opening," in *Historical Memorials Relating to the Independents and Congregationalists from Their Rise to the Restoration of the Monarchy,* by Benjamin Hanbury, 1:230.
120. Miller, pp. 92-93.

ciple of complete separation of church and state was Robert Browne (1550-1633). Some have scorned his name and discredited his leadership because of his later reconciliation to the English church, which he had so fiercely attacked.|| Despite his abandonment of Congregational professions, which abandonment Walker feels was "the result of mental breakdown consequent upon disappointments and imprisonments rather than any real denial of the beliefs for which he had proved himself ready to suffer,"[121] he remains the English leader of Separatist principles.#

There were two basic principles that the Separatists promoted, and in these important respects they differed from Presbyterianism. In the first place they demanded a regenerate membership. Only persons who could demonstrate that they were "redeemed by Christ vnto holiness & happiness for ever"[122] could be church members. They could not afford to admit any of the wicked and ungodly, for to do so would infect and corrupt the rest. When a new organization was to be founded, the "visible saints" were to come together, profess their faith, and take a covenant of allegiance to Christ as their king and prophet, and promise to be bound by His laws. This covenant and confession were to be undertaken voluntarily.[123] Therefore, no official could force a church to be gathered, constrain an individual to join, or compel "the church to receive any without

||One of his most important tracts, *A Treatise of reformation without tarying for anie, and of the wickednesse of those Preachers, which will not reforme till the Magistrate commaunde or compell them,* carries its burden in its title. It is a strenuous argument for instant separation from the established church and a special attack upon the position of the Puritans who were waiting within the Church of England for its reform by civil authority.

121. Williston Walker, *A History of the Congregational Churches in the United States,* pp. 31-32.

#Cf. Ibid., p. 32: "Whatever his defects may have been, he enjoys the distinction not only of being the first to formulate Congregational polity, but the earliest Englishman also to proclaim the doctrine that church and state should be mutually independent. A man of such clearness of insight, and who made such large contributions to Congregational development, cannot be denied a prominent place in the history of Congregational beginnings."

122. Walker, *Creeds and Platforms,* p. 19.

123. John Robinson, *Works,* ed. Robert Ashton, 2:316.

assurance by public profession of their own faith; or to retain any, longer than they continue to walk orderly in the faith."[124] Thus, they felt that Calvin, the Church of England, and the Puritans had all been wrong when they said the marks of a true church were preaching of the Word and administration of the sacraments, for the Word could be preached and the sacraments be administered to "assemblies of unbelievers."[125] The real marks of a true church were faith and order; only where God had called a company of His own together could faith be found, and order could exist only where such a company administered it.

While this first distinctive was internal to the church, the second was external. The individual assemblies of believers were directly related to Christ. Every believer, being of the elect, was made, according to Browne, "a Kinge, a Priest, and a Prophet vnder Christ, to vpholde and further the kingdom of God."[126] Every such group was therefore self-sufficient, independent of all external compulsion, and competent to manage its own affairs. No minister had authority outside his own local assembly.

The views of Browne are ably summarized by Walker:

> To his thinking a Christian church is a body of professed believers in Christ, united to one another and to their Lord by a voluntary covenant. This covenant is the constitutive element which transforms an assembly of Christians into a church. Its members are not all the baptized inhabitants of a kingdom, but only those possessed of Christian character. Such a church is under the immediate headship of Christ, and is to be ruled only by laws and officers of his appointment. To each church Christ has entrusted its own government, discipline, and choice of officers.[127]

124. Benjamin Hanbury, *Historical Memorials Relating to the Independents and Congregationalists from Their Rise to the Restoration of the Monarchy*, 1:52.
125. Robinson, 3:428.
126. Walker, *Creeds and Platforms*, pp. 22-23.
127. Walker, *A History of the Congregational Churches*, p. 38.

These principles, especially that of separation of church and state, were later to prove most influential in the growth and development of the church in the United States. Together with the Anabaptists,** the Separatists from England did much to preserve a free church with a regenerate membership.

V. AMERICAN DEVELOPMENT

Generally speaking it is not necessary to examine the history of the doctrine of the nature of the church in America, for there has been no development of the doctrine as such. The American scene did, however, offer a wide door of liberty for the practice of certain doctrinal developments that came out of the Reformation and were not allowed freedom of expression under the established church system of Europe. The views of the Anabaptists concerning the nature of church and state have already been discussed. As to their influence in American life, Rufus Jones has expressed a judgment that is shared by William Warren Sweet and other historians of American Christianity:

> Even as it was, in spite of all the handicaps, Anabaptism proved to be one of the most virile and contagious of all the new religious ideals of the reforming epoch. . . . As has happened many times before and since, with movements that have been showered with scorn and opprobrium, the conquered and defeated became in the end the conqueror . . . when nearly every one of the constructive principles of the Anabaptists got written into the Constitution of the United States, or got expressed in some important branch of American Christianity.[128]

That this appraisal of what happened in America is a true one

**Although no evidence of direct influence upon the Separatists by the Anabaptists has been found, yet there are distinct intimations of the same. Cf. Walker, *A History of the Congregational Churches*, p. 36: "the similarity of the system which he [Browne] now worked out to that of the Anabaptists is so great in many respects that the conclusion is hard to avoid that the resemblance is more than accidental."

128. Rufus Jones, *Mysticism and Democracy in the English Commonwealth*, pp. 32-33.

is verified by Franklin Littell, the modern authority on the free church movement:

> The American system is different from that set up first at Westphalia (1648), repeated in the time of the Toleration Act in Britain (1690), in which the government supports one or more religions and permits others to exist relatively undisturbed. It is different from any Roman Catholic teaching, the most liberal of which can only concede the value of liberty if itself a minority, or grant toleration if suppression will not succeed. It is different in kind from the Protestantism of Europe, which also produced establishments here in America during the colonial period. These colonial "state churches," which were perpetuated in some measure until 1819 in Connecticut and until 1833 in Massachusetts, resulted in all the familiar problems: internal latitudinarianism, rending of society by persecution and forced emigration, abridgement of related liberties of citizens. The American system, as it came to be expressed in the provisions of the Virginia Bill of Rights (1778), represented the triumph of Free Church principles in the New World.[129]

Another development that was separate from,†† although not uninfluenced by, the Anabaptist free church movement was that of the Puritans in New England. As has been seen, the nonseparating Puritans in England had developed free church beliefs, but they could not practice their beliefs because of their restriction within the hierarchy of Anglican polity. Thus, with the free air and exigencies of discovery of new land and emergence of new government, they burst the old wineskins. If they could not abolish the hierarchy, Puritans could remove it by

129. Franklin Hamlin Littell, *The Free Church*, pp. 50-51.

††That there is a distinction to be made is clear in that when Browne accused the Salem ministers of becoming Separatists, Higginson and Skelton replied they were "neither Separatists nor Anabaptists." Cf. Cotton Mather, *Magnalia Christi Americana; or, The Ecclesiastical History of New-England, from Its First Planting in the Year 1620 unto the Year of Our Lord 1698*, 1:73.

putting between it and themselves a ditch so wide "they could not leap over with a lope-staff."[130]

It must not be thought, however, that this leap across the ocean implied a break with the Church of England. The Puritans had no intention of separating as the Pilgrims had done. Francis Higginson, one of the two ministers of the first Puritan church on Massachusetts soil, is reputed to have exclaimed as the last headlands of England faded from view:

> We will not say, as the separatists were wont to say at their leaving of England, "Farewel, Babylon!" . . . but "farewel, the Church of God in England! . . . We do not go to New England as separatists from the Church of England; though we cannot but separate from the corruptions in it.[131]

They still looked to the Church of England as the mother church. As some said: "We . . . esteem it our honor to call the Church of England . . . our dear mother."[132] Thus, somewhat amazed, Walker states:

> All the more remarkable it is, then, in view of the worldly and educational superiority of the Puritans over the Pilgrims, and their anti-Separatist feelings, that the Puritan churches organized in New England adopted the principles of Separatist Plymouth in their formation and government. No step in the development of Congregationalism is more obscure or more important than this Congregationalizing of English Puritanism.[133]

Some have charged that the non-separating Puritans feared being charged as schismatics. Thus, they felt that the great ocean put something of an invulnerable defense between them

130. Edward Johnson, *The Wonder Working Providences of Zion's Saviour in New England*, p. 20.
131. In Mather, 1:362.
132. Alexander Young, ed., *Chronicles of the First Planters of the Colony of Massachusetts Bay, 1623-1636*, p. 296.
133. Walker, *A History of the Congregational Churches*, p. 100.

and the sharp eye of Archbishop Laud in England. Miller observes:

> Behind this bulwark the churches could become completely Congregationalized, even to the point where they would no longer be distinguishable from Separatist organizations, and yet as long as there had been no formal Separation, as long as the churches could claim to be simply purified and transported English parishes, the principle of uniformity had not been infringed. Massachusetts was not schismatical.[134]

Whether such duplicity can be laid at the feet of the Puritans will no doubt be debated. Perhaps it was the only line of circumstances left open to a people who were at one and the same time convinced of the absolute truth of a dissenting program and of the absolute necessity for orthodox uniformity. Perhaps they were weary from sixty years of fruitless controversy. At any rate the principles of the Separatists found in the Puritan churches of New England an outworking that they had not experienced in the restricted atmosphere of the Church of England. Thus, while they refused to adopt the principle of separation, yet they did insist on the autonomy of the local church and the necessity of a regenerate membership.

America to the Puritans spelled opportunity, for it meant the cessation of protest and the beginning of construction. Cotton Mather declared:

> It is one thing for the church, or members of the church, loyally to submit unto any form of government, when it is above their calling to reform it, another thing to chuse a form of government and governore discrepant from the rule.[135]

This is not meant to imply that the Puritans established religious liberty, for as Walker states:

> Neither Pilgrims nor Puritans had any thought of establishing liberty for men to do as they pleased; nor would any gen-

134. Miller, p. 139.
135. Thomas Hutchinson, *The History of the Colony of Massachusetts Bay*, 1:494.

> eral toleration, such as we now justly value, have furnished motives definite enough to have led our ancestors to the New World.[136]

Their aim was not a democracy but a theocracy or a holy commonwealth, which Richard Baxter defined as "a Government of the Society of God's subjects by a sovereign subordinate to God, for the common good, and the Glory and Pleasing of God."[137] This ideal they realized to a certain extent. Just as they had specific requirements for entrance into the church, so they had specific requirements for entrance into the civil body. Their aim was that

> all should be done in accordance with the direction of the Bible, the laws, and the terms of the civil contract. Thus, Church and State walked side by side because they agreed with one restriction that the magistrate should not have spiritual power and the church authority should not have civil authority. Thus, there was erected this "equal correspondence in jurisdiction."[138]

The illustrations of some overstepping of this line of demarcation, however, were numerous. A glaring example is the fact that church membership soon became imperative for election to office. Thus, it was only in theory that state and church were distinct, for in practice they were not.[139] It remained for Roger Williams and other to bring to bear true principles of religious liberty and the separation of church and state.

VI. SUMMARY

In this brief survey of the history of the doctrine of the church, several trends can be noted. It is quite evident that in the earliest writings of the Fathers there was a strong emphasis

136. Walker, *A History of the Congregational Churches*, p. 99.
137. Richard Baxter, *A Holy Commonwealth; or, Political Aphorisms Opening the True Principles of Government.*
138. George W. Dollar, "The Life and Works of the Reverend Samuel Willard," p. 171.
139. Ibid., p. 172.

on the local church, especially on the unity of that group as a fellowship of believers. But there is sufficient evidence to indicate that these writers were not unaware that these local churches were visible representations of the church, the body of Christ, to which all believers in Christ belong. It was not long, however, until the rise of persecution without and heresies within brought about the desire for organizational unity of all the churches and centralization of power. The doctrinal climax of this development was seen in the ecclesiology of Cyprian and Augustine. The historical outworking of this development was seen in the rise of the papacy, and the universal church on earth. Contrary to the early church emphasis, the New Testament teaching concerning the local church had disappeared from their thinking. The church was equated with the earthly kingdom of God headed by the pope, Christ's visible representative on earth. Outside of this earthly hierarchal organization, there was no salvation or forgiveness of sin.

Only a partial recovery of the early church teaching was made in the major streams of Reformation thought. The major Reformers were still interested in maintaining the medieval pattern of the universal church on earth, but they desired to purify its doctrine. The Lutheran, Reformed, and Anglican churches all saddled their members with a state-controlled church. They made a break with the organizational unity of the Roman church, but they put a sacramental unity in its place. Although they attempted to separate ecclesiology and soteriology, they never quite succeeded, for they felt there was no salvation outside the universal church on earth.

A more thorough reform was made by the radical Reformers, who demanded a complete separation of the church from the state. They emphasized that the church was a voluntary gathered assembly of baptized believers exercising discipline apart from control by the state. Among these radical Reformers were the Anabaptists of the continental Reformation and the Separatists of the English Reformation. The ecclesiology of these groups has had a notable influence on the growth and development of the church in America.

The history of the church in America has not developed the doctrine of the church beyond that which was evident in the four streams of Reformation thought.[140] Rather, it has adopted and maintained one or another of the various ecclesiological presentations that came out of the Reformation. It has been noted, however, that the free atmosphere of the American scene provided a choice opportunity for the propagation of the free church principles. Peters writes:

> It is our conviction that the great ideals of Luther have expressed themselves most fully in the Evangelical State Churches of Germany and the Scandinavian countries. The ideals of the great English Reformers live on in the Church of England. The Dutch Reformed State Church of Holland expresses the doctrines of Calvin. The ideals of the sixteenth century Anabaptists are coming at least in part to their own in the *free church life* of America and elsewhere.[141]

Thus, while there was no development of new doctrine, there was a place to practice that which had previously been restricted by established church systems. Therefore, it is not the purpose of this book to examine the ecclesiology that each of the denominations has adopted in American history, but rather to witness the varying emphases that for the most part have come out of the Reformation and are present on the contemporary scene.

140. Christian Rudolph LaVere, "The Doctrine of the Church," in *Twentieth Century Encyclopedia of Religious Knowledge,* ed. Lafferts A. Loetscher, 1:254.
141. G. W. Peters, "Major Theological Tenets of Sixteenth Century Anabaptist-Mennonitism," pp. 2-3.

3

THE CONTEMPORARY VIEWPOINTS

The contemporary viewpoints of the nature of the church present a pattern equally as variegated as that of the Reformation. The doctrine has become especially significant in the light of the recent, rapid rise of interest in the ecumenical movement. This push for unity is not an emphasis confined to a few denominations, but it has its ardent advocates in practically every religious group.

I. Roman Catholic

On January 25, 1959, a Reuters dispatch from Rome carried to the world the news that Pope John XXIII was intending to convene "an ecumenical council for the universal church." The dispatch concluded:

> The convocation of the ecumenical council, in the thoughts of the Holy Father, aims not only at the edification of Christian peoples, but is intended also as an invitation to the separated communities in quest of unity, to which end so many hearts aspire in so many parts of the earth.[1]

This desire for the unity of Protestantism and Roman Catholicism is shared by the Protestants as well as the Roman Catholics. A leading liberal Protestant theologian, Robert McAfee Brown, writes:

1. In Franklin H. Littell, "The Pope's Ecumenical Council," *Christian Century* 76:224.

> In various parts of the world there is actual encounter and interchange going on between Catholics and Protestants. A good deal of this is at the level of theological discussion which comes to grips in a fundamental way with the issues that have kept Christendom divided.[2]

Quoting from a report by Father Gerard Hughes, S.J., Brown writes:

> Many of the questions raised between Catholics and Protestants on the nature of the Church, her essential visibility . . . are now being discussed in Protestant Episcopal Synods, in theological conferences, and in many Protestant theological periodicals. Protestants are ridding themselves of that very restricting prejudice which tends to dismiss serious discussion of specifically Catholic teaching and practice as *a priori* suspect and a betrayal of Reformation principles.[3]

In light of this ecumenical dialogue, one is constrained to ask what is the church according to Rome?

The Roman Catholic teaching on the nature of the church falls into two divisions, namely, the mystical body of Christ and the church on earth.[4] It should be noted, however, that these designations do not refer to two different churches, for the constituency of each one is the same. Furthermore, although they speak of the invisible and visible elements of the church, they never speak of the invisible church. Graham contends that this terminology sets up a false antithesis and "suggests that one might belong to Christ's Mystical Body without being incorporated, simultaneously and in the same degree, in the visible Catholic Church—which is impossible."[5] Van Noort poses the question:

2. Robert McAfee Brown and Gustave Weigel, S.J., *An American Dialogue: A Protestant Looks at Catholicism and a Catholic Looks at Protestantism*, p. 85.
3. Ibid., p. 86.
4. E. Myers, "The Mystical Body of Christ," in *The Teaching of the Catholic Church*, ed. George D. Smith, 2:659.
5. Aelred Graham, "The Church on Earth," in *The Teaching of the Catholic Church*, ed. George D. Smith, 2:709.

> Did Christ personally found a visible Church, one which by its very nature would have to be an external (public) society, so that an invisible Church could not possibly be the true Church of Christ? For once one proves that the one and only Church which Christ founded is visible from its very nature, then it necessarily follows: (a) that an invisible Church such as that to which Protestants appeal is a pure fiction, and (b) that all the promises which Christ made to His Church refer to a visible Church.[6]

There is a clear distinction to be made, however, between the visible and invisible elements. Myers explains:

> Man is a sense-bound creature and the appeal of sense is continuous. Our Lord has taken our nature into consideration. The merely invisible we can accept on his authority. But he has given us a visible Church. . . . We accept Our Lord's gift to us with gratitude and strive to avail ourselves of its visible and invisible character. He has willed that as individuals we should be united with him by sanctifying grace, and that at the same time we should be united to one another with a unique collectivity, an unparalleled solidarity, which is the reality designated as the Mystical Body of Christ. And he has further willed that all the members of that Mystical Body should be members of the visible organised [sic] hierarchical society to which he has given the power of teaching, ruling, and sanctifying. That visible Church is to be the unique indefectible Church which is to last until the end of time, and in its unity to extend all over the world.[7]

Because of this close identification between the mystical body and the visible organization, it is not difficult to understand the Roman Catholics' conclusion that there is no salvation outside the visible church. If the membership of the body of Christ is identical with the membership of the visible church, and if the

6. G. Van Noort, *Dogmatic Theology,* ed. J. P. Verhaar, trans. and rev. John J. Castelot and William R. Murphy, 2:12-13.
7. Myers, 2:662.

Holy Spirit only gives life to those united to the body of Christ, then there is no life outside the visible church. Following in the teaching of Augustine, Myers writes:

> The Church is the body of Christ and the Holy Ghost is the soul of that body; for the Holy Ghost does in the Church all that the soul does in the members of one body; hence, the Holy Ghost is for the body of Jesus, which is the Church, what the soul is for the human body. Therefore, if we wish to live of the Holy Ghost, if we wish to remain united to him, we must preserve charity, love truth, will unity, and persevere in the Catholic faith; for just as member amputated from the body is no longer vivified by the soul, so he who has ceased to belong to the Church receives no more the life of the Holy Spirit. "The Catholic Church alone is the body of Christ . . . outside that body the Holy Spirit gives life to no man . . . consequently those who are outside the Church have not the Holy Spirit."[8]

The body of Christ, which is the church, took its rise from the death of Christ on Calvary. "At that moment, the Church, like a second Eve, a new 'mother of all the living,' was born from the Saviour's side."[9] With the rending of the veil of the temple "the Old Law was abolished and the Messianic Kingdom on earth came into being."[10] Although the church was brought to birth by the atoning act of Christ, it was not formally constituted until the coming of the Holy Spirit at Pentecost to animate the organism of the mystical body and to give life to the visible social organism.[11] Since that time, the Roman Catholics' claim, the true church has been characterized by the properties* of visibility, indestructibility, infallibility, unity, holiness, catholicity, and apostolicity.[12]

In the light of the Roman Catholic doctrine of the church,

8. Ibid., 2:666.
9. Graham, 2:694.
10. Ibid.
11. Ibid., 2:694-95.
*The church's properties are those qualities that flow from its very essence and are a necessary part of it.
12. Van Noort, 2:102-55.

those aspirants of ecumenicity should give careful attention to the Roman demands. Listen to their offers:

> Any "return," corporate or individual, must involve recognition of the Pope as the vicegerent of Christ. Once an individual has reached the point of recognizing this truth, he cannot stay outside Catholic unity, since he would in that case be refusing obedience to Christ in the person of his earthly vicar.[13]

Equally as outspoken is Adam:

> The Catholic Church feels and knows herself as the Church of Christ in the emphatic, exclusive sense: as the visible revelation in space and time of the redemptive powers which proceed from Christ her Head, as the Body of Christ, as the *one means of salvation* [italics in the original]. . . . To admit even the possibility that the final union of Christendom could take place other than in her and through her would be a denial and betrayal of her most precious knowledge that she is Christ's own Church. For her there is only one true union, reunion with herself.[14]

The last sentence of Adam's statement may well be prophetic.

Although the biblical concept of the church will be set forth in the next chapter, DeWolf's evaluation of the Roman concept should be noted at this point.

> Such a conception of the church is indefensible at three points. First, it identifies the spiritual body of men under Christ with the externally formed organization. Second, it identifies the total true church with one particular organization which very obviously has no monopoly on the fruits of the Spirit. Third, by its assignment of supreme authority on earth to this one organization and more specifically to one man, it is guilty of the most arrogant and sinful presumption.[15]

13. John Murray Todd, *Catholicism and the Ecumenical Movement*, p. xii.
14. Karl Adam, *One and Holy*, trans. Cecily Hastings, p. 93.
15. L. Harold DeWolf, *A Theology of the Living Church*, p. 323.

II. PROTESTANT

The task of classifying the diversity of opinions on the subject under consideration set forth by Protestant writers would be virtually impossible. At best only a sampling is possible. Therefore, representative writers of the more popular viewpoints have been chosen in order to give a general picture of the contemporary Protestant outlook.

LIBERAL

The emphasis on the social gospel in liberalism had a strong influence on the liberals' concept of the church. Hordern states:

> Liberals in general had little concept of the Church. To many liberals the Churches were simply social organizations of men gathered together because of a common religious and ethical concern. The necessity of the Church was purely practical: men are able to do more when organized than as individuals alone.[16]

The leading concept among leading liberal theologians was that the church is a spiritual society with the task of spreading the "social gospel," which act paves the way for the coming kingdom.[17] Very little interest was generated toward an answer to the question, What is the church?

Because of their blind optimism as to the essential goodness of man and his possibility of progress, they saw little need for the local churches, which simply impeded this progress by feverishly clinging to their ecclesiastical dogmas and traditions. In his survey of the movement, Lightner writes:

> They had little faith in the existing organized churches to make any sizable contribution to either the spiritual change of the individual or the radical transformation of society as a whole. In fact, they looked at the churches as elements which needed to be overcome before society could be changed.[18]

16. William Hordern, *A Layman's Guide to Protestant Theology*, p. 116.
17. William Adams Brown, *Christian Theology in Outline*, p. 57.
18. Robert P. Lightner, *Neo-Liberalism*, p. 74.

With this low view of the church—a view that regarded the church as being extraneous to the Christian faith and a strictly human, mundane organization—it is understandable that liberalism has not made any significant contribution to the understanding of the nature of the church. Furthermore, it is not surprising that one of the major elements in the "remaking of liberalism"[19] was a heightened concept of the church.

Neoliberalism

The new sense of the importance of the church in neoliberalism has resulted, at least in part, from a dissatisfaction with the condition of the liberal churches. Horton, himself a liberal, complains:

> In the modern liberal churches, religious credos are no longer fighting slogans, rallying points for common loyalty and collective action; they are matters of private opinion, about which it is impolite to question a man. The liberal churches themselves have no corporate life, no common consciousness; they are collections of religious individuals, each carrying on his private and peculiar type of commerce with God, but occasionally gathering for worship in the same place, where they may listen to some exceptionally gifted preacher air his private religious opinions—after which they go their separate ways as before.[20]

Then, Horton proceeds to hammer away at the fact that the church has become a worldly institution, a factor in contemporary culture, which smiles at the Puritans for their fear of worldly amusements, worldly adornments, and worldly conversation.[21]

Dissatisfaction was not the only factor, however. Part of the interest is due to the ecumenical impetus toward unity.

> Ever since the protest of Bishop Charles Brent that matters

19. Hordern, p. 115.
20. Walter Marshall Horton, *Theology in Transition*, p. 120.
21. Ibid., p. 121.

> of faith and order could hardly be exempt from ecumenical discussion, and the subsequent initiation of the World Conference on Faith and Order, most large ecumenical gatherings have featured a solemn conclave considering the nature of this divided church which is really one.[22]

What concept of the church has this reaction produced? One prominent initial factor is the insistence upon a distinction between the spiritual church and the organized church. Neoliberals have come to believe that there is a church over and beyond the split denominations. It is a living society, begun in the work of Jesus and continuing that work through the ages. It is not just another social organization to be explained in sociological terms; it is a divine institution, founded by God.[23]

One of the clearest and most complete delineations of the neoliberal viewpoint of the church is that given by DeWolf. He refers to the true church as the spiritual church and is careful to distinguish it from the invisible church concept. Speaking of what the church is not, he explains:

> Strictly speaking, it is not visible to the eye. But neither is it something outside human experience. The spiritual church is not the ideal of what the church ought to be. Neither is it the mere aggregate number of all the individuals known to God as "saved" or destined to salvation.[24]

Positively speaking, he defines the spiritual church as "that unique and powerful fellowship of sharing created by the power of the Holy Spirit and spoken of hitherto as the *koinonia*."[25] As suggested by the use of *koinonia*,† "it is the real spiritual fellowship of all those persons who have committed themselves to the reign of God, whose Word was made manifest in Christ Jesus."[26]

22. Christian Rudolph LaVere, "The Doctrine of the Church," in *Twentieth Century Encyclopedia of Religious Knowledge*, ed. Lafferts A. Loetscher, 1:254.
23. Hordern, p. 116.
24. DeWolf, p. 318.
25. Ibid.

†This is a common term for the church among neoliberal writers.

26. DeWolf, p. 318.

> A person is only a part of this church as long as he is living continuously under the dominion of Christ. Although Paul said of the Corinthian Christians, "you are the body of Christ," it is apparent that this was strictly true only at times. It was not constantly true of those people.[27]

He continues:

> They knew well what it was to be the church, but they were not always the church. They were the church, the body of Christ, only when they truly accepted Jesus Christ as head.[28]

It is quite plain, then, that this concept includes nothing of a positional relationship in the body of Christ because of the new birth. Rather, one's relationship is always changing in accordance with the person's committal to the Lordship of Christ in his life. Furthermore, one could never be sure of his salvation for "the spiritual church is essential both as means and as meaning of salvation."[29] Membership in the body of Christ is the cause rather than the result of salvation.

Thus, while the neoliberals' change in their view of the church is probably the most outstanding concession that they have made in their "break" with old liberalism, it is also one of the most deceptive. Roth observes:

> The side of liberalism which did collapse . . . was its cavalier optimism, exposed as it was by the two wars and the great depression. But out of its shallow grave arose a new spirit for our age. This is the principality or power which we call *existentialism.*[30]

This chastened liberalism, which sees reality only in the historical experience, the true *existence,* has had a marked effect on the doctrine of the church. Roth continues:

27. Ibid., p. 319.
28. Ibid.
29. Ibid., p. 320.
30. Robert P. Roth, "Existentialism and Historic Christian Faith," *Christianity Today,* 5:4.

> The concept of the Church is quite radically changed by the existentialists because of their category of Inwardness or Subjectivity. This subjectivism is not the romantic subjectivity of the liberals which was centered in a feeling of dependence upon God. Such a feeling would make God a projection of the human heart. Existentialists would consider this the idolatry of using God as a disposable object, and God is never an object. Always he is Subject; always Thou, never It. The divine Thou can never be manipulated. He can only be spoken to in answer to his call. The call comes to me inwardly, not objectively or mechanically or casually. God always treats me as subject too and never as an object. Hence the relation between man and God is neither a cognitive one which can be apprehended by means of a set of propositions nor an emotional one which can be grasped by a genuine feeling. The relationship is rather one of speaking and responding to God's Word, hence it is one of decision. But no man can make this decision for another. Each must do his own believing just as he must do his own dying. The result of this doctrine, which is a one-sided truth, is an extreme individualism with no proper place for the sacramental community of the Church. Indeed for most existentialists the Church, as a visible structure, only gets in the way of the decisive conversation between the I and the Thou.[31]

Neoliberalism regrets the necessity of the organized church, but admits that it cannot get along without it. They infer that Christ did not plan for an organization to perpetuate the fellowship but that some such structure was inevitable. They warn that the organized church continually threatens to stifle or betray the spiritual church. But despite the perils and temptations inherent in organization, the organized church is necessary. DeWolf concludes:

> For better or for worse we are in the world. In the world, life, whether individual or social, requires embodiment in some structural means of nurture and expression.[32]

31. Ibid., 5:4-5.
32. DeWolf, p. 321.

Thus, the task of the church, according to neoliberals, is to *be* the church, cultivating and expressing the sacred *koinonia.*

Neoorthodox

" 'Where two or three are gathered together in my name there am I in their midst'—that is the Church."[33] This oft repeated formula of Barth seems quite simple, but behind it in Barth's thinking are concepts that are not always easy to grasp; yet, the doctrine of the church is more central in his theology than in that of many of his contemporaries. Hunt says that Barth's theology "has raised into the forefront in unparalleled fashion the doctrine of the church."[34]

There seems to be a striking similarity between the neoliberal and neoorthodox concepts of the church when one first reads Barth's challenge, "Let us be the Church."[35] And it is true that there seems to be something of a fluid nature to it. Something of this is seen in his definition of the church as "the living congregation of the living Lord Jesus Christ."[36] This gathering of believers is only a church insofar as certain conditions exist. When they cease, the church ceases. Barth explains:

> *What the Church is:* the congregation *is,* or *exists,* where and in so far as it dares to live by the act of its living Lord.
>
> *The danger* menacing the Church: the congregation fails to *exist* when, and in so far as the foundations of its life are shaken by its own sins and errors.[37]

This living, acting aspect is further emphasized when he refers to the congregation as the "event" by which he means that "the Church is not constituted once for all, but that it is continually

33. Karl Barth, *Dogmatics in Outline,* p. 143.
34. George L. Hunt, ed., *Ten Makers of Modern Protestant Thought,* p. 65.
35. Barth, p. 141.
36. Karl Barth, "The Church—The Living Congregation of the Living Lord Jesus Christ," in *Man's Disorder and God's Design,* by the World Council of Churches, 1:67.
37. Ibid.

being re-created by renewed divine activity."[38] "In this congregation the work of the Holy Spirit becomes an event."[39]

There are striking differences, however, between Barth's view and that of the neoliberal. The existence of the church in neoliberalism rests in man's determination to make Christ Lord. The emphasis is still on man. Barth is careful to emphasize, however, that this is a work of the Holy Spirit. He cautions:

> Woe to us, where we think we can speak of the Church without establishing it wholly on the work of the Holy Spirit. . . . The Christian congregation arises and exists neither by nature nor by historical human decision, but as a divine *convocatis*. Those called together by the work of the Holy Spirit assemble at the summons of their King.[40]

A second major difference between neoliberalism and neo-orthodoxy is in their respective attitudes toward the local church. Whereas DeWolf feels that the local organization is a necessary evil,[41] Barth feels that it is *the church*. He states:

> By men assembling here and there in the Holy Spirit there arises here and there a visible Christian congregation. . . . If the Church has not this visibility, then it is not the Church. When I say congregation, I am thinking primarily of the concrete form of the congregation in a particular place.[42]

Furthermore, he cautions against the use of the term "invisible."

> It is best not to apply the idea of invisibility to the Church; we are all inclined to slip away with that in the direction of a *civitas platonica* or some sort of Cloud-cuckooland, in which Christians are united inwardly and invisibly, while the visible Church is de-valued.[43]

Finally, Barth believes that the one, holy, universal church

38. Ibid., 1:68.
39. Barth, *Dogmatics in Outline,* p. 143.
40. Ibid., p. 142.
41. DeWolf, pp. 321-22.
42. Barth, *Dogmatics in Outline,* p. 143.
43. Ibid.

exists in each of these congregations. A group of believers stands on the earth at a definite place and there is the church, the one church. He states:

> The mystery of the Church is that for the Holy Spirit it is not too small a thing to have such forms. Consequently, there are in truth not many Churches but *one* Church in terms of this or that *concrete* one, which should recognise itself as the one Church and in all the others as well. . . .
>
> I believe that the congregation to which I belong, in which I have been called to faith and am responsible for my faith, in which I have my service, is the one, holy, universal Church.[44]

Each member of that local congregation is appointed to the task of making the one, holy, universal church visible in that place.[45] Another neoorthodox theologian, William Childs Robinson, explains:

> Thus it is not the addition of churches which makes the whole church, nor is the whole church divided into separate congregations. But wherever the church meets she exists as a whole, she is the church in that place.[46]

This church becomes visible by being continually occupied with the exposition and application of the Scripture, by fulfilling its service as an ambassador of Jesus Christ, and by having as its aim the Kingdom of God. When these things are missing, it is no longer a church.[47]

Neoevangelical

Among those who call themselves orthodox are two movements, fundamentalism and neoevangelicalism. The latter of these is especially difficult to define because of the wide variety of theological viewpoints among its adherents. One leading

44. Ibid., pp. 143-44.
45. Ibid., p. 145.
46. William Childs Robinson, "Church," in *Baker's Dictionary of Theology*, ed. Everett F. Harrison, p. 124.
47. Cf. Barth, *Dogmatics in Outline*, pp. 146-47.

neoevangelicalist assures his readers that "there is a solidarity of doctrine between fundamentalism and evangelicalism."[48] That such is not always the case, however, is pointedly expressed by Walvoord.

> An evangelical is free to believe all that fundamentalists believe theologically . . . or, if he prefers, he can deny all the fundamentals and still claim the same name, as does Cecil John Cadoux in his *The Case for Evangelical Modernism.* In a word, the designation *evangelical* only declares one in favor of the evangel, or the gospel, but it does not in itself define the term theologically. Its meaning depends upon the one who uses the term.[49]

Thus, there is a wide latitude in the usage of the term *evangelical.* A certain clarification and limitation has been achieved, however, in the term *neoevangelical,* which others have applied to this specific group within evangelicalism.

In the area of the doctrine of the church, there is general agreement among neoevangelicals as to their basic differences from fundamentalism. In fact both groups seem quite sure that the other has neglected or misinterpreted the doctrine of the church. Ockenga charges:

> The cause of the fundamentalist defeat in the ecclesiastical scene lay partially in fundamentalism's erroneous doctrine of the Church which identified the Church with believers who were orthodox in doctrine and separatist in ethics. Purity of the Church was emphasized above the peace of the Church.[50]

Contrariwise, Young counters:

> It is when we come to the question of attitudes, that this writer believes the New Evangelicalism to be weak. For one thing its leaders are outspoken opponents of the "come-outer"

48. Harold John Ockenga, "Resurgent Evangelical Leadership," *Christianity Today* 5:13.
49. John F. Walvoord, "What's Right About Fundamentalism," *Eternity* 8:35.
50. Ockenga, 5:12.

> groups. . . . Those who left the organization known as the United Presbyterian Church in the U.S.A. did so, not because they were separatists at heart but because they deeply believed in the unity of the true church and were concerned for the purity of its doctrine.
>
> With this attitude toward the church the New Evangelicalism has little or no sympathy. Indeed, if we understand it aright, it seems little concerned as to how a man obeys his ordination vows. . . .
>
> Perhaps it is not incorrect to say that the New Evangelicalism would like to build up the church without any reference to the church. It stresses evangelism, and does not always show itself discriminate with respect to those whom it invites to support it. It stresses scholarship and education. In fact it stresses just about everything except the all-important doctrine of the church.[51]

Thus, both sides are calling for a deeper understanding of the doctrine of the church. The neoevangelical charges that the fundamentalist has forgotten the unity of believers, while the fundamentalist charges that all too frequently church membership is meaningless. The point of tension, then, revolves around the question, "Which is more important, purity or unity?"[52]

The neoevangelical is willing to sacrifice purity for unity and opportunity. Ockenga states:

> An up-to-date strategy for the evangelical cause must be based upon the *principle of infiltration* [italics not in the original]. . . . It is time for firm evangelicals to seize their opportunity to minister in and influence modernist groups. Why is it incredible that the evangelicals should be able to infiltrate the denominations and strengthen the things that remain, and possibly resume control of such denominations? Certainly they have a responsibility to do so unless they are expelled from those denominations.[53]

51. Edward J. Young, "Where Are We Going?," *The Presbyterian Guardian* 28:154.
52. John W. Sanderson, *Fundamentalism and Its Critics*, p. 37.
53. Ockenga, 5:14-15.

Carnell has recently criticized Machen's withdrawal from the Presbyterian Church U. S. A. as a failure to understand the nature of the church. He questions:

> Does the church become apostate when it has modernists in its agencies and among its officially supported missionaries? The older Presbyterians knew enough about Reformed ecclesiology to answer this in the negative. Unfaithful ministers do *not* render the church apostate.[54]

He goes on to say that "Christ and the apostles did *not* decide the nature of the church by the presence or absence of heretics in the church."[55] Thus, it is Carnell's contention that a minister must stay in the denomination unless the gospel is removed from the creed or confession.[56] It was Machen's experience, however, that when the liberals had gained control they were content for the most part to allow the credal statement to stand. Sanderson notes:

> A desire to change the creeds did not develop, and has not developed to our day. The words are allowed to remain the same, and if they are interpreted at all, they are viewed as symbols of spiritual truth, not as historical facts.[57]

Thus, because the neoevangelicals seem to think that a rapprochement can be effected with liberalism and neoorthodoxy, they are willing to subordinate doctrinal particularity. If a strict doctrine of the purity of the local church inhibits the gospel preacher, he ignores the doctrine completely, or turns his attention to only those aspects that do not interfere. He is willing to sacrifice the preaching of the "whole counsel of God."

Not only is the neoevangelical advocating infiltration into modernistic denominations, but he is desirous of wiping out denominational barriers and achieving the unity of the visible

54. Edward John Carnell, *The Case for Orthodox Theology*, p. 115.
55. Ibid., p. 136.
56. Ibid., p. 157.
57. Sanderson, p. 41.

church on earth. Carnell believes that the physical divisions and denominational distinctives "are an index to our blindness, not our vision, for if we knew Christ as we ought, we would succeed in mediating the gospel without dividing brother from brother."[58] This prescription for unity is quite different from that of Charles Hodge, who could hardly be classed as one with cultic mentality. He states:

> One of the greatest evils in the history of the Church has been the constantly recurring efforts to keep men united externally who were inwardly at variance. Such forced union must be insincere and pernicious. It leads to persecution, to hypocrisy, and to the suppression of the truth. Where two bodies of Christians differ so much either as to doctrine or order as to render their harmonious action in the same ecclesiastical body impossible, it is better that they should form distinct organizations.[59]

Perhaps it would be better to promote and pursue spiritual fellowship where possible, and not attempt a visible, universal church on earth. Even Barth has a word here:

> It was and is needful that someone somewhere should make a stand against the excessive claims of all church movements, and assert that the union of the churches is a thing which cannot be manufactured, but first must be found and confessed, in subordination to that already accomplished oneness of the Church which is in Jesus Christ.[60]

In the final analysis, the neoevangelical is more interested in the opportunities of outreach through unification and infiltration than he is in the purity of the membership and testimony of the local church. The nature of the church is not contradicted by the inclusion of unbelievers. It must be remembered that this is the attitude and mood of the movement, and these things

58. Carnell, p. 131.
59. Charles Hodge, "The Unity of the Church," *Eternity* 9:27.
60. Karl Barth, *The Church and the Churches*, pp. 64-65.

may not undiscerningly be ascribed equally to everyone who calls himself a neoevangelical.

Fundamentalist

The fundamentalist movement is so named because of its historical adherence to the basic fundamentals of the faith. The *Oxford Dictionary of the Christian Church* defines fundamentalism as "strict adherence to traditional orthodox tenets held to be fundamental to the Christian faith."[61] Although it has its roots in the Protestant Reformation, the movement, as it is known today, arose as a protest against liberal theology, which swept over America after the Civil War. The initial impetus of the movement was seen in the prophetic conferences that began with a great rally in New York in 1877. The movement attracted interest and alerted conservatives to the dangerous infiltration of liberalism in theology. The doctrinal beliefs of the group were committed to writing by many outstanding conservative scholars and published in twelve volumes in 1909 under the title *The Fundamentals: A Testimony to the Truth.*[62]

Although the doctrine of the nature of the church was not set forth as one of the five basic fundamentals, yet it was intrinsic to the whole movement. The very impetus to the movement was the current low view of the church: unbelievers were allowed to participate and even preach and teach in the church. Machen writes:

> But what is the trouble with the visible Church? What is the reason for its obvious weakness? There are perhaps many causes of weakness. But one cause is perfectly plain—the Church of today has been unfaithful to her Lord by admitting great companies of non-Christian persons, not only into her membership, but into her teaching agencies. . . . What is now meant is not the admission of individuals whose confessions of faith may not be sincere, but the admission of great companies

61. Frank Leslie Cross, *The Oxford Dictionary of the Christian Church*, p. 533.
62. Walvoord, 8:7.

> of persons who have never made any really adequate confession of faith at all and whose entire attitude toward the gospel is the very reverse of the Christian attitude.[63]

Because of the presence of such rank unbelief in the churches, the fundamentalists cried out for a separation of the two parties, liberalism and Christianity, in the church. Again, Machen states: "If the liberal party, therefore, really obtains control of the Church, evangelical Christians must be prepared to withdraw no matter what it costs."[64] This plea for separation could not help but raise certain questions. Is separation contrary to the Scriptural exhortations to unity? Is schism within the visible church a heresy, or is it an act of obedience on the part of an individual to the Word of God? These questions flow out of the more central issue, What is the nature of the church? What is the church all about?

The answer of the fundamentalists was to make a sharp distinction between the nature of the visible church and the nature of the body of Christ, which is the true church.[65] They rebelled at the attitude of some who argued that discipline and a possible separation when discipline fails are a contradiction of the unity of the body of Christ. Unfortunately, in their reaction their tendency was to overstate the case and to give the impression that there are two distinct and separate churches, the invisible and the visible, with no relation whatsoever between the two. Ryle states:

> The one true church is composed of all believers in the Lord Jesus. . . .
>
> It is a church which is dependent upon no ministers upon earth. . . .
>
> This is the only church which possesses true unity. . . .
>
> This is the only church which possesses true sanctity. . . .

63. J. Gresham Machen, *Christianity and Liberalism*, p. 159.
64. Ibid., p. 166.
65. John C. Ryle, "The True Church," in *The Fundamentals for Today*, ed. Charles L. Feinberg, 2:505-8.

> This is the only church which is truly catholic. . . .
> This is the only church which is truly apostolic. . . .
> This is the only church which is certain to endure unto the end. . . .
> This is the church which does the work of Christ on earth.[66]

Although much of what Ryle says is true, it tends to be a one-sided truth. The typical fundamentalist emphasis minimized the importance of unity in the local church with its obvious corruptions. Paul teaches that the local church is the "church of the living God, the pillar and ground of the truth" (1 Tim 3:15). Peter teaches that the local church is the medium for the manifestations of the excellencies (attributes) of Him who has called us out of darkness into His marvelous light (cf. 1 Pet 2:9). Thus, the local church is to be the manifestation of what God is like.

Despite this weakness of fundamentalism, it fought a battle against impressive odds when almost every scholarly citadel of the faith capitulated. At its core fundamentalism had the truth of God and it cherished that truth. One can heartily agree with Sanderson when he says that "the critic of Fundamentalism today can thank his God that someone fought for the most important doctrines of the faith."[67]

Furthermore, fundamentalism today is making an effort to study the doctrine of the church against the background of today's needs and opportunities. This is not meant to imply that fundamentalists have become soft in their separatist stand, for even in these days when everyone is talking of union, the creeping liberalism within the Lutheran Church—Missouri Synod constituency was dealt a dramatic rebuke by its sister synod, the Wisconsin Evangelical Lutheran Synod. The resolution suspending fellowship reads:

> Whereas the Wisconsin Evangelical Lutheran Synod has

66. Ibid.
67. Sanderson, p. 14.

> lodged many admonitions and protests with the Lutheran Church—Missouri Synod during the past 20 years to win her from the path that leads to liberalism in doctrine and practice . . . and, whereas, our admonitions have largely gone unheeded and issues have remained unresolved; and . . . whereas the Commission on Doctrinal Matters has faithfully carried out its directions to continue discussions but now regretfully reports that differences with respect to the Scriptural principles of church fellowship . . . have brought us to an impasse . . . therefore, be it resolved that we now suspend fellowship with the Lutheran Church—Missouri Synod on the basis of Romans 16:17-18 with the hope and prayer to God that the Lutheran Church—Missouri Synod will hear in this resolution an evangelical summons to "come to herself" (Luke 15:17) and to return to the side of the sister from whom she has estranged herself.[68]

On the other hand, however, fundamentalists are attempting to resolve the purity-unity tension point. As a leading contemporary educator, John F. Walvoord, says:

> There should be no needless division within the organized church. There is constant exhortation to preserve a unity of fellowship in the instructions of Christ to the seven churches of Asia. Even though some of them had departed from the faith, it is significant that those who formed a part of these local congregations are not given any mandate to withdraw from that fellowship but rather are commanded to preserve their own testimony and do what they can to alleviate the situation. They were to accept persecution that would result from their faithfulness to the Lord and they were under no circumstances to compromise their testimony.[69]

In an attempt to find a practical, workable, and scriptural ap-

68. In "Wisconsin Lutherans Break With Missouri Synod," *Christianity Today* 5:989.
69. John F. Walvoord, "The Nature of the Church," *Bibliotheca Sacra* 116:297-98.

proach to the problem of unity in the visible organization, Walvoord continues:

> Such a practical program would involve, first the principle that believers should not be in organic relationship with an ecclesiastical organization which is predominantly non-Biblical and non-Christian in its actual belief. Second, needless divisions and conflicts within the church should be avoided and minor differences and doctrines should be submerged in the interest of the common task. Third, it is better for organizations having differing theological convictions to carry on their ministry separately than to attempt to work together with no sound theological agreement.[70]

Such endeavors to solve the present tension of the nature of the church will go far toward stabilizing fundamentalism as a movement.

One final problem of the contemporary scene needs to be discussed. Among men who are interested in doctrinal particularity there will always be theological debate, and this is as it should be. There is nothing obscurantist about those people who want to raise questions about the sharpness of theological definition. Among contemporary fundamentalists, there is a definite difference of opinion concerning the present existence of a universal church. Some feel that the universal church is in existence today and that it is the pattern of the local church. Others claim that the only church spoken of for this age in the Scripture is the local church. The former believe that the universal church is the body of Christ, whereas the latter believe the local church to be the body of Christ. Thus, these two viewpoints will be set forth briefly.

Universal-local church theory. This is the viewpoint held by those who follow generally in the Reformed doctrine of the nature of the church. In this view a distinction is made between

70. Ibid., 116:301.

the visible church and the invisible church.[71] McClain prefers the designations local and universal.‡

Those holding to this distinction claim that it gains its validity from the times that *ekklesia* is used in the New Testament but cannot refer to the local church or churches. Summers writes:

> While the term "church" predominately in the New Testament refers to a local body of people who have been called out redemptively by Christ, it is most difficult to escape the impression that in this letter [Ephesians] Paul ideally is enlarging the significance of the word to make it embrace all true believers. These make up the spiritual body of which Christ is the head; they fill out the remainder of the body. All together believers and Christ make one great spiritual body.[72]

These men hasten to add, however, that these are not separate churches but are different aspects of the one body of Jesus Christ. The universal church contains only true believers, and includes those on earth and in heaven. The local churches have to do with men on earth only, but may include both true believers and mere professors.[73] Kuiper declares:

> Very strictly speaking, the membership of the visible church coincides with that of the invisible church. And since the invisible church consists of the regenerate, only they rate as members *of* the visible church. To use a biblical expression, only the regenerate are of the visible church (1 John 2:19). However, it cannot be denied that there may be, and actually are, unregenerate persons *in* the visible church.[74]

There are varying expressions and opinions as to the relationship between these two aspects of the one church. McClain

71. R. B. Kuiper, *The Glorious Body of Christ,* p. 26.
‡Alva J. McClain, "The Church." Other terms, such as external and spiritual, real and ideal, organization and organism, have been suggested.
72. Ray Summers, *Ephesians: Pattern for Christian Living,* pp. 30-31.
73. Ibid.
74. Kuiper, p. 26.

says, "The *Local* Church is the Universal Church manifested in any particular place."[75] Shelley puts it well:

> There is then only one church but it may be viewed universally because viewed from union with its Head, or it may be viewed locally because viewed from the membership in a particular place.[76]

A slightly different explanation of the relationship between the universal church and the local church is elucidated by the late W. O. Carver, who interprets the figure of the body of Christ more realistically.

> The universal church and its local manifestations as congregations are distinctly divine in origin and in meaning. They are God's creation, the people of God, and of his Christ. They constitute a new humanity produced, preserved, and empowered as God's representative in the midst of "all the families of earth." The church is the congregation of the true Israel of God, continuing, interpreting, and supplanting the Old Testament Israel in terms of "God's saints in Christ Jesus. . . ."
>
> This "new humanity" consists of those who have accepted God's grace and have committed themselves to it. . . . These sanctified individuals voluntarily unite—as a church in the local sense—to give expression to their common experience of redemption, through worship, fellowship, and witnessing to the gospel of the Lord Jesus Christ. . . .
>
> Each group of believers becomes in its own location the body of Christ. Each is distinctly a temple of God in the Holy Spirit and is so sacred that whoever destroys it will himself be destroyed (1 Cor. 3:17). Its unity, its fellowship, and its representative character is such that factions and divisions in that body divide Christ and bring him condemnation (1 Cor. 10:14). Each member of each church is "baptized into the

75. McClain.
76. Bruce Shelley, *Introducing Laymen to Their Church: Studies in Ecclesiology,* p. 3.

fellowship" and repudiates or neglects that fellowship to his own sickness and even spiritual death. . . .

The congregation, a local manifestation of the church, begins in, and follows from, the fact that the total body of the redeemed constitutes the continuing, growing body of Christ. While the exact expression is never used, this comprehensive spiritual church is *the continuation of the incarnation* [italics not in the original]. In the book of Ephesians Christ and the church are so intimately related as to constitute one entity, neither being complete except in relation to the other. . . . By the fact of his salvation the believer becomes a member of the church, "a member of the body of Christ." Under the impulse of the Spirit, this member of the spiritual church voluntarily takes his place in the local fellowship and assumes his responsibility as a Christian in that church, for that local church is a concrete, organized expression of the one spiritual church. This conception of the one church as the body of Christ is more than a figure of speech. It is a spiritual reality apart from which there is no salvation and no true Christianity. . . .

In the measure of its genuineness and integration and unity and love and its loyalty to its Head, each congregation is, in its situation, God's local humanity, Christ's local body.[77]

This writer has been quoted at length because he is representative of a view that has become quite popular in recent years. This viewpoint interprets the phrase "the body of Christ" with strict realism and sees the church as "the extension of the incarnation." In the main, this is the view of most Roman Catholic writers, but there is a reception of it even among fundamentalists. However, most evangelical writers tend to interpret the phrase analogically, in terms of fellowship.[78] Further discussion concerning this interpretation will be entered into in chapter five, where the figures of the church will be discussed. Suffice it to note at this point that there are varying opinions as to the

77. W. O. Carver, "Introduction," in *What Is the Church?*, ed. Duke McCall, pp. 6-12.
78. Owen R. Brandon, "Body," in *Baker's Dictionary of Theology*, ed. Everett F. Harrison, p. 102.

exact relationship between the universal church and the local expressions of that church. But all of these men are in agreement that the ecclesiological expressions of the New Testament cannot be restricted to the local organized bodies.

Local church theory. Another viewpoint that has gained momentum recently, mainly in fundamental Baptist groups, is the concept that denies that there is any such thing as a universal or invisible church in this age and affirms that the New Testament church is a local company of baptized believers who have made a credible profession of salvation in Christ, organized for worship, fellowship, the proclamation of the Word, and the observance of the ordinances.[79]

This viewpoint is not entirely recent, for it had already gained specific expression over a century ago in the movement known as Old Landmarkism.[80] The founder of the movement, J. R. Graves, a leading pastor and writer of the day, identified the church with the Kingdom and thus argued that it must be a visible organization. "The church and kingdom of Christ is an institution, an organization; he, as God of heaven, 'set it up,' he built it, and it must therefore be visible."[81] This, then, led to this denial of any idea of an invisible church or any worldwide organization.

> And this, too, is manifest, that the only church that is revealed to us is a visible church, and the only church with which we have any. . . . duties to perform, is a *visible* body. . . . If this is visible, he has no invisible kingdom or church, and such a thing has no real existence in heaven or earth.[82]

The background of Graves sheds light on his rejection of the universal church. Torbet writes:

79. Chester E. Tulga, *New Testament Baptists and the Nature of the Church,* p. 13.
80. John E. Steely, "The Landmark Movement in the Southern Baptist Convention," in *What Is the Church?,* ed. Duke McCall, p. 134.
81. J. R. Graves, *Old Landmarkism: What Is It?,* p. 32.
82. Ibid.

> Graves came from New England, where in colonial days Baptists had experienced persecution at the hands of the Congregational state church. As a result these Baptists had come to fear the concept of the universal church, for with it they associated state-churchism. . . . They were convinced that the safeguard of soul liberty lay in the freedom of the local church to receive members upon its own requirement of a personal experience of the grace of God and a confession of that experience in believer's baptism. They viewed any ecclesiastical authority which might develop outside the local church as a threat to the true nature of the church.[83]

This movement originated by Graves has been a flourishing force in the Southern Baptist Convention.[84] Fifty years after Graves's statements, B. H. Carroll, president and professor of theology at Southwestern Baptist Theological Seminary, wrote:

> All teaching in the direction that there now exists a general assembly which is invisible, without ordinances, and which is entered by faith alone, will likely tend to discredit the particular assembly, which does now really exist and which is the pillar and ground of the truth.[85]

A contemporary writer, Roy Mason, expresses the sentiment of the North American Baptist Association concerning the universal or invisible church.

> This theory, which plays exegetical tricks, employs specious arguments and minimizes the importance of true churches of Christ, is a theory that has been and is a curse to the cause of Christ. It is one of the most widespread and hurtful heresies of our day.[86]

The feeling he exhibits is natural, since the North American

83. Robert G. Torbet, "Landmarkism," in *Baptist Concepts of the Church,* ed. Winthrop Still Hudson, pp. 172-73.
84. Steely, p. 134.
85. B. H. Carroll, *Ecclesia—The Church,* p. 13.
86. Roy Mason, *The Church That Jesus Built,* p. 25.

Baptist Association believes that *ekklesia* refers only to a local church.

Many of those who limit the church of the present age to the visible organization, however, do not identify the church with the Kingdom, as did J. R. Graves. Being premillennial, they believe the Kingdom is to be visibly erected in the future, but they deny the existence of the invisible, universal church in this age.[87]

A great diversity of opinions as to the explanation of the nature of the church has been set forth in this chapter. This diversity demands a thorough examination of the biblical use of the word *ekklesia*. That is the task of the following chapter.

87. Cf. Tulga; Richard V. Clearwaters, *The Local Church of the New Testament;* Edward H. Overby, *The Meaning of Ecclesia in the New Testament.*

4

THE USAGE OF THE WORD *EKKLESIA*

The word *ekklesia* was not a creation of the Christian church. When the Christian church annexed it for its purposes, *ekklesia* was already a word with a history, and a double history—both Jewish and Greek. Therefore, it is necessary to an adequate treatment of the doctrine of the church to understand the linguistic associations that the word *ekklesia* brought with it into New Testament usage.

Knowing a Greek word fully means knowing the history of the word. In any given instance, before the meaning of a word can be finally concluded its etymology, its development, and its immediate context must be taken into account, for they determine the word's meaning.[1] Although *ekklesia* is a word that in reality only finds its true and ultimate meaning in Christ, normal linguistic developments have nevertheless been employed as means under the guidance of the Holy Spirit. In the case of *ekklesia* their contribution is considerable. Trench explains:

> There are words whose history it is peculiarly interesting to watch, as they obtain a deeper meaning, and receive a new consecration, in the Christian Church; words which the Church did not invent, but has assumed into its service, and employed in a far loftier sense than any to which the world has ever put

1. See A. T. Robertson, *A Grammar of the Greek New Testament in the Light of Historical Research*, p. 31 ff.

> them before. The very word by which the Church is named is itself an example—a more illustrious one could scarcely be found—of this progressive ennobling of a word. For we have [*ekklēsia*] in three distinct stages of meaning—the heathen, the Jewish, and the Christian.[2]

The first source for investigation, then, is the classical or nonbiblical Greek.

I. USAGE IN THE CLASSICAL GREEK

ETYMOLOGICAL MEANING

Words have both etymological and connotational meanings, and both must be considered. The etymology of *ekklesia* is quite simple and would answer any doubts as to meaning if the question could be settled by etymology alone. The noun *ekklesia* comes from the preposition *ek* (out) and the verb *kaleo* (to call or to summon).[3] Robertson states:

> The root *kal* appears in the Latin *cal-endae, con-cil-ium, nomen-clā-tor;* in the Old High German *hal-ôn,* "to call." Originally *ekklesia* was a calling-out of the people from their homes.[4]

Liddell and Scott define *ekklesia* as "an assembly of the citizens summoned by the crier, the legislative assembly."[5] Trench attempts to add the idea of separation:

> *He ekklesia* was the lawful assembly in a free Greek city of all those possessed of the rights of citizenship for the transaction of public affairs. That they were *summoned* is expressed in the latter part of the word; that they were summoned *out of* the whole population, a select portion of it, including neither the populace, nor the strangers, nor yet those who had forfeited their civic rights, this is expressed in the first.[6]

2. Richard Chenevix Trench, *Synonyms of the New Testament,* p. 1.
3. Marvin R. Vincent, *Word Studies in the New Testament,* 1:93.
4. Robertson, p. 174.
5. Henry George Liddell and Robert Scott, *A Greek-English Lexicon,* p. 206.
6. Trench, pp. 1-2.

CONNOTATIONAL MEANING

If etymology alone were the sole consideration, Trench's definition would be quite adequate; however, he has not given proper attention to the connotational meanings, which have more to do with actual usage. This elaboration of the idea of segregation reads far too much into the classical usage. A distinction should be maintained between the etymology of a word and its meaning at some particular time in history. For example, *hussy* came from *huswife*, which means housewife; today it means a worthless woman or girl. *Ekklesia* comes from *ekkaleo* (to call out), but in the times prior to the New Testament it meant assembly or called out assembly. To say it means "the called out" is not correct. Broadus writes:

> The Greek word *ekklesia* signified primarily the assembly of citizens in a self-governed state, being derived from *ekkaleo,* to call out; i.e. out from their homes or places of business, to summon, as we speak of calling out the militia. The popular notion that it meant to call out in the sense of separation from others is a mistake.[7]

In an exhaustive research on the history of the development of *ekklesia,* Baker points out why the idea of segregation is untenable.

> The written language of the Greeks is usually dated from three to four centuries after they had settled in the peninsula. By this time the conception of an ecclesia had been well-established. It is generally agreed that when the derivative of the verb meaning "to call out" was applied to this assembly, the idea was not of segregation but of summoning. It would contradict the early Greek spirit to suppose that the "Calling" eliminated some from the meeting which would determine their common fate. It is probable that the earliest ecclesia found the members acting more in the capacity of warriors and

7. Alvah Hovey, ed., *An American Commentary on the New Testament,* (no vol. nos. given), *Commentary on the Gospel of Matthew,* by John A. Broadus, p. 358.

> fathers than as citizens. . . . It would hardly be fitting to interpret the word found in the New Testament as carrying an etymology so susceptible to Christian teachings when surrounding the Christian ecclesia were numerous wicked and seditious (and more ancient) ecclesiai bearing the same name.[8]

Hort, along with other competent scholars, confirms this when he writes: "There is no foundation for the widely spread notion that *ekklesia* means a people or a number of individual men *called out* of the world or mankind."[9] In other words, it does not mean a body of people who have been picked out from the world. It has not in it that exclusive sense. It means a body of people who have been summoned out. The summons was not to any selected few—it was not exclusive; it was a summons from the state to every man to come and shoulder his responsibilities. In itself the idea of segregation is etymologically possible and, of course, entirely scriptural, but it was never so used even in later times when it acquired religious associations.

To the Greek-speaking people, therefore, *ekklesia* came into use as the designation for the regular assembly of a self-governed state's citizens (who were called out from their homes or places of business by the herald) so that they could discuss and decide public business.[10] This meaning seems to be reflected in the following quotations cited by Carroll from classical writers:

> Thucydides 2, 22:—"Pericles, seeing them angry at the present state of things . . . did not call them to an assembly (ecclesia) or any other meeting."
>
> Demosthenes 378, 24:—"When after this the assembly (ecclesia) adjourned, they came together and planned. . . . For the future still being uncertain, meetings and speeches of all sorts took place in the market-place. They were afraid an assembly (ecclesia) would be summoned suddenly. . . ."

8. Robert A. Baker, "An Introduction to the Study of the Development of Ecclesiology," p. 25.
9. Fenton John Anthony Hort, *The Christian Ecclesia*, p. 5.
10. J. C. Lambert, "Church," in *The International Standard Bible Encyclopaedia*, ed. James Orr, 1:651.

> Aristophanes Act. 169:—"But I forbid you calling an assembly for the Thracians about pay."[11]

As time passed, the original meaning of the word seems to have disappeared from common usage.[12] Instead of referring to the popular assembly of citizens called out by the herald to transact public affairs, the word came to mean simply *an assembly,* irrespective of its constituents and how they were gathered or summoned. In Athens it signified the constitutional assembly.[13] Campbell states that in Athens the assemblies that had to be specially summoned to deal with urgent matters were called *sugkletoi.* In contrast were the *ekklesiai,* which met on days fixed beforehand and, therefore, did not need to be specially summoned.[14] He declares further that when the denominative verb *ekklesiadzein* is used of convening an *ekklesia,* it is sometimes used of assemblies that were not assemblies of citizens and, so far from being duly summoned, were probably not summoned at all.[15] Furthermore, even in New Testament times an assembly of almost any kind could be called an *ekklesia,* for in Acts 19 the disorderly mob that rushed into the theater at Ephesus, for the most part without knowing why it had come together, is twice called an *ekklesia.*

Campbell notes further that in ordinary usage *ekklesia* always meant only an assembly, a meeting, and not the body of people who assembled or met together. At Athens the *boule,* or council, was a body that existed even when it was not actually in session, but there was an *ekklesia* only when the citizens were actually assembled. Consequently, there was a new *ekklesia* every time they assembled.[16]

11. B. H. Carroll, *Ecclesia—The Church,* p. 28.
12. Robertson, p. 28.
13. Ibid.
14. J. Y. Campbell, "The Origin and Meaning of the Christian Use of the Word *Ekklesia,*" *Journal of Theological Studies* 49:131.
15. Ibid., 49:131-32.
16. Ibid., 49:132.

CONTRIBUTION TO NEW TESTAMENT WRITING

Having noted the salient factors in the classical usage of *ekklesia,* one ought next to determine what bearing they have upon the New Testament usage. Dana feels the contribution is quite significant:

> There were in the classical usage of this term four elements pertinent to its New Testament meaning: (i) the assembly was local; (ii) it was autonomous; (iii) it presupposed definite qualifications; (iv) it was conducted on democratic principles.[17]

Others are much less optimistic concerning the value of the classical usage. Johnston declares: "Non-Biblical Greek affords little aid for appreciating its meaning, for there *ekklesia* is never the *title* of a religious group."[18] In fact, Craig states: "The Greek word *ekklesia* had no special religious connotation."[19] Hoskyns and Davey declare that "classical and contemporary usage provides no analogy"[20] for an interpretation of the *ekklesia* of the New Testament. They support their conclusion by noting the manner in which the writers of the New Testament refer to *ekklesia.*

> In the Hebraic-Christian tradition *ekklesia* which is by its very nature exceptional, is evident from their use of the definite article. Yet the phrase, *the ekklesia,* used absolutely, though consistent in the New Testament, is *never once found in secular writings* [italics not in the original].[21]

Kicklightner speaks to the same point:

> In the Hebraic-Christian tradition *ekklesia* was more than *an* assembly; it was *the* assembly. The use of the definite article with *ekklesia* in Christian literature is an evidence of its

17. H. E. Dana, *A Manual of Ecclesiology,* p. 26.
18. George Johnston, *The Doctrine of the Church in the New Testament,* p. 35.
19. Clarence T. Craig, "The Church of the New Testament," in *Man's Disorder and God's Design,* by the World Council of Churches, 1:32.
20. Edwyn Hoskyns and Noel Davey, *The Riddle of the New Testament,* p. 21.
21. Ibid.

> exceptional nature and suggests a peculiar connotation, which must have made it somewhat meaningless to a contemporary Greek unfamiliar with Jewish or Christian practices.[22]

The lack of the definite article in the classical writings indicates that something about the essential nature of the religious *ekklesia* found no analogy in the secular *ekklesiai.* Thus, whatever similarities may be found, they are only *external, organizational* similarities. In this regard one can certainly agree with at least the first two elements of contribution that Dana sets forth—that the assembly was local and that it was autonomous.[23] But it must be remembered that these were simply organizational similarities without religious meaning. Baker cautions:

> Organizational similarities, whether they do or do not exist, are not the criterion of the character of the Christian ekklesia. Such a similarity is incidental as compared with the mission and message of the Christian ekklesia. It is the *difference,* not the similarity, which distinguishes the Christian ekklesia from anything else in history.[24]

It remains, then, to determine if the word *ekklesia* received a religious meaning or connotation in the Septuagint.

II. USAGE IN THE SEPTUAGINT

IMPORTANCE OF THE SEPTUAGINT USAGE

Several factors make the Septuagint an indispensable aid for finding the meaning of certain New Testament words and concepts. First, this Greek version of the Hebrew Scriptures was the Bible of the early church. Deissmann challenges the aspiring student:

> Take the Septuagint in your hand and you have before you

22. R. W. Kicklightner, "The Origin of the Church," in *What Is the Church?,* ed. Duke McCall, p. 30.
23. Dana, p. 26.
24. Baker, p. 49.

> the book that was the Bible of the Jews of the Dispersion and of the Proselytes from the heathen; the Bible of Philo the philosopher, Paul the Apostle, and the earliest Christian missions; the Bible of the whole Greek-speaking world; the mother of influential daughter-versions; the mother of the Greek New Testament. . . . Paul, the preacher and propagator of the Gospel, is not comprehensive without the Septuagint. He is not only the great Christ-Christian, but also the great Septuagint-Christian.[25]

Exclusive of the synoptic gospels, there are about six hundred New Testament verses that are quoted from the Septuagint. Roughly, this would equal Philippians, Colossians, Philemon, 1 and 2 Timothy, Titus, and 1 and 2 Thessalonians. More than half of the quotations from the Old Testament found in the New Testament are taken from the Septuagint.[26]

A second factor of importance concerns the Alexandrian Jews who were the translators of the Septuagint. While they had a thorough knowledge of Hebrew, they were at the same time familiar with the Greek of their time. Sanford expresses well the importance of this bilingual ability:

> Their task was to translate the Hebrew Old Testament into Greek, fitting Hebrew Idiom into the mold of Greek so that the meaning of the Greek words would convey to the Greek speaking people the thought of the Hebrew. For example, in those instances where the thought of the Hebrew word signified simply an assembly, the task of the translators was to select the Greek word that denoted an assembly. Only the Greek word that conveyed accurately the thought of the Hebrew word was to be selected.[27]

These factors, then, make evident the need for the study of the word *ekklesia* in the Septuagint, and one can easily sympathize with the feeling of Deissmann when he says:

25. G. A. Deissmann, *The Philosophy of the Greek Bible*, trans. Lionel R. M. Strachan, pp. 8-9.
26. Robertson, p. 99.
27. Carlisle J. Sanford, "The Concept of *Ekklesia* in Matthew," p. 15.

> It is one of the most painful deficiencies of biblical study at the present day that the reading of the LXX has been pushed into the background, while its exegesis has been scarcely ever begun. . . . A single hour lovingly devoted to the text of the Septuagint will further our exegetical knowledge of the Pauline Epistles more than a whole day spent over a commentary.[28]

One caution should be observed, however, in this very worthwhile study of the Septuagint. As valuable as it is for the historical background of a word, one must not assume that a New Testament word necessarily has the same sense that it has either in the Septuagint or the classical writings.[29] The New Testament has ideas of its own, and they will be considered later. The following study will determine how faithful the translators of the Septuagint were in their selection and use of the word *ekklesia.*

COMPARISON OF EDHAH AND QAHAL

An investigation of the Septuagint use of the word *ekklesia* includes a consideration of the Hebrew words *qahal* and *edhah* (the two principal Hebrew words for "gathering" or "assembly") along with the related use of the Greek *sunagoge* to translate these two words. According to Hatch and Redpath, the word *ekklesia* is used in seventy-seven passages in the Septuagint Old Testament.[30] Using Kittel's latest edition of *Biblia Hebraica,* one who examines the passages cited by Hatch and Redpath will see that where the Hebrew word is present for comparison, *ekklesia* is always used to translate some nominal form of the word *qahal.*[31]

The fact that the presence of the word *ekklesia* in the Septuagint only finds usage as a translation of *qahal* brings up the question Why should any further synonyms, such as *edhah* be

28. Deissmann, pp. 293-94.
29. Robertson, p. 100.
30. Edwin Hatch and Henry A. Redpath, *A Concordance to the Septuagint and the Other Greek Versions of the Old Testament,* 1:433.
31. Rudolpf Kittel, *Biblia Hebraica.*

considered? Some would say that such a consideration only confuses the issue. For example, Carroll says:

> In determining this question [i.e. the meaning of *ekklesia* in the Septuagint] have nothing to do with the meaning of *qahal* in its other connections. Rigidly adhere to the passage where *ecclesia* translates it. Because a word sometimes serves for another purpose, do not foist on it all the meanings of the other word.
>
> It is well enough to illustrate by synonyms, but do not define by them.[32]

Such an approach, however, seems to miss some of the greatest value of word study. One cannot understand the contrasts of meaning within a word until he sees the breadth of the word. The very fact that *qahal* is translated by seven different Greek words demonstrates the breadth of the word and demands a complete study in order to understand what facet of the word is brought out when it is so often translated by *ekklesia.* Concerning these subtle distinctions within words, Trench explains:

> And instructive as in any language it must be, it must be eminently so in the Greek—a language spoken by a people of the subtlest intellect; who saw distinctions, where others saw none; who divided out to different words what others were often content to huddle confusedly under a common term; who were themselves singularly alive to its value, diligently cultivating the art of synonymous distinction . . . and who have bequeathed a multitude of fine and delicate observations on the right discrimination of their own words to the afterworld.[33]

It is important, therefore, to find the fine nuances of thought that are distinguished by the Greek in the broad Hebrew term. It must be remembered, however, that the main issue at stake in this study is, What does *qahal* mean in those passages where it is translated by *ekklesia?*

32. Carroll, pp. 44-45.
33. Trench, p. vii.

The first step, then, is a study of the breadth of meaning in *qahal* itself. The lexicon defines *qahal* as an *assembly, congregation, convocation.* Its meaning has been divided as follows: first, an assembly specially convoked for evil counsel (Gen 49:6); for civil affairs (Prov 5:14); for war or invasion (Num 22:4); for a company of returning exiles (Jer 31:8); for religious purposes (Deut 5:19); and second, a congregation as an organized body: of Israel (Mic 2:5); a restored community in Jerusalem (Ezra 10:12); of angels (Psalm 89:6); more generally, a company, assembled multitude (Gen 35:11).[34] Disregarding variants, the word *qahal* is translated by seven Greek words in the Septuagint. Suffice it to say that *qahal* is a broad term, which breadth is not, perhaps, even grasped completely by noting the lexical definition given above. Baker spells out the distinction within the word more plainly:

> It is used *definitely* to refer to a particular meeting at a particular place; it is used indefinitely to refer to a local meeting at a particular place; it is used of meetings for wickedness, for politics, for war, for religion; it is used for a group of people that would never be able to assemble as a group (Gen. 28:3, 35:11, 48:4); it is used of a nation or perhaps a group of nations (Ezek. 32:22); it is used of a wicked Gentile army (Ezek. 38:4).[35]

The breadth of *qahal,* therefore, as pointed out, makes it evident that the Hebrew concept of *qahal* was of an untechnical noun that only gained particularity by the context. After noting this nontechnical usage of the word, one is able to see the fallacy of those definitions that explain it as the technical term for the redeemed community or the church in the Old Testament. An example of such thinking is given by T. F. Torrance:

> Two further elements in the concept of *qahal-ekklesia*

34. Francis Brown, S. R. Driver, and Charles A. Briggs, *A Hebrew and English Lexicon of the Old Testament,* based on the lexicon of William Gesenius as trans. Edward Robinson, p. 874.
35. Baker, p. 67.

> should be noted here: (a) The fact that *qahal* comes from the same root as *qol,* the word for "voice," suggests that the Old Testament *qahal* was the community summoned by the Divine Voice, by the Word of God. It was the people of the voice of the Word of God. Of that concept *ekklesia* is a very apt translation, indicating as it does the community of "the called" (*kletoi*) of God. *Ekklesia* is church, not in any sociological or political sense of assembly, and it is not, therefore, in any sociological or political continuity with Israel. It is church as act of God, as the community called into being and created by God's Word. (b) In line with that is the fact that the Old Testament *qahal* was first established at Sinai when God came and spoke, when his Voice was heard by all Israel, and his Word founded the covenant community. That was known as "the day of the *qahal,*" and so *qahal* came to have a special significance as the community brought into covenant relation with God for sacrifice and worship, and for the special end of revelation. *Qahal* denotes the Old Testament church actively engaged in God's purpose of revelation and salvation, that is, caught up in the mighty events whereby God intervenes redemptively in history, and involved in the forward thrust of the covenant toward final and universal fulfillment. *Qahal* is the community expecting eschatological redemption. In that sense, it is appropriated in the New Testament to denote the community in which the covenant promises of God to Israel are fulfilled in Jesus Christ and in the pouring out of his Spirit. Far from being an off-shoot of Israel, the Christian Church is Israel gathered up in Jesus Christ who recapitulates in himself the historico-redemptive service of Israel.[36]

These words from such a well-known contemporary spokesman are most significant because they express the viewpoint of many who see the origin of the church in the Old Testament and see the New Testament *ekklesia* as simply the development of the Old Testament *qahal.* One severe fallacy of this interpretation is the usage of *qahal* as a technical term. In direct opposition

36. T. F. Torrance, "The Israel of God," *Interpretation* 10:305-6.

to this viewpoint, Schmidt says of both *edhah* and *qahal:* "The absence of a consistent usage in translation shows that neither of these Hebrew words is in itself a technical term."[37]

There is another word that must be considered because, even though it is never translated by *ekklesia,* it does have a very close relation to *qahal.* Both *edhah* and *qahal* refer to an assembly or gathering, yet *ekklesia* is never used to translate *edhah.* Furthermore, *edhah* is of interest in this study because it is translated approximately one hundred and thirty times from Exodus to Proverbs by the word *sunagoge,* which is the same Greek word that is many times used to translate *qahal.** This raises a question then as to what is the distinctive difference in these two synonyms—a difference that allows *ekklesia* repeatedly to translate *qahal* but never to translate *edhah.*

The lexical meaning of *edhah* is given as *congregation*—a company assembled together by appointment, or acting concertedly. Its usage is given variously as referring to people, to the righteous, to evildoers, to animals (such as a swarm of bees), to a whole assembly of Israel.[38] Many times it seems to approximate the meaning of *qahal.*†

In comparing the meaning and usage of these two words, then, opinions that are in direct contradiction with each other have been set forth. On the one hand there is the view of Bannermann, who quotes with approval from Vitringa:

> The Hebrew *eda* corresponds to the Greek *sunagoge,* as *qahal* does to *ekklesia.* . . . *Sunagoge,* like *eda,* always means a meeting assembled or congregated, although possibly bound together by no special tie; but *ekklesia,* like *qahal,* denotes a number of persons who form a people, joined together by laws and other bonds, although it may often happen that they are

37. Karl Ludwig Schmidt, "The Church," in *Bible Key Words from Gerhard Kittel's Theologisches Wörterbuch zum Nuen Testament,* ed. and trans. J. R. Coates and H. P. Kingdon, 1.2:55.

**Qahal* is translated in the Septuagint by no fewer than seven Greek words.

38. Brown, Driver, and Briggs, p. 417.

†Cf. Num 10:2?; 16:2; 16:5ff.; 26:10ff.

> not assembled together, and that it is impossible that they should be so.[39]

He makes his distinction very clear in the following illustration:

> When, for example, believers are scattered through different parts of a country, so that they have no opportunity of meeting together, then indeed they cease to be an *eda,* a *sunagoge;* but they do not cease to be a *qaha,* an *ekklesia.* In other words, they do not, in such a case, cease to form one body, which is united together in the very closest bonds by the Holy Spirit in faith.[40]

On the other hand, Hort expresses an opposite view:

> Neither of the two Hebrew terms was strictly technical: both were at times applied to very different kinds of gatherings from the gatherings of the people, though *qahal* had always a *human* reference of some sort, gatherings of individual men or gatherings of nations. The two words were so far coincident in meaning that in many cases they might apparently be used indifferently: but in the first instance they were not strictly synonymous. *Edhah* (derived from a root *ydh* used in the Niphal in the sense of gathering together, specially gathering together by appointment or agreement) is properly, when applied to Israel, the society itself, formed by the children of Israel or their representative heads, *whether assembled or not assembled* [italics not in the original].
>
> On the other hand *qahal* is properly their *actual meeting together* [italics not in the original]: hence we have a few times the phrase *qahal edhah* "the assembly of the congregation."[41]

What is the answer, then, to these contradictory statements? The answer will undoubtedly be found by making a thorough inductive study of each usage of *edhah* and *qahal* in the Old Testament. This Bannerman did not do. He, along with Trench, Cremer, and (in substance) Schurer was governed

39. D. Douglas Bannerman, *The Scripture Doctrine of the Church,* p. 92.
40. Ibid.
41. Hort, pp. 4-5.

in his thinking by the findings of Vitringa.[42] One who, like Hort, has made an exhaustive inductive study is Baker. Speaking of these words as they refer to assembled people, he sets forth the following distinction:

> It seems apparent from this inductive study, that *eda* contemplates the people considered as a group—a congregation or company not exercising the prerogatives of specific autonomous action. The American Standard Version of the Bible retains this distinction by translating the word as "congregation" or "company." On the other hand, *qahal,* in its farthest point from *eda,* contemplates the people as assembled in a physical meeting for a specific purpose, immediately or remotely displaying the prerogatives of autonomous action. . . . There is a broad band of meaning in which they are very similar in content yet looking in an opposite direction. That is, *qahal,* as translated by *sunagoge, includes* as its meaning the assembled congregation of Israel (Numbers 16:33) *in spite of the fact* that the congregation did not specifically exercise immediate autonomous prerogatives. *eda,* on the other hand, as translated by *sunagoge, includes* as its meaning the assembled congregation of Israel (Judges 20:2, 3, 7) *because* the congregation is not exercising autonomous prerogatives.[43]

Thus, in the only place the two words can be compared (i.e., the mutual translation by *sunagoge*) the distinctive element of *qahal* seems to be the necessity of a physical meeting for a specific purpose, immediately or remotely displaying the prerogatives of autonomous action.

Relation of ekklesia *to* qahal.

Now, to approach the crux of the whole issue: namely, the specific meaning of *qahal* in those passages where it is translated by *ekklesia.* Of the one hundred and twenty occurrences of *qahal* in the Hebrew Old Testament, it is translated in the Sep-

42. Bannerman, p. 90.
43. Baker, pp. 141-42.

tuagint by *ekklesia* seventy-seven times, or 64 percent of the time. Thus, *ekklesia* apparently reproduces the typical Old Testament significance of the Hebrew *qahal.* And when one narrows the study of *qahal* down to these specific passages that are translated by *ekklesia,* he finds that *qahal* is always used of an actual assembly or meeting of some kind. Schmidt says:

> In the LXX *ekklesia* has no ecclesiastical significance; it simply means "gathering" and denotes either coming together, as at Deut. ix, 10; xviii, 16 (*yom haggahal*: Luther "Versammlung"; R.V. "assembly") or being together, as at I Kings viii, 65 (*qahal qadhol*): Luther "Versammlung"; R.V. "congregation"). *The nature of the gathering depends entirely upon the nature of those who compose it* [italics not in the original].[44]

Thus, in Psalm 26:5 the *ekklesia* is an assembly of evildoers. In Ezekiel 32:22-23 it refers to the military host of Asshur, the world power overthrown by the Chaldeans. First Chronicles 13:1-2 indicates the word is used of a meeting of military officers rather than the army as a whole. In other passages, such as Deuteronomy 31:30 and Joshua 8:35, the word is used of the assembly of Israel. It is easily seen, then, that *ekklesia* is not a technical term in the Septuagint. Rather, the content of the word *ekklesia* was determined by its modifiers. Thus, there may be found wicked *ekklesiai, ekklesiai* of saints, and so forth. The word *ekklesia* may be likened to a vehicle, whose content depends on its modifiers and environment. The assembly may be religious, political, military, judicial, national, or racial. The word does not signify the nature or the purpose of its constituency: it only points to the constituency's group identity and autonomous prerogatives. One thing must be stressed, and that is that the word always describes a corporeal, physical unity of people. In other words, one must be physically present in the assembly itself to constitute a member of the *ekklesia.* If there were some absent who should have been present, they are not

44. Schmidt, p. 51.

members of the *ekklesia.* A mental or spiritual unity is not contemplated. The Jews preparing the Septuagint did not think in terms of "the *ekklesia*" as an abstract institution; they conceived of it as "an *ekklesia*" whenever it met.[45]

By way of summary of the Septuagint usage, then, it has been seen that an *ekklesia* may meet for any purpose, but there always seems to be some deliberative purpose for the meeting. Secondly, this *ekklesia* seems to be autonomous in nature. Thirdly, whereas the qualifications for the constituency may vary to a great extent, yet one qualification is constant, never varying: to be a member of an *ekklesia* a person must be physically present at the assembly. The *ekklesia* is never contemplated as a spiritual fact, independent of spatial and temporal limitations. Finally, as was the case in the classical writings, there is no evidence whatever that the word acquired a specifically religious connotation in the Septuagint. All uses of the word never go beyond the simple meaning of *an assembly.* Thus, there is no place for reading the church back into the Old Testament on the basis of the prevalent usage of *ekklesia.* As Carroll exclaims: "The testimony here is univocal. It is as solidly one thing as the Macedonian phalanx."[46]

III. USAGE IN THE NEW TESTAMENT

RELATION TO PREVIOUS USAGE

By the time of the writing of the New Testament, the word *ekklesia* already had an extensive history of its own—a background in both Greek and Jewish writings. From its etymological meaning *to call out,* the word in the classical Greek period came to signify *an assembly* irrespective of its constituents and how they were gathered or summoned. Furthermore, *ekklesia* did not acquire any different significance in the Septuagint. All the uses of the word never go beyond the simple meaning of an

45. Baker, pp. 98-99.
46. Carroll, p. 44.

assembly. Thus, when the writers of the New Testament, whose Bible was the Septuagint, used *ekklesia,* they were not inventing a new term. They found the term in common use and simply employed what was at hand.

A question arises, however, as to whether the New Testament writers used the term in its established nontechnical and general sense or in a specific and technical sense. In other words, although the etymological associations of *ekklesia* have their unquestionable bearing upon the significance of the term, the deciding evidence must be drawn from an exhaustive investigation of its actual use in the New Testament. While it is true that historical continuity seems to demand that the early appearance of the word *ekklesia* in any new literature should simply suggest "assembly," it is also true that the Holy Spirit frequently lifts words from their current usages to a higher plane of meaning and packs into them such vast new content as their etymologies will scarcely account for. Whitney states: "Philologists agree that the final authority on any word does not lie in its etymology or historical connotation but *in its actual use.*"[47] Robertson remarks: "one must not assume that a N.T. word necessarily has the same sense that it has either in the LXX or in the *koine*. The N. T. has ideas of its own."[48] He lists *ekklesia* among those words of which he says: "the main point to note is the distinctive ideas given to words already in use."[49]

For this reason it is hardly possible to agree with Davidson's view of the complete Old Testament causality in accounting for the Christian *ekklesia*. With him the church is simply an unconscious development of early Christians, continuing Judaism.[50] A more balanced approach seems to be that of Cameron, who admits a historical continuity but denies complete Old Testament causality for New Testament doctrines. He writes:

47. W. D. Whitney, *The Life and Growth of Language,* p. 48.
48. Robertson, p. 100.
49. Ibid., p. 115.
50. Richard Davidson, "The Old Testament Preparation for the New Testament Doctrine of the Church," *Review and Expositor* 38:49-56.

> I am not so sure, as many critics are today, that all of our Lord's principles were rooted in the Old Testament as if it anticipated and foreshadowed all. No doubt some of His principles were related to many in the Old Testament. But did anything like the sovereignty of God or his unity contained in the Old Testament require merely a stage or two of development to transform them into the wealth of thought and practice of Jesus? The difference is so wide that it seems that the ordinary confined idea of development is not wide enough to account for the New Testament as it stands. There is so much more in the New Testament than can be said to have grown up by gradual process from the soil of the Old Testament, so much more than found enough in the Old Testament to initiate a process at all.[51]

As one approaches the study of *ekklesia* in the New Testament, then, he should be cognizant of the etymological associations and historical connotations of the word and he should also be open to any new content that the Holy Spirit may have given to it.

According to Moulton and Geden there are one hundred and fourteen occurrences of *ekklesia* in the New Testament.[52] Except for three occurrences in Matthew, it is absent from the gospels. Also, it does not occur in 2 Timothy, Titus, 1 Peter, 2 Peter, 1 John, 2 John, or Jude. Especially remarkable is its nonappearance in the Petrine epistles.

It is not necessary that this study should make a detailed examination of every occurrence of *ekklesia*. Rather, representative usages and most important passages will undoubtedly be sufficient to yield perfectly valid conclusions.

USAGES ACCORDING TO LITERARY CLASSIFICATIONS

Because this is an inductive study of the usages of *ekklesia* by the New Testament writers, it is proper that their usages be

51. James R. Cameron, *God the Christlike*, p. 184.
52. W. F. Moulton and A. S. Geden, *A Concordance to the Greek Testament*, pp. 316-17.

classified according to literary classifications rather than theological classifications, which were developed after the time of the New Testament writers. After these literary usages have been determined, they will then be classified according to their proper theological divisions.

Nontechnical usage

It should be reiterated that at the beginning of the Christian era the word *ekklesia* had no etymological associations or historical connotations that carried its meaning beyond the idea of an autonomous physical assembly. Baker declares:

> It must be insisted that if the distinctly Christian ekklesia had a particular content different from the secular ekklesia that met on the next street, the source of that different content may be exhausted in Jesus Christ.[53]

The Septuagint *ekklesia* was *not* a Christian *ekklesia,* and there are New Testament *ekklesiai* that are not Christian *ekklesiai.* Jesus said, "I will build *my ekklesia.*" The pronoun *mou* (my) is in the emphatic position in the Greek text, suggesting that the distinctiveness was not to be associated with the *word ekklesia* but with the *content* of the *ekklesia.* When Jesus established "my *ekklesia*" it was as different from the Old Testament *ekklesiai* as it was from the numerous *ekklesiai* that existed in every city. McDaniel notes: "The technical New Testament ekklesia was the 'Jewish ekklesia,' the 'Greek ekklesia,' etc."[54] Thus, the content of *ekklesia* is determined by its modifiers. It is true that there were points of similarity between the *ekklesia* that Jesus established and the other *ekklesiai,* but these are not the vital issue. It is the *difference* between these *ekklesiai* that constitutes the significant factor. Baker illustrates:

> The difference between a "gambling" *house* and "God's" *house* . . . does not consist in the conception of the word

53. Baker, p. 181.
54. George W. McDaniel, *The Churches of the New Testament,* p. 9.

> "house," nor do coincidental structural similarities affect the conception. The distinctive factor is in the content ascribed—whether "gambling" or "God."[55]

Thus, the distinctive factor of an *ekklesia* was found in the content ascribed to it by the modifiers.

With these factors in mind, one is prepared to classify the various ways in which *ekklesia* is used in the New Testament. Historical continuity seems to demand that the literal or nontechnical use of the word *ekklesia* would simply refer to an autonomous group of people *physically* united. Physical unity is the characteristic of the nontechnical *ekklesia.*

There are five *nontechnical* uses of the word *ekklesia* in the New Testament. The first passage illustrative of this usage is Acts 7:38: "This is he who was in the *ekklesia* in the wilderness." Stephen is here speaking of the gathering of Israel before Mount Sinai for the receiving of the Law. *Ekklesia* here has its common significance of a physical assembly, as used in the Septuagint. A similar passage occurs in Hebrews 2:12: "In the midst of the *ekklesia* I will sing praises to thee." This is a quotation of a Septuagint passage (Psalm 22:22) in which *ekklesia* is used to translate *qahal.* Obviously, there is not even remote reference to the New Testament idea of the church.

A more significant passage is the account in Acts 19:23-41, which "seems to present conclusive evidence that the word *ekklesia* has broadened its meaning far beyond the strictly classical sense."[56] Thus, these verses have been a cause of difficulty for those who have based their concept of *ekklesia* in the New Testament strictly on the classical usage.[57] Here Luke is describing an assembly of Greeks who met together because Paul's preaching had hurt the idol makers' business. Notice the description of the assembly:

55. Baker, p. 185.
56. Ibid., p. 194.
57. Cf. Carroll, p. 6.

> And the whole city was filled with confusion: and having caught Gaius and Aristarchus . . . they rushed with one accord into the theatre. . . . Some therefore cried one thing, and some another: for the assembly was confused; and the more part knew not wherefore they were come together (Acts 19:29-32).

That this wholly irregular, disorganized mob in a state of confusion should be considered as any kind of *ekklesia* is quite different from the classical Greek usage. On the same occasion, however, the town clerk spoke of convening a regular or lawful *ekklesia* (v. 39). Thus, both a riotous mob and an orderly and authoritative legislature were termed as *ekklesiai*. Concerning these assemblies, F. F. Bruce explains:

> There were regular assize-days—the days when the convention of citizens met under the presidency of the provincial governor. . . . If the matters which caused them concern were such as might more suitably be dealt with by the citizen body of Ephesus, they should wait for one of the regular meetings of the civic assembly (of which there were three in each month) instead of convening an irregular and riotous assembly like this.[58]

Thus, the more popular type of *ekklesia* under the Greeks had become a more formal, regulated *ekklesia* with the Romans.[59]

Because words are constantly changing and developing in meaning,[60] it would be natural that some of the usages would be on the borderline of the nontechnical use, or in what may be called the subtechnical use. Four occurrences of *ekklesia* in the early writings of Paul should be classified as subtechnical. These are found in the very earliest of the epistles, when *ekklesia* had not taken on a very definite Christian content. Notice the extensive descriptive modifiers: "the church of the Thessalonians which is in God the Father and in the Lord Jesus Christ" (1

58. F. F. Bruce, *Commentary on the Book of the Acts,* pp. 401-2.
59. R. J. Knowling, "The Acts of the Apostles," in *The Expositor's Greek Testament,* ed. W. Robertson Nicoll, 2:419.
60. Cf. Robertson, pp. 31-48.

Thess 1:1); "the churches of God which in Judea are in Christ Jesus" (1 Thess 2:14); "the church of the Thessalonians in God our Father and the Lord Jesus Christ" (2 Thess 1:1); "the churches of God" (2 Thess 1:4).

Some characteristics common to these four uses indicate that *ekklesia* had not yet come to be identified definitely with a *Christian* assembly. The nature and extent of the modifiers suggest this. For example, in the opening verses of each epistle, *ekklesia* is followed by the adjective form of the city, modifying it as to place, then it is further modified by a locative of sphere, defining the particular *kind* of *ekklesia*; i.e., the kind of *ekklesia* that is "in God our Father and the Lord Jesus Christ."[61]

Because it has previously been demonstrated that in pre-New Testament times, the word *ekklesia* received its content from its modifiers, and that various *ekklesiai,* other than Christian assemblies, existed in every city, it seems clear that Paul's modifying descriptions of the *ekklesia* were of necessity added because the word *ekklesia* had not yet become a technical Christian word. Ramsay agrees with this interpretation.

> In Lukan and Pauline language two meanings are found of the term ekklesia. It means originally simply "an assembly"; and, as employed by Paul in his earliest Epistles, it may be rendered "the congregation of the Thessalonians." It is then properly construed with the genitive, denoting the assembly of this organized society, to which any man of Thessalonica may belong if he qualifies for it.[62]

When Origen compared the *ekklesia* of God with the *ekklesia* in various cities as they existed side by side, he seemed to have made this same distinction.

> For the Church [*ekklesia*] of God, e.g., which is at Athens, is a meek and stable body, as being one which desires to please

61. Baker, p. 195.
62. W. M. Ramsay, *St. Paul: The Traveller and Roman Citizen,* p. 124.

> God, who is over all things; whereas the assembly [*ekklesia*] of the Athenians is given to sedition.[63]

Moffatt also takes the view that it was necessary for Paul here to modify fully the *kind* of *ekklesia* he had in mind.

> An implicit contrast lies in the following words (so in 2: 14); there were *ekklesiae* at Thessalonica and elsewhere (cf. Chrysostom and Orig., Cels. III xxix-xxx) which had not their basis and being *en . . . christoi.*[64]

Plummer also remarks:

> The word *ekklesia* "assembly" still needs a modifier to show that a Christian assembly is referred to, hence "the churches of God"; the unmodified *ekklesia,* like our word "church," soon became sufficient.[65]

It is interesting to note that in Paul's later epistles *ekklesia* is not characterized by these extensive qualifying phrases in order to define its content. This seems to be assumed.

Technical usage

In the literary development of words there is an unconscious process whereby when words are applied in a restricted way to a particular field, they oftentimes assume what is termed a *technical* character, caused by the transference of ideas.[66] The word *ekklesia* was so affected. It became so completely identified with a new kind of assembly—an assembly with a spiritual or Christian unity—that it was applied to that type of assembly. The spiritual or Christian characteristic became accepted as a part of the word itself. Thus, there came to be a new content in the use of the word *ekklesia* as applied to the Christian assembly. Previously there seemed to be a necessity of so modifying

63. Origen *Origen Against Celsus* 3. 30.
64. James Moffatt, "The First and Second Epistles to the Thessalonians," in *The Expositor's Greek Testament,* ed. W. Robertson Nicoll, 4:23.
65. Alfred Plummer, *A Commentary on St. Paul's First Epistle to the Thessalonians,* p. 3.
66. G. A. Deissmann, *Light from the Ancient East,* trans. Lionel R. M. Strachan, pp. 113-14.

the word as to differentiate if trom the secular *ekklesiai.* The New Testament usage bears out this usage in a surprisingly consistent way. Eleven times in the New Testament the modifying phrase "of God" is affixed to the word *ekklesia,* apparently to identify its spiritual nature. Significantly, this phrase is added primarily in the earlier epistles of Paul. Hort observes:

> Everyone must have noticed St Paul's fondness for adding *of God* to ekklesia. . . . With the exception however of two places in I Tim. (iii. 5, 15), where the old name is used with a special force derived from the context, this name is confined to St Paul's earlier epistles, the two to the Thessalonians, the two to the Corinthians, and Galatians.[67]

Thus, in the development of the word *ekklesia,* the technical use of the word came to mean not only a physical assembly, but a physical assembly characterized by a distinctly Christian unity. This is the usage, then, that became overwhelmingly predominant in the New Testament. Here was a new kind of *ekklesia*—a Christian *ekklesia*—and it was distinct from every other *ekklesia* because it had the content that Jesus Christ gave it. This Christian *ekklesia* may be defined, then, as a local assembly spiritually united in Christ, with an autonomous nature.

Most of the New Testament usages are technical and in most every case they can be easily recognized as such because they have the two characteristics of the technical usage—both physical and spiritual unity. Compare for example such expressions as "the church which was in Jerusalem" (Acts 11:22); "the church that was at Antioch" (Acts 13:1); and "the church of God which is at Corinth" (1 Cor 1:2). These passages leave no doubt as to the local meaning of the term.

A passage that has caused considerable dispute, however, is Matthew 18:17: "and if he shall neglect to hear them, tell it unto the *ekklesia:* but if he neglect to hear the *ekklesia,* let him be unto thee as a heathen man and a publican." The great ma-

67. Hort, p. 107-8.

jority of scholars agree that the *ekklesia* here is a specific assembly with which the offender is connected. The disagreement centers on what kind of assembly is referred to and whether or not such an assembly was then in existence or was at that time still future. Robertson writes:

> The problem here is whether Jesus has in mind an actual body of believers already in existence or is speaking prophetically of the local churches that would be organized later.[68]

There are basically two interpretations that represent this *ekklesia* as already in existence at the time Christ spoke these words. One such view claims this as simply a reference to the local Jewish synagogue. Hort contends:

> The actual precept is hardly intelligible if the *ekklesia* meant is not the Jewish community, apparently the Jewish local community, to which the injured person and the offender both belonged.[69]

Several factors make this view seem quite improbable. First, why does Christ have a preference for *ekklesia* instead of synagogue if He is speaking of the Jewish community? As a matter of fact, the term *ekklesia* is never applied elsewhere in Scripture to the synagogue. Gaebelein says: "If the Lord had meant synagogue the Holy Spirit surely would have used the Greek word 'synagogue' instead of 'ecclesia.'"[70] Secondly, in what sense could the following verses be applied to the synagogue? The content of these verses is that which was to be given to the followers of Jesus according to Matthew 16:18-20, and there they are clearly distinct from the Jewish synagogue. Finally, why would Christ refer His disciples to an assembly that was opposed to Him and His followers? The people knew that already the synagogue and the Sanhedrin were arrayed against Him. John 12:42 states that many of the rulers believed on

68. A. T. Robertson, *Word Pictures in the New Testament*, 1:149.
69. Hort, p. 10; cf. also Alfred Plummer, *An Exegetical Commentary on the Gospel According to St. Matthew*, p. 253.
70. Arno C. Gaebelein, *The Gospel of Matthew*, p. 384n.

Christ "but because of the Pharisees they did not confess it, lest they should be put out of the synagogue." Thus Sanford writes that "Christ could not have meant to direct His disciples to apply to an assembly which was estranged from them for the purpose of restoring brotherly relations among themselves."[71]

Others hold that the *ekklesia* referred to is the existing community of believers. A. B. Bruce calls it "the brotherhood of believers" and says that for the time being the twelve were the nucleus of the local *ekklesia.*[72] This view seems improbable, however, for there is no evidence that there existed such a group of believers so constituted as to execute these directions for discipline. Simpson declares: " 'Tell it to the *ecclesia*' can hardly refer directly to communities of Jesus' disciples, as these did not exist in the time of the Galilaean ministry."[73] Furthermore, the following verses speak in general terms showing that the *ekklesia* refers to an assembly of believers so constituted and not simply to a specific community in the time of Christ. There does not, therefore, seem to be any evidence in this passage, or elsewhere, to prove that during Christ's ministry He founded an assembly having the external authority to execute the discipline referred to in this passage.[74]

The most tenable view seems to be that Christ spoke of the *ekklesia* in anticipation of the local Christian assemblies that would be organized after the advent of the Holy Spirit and the formation of the body of Christ on the day of Pentecost. Prior to that time no *ekklesia* that could hear and adjudicate matters of dispute arising among its members existed. Gaebelein says: "The injunction given here could not have been kept at the time when the Lord gave it, nor before the day of Pentecost."[75] Toussaint states:

71. Sanford, p. 38.
72. Alexander Balmain Bruce, "The Synoptic Gospels," in *The Expositor's Greek Testament,* ed. W. Robertson Nicoll, 1:240.
73. J. G. Simpson, "Church," rev. Clifton Grant, in *Dictionary of the Bible,* ed. James Hastings, rev. Frederick C. Grant and H. H. Rowley, p. 160.
74. Sanford, p. 39.
75. Gaebelein, p. 89.

> "Where two or three are gathered together in my name there am I in the midst of them" [Matt. 18:20] clearly implies a time when Christ will be absent from His disciples, a time in which the church would exist.[76]

Marsh explains further:

> During his earthly ministry he called individuals to himself, but he formed no organization. He made preparation for the latter, but complete preparation was not made until after his resurrection and ascension, and the consequent outpouring of the Holy Spirit on the day of Pentecost. . . . In whatever he said of the terms of discipleship he anticipated the establishment and development of the New Testament church.[77]

Thus, it seems that the *ekklesia* of Matthew 18:17 may be taken in the technical usage, which necessitates physical assemblage and spiritual unity in Christ. It has that distinctly Christian content designated in Matthew 16:18-20, the only other reference to this *ekklesia* in the gospels.

Metaphorical usage

It has been previously demonstrated that in its common historical and nontechnical usage the word *ekklesia* simply means "an assembly"—a physical unity. In the development of the word, however, it took on a specific Christian content and came to be used in a technical sense meaning "a Christian assembly"—both physical and spiritual unity. Concerning this development Dargan has observed that the meanings shade off into one another, not in abrupt, sudden changes, but in gradual, almost imperceptible growth.[78] Nor did this growth stop with the technical sense. Just as it was noticed that the word as it is used in the early epistles went a little beyond the nontechnical usage, so there are some usages that seem to go beyond the technical

76. Stanley Dale Toussaint, "The Argument of Matthew," p. 239.
77. W. H. H. Marsh, *The New Testament Church*, p. 81.
78. E. C. Dargan, *Ecclesiology*, p. 29.

meaning. Concerning this constant development of the word *ekklesia,* Dargan writes:

> While in a great majority of places where the word *ekklesia* occurs the meaning is unmistakably that of the local church, [i.e., the technical meaning], there are yet a few very interesting and weighty passages where this well-defined conception gives place to one that is more general and indefinite. This is in accord with a well-known phenomenon of language. Of many terms it is true that when once they pass from the strict and established sense in which they are chiefly and clearly employed, they take on a number of secondary meanings which shade into each other by degrees. It is thus with the word *ekklesia.*[79]

It seems best to use a literary classification and designate these usages that go beyond the technical use as metaphorical usages. These are the usages that arouse the most debate. Of these disputed passages, there are four that deal with Paul's persecution of the *ekklesia* (Cf. Acts 9:31; 1 Cor 15:9; Gal 1:13; Phil 3:6). The passage in Acts is the historical reference of the rest of the passages. In Acts 8:1 Luke describes how a great persecution arose against the *ekklesia* at Jerusalem, and the members were all scattered abroad throughout all the regions of Judea and Samaria, except the apostles. Acts 8:3 continues by describing how Saul made havoc of the *ekklesia,* entering into every house and hauling men and women to prison. Acts 9:31 closes the incident of Paul's persecution by saying:

> Then had the *ekklesia*‡ rest throughout all Judaea and Galilee and Samaria and was edified; and walking in the fear of the Lord, and in the comfort of the Holy Ghost was multiplied.

79. Ibid., p. 30.

‡Some manuscripts have the plural, *ekklesiai,* with the following verbs plural. This is the reading of the Textus Receptus. The great weight of manuscript evidence, however, favors the singular throughout. Cf. Robertson, *Word Pictures,* 3:128: "The singular reading is undoubtedly the true reading here (all of the great documents have it so)." The variant suggests an effort at explanation, perhaps, of such passages as Acts 15:41 and 16:5.

The problem, of course, is seen in the fact that one *ekklesia* is represented as being in three distinct geographical areas at the same time. How can there then be the physical unity demanded by *ekklesia?* Some easily dismiss the problem by identifying it with the local church at Jerusalem. Overby states: "This was the church at Jerusalem which was scattered, Acts 9:1, the only church Scripture tells us he persecuted."[80] Likewise, Dana agrees that "the only Christian church of any kind in existence at the time was the local church at Jerusalem, hence the reference can only be local."[81] This solution presents two problems. First, by this time there were churches scattered over Judea, Galilee, and Samaria (cf. Gal 1:22), so it need not refer to the local church at Jerusalem. Second, even if the scattered people had been members of the Jerusalem *ekklesia,* that does not solve the problem of Luke's calling an unassembled group throughout Judea, Galilee, and Samaria an *ekklesia* where there was no physical, local gathering.

Robertson feels that Luke "employs the term *ekklesia* in a geographical or collective sense covering all of Palestine."[82] Hort agrees that "it was no longer the Ecclesia of a single city, and yet it was *one.*"[83] However, such an interpretation does not coincide with the physical unity demanded by *ekklesia.* It is apparent from the language that the Christians did not return to one place and constitute an *ekklesia.* The most thorough and helpful analysis seems to be that of Baker, who explains:

> Verses 1 and 3 of the eighth chapter suggest a most striking fact. Luke says that there was a great persecution against the *ekklesia* (accusative singular) and *they all* (nominative plural) were scattered abroad, *except the apostles.* In this verse Luke makes the *members* of the ekklesia the equivalent of the ekklesia itself. "They all" could have no antecedent except "members of the ekklesia" and these were called simply "the

80. Edward H. Overby, *The Meaning of Ecclesia in the New Testament,* p. 15.
81. H. E. Dana, *Christ's Ecclesia,* p. 41.
82. Robertson, *Word Pictures,* 1:149.
83. Hort, p. 55.

> ekklesia." The exception made with respect to the apostles shows that this is exactly what he means—the people, whether assembled or scattered, *were* the *ekklesia.* Even with the apostles left in Jerusalem, the scattered disciples constituted the ekklesia. . . . Verse 3 is consistent with this view. "Saul made havoc of the *ekklesia* by entering in, house by house" (a distributive use of *kata,* with the participle *eisporeuomenos* having the force of mode or manner). If the members of the ekklesia were in their houses, they could not be assembled in physical unity. They, themselves, whether physically united or not, constituted the ekklesia. Likewise, the passage in 9:31 is favorable to this view. The very functions ascribed to the ekklesia of verse 31 suggest personality. "The ekklesia throughout all Judaea and Galilee and Samaria had peace" being edified and *they walked* in *fear* of the Lord and *comfort* of the Holy Spirit and were multiplied.[84]

If this exegesis is correct, and it seems that it is, then there is need for a broadening of the concept of *ekklesia.* Here is another step in its development. Previously, it has been shown that the nontechnical usage involved simply a physical unity. As this came into Christian usage, however, it took on a specific content, thus giving it a dual unity—both physical and spiritual. Thus, the difference between secular and Christian *ekklesiai* was not in the fact of meeting, but in the *kind of person* who was attending the meeting. Now, then, it has been found that in Acts 9:31 the normal process of transference of ideas has resulted in the application of the name of the assembly to the continuents themselves. Here, then, is an illustration of that "phenomenon of language" of which Dargan speaks, by means of which a "well defined conception gives place to one that is more general and indefinite."[85]

> It is a clear indication of the development of the word ekklesia as the word leaves the conception of a *physical* as-

84. Baker, p. 210-11.
85. Dargan, p. 30.

> sembly and approaches the *spiritual* assembly. The Locative of Place, the literal necessity for an ekklesia, is giving way to the Locative of Sphere *en Christo,* the metaphorical concept. This does not mean that the *literal* has disappeared; it means that the *spiritual* had been emphasized as an independent concept.[86]

Thus, in addition to the nontechnical or plain use, the concept of a spiritual or Christian unity has developed a metaphorical usage of *ekklesia.* In Acts 9:31, 1 Corinthians 15:9, Galatians 1:13, and Philippians 3:6 the physical unity cannot be maintained, but these scattered members of Christ's body have one characteristic that makes them constitute an *ekklesia*—a spiritual unity. Robertson refers to them as an "unassembled assembly" and reminds his readers that "the words do not remain by the etymology, but travel on with usage."[87]

In addition to this group of passages, fourteen other uses of the word *ekklesia* should be classified as metaphorical.§ Most students of the nature of the church agree that there is this metaphorical usage, only they have used different terms in describing it. But whether the term is "spiritual" or "ideal" or "universal" or "invisible," it is metaphorical from the literary viewpoint. These terms do not have the nontechnical idea of spatial or physical unity; rather, they maintain a spiritual or Christian unity. It remains then to examine in detail some of these fourteen remaining instances of the metaphorical usage.

One of the most controversial of these verses is Matthew 16:18; "And I say also unto thee, That thou are Peter and upon this rock I will build my church, and the gates of hell shall not prevail against it." Several questions should be studied in a detailed examination of this passage. Who is the rock? What are the "keys of the kingdom"? What is meant by binding and loosing? But the question that concerns this writer is that of

86. Baker, p. 213.
87. Robertson, *Word Pictures,* 1:101.
§For a listing of all the uses of *ekklesia* in the New Testament, refer to Appendix 2.

what the word *ekklesia* means here. Several factors indicate that Matthew did not use the word *ekklesia* in its established nontechnical sense, or even in the technical Christian sense, but, rather, in the metaphorical sense to refer to an entirely new entity. The first distinctive element in this promise of Christ is that this building is a personal project. Notice should be taken of the personal pronoun *mou* in the emphatic position and genitive case. This shows that this *ekklesia* was to be peculiarly related to Christ. It was to be *His ekklesia.* It was to be characterized by the content Jesus gave it, as over against some other kind of *ekklesia.* Sanford writes:

> It is entirely possible that *mou* here indicates Christ's *ekklesia* is to be characteristically different from the only existing religious assembly known to those Christ addressed, namely, the synagogue. In any case, the use and position of *mou* in the sentence does show the *ekklesia* has a unique relationship to Christ, and this distinguishes this *ekklesia* from all else.[88]

The second distinctive factor is that this *ekklesia* was a future project. This is seen in the verb *oikodomeso,* which is a future tense and of which Robertson says it is possibly a durative volative future.[89] Thus, the phrase may be translated "I will" instead of "I shall." It was not to be any *ekklesia* that existed before or during Christ's previous ministry, but an *ekklesia* that was to be built in the future. This fact alone deals the death blow to any teaching that sees Jesus' *ekklesia* as simply the continuation of the Old Testament *ekklesia.* The first person singular of the verb shows that Christ Himself was to be the builder, and there is no indication that Christ merely meant that He would make a new beginning in the development of any existing *ekklesia,* for He is dealing here with the founding of an *ekklesia,* not the rebuilding of one. Vincent states:

88. Sanford, p. 23.
89. Robertson, *A Grammar of the Greek New Testament,* p. 889.

> In Christ's words to Peter the word *ekklesia* acquires special emphasis from the opposition implied in it to the synagogue. The Christian community in the midst of Israel would be designated as *ekklesia,* without being confounded with the *sunagoge,* the Jewish community.[90]

The third distinctive factor is that this was to be a permanent project. The Lord declares that "the gates of hell shall not prevail against it." Since it is generally conceded that the phrase "gates of hell [hades]" to the Jew designated death,[91] the thought of the clause would be that this *ekklesia* built by Christ could not succumb to the power of death. This could not have referred to the local *ekklesia* at Jerusalem, for it did succumb to the power of death. Such is also the case with other local churches. Van Gilder exclaims:

> No local church can be assured of perpetuity, and one that can claim continuous existence for more than a hundred years can boast of its antiquity. Death *does* swallow local churches.[92]

Realizing that this passage speaks too exclusively to be applied to the local church, others have defined the usage as "the local significance, used in a generic sense."[93] Applying this generic idea, Tulga says:

> The church is here conceived of as an institution, an institution to be built. It cannot mean a local church and the context forbids its interpretation as an invisible church.[94]

Such a view does not seem to accord with the scriptural revelation of the organizational church on earth in the last days. The organized church will ultimately be repudiated by Christ Himself (Rev 3:16), who will allow it to be judged and destroyed by the world ruler (Rev 18:8). The development of the history of the visible church is given prophetically in many passages of

90. Vincent, 1:93.
91. C. Clare Oke, "My Testimony," *The Expository Times* 37:47.
92. H. O. Van Gilder, *The Church Which Is His Body,* p. 18.
93. Dana, *A Manual of Ecclesiology,* p. 40.
94. Chester E. Tulga, *New Testament Baptists and the Nature of the Church,* p. 12.

the New Testament. Even though believers in the Lord Jesus Christ have the Word of God, it is seen that the visible church is to be characterized by progressive unbelief and apostasy. Concerning this earthly institution, which is ultimately to be destroyed by the Lord Jesus Christ (cf. Rev 17), Ryrie says:

> The true and professedly true elements will co-exist until the rapture. When the believing element is removed at the rapture. . . . the Church does not cease to exist or function, but becomes a truly and completely apostate Church. The eschatology of this organization is recorded in Rev. 17 under the figure of Babylon the harlot. This is the Church organization which during the first part of the tribulation unites Church and State (v. 2), rules the beast (vv. 3, 11), displays herself with great grandeur and pomp (v. 4), is organized as a federation (v. 5), and reigns with cruel ruthlessness (v. 6). When Antichrist shows his true colors by demanding worship of himself he must destroy this rival. So complete is that destruction (v. 16) that it may be said that organized Christendom comes to an end at that time.||

Thus it could hardly be said that this visible institution will not eventually succumb to the powers of death.

What then was the contrast Jesus had in mind with the for-

||Charles Caldwell Ryrie, *Biblical Theology of the New Testament,* p. 356; Cf. also J. Dwight Pentecost, *Prophecy for Today,* pp. 126-27: "And as we thread our way through these passages of Scripture, we find that the Word of God pictures the Church in a state of degeneracy and corruption, or ethical and moral malpractice as well as doctrinal error and heresy. And at the time when Jesus Christ comes to take to Himself every true believer by translation, He is going to leave on this earth all who may have professed to be believers in Jesus Christ as the Way, the Truth, and the Life, and have never received eternal life from Him. And the great, professing, visible but unregenerate church, as Revelation 2 says, will go into the Tribulation period to experience the wrath of God. And that visible church which will go into the Tribulation period is characterized in Revelation 3:20 as separated from the Lord Jesus Christ, that great Head of the Church, for He says 'I stand at the door and knock.' That means that Jesus Christ is on the outside, not on the inside. Even though they profess to know Him and follow Him and worship Him, He is a stranger to them and they to Him, and He has to stand on the outside and knock to seek admission. Here is a church that gives lip service to the Lord Jesus Christ, that professes to be His Bride, that professes to be united to Him in this mystical marriage, but which is truly a stranger and which the Apostle John in Revelation 17 calls 'the great harlot.' "

mer *ekklesia?* It could not have been a local or institutional *ekklesia.* Rather, as was seen in Acts 9:31, the contrast seems to extend to a *spiritual ekklesia* with the content Jesus gave it, as over against a *spatial* or corporeal *ekklesia* of the Old Testament. Thus, Jesus seems to be saying, "You are familiar with the *ekklesia* of the Old Testament. But I am going to construct personally an *ekklesia* that will be characterized by the content that I will give it and it shall endure forever."

Another use of the word *ekklesia* has occasioned differences of opinion not only in classification but in the interpretation of the phrase; that use is in Hebrews 12:23.

> But ye are come unto mount Sion, and unto the city of the living God, the heavenly Jerusalem, and to an innumerable company of angels, to the general assembly and the church of the firstborn, which are written in heaven, and to God the Judge of all, and to the spirits of just men made perfect, and to Jesus the mediator of the new covenant, and to the blood of sprinkling, that speaketh better things than that of Abel (Heb 12:22-24).

Overby, who insists that the local *ekklesia* is the only one known in the New Testament, says: "These members of a church are said to be enrolled in Heaven not there in actual location."[95] He further explains:

> New Testament churches are here now yet they have a close connection with Heaven because their members are enrolled in Heaven. The writer is reminding them of their great privileges as saved by grace by these eight things they have come to at their conversion. . . . A New Testament church is composed of professed Christians, those who have a common destination; they are enrolled in Heaven. To renounce our profession means to give this great privilege up.[96]

In response to this view, one simply wonders how an unsaved

95. Overby, p. 26.
96. Ibid.

church member's name could be written in heaven (for the local church has both saved and unsaved) and, further, how one whose name was written in heaven could be erased if he left the local assembly. The enrollment has been settled since the foundation of the world (cf. Rev 13:8; 17:8). Christ assured His disciples that they should rejoice because their names are already written in heaven (cf. Luke 10:20).

Another viewpoint explains this as the church viewed prospectively. Tulga is representative of the view:

> Here are the elect of all ages. This is not the visible assembly on earth, neither is it an invisible assembly but the assembly in glory of the saints of God.[97]

To this view agrees Carroll, who says:

> If one part of the membership is now in heaven, another part on earth, another part not yet born, *there is as yet no assembly,* except in prospect. . . . We may, however, properly speak of the General Assembly now, because . . . the mind may *conceive* of that gathering as an accomplished fact. . . . When the calling out is ended, and all the called are glorified, then the present concept of a General Assembly will be a fact. Then and only then actually, will all the redeemed be an *ecclesia.*[98]

Kuiper disagrees with this, however, and claims this as a picture of the militant church on earth but closely identified with the triumphant church in heaven.[99] These variant views, along with numerous others, demand that close attention be given to the grammar of this passage.

Crucial to the explanation of the nature of the *ekklesia* in this passage is an understanding of the argument of the book of Hebrews. Basically it is a contrast of the superiority of Christ and the new dispensation to the law of Moses and the old dis-

97. Tulga, p. 12.
98. Carroll, p. 62.
99. R. B. Kuiper, *The Glorious Body of Christ,* pp. 34-35.

pensation. In the immediate context this contrast is brought out forcefully by the use of the adversative conjunction *alla* in verse 22. The privileges of the Christian believer in this present age are set in contrast to the terrors of the Law. Thus, verses 22-24 speak of present privileges that believers in this age have entered into. The present possession of these privileges is proven by the use of the perfect active indicative verb *proseleluthate*. In some sense they have now entered into these privileges, which will continue and have their completion or consummation later.# Thus, this is proof that believers today are in this *ekklesia*.

The passage itself identifies this *ekklesia* by the use of the descriptive genitive *prototokon,* "firstborn ones." In the previous context (vv. 16-17) the writer has been giving the warning example of Esau, the firstborn of Isaac, who for a morsel of meat sold his birthright. This seems to prepare the way for such a designation and remind one of the high privileges of those included in this *ekklesia*. Sauer writes: "The word 'firstborn' is used in order to express the special position of grace of the CHURCH."[100] The apostle James has written: "Of His own will He brought us forth by the word of truth, that we should be a kind of firstfruits of His creatures" (James 1:18). Sauer goes on to explain that in the light of the Jewish-Christian audience this reference to the firstborn must be explained and understood by reference to the Old Testament sense. The essential idea of being "firstborn" is priority of rank or dignity, and not the time of birth (cf. 1 Chron 26:10). The same truth is the force of Colossians 1:15, where Paul says that Christ is the "firstborn of all creation," emphasizing preeminence, not time of birth. In the Old Testament economy, the rights of the

#Cf. Robertson, *A Grammar of the Greek New Testament,* p. 893: "The perfect looks at both ends of the action. It unites in itself as it were present and aorist, since it expresses the continuance of completed action. That is to say the perfect is both punctiliar and durative."

100. Erich Sauer, *In the Arena of Faith: A Call to a Consecrated Life,* p. 126.

firstborn were threefold: position of authority, priestly service, and a double portion of the inheritance.[101]

> Seen from the point of view of the New Testament all this is symbolic and typical language pointing to the spiritual possessions of the church. By the church being called "the assembly of the firstborn which is written in heaven" (Heb. 12:23), in connection with these Old Testament ordinances of the birthright, a threefold spiritual possession is indicated: Outstanding and glorious fulness of heavenly blessings, spiritual and heavenly priesthood, and God-given kingship and rule.[102]

The use of *prototokon* not only gives light as to the present privileges being exercised by the *ekklesia,* but it also relates this *ekklesia* distinctly to Christ. Colossians 1:18 states that Christ "is the head of the body, the church, who is the beginning, the firstborn from the dead." His headship has been made a fact, in that He has become the beginning, the firstborn *from among* the dead. It is fitting, then, that He should be Head of the *ekklesia* of firstborn ones by virtue of His resurrection. He is the beginning of the *ekklesia* of the firstborn ones. Thus, the use of *prototokon* to show the exercise of these present privileges as well as the present headship of Christ is another proof that this *ekklesia* is in existence today.

A final proof of the present existence of this *ekklesia* of firstborn ones is the usage of the perfect passive participle *apogegrammenon.* Members of the *ekklesia* of firstborn ones are enrolled as citizens of heaven even while on earth (cf. Phil 3:20; 4:3; Rev 13:8, etc.). The apostle Paul states:

> Now therefore ye are no more strangers and foreigners, but fellowcitizens with the saints, and of the household of God; and are built upon the foundation of the apostles and prophets,

101. Ibid., pp. 126-30. Cf. also George N. H. Peters, *The Theocratic Kingdom of Our Lord Jesus, the Christ, as Covenanted in the Old Testament and Presented in the New Testament,* 2:609.
102. Sauer, p. 131.

> Jesus Christ himself being the chief corner stone (Eph 2:19-20).

It is fitting that this *ekklesia* built upon Christ, who is the First-born (cf. Rom 8:29; Col 1:15, 18; Rev 1:5), should be called "the *ekklesia* of firstborn ones." Christ, as the Firstborn, was to be related to others who were to be conformed to His image because He is the "Firstborn *among many brethren*" (cf. Rom 8:29).

The foregoing examination of this passage has been set forth to demonstrate that the *ekklesia* mentioned in Hebrews 12:23 is presently in existence. It is obvious to all, however, that this *ekklesia* has never had a physical assemblage on earth. Thus, this is another example of the metaphorical usage of ekklesia, which usage stresses the spiritual unity apart from any present physical unity. It gives the heavenly charter of the church below, the invisible side of sonship and citizenship.[103]

Another passage in which the word *ekklesia* seems to imply something beyond the technical usage is 1 Corinthians 12:28. After discussing the oneness of the body into which believers come and asserting that "*ye* are Christ's body [no article] and members in particular," Paul says, "And God hath set some in the *ekklesia,* first apostles, secondarily prophets." From the text of this entire chapter it seems that Paul is using *ekklesia* as the equivalent of *soma* (body—used eighteen times in the last twenty verses of this chapter). The figure of the body, which figure is developed in verses 14-26 with deliberateness and completeness, is in verse 27 and following applied in detail to the church. In the former he writes of the human body and in the latter of the spiritual body. In the process Paul makes it quite clear that the company comprehended within the "one body" is much more extensive than the local *ekklesia.* He does so, first of all, by including himself within the membership: "For by

103. For an extended grammatical and syntactical defense of this position see Sauer, pp. 125-66; also Franz Delitzsch, *Commentary on the Epistle to the Hebrews,* trans. Thomas L. Kingsbury, 2:350-52.

[*en*] one Spirit are we all [*hemeis pantes*] baptized into one body." Obviously this is not meant to assert that Paul had left his membership in the church at Corinth when he departed five or six years before.

The nature of the act of God here also implies something broader than the local *ekklesia.* The aorist tense of *etheto* suggests that this was a work of God accomplished at a point of time in the past. Robertson and Plummer suggest that the correspondence with the human analogy in verse 18 must be marked in translation, "And some God placed in His Church."

> Just as God in the original constitution of the body placed differently endowed members in it, so in the original constitution of the Church He placed . . . differently endowed members in it. . . . The Church is the Church Universal, not the Corinthian Church; and this is perhaps the first Epistle in which we find this use.[104]

Most commentators agree that in this passage Paul universalizes the concept of *ekklesia.* Even Dana states:

> This passage unquestionably denotes some general idea of the church since it is not possible to apply the statement to the particular congregation at Corinth. No apostle ever held an official relation to any one church as distinct from another. . . . On the other hand he could not mean "the Church" in the sense of an ecclesiastical organization, for nothing of the kind existed in his day. . . . This use we may call the ideal or spiritual sense of *ekklesia.*[105]

The *ekklesia* here, then, cannot be a nontechnical or a technical usage, for there is no physical unity. The only unity is a spiritual unity in Christ. The emphasis has been transferred from the meeting itself to the persons meeting. Thus, the metaphorical usage of *ekklesia* sees a complete spiritual unity in Christ, without spatial assemblage.

104. Archibald Robertson and Alfred Plummer, *A Critical and Exegetical Commentary on the First Epistle of St. Paul to the Corinthians,* p. 278.
105. Dana, *A Manual of Ecclesiology,* pp. 44-45.

The peak of the development in Paul's usage of *ekklesia* is seen in Ephesians and Colossians, which were written several years later than 1 Corinthians, where he used *ekklesia* metaphorically for the first time. In Ephesians and Colossians the word *ekklesia* occurs thirteen times and in only two instances (Col 4:15, 16) can the technical meaning be attached to it. Some things common to all of these eleven occurrences should be noted. In each case the word *ekklesia* occurs in the singular together with the definite article, which facts seem to give support to the one universal *ekklesia* absolutely. The "localists," however, maintain that these occurrences of *ekklesia,* as do all others, refer to the particular local assembly. They understand these to be instances of the generic usage of *ekklesia* that, whenever it finds concrete expression or takes operative shape, is always a particular assembly.[106] It must be admitted that the generic usage is a grammatical possibility. Robertson says that "it is very common to find the singular used with the article in a representative sense for the whole class."[107] Overby explains further: "In such cases the word may be singular and yet not refer to any particular object of the class but to every object of that class."[108] Because the grammatical possibilities may support either viewpoint, it then becomes necessary to examine the context to determine the most probable solution.

Of the eleven occurrences of the word *ekklesia* in Ephesians and Colossians, only two are in Colossians, so these will be examined first. Speaking of Christ, Paul says: "And he is the head of the body, the church" (Col 1:18). The phrase *tes ekklesias* is in the genitive case, which is the specifying case, and it seems to be used here in its truest form as a genitive of apposition. This is further emphasized by the phrase "the body which is the church" *(tou somatos autou, ho estin he ekklesia)* (v. 24). This not only serves to equate the two, but it also

106. Carroll, p. 6.
107. Robertson, *A Grammar of the Greek New Testament,* p. 757.
108. Overby, p. 14.

sheds light on the nature of the *ekklesia.*** For the most part this truth concerning the "body" will be examined in the following chapter. Its particular importance at this point, however, concerns membership of the *ekklesia.* Previously, Paul has already called believers of this age (i.e., believers who have been baptized by the Holy Spirit) the body of Christ (Rom 12:5; 1 Cor 12:13, 27), a unified organism. Believers today are members of one body in Christ, who is their Head. The new thing that Paul does here is to combine the metaphors body and church and to speak of Christ as the Head of the body, which is His church. When this fact is coupled with synonymity of the body and the *ekklesia* in Colossians 1, it must be concluded that the *ekklesia* there includes more than a local assembly and extends to all believers in this age.

This metaphorical usage is further emphasized by the comparative study in the context. The contrast is between the headship of Christ in the realm of nature (vv. 15-17) and the realm of Spirit, or grace (vv. 18-20). Robertson states:

> The local use of the word "church," which is common enough in the New Testament, is not permissible here, for the contrast is with the material universe, a general conception.[109]

In the epistle to the Ephesians Paul reaches the epitome of his development of the doctrine of the church. In both Colossians and Ephesians Christ appears as the Head of the church, but the emphasis in Colossians is on the headship, whereas in Ephesians it is on the church.[110] The context of the first occurrence of the word *ekklesia* in Ephesians says that Christ is "head over all *things* to the church, which is his body, the fulness of him that filleth all in all" (vv. 22*b*-23). The order of the pre-

**Cf. Henry Alford, *The Greek Testament,* rev. Everett F. Harrison, 2:204-5: "The genitive is much more naturally taken as one of apposition, inasmuch as in St. Paul, it is the church which *is,* not which possesses the body."

109. A. T. Robertson, *Paul and the Intellectuals: The Epistle to the Colossians,* ed. and rev. W. C. Strickland, p. 49.

110. A. S. Peake, "The Epistle to the Colossians," in *The Expositor's Greek Testament,* ed. W. Robertson Nicoll, 3:507.

sentation of *soma* and *ekklesia* in this passage is the opposite of that in Colossians 1:18 and 1:24, although in each case the grammatical relation is one of apposition. This interchangeableness further emphasizes the synonymity of the two terms. This fact is reinforced by the explanatory use of the relative pronoun *hetis,* which may be translated "which in fact is."[111] Thus, Christ is head of the *ekklesia,* which in fact is His body. Salmond comments: "The *etis* . . . has something of its qualitative force, pointing to what belongs to the nature of the Church."[112] It has already been demonstrated that the use of the modifier "body of Christ" demands the metaphorical usage of the word *ekklesia* because it includes all the redeemed of this age. Also, not only *all* the redeemed, but *only* the redeemed are included in the body, which has an organic connection with the Head. Further support of this usage is the last clause of verse 23, which is in apposition with "his body": "the fulness of him that filleth all in all." This phrase is very difficult to interpret, partly because of the extreme grandeur of the concept and partly because of the dispute as to whether *pleroma* should be taken in the active or passive sense, "that which is filled." The passive is the choice of most commentators. Thus, Salmond suggests:

> The idea is that the Church is not only Christ's body but that which is *filled* by *Him.* In Col. i. 19, ii. 9 the whole *pleroma,* or every plenitude of the Godhead, the very fulness of the Godhead, the totality of the Divine powers and qualities, is said to be in Christ, so that He alone is to be recognized as Framer and Governor of the world, and there is neither need nor place for any intermediate beings as agents in those works of creating, upholding and administering. Here the conception is that this plenitude of the Divine powers and qualities which is in Christ is imparted by Him to His Church, so that the latter

111. Robertson, *Word Pictures,* 4:522.
112. S. D. F. Salmond, "The Epistle to the Ephesians," in *The Expositor's Greek Testament,* 3:282.

> is pervaded by His presence, animated by His life, filled with His gifts and energies and graces. He is the sole Head of the universe, which receives from Him what He Himself possesses and is endowed by Him with all that it requires for the realisation of its vocation.[113]

It seems quite evident that the *ekklesia* here described is not the local *ekklesia.* Rather, it refers to the entire body of those spiritually joined to Christ. Van Gilder questions:

> How can any local church be regarded as the fulness, or completeness of Christ? And if it could be shown that some local church does exist, or has existed, somewhere which justifies this description, how can any other local church ever justify its existence? The term is exclusive; if one local church is the fulness—not filled *with,* mind you, but the fulness *of* Him—then a second local church would be superfluous, and could not be His body![114]

Most serious, of course, is the very practical fact that either the body of Christ is more than a local *ekklesia,* or membership in a local *ekklesia* is necessary for salvation. Although this is agreeable to Roman Catholicism, it is not received by Protestant Christianity.

Having seen very definitely that the apostle Paul does use the word *ekklesia* in a metaphorical sense, it is not necessary to examine each use in Ephesians at this point, for they will be discussed subsequently with regard to the figures of the church. There are some general observations that should be made, however, concerning these metaphorical usages in Ephesians. Having admitted that the local meaning is not possible in Ephesians, Dana significantly notes:

> In the eleven times that Paul uses *ekklesia* in something other than the local sense he relates it in some way to the au-

113. Ibid., 3:282.
114. Van Gilder, p. 16.

> thority and preeminence of Christ, the central theme of these epistles. In the earlier epistles of Paul the *ekklesia* is viewed in its functional relation to the work of the kingdom. In Ephesians and Colossians it is viewed in its spiritual relation to the person of Christ. In the earlier epistles Paul is dealing with the problem of the churches as practical agencies of redemption; here he is dealing in the abstract with the church idea in relation to the great metaphysical problem of the person of Christ. There he is dealing with the churches on the side of their active ministry; here he is dealing with the church on the side of its divine relationship. Consequently, conclusions derived from the conception of the church represented in these epistles should have no bearing upon the matter of church polity. The "body of Christ" of which Paul speaks is not an ecclesiastical organization bound by an ascending order of official links to an oligarchical or hierarchical head, but an ideal, spiritual body in sacred and vital connection with Christ its divine founder as its head.[115]

These observations of Dana should be indelibly inscribed upon the minds of contemporary students of the nature of the church. They are exceedingly important especially in the light of the contemporary push for a one-world church organization. In the same vein of thought, Hort remarks that his view of *ekklesia* does not come from the *historical* side, but from the *theological* consideration of the believer's relation to Christ;[116] and that this *ekklesia* does not consist of the aggregate of all individual *ekklesiai,* but consists of all *believers* in their immediate relationship to Christ.[117]

These two statements cannot be emphasized too strongly. That is to say, this metaphorical use of the word *ekklesia* is in the realm of *conception,* not ecclesiastical practice; and individual *ekklesiai,* banded together by any sort of tie, whether name

115. Dana, *A Manual of Ecclesiology,* pp. 52-53.
116. Hort, p. 148.
117. Ibid., p. 168.

or organization, do not constitute this *ekklesia.*†† It is an *ekklesia* growing out of the immediate relationship of an individual believer to God in Christ.

Briefly summarized, then, the Christian usage of *ekklesia* in the New Testament is divided into two ideas. There is the technical *ekklesia,* which is an autonomous group of people united both physically and spiritually in Christ. Then there is the metaphorical *ekklesia,* which implies spiritual unity alone, without reference to physical unity.

USAGES NOT FOUND IN THE NEW TESTAMENT

Although we have classified the literary usages of *ekklesia* in the New Testament, the problem of definition is still not complete. Because of the numerous popular expressions of the church, it is important that the usages that are nonexistent in the New Testament be clearly set forth as something extrabiblical.

Never used of a physical structure

In defining the word *ekklesia,* Webster states that it is "A church, either the body of members or building."[118] Nowhere in the New Testament, however, does the word *ekklesia* mean a building. The *ekklesia* of the New Testament is never a structure composed of stones and lime, or bricks and mortar. A statement such as "I pass the church every day on my way to work" would have been unintelligible to the writers of the New Testament. Barclay states:

> We know that in the very early days the gatherings of the Christians must have been small, for it was not until the early

††Cf. Baker, pp. 69-70: "The singular and the plural are used interchangeably, but this does not mean that the ecclesia is made up of or divided into ecclesiai. It means rather that *the* ecclesia is present in a certain place (Acts 13:1; 20:28), and this is not affected by the mention of the ecclesiai elsewhere. . . . 1 Cor. 1:2 and 2 Cor. 1:1 support the idea that the church is not the accumulation of small communities but is truly present in its wholeness in every company of believers."

118. *Webster's New International Dictionary of the English Language,* s.v. "ecclesia."

> third century that anything in the nature of church buildings came into being. In the early days the Christians were still meeting in any house which had a room large enough to give them accommodation.[119]

It is obvious, then, that if church buildings were nonexistent, there could be no reference to them in the use of the word *ekklesia*. On the other hand, the Scriptures make it plain that the *ekklesia* is the body of people at worship, not the building in which they worship. Thus, Paul speaks of the *ekklesia* that is in the house of Aquila and Priscilla (Rom 16:5); of the *ekklesia* in the house of Nymphas in Laodicea (Col 4:15); of the *ekklesia* in the house of Archippus (Philem 2).

Never used of a state or national church

It is common today, especially in European countries, for one particular church to be governed and supported by the state. It is interesting to note that all the leading Reformers, who so heroically freed the church from the Roman Catholic Church and the pope, fastened a state church upon the people wherever they went[120] and that the churches that stood for absolute religious liberty were persecuted by these state churches. Berkhof explains this national church system.

> It proceeds on the assumption that the church is a voluntary association, equal to the State. The separate churches or congregations are merely sub-divisions of the national Church. The original power resides in a national organization, and this organization has jurisdiction over the local churches.[121]

Speaking of the results of such a system, Berkhof continues:

> This system disregards altogether the autonomy of the local churches, ignores the principles of self-government and of

119. William Barclay, *The Mind of St. Paul*, p. 232.
120. G. W. Peters, "Major Theological Tenets of Sixteenth Century Anabaptist-Mennonitism."
121. Louis Berkhof, *Systematic Theology*, p. 581.

> direct responsibility to Christ, engenders formalism, and binds a professedly spiritual Church by formal and geographical lines.[122]

One of the most serious objections to such a system is that it results in an unregenerate church membership, which Littell chooses to call "baptized heathenism."[123] Neve notes that "all citizens are by birth members of the church as long as they have not explicitly left it."[124]

It is the opinion of this writer that such a system finds no support in the New Testament use of *ekklesia.* It is true that *ekklesia* in its metaphorical usage comprehends a group far greater than the local church, but the New Testament never gives any grounds for ecclesiastical organization on a broader basis than the local church. Forrester declares: "Church government in the New Testament applies only to local bodies."[125]

> The management of their business was in their own hands. Paul wrote the church at Corinth: "Let all things be done decently and in order" (1 Cor. 14:40). In that comprehensive injunction, given to a church, is implied control of its affairs by the church.[126]

Thus, the authority of the local church is final as far as its own affairs are concerned (cf. Matt 18:17). There is no higher court.

This fact should sound a solemn note of warning to those churches and church-related agencies that are increasingly succumbing to the lure of tax funds made available by the welfare state. Lowell declares:

> It is only fair to sound a note of warning as the Church seems to move in that direction. If the Church succumbs to the lure of the state's gold and becomes merely one of many

122. Ibid.
123. Franklin Hamlin Littell, *The Free Church,* p. 3.
124. J. L. Neve, *Churches and Sects of Christendom,* p. 159.
125. E. J. Forrester, "Church Government," in *The International Standard Bible Encyclopaedia,* ed. James Orr, 1:654.
126. Ibid., 1:655.

> social functionaries, her loss will be irreparable. Certainly she will forfeit whatever claim she may exert as a unique society. Under such circumstances the Church becomes, in effect, another secular institution. That is, she ceases to be the Church and becomes something else.[127]

The only church known in the New Testament is a church separate from control or support by the state.

Never used of a denomination

People often speak of the various denominations as churches, as, for instance, the Protestant Episcopal Church, the Lutheran Church in America, the United Presbyterian Church in the U.S.A.; but this use of *ekklesia* is never found in the Scriptures. This is not meant to imply that denominations are evil, per se, but only to stress that the New Testament knows of no ecclesiastical organization on a broader level than the local church. Berkhof states:

> Scripture does not contain an explicit command to the effect that the local churches of a district must form an organic union. Neither does it furnish us with an example of such a union. In fact, it represents the local churches as individual entities without any external bond of union.[128]

It is not the purpose of this book to debate the reasonableness or unreasonableness of organic union of churches into denominations. Suffice it to say that Scripture knows of no such organic union.

The plea for organic union has usually developed from principles of expedience or convenience. Hodge writes:

> Believers have feelings to be exercised, exigencies to be met, and duties to be performed, which assume and demand organic union with fellow believers. . . . There is no reason why indi-

127. C. Stanley Lowell, "What Is the Church's Real Task?," *Christianity Today* 5:516.
128. Berkhof, p. 590.

> vidual churches should remain isolated, without organic, visible union with other churches.[129]

One cannot deny that advantages do accrue through interchurch fellowship, but the practice of securing these advantages through organic union finds no precedent in the Scriptures.

Oftentimes this plea for organic union is based on an appeal to the prayer of Christ in John 17:23, "that they may be one, even as we are one." This is interpreted as a desire for visible, organic union. The ultimate result of such reasoning is precisely what is being presented in the present ecumenical drive for a one-world church.

Ecumenicists speak of "the scandal of our apartness"[130] and Hitt chides:

> The interdenominational organizations of evangelicalism have little time left to decide whether they are going to align themselves with the separatists who believe hopefully that the church can be made "pure" or with the majority of Christendom moving in the growing ecumenical tide. . . . Conservative Christians who have been preoccupied with the doctrine of the Scriptures must now concentrate on the doctrine of the church.[131]

Others seriously doubt, however, that organic union will automatically bring spiritual power. Perhaps Tenney is closer to the real meaning of John 17 when he says:

> A clear distinction should be drawn between four closely allied concepts: unanimity, uniformity, union, and unity. Unanimity means absolute concord of opinion within a given group of people. Uniformity is complete similarity of organization or of ritual. Union implies political affiliation without necessarily including individual agreement. Unity requires oneness of inner heart and essential purpose, through the pos-

129. Charles Hodge, "The Unity of the Church," *Eternity* 9:21.
130. Lesslie Newbigin, "The Scandal of Our Apartness," *Eternity* 12:13.
131. Russell T. Hitt, "Church Merger: Threat or Hope?" *Eternity* 12:28.

> session of a common interest or a common life. No one of these is dependent on any other. Unanimity of belief does not necessarily mean uniformity of ritual; nor does uniformity of ritual presuppose organic union; nor does organic union involve unity of spirit. . . . Unity, however, prevails wherever there is a deep and genuine experience of Christ; for the fellowship of the new birth transcends all historical and denominational boundaries. . . . Such unity was what Jesus petitioned in His prayer, for He defined it as the unity which obtained between Himself and the Father, "as thou, Father, art in me, and I in thee, that they also may be in us" (21). . . . Jesus did not pray for absolute unanimity of mind, nor for uniformity of practice, nor for union of visible organization, but for the underlying unity of spiritual nature and devotion which would enable His people to bear a convincing testimony before the world.[132]

History has demonstrated that organic union does not necessarily produce this kind of unity. Perhaps it would be best to adhere to the scriptural example of limiting ecclesiastical organization to the autonomous local church.

Never used of the kingdom of God or the kingdom of heaven

It has been the practice of a large majority of professing Christendom to identify the church with the kingdom. This view has its basic foundation in the teachings of Augustine. The previous study of this church Father in chapter two has demonstrated the truth of Berkhof's statement that "Augustine viewed the kingdom as a present reality and identified it with the Church."[133] A further development occurred, however, when this idea was adopted by the Roman Catholic Church, which made the boundaries of the kingdom conterminous with those of their visible ecclesiastical system. Berkhof explains:

132. Merrill C. Tenney, *John: The Gospel of Belief: An Analytic Study of the Text*, pp. 248-49.
133. Berkhof, p. 569.

> For him [Augustine] it was primarily identical with the pious and holy, that is, with the Church as a community of believers; but he used some expressions which seem to indicate that he also saw it embodied in the episcopally organized Church. The Roman Catholic Church frankly identified the Kingdom of God with their hierarchical institution.[134]

Marsh speaks even more specifically:

> Romanism identifies the two in every respect. . . . This is a fundamental principle of the ecclesiastical system of the Roman Catholic Church. . . . Their functions are identical; they have the same earthly administration. In both the pope is the viceregent of Christ. Very much in the theology of the Roman Church is based on the identity of the two.[135]

Berkhof states that the Reformers returned to Augustine's view that the kingdom is "in this dispensation identical with the invisible church."[136] Thus, it should be carefully noted that the Reformers only limited or modified the Roman conception. They did not question the identification of the church with the kingdom, but they protested against the external view of the kingdom of God, which view they countered by distinguishing between the church invisible and visible. Marsh notes that the "logical and ecclesiastical outcome in the Reformation was the establishment of state churches."[137]

Hort states that since Augustine's time the kingdom of heaven has been simply identified with the Christian *ekklesia.*[138] The emphasis on religious liberty in America, especially by the free church movement, has rendered the form this teaching assumed in the Reformation obsolete, but the substance is still retained in Reformed theology. The identification goes further. Charles Hodge states:

134. Ibid.
135. Marsh, pp. 75-76.
136. Berkhof, p. 569.
137. Marsh, p. 76.
138. Hort, p. 19.

> As Christ has enjoined upon his people duties which render it necessary that they should organize themselves in an external society, it follows that there is and must be *a visible kingdom of Christ in the world.* They therefore form themselves into churches, and *collectively constitute the kingdom of Christ on earth.*[139]

So also, A. A. Hodge identifies the kingdom, in the parables of the sower, the tares, and the net, with the visible church, which was established as an outward, visible society by the Abrahamic covenant and has remained identical in all dispensations.[140] Thus, Berkhof has not stated the case quite accurately, as far as Reformed theologians are concerned, when he says that the kingdom is identical with the invisible church. Rather, they have the same tendency that Augustine later had, and that is to equate the kingdom with the visible church.

In the mind of this writer, however, there are some very important reasons why it is utterly untenable to equate the kingdom with either the visible or the invisible church. In the first place, the term *ekklesia* is never used with reference to the kingdom. There are one hundred and fourteen occurrences of *ekklesia* in the New Testament, but in no instance is it equated with the kingdom. There are those who have attempted to equate the *ekklesia* with the "kingdom of heaven" of Matthew 16:19. Berkhof declares: "It is quite evident that the terms 'church' and 'kingdom of heaven' are used interchangeably here."[141] More recently Hanke has boldly asserted that in Matthew 16:19 " 'the kingdom of heaven' is employed in such a way as to make the two expressions the 'church' and the 'kingdom' synonymous and capable of translation into each other's terms."[142] Close examination, however, reveals that there is nothing in the passage or in its context that would even

139. Charles Hodge, *Systematic Theology,* 2:604.
140. Archibald Alexander Hodge, *Outlines of Theology,* pp. 616-21.
141. Berkhof, p. 593.
142. Howard A. Hanke, *Christ and the Church in the Old Testament: A Survey of Redemptive Unity in the Testaments,* p. 113.

suggest such identification. In fact, the case is just the opposite. The *ekklesia* of Christ is qualified by the personal pronoun, which contrasts it not only to the kingdom but to every other *ekklesia*. Furthermore, it is stated that the *ekklesia* is to be built and that "the gates of hades shall not prevail against it." Neither of these particulars is expressly affirmed of the "kingdom of heaven."

A second argument against equating these terms is their basic etymological and connotational meanings. It has been demonstrated previously that the basic idea of an *ekklesia* was that of an autonomous physical assembly of the citizens of the local community met to transact business of common concern on democratic principles. The word *ekklesia* would bring to mind a conception not only not identical with, but also in every particular the antithesis of, that suggested by the word *basileia* (kingdom). Thomas effectively sets forth this antithesis.

> The early Greek *basileus,* who had been an absolute local or tribal ruler, had long since vanished, as Aristotle explains in his "Politics." The title was now restricted exclusively to the head of the Roman Empire—the one sole master of the "habitable world." The word *basileia* had, therefore, come to carry with it the inevitably associated notion of world range and mastery. Our Lord's allusion to a new *basileia* . . . must suggest instantly and logically the idea of rivalry with Caesar, and not of local insurrection or insubordination only; for two world-empires could not exist together (Acts 17:7). . . . Had the word *basileia,* used by him as describing the new *regime* to be set up, meant to the ordinary hearer only a local and subordinate *regime,* its threatened establishment would have been insubordination only—a less serious offense. But if the broader meaning necessarily attached to the word, he could not escape the charge afterward actually made of attempted world rivalry with Caesar.
>
> But over against this single, comprehensive, world-extensive conception, the word *ekklesia* set up an idea as distinctly

> local, partitive and multiple. The empire was, and must be, one. But there might be as many *ekklesiai* as there were Greek cities. . . . The *basileia* was centered in the *basileus,* as its etymological form indicates, and was therefore necessarily monocratic: the *ekklesia,* from like etymological implication, must derive its central significance from the whole body of people assembled, and be democratic. The autonomy of the local group, as contrasted with the individual lordship over it, was essential to the conception of the thing itself.[143]

Thus, the *ekklesia* and the *basileia* may more properly be contrasted than compared. The terms in the original were as opposite in their current acceptance as the present terms *monarchy* and *democracy;* hence, it seems entirely unreasonable to conceive of the New Testament writers as seeking to make them synonymous.

A third argument for a definite distinction between the *ekklesia* and the *basileia* is seen in their manner of introduction in the gospel of Matthew. Sanford notes:

> In Matthew 3:4 the "kingdom of heaven" is simply announced, without explanation by use of the definite article. Since Israel was looking for a Messianic kingdom, acquaintance with it is taken for granted.‡‡ On the other hand, the *ekklesia* is introduced in Matthew 16:18 by *mou* as being peculiarly related to Christ. The sufferings and death of Christ are not present in the context in which the "kingdom of heaven" is offered; whereas, they are clearly and emphatically declared in the context in which the *ekklesia* is introduced (Matt. 16:21).[144]

143. Jesse B. Thomas, *The Church and the Kingdom,* pp. 213-15.

‡‡Cf. James Orr, "Kingdom of God, of Heaven," in *A Dictionary of the Bible,* ed. James Hastings, 2:849: "In announcing the approaching advent of the 'kingdom of heaven,' Jesus had in view the very kingdom which the prophets had foretold." Also, Alva J. McClain, *The Greatness of the Kingdom,* p. 275: "The Kingdom announced by our Lord and offered to the nation of Israel at His first coming was identical with the Mediatorial Kingdom of Old Testament prophecy, and will be established on earth at the second coming of the King."

144. Sanford, p. 29.

Rowe adds the following very significant distinctions:

> The one is an offer as being "at hand" (Matt. 3:2; 4:17); the other is an "I will" declaration (Matt. 16:18). The one is an offer of a prophesied entity; the other is itself a prophesied entity in its very introduction. The kingdom is a major theme of antiquity; the church now appears prophetically as a wholly new entity. The kingdom is offered prior to the hostility and rejection on the part of the Jews which followed; the church is introduced prophetically and at the end of this period of intense hostility and rejection.[145]

The manner and time of its introduction, therefore, demonstrates the fallacy of making the *ekklesia* and the *basileia* identical or synonymous.

A fourth argument that supports this distinction is seen in the usage of the terms throughout the New Testament. As one opens the New Testament to the gospels he is immediately impressed with the incessant recurrence of the *basileia,* while the *ekklesia* only occurs three times—and those in a prophetic sense. Upon coming to the transition book of the Acts of the Apostles, the reader is made aware that Christ had been speaking to His disciples concerning the *basileia;* thus, they ask when it will be restored again to Israel. The answer of the Lord does not deny a future restoration of the *basileia,* but it informs them that it is not for them to know the times or the seasons. Then, in this transitional book of Acts, attention turns with increasing momentum from the *basileia* to the newly established *ekklesia.* The *basileia* is no longer the center of interest. Craven significantly remarks: "There is no critically undisputed passage in the Scriptures which declares, or necessarily implies, even a partial establishment [of the Kingdom] in New Testament times."[146] As one comes to the epistles he is immediately con-

145. Harley Edward Rowe, "The Kingdom in Matthew," p. 19.
146. E. R. Craven, "Excursus on the Basileia," in *A Commentary on the Holy Scriptures: Critical, Doctrinal, and Homiletical,* by John Peter Lange et al., ed. and trans. by Philip Schaff. *Revelation,* ed. E. R. Craven, p. 95.

fronted with the fact that each one of them was sent under various forms of address to an *ekklesia* or to members of *ekklesiai.* Even the letters enclosed in Revelation 2 and 3 are sent respectively to seven local churches. In no case, however, is there an epistle of the New Testament addressed to the saints of the *basileia.*§§ But the picture changes with the arrival at the book of Revelation, the panoramic view of "things to come." It is entirely fitting, therefore, that this book should be primarily concerned with the *basileia.* Peters writes:

> It is only through this doctrine of the Kingdom that the Apocalypse can or will be understood and consistently interpreted. The reason for this lies in the simple fact that it announces the Coming and the events connected with the Advent of the Theocratic King.[147]

Thus, this entire advancing change of emphasis from *basileia* to *ekklesia* and back to the *basileia* yet to come may not be overlooked. Together with the previous arguments it serves to emphasize the fact that the *ekklesia* and the *basileia* are two distinct entities in the eternal program of God.

It should be further noted that these two entities will be distinct for all eternity. Even when the entire *ekklesia* (metaphorical sense) is gathered together in absolute perfection because conformed to the glorified humanity of the Son of God, it will still be a distinct constituency. Marsh states:

> There is nothing in either the teachings of Christ or of the apostles identifying the church invisible when it becomes the

§§Cf. Gosta Lindeskog, "The Kingdom of God and the Church in the New Testament," in *This is the Church,* ed. Anders Nygren with Gustaf Aulen, trans. Carl C. Rasmussen, pp. 138-39: "It is clearly a fact that the thought of the kingdom of God rules Jesus' own preaching, while very little is said in the Gospels about the church. But in the epistles the situation is virtually the opposite. A simple counting of the words shows that 'the kingdom of God' (or 'the kingdom of heaven') occurs about one hundred and twenty times in the Gospels, and eight times in Acts. In the rest of the books it is found only a total of twenty-four times. . . . This striking difference between the Gospels and the other books, in the use of the expression 'the kingdom of God,' can obviously not be an accident."

147. Peters 3:366.

> church triumphant with the kingdom when consummated. Instead they teach that the church invisible is to be ultimately glorified with Christ its Head *in* his kingdom, and is then to be the glory of his kingdom; but the kingdom itself is to comprehend all the fullness of his mediatorial domain.[148]

The *ekklesia* will never be merged into the *basileia* in any such sense as to lose its identity. In Hebrews 12:23 several distinct groups are specified as distinct inhabitants of the new Jerusalem. Chief among these is the church from which the city receives its dominant characteristic as the Lamb's wife (Rev 21:9). Speaking of this eternal city, Pentecost states:

> The city is to be inhabited by God, by the church, by the redeemed of all ages, together with the unfallen angels. However, this city seems to take her chief characterization from the bride who dwells there.[149]

They are not the subjects of the *basileia,* but they are to *reign with Him in the basileia.* The apostle John sings out with a paean of praise that Christ "hath made us kings and priests unto God and his Father; to him be glory and dominion forever and ever. Amen" (Rev 1:6; cf. also Matt 19:28; 1 Cor 6:2; 2 Tim 5:10).

Much space has been devoted to a defense of this distinction between the *ekklesia* and the *basileia* not only because of a desire to present accurately the various phases of the eternal program of God but also to avert very subtle dangers that arise when the two are confused. Thus, McClain warns:

> The identification of the Kingdom with the Church has led historically to ecclesiastical policies and programs which, even when not positively evil, have been far removed from the original simplicity of the New Testament *ekklesia.* It is easy to claim that in the "present kingdom of grace" the rule of the saints is wholly "spiritual," exerted only through moral principles and influence. But practically, once the Church be-

148. Marsh, pp. 127-28.
149. J. Dwight Pentecost, *Things to Come: A Study in Biblical Eschatology,* p. 576.

> comes the Kingdom in any realistic theological sense, it is impossible to draw any clear line between principles and their implementation through political and social devices. For the logical implications of a present ecclesiastical *kingdom* are unmistakable, and historically have led in only one direction, i.e., political control of the state by the Church.[150]

Thus, the *ekklesia* must beware lest she lose her pilgrim character and become an *ekklesia* that is not only in the world, but also *of* the world.

Finally, it should be realized that although the *ekklesia* and the *basileia* are distinct, yet there is a very definite relationship between the two. Numerous explanations of this relationship have been suggested. Dana believes: "The spiritual *ekklesia* simply expresses a relation to Christ and between his saints, while the local *ekklesia* is an active agency of the kingdom."[151] Fairbairn states that "the church was to promote the ends, realize the ideals of the Kingdom."[152] A similar view is developed by Ladd when speaking of the use of the "keys" and the future kingdom of heaven (Matt 16:19). He says, "No longer is the Kingdom of God active in the world through Israel; it works rather through the Church."[153] He states further:

> The kingdom is not the church. The apostles went about preaching the kingdom of God (Acts 8:12; 19:8; 28:23); it is impossible to substitute "church" for "kingdom" in such passages. However, there is an inseparable relationship. The church is the fellowship of men who have accepted his offer of the kingdom, submitted to its rule, and entered into its blessings.[154]

None of these definitions is entirely satisfactory, however, because they do not distinguish between present and future

150. McClain, pp. 438-39.
151. Dana, *A Manual of Ecclesiology*, p. 57.
152. A. M. Fairbairn, *Studies in the Life of Christ*, p. 110.
153. George Eldon Ladd, *The Gospel of the Kingdom*, p. 113.
154. George Eldon Ladd, "Kingdom of God," in *Baker's Dictionary of Theology*, ed. Everett F. Harrison, p. 313.

relationships. Concerning the future relationship, Peters clearly states:

> The Church is represented as Christ's body, simply because that body are "co-heirs," joint inheritors with Him in the Kingdom, and, therefore, they are purposely called *"the subjects of the heavenly kingdom."*[155]

As co-heirs of the *basileia* with Christ, the *ekklesia* is as related to the *basileia* as Christ. Although only the bride of the King, the *ekklesia* is pictured as the "ruling aristocracy, the official administrative staff, of the coming kingdom."[156]

The kingdom is thus the goal|| || of the pilgrimage of the *ekklesia* during this age. But being already related to this kingdom through the reception of its power in the gospel, the church has a definite function to perform even now. Skydsgaard explains the position of the church in the present economy of God.

> The church has a double nature in that she already participates in the new age of the Kingdom in which God acts and works and speaks, and yet at the same time she still lives on earth and in the old aeon.[157]

During this time, God is preparing a spiritual nucleus for the future kingdom, which will be established on earth at the return of Christ. McClain adds:

> He is gathering to Himself a body of people . . . who are destined to be associated with Him in the coming kingdom. Upon them, from His present throne in the heavens, He is abundantly able to bestow certain of His regal blessings even before the arrival of the Kingdom.[158]

155. Peters, 1:597.
156. Erich Sauer, *From Eternity to Eternity,* trans. G. H. Lange, p. 93.
|| ||Cf. K. E. Skydsgaard, "Kingdom of God and Church," *Scottish Journal of Theology* 4:386: "In the Kingdom of God the Church has her ultimate frontier; from the Kingdom she receives all her substance, her power and hope. In the age of the Church everything is characterized by the sign *till He come* and stands constantly under the unfulfilled *not yet,* under the Quousque Domine?"
157. Skydsgaard, 4:386.
158. McClain, p. 440.

The total picture of the relation of the *ekklesia* to the kingdom program of God is very clearly summarized by Sauer:

> As to their persons, they are citizens of the kingdom: as to their existence they are the fruit of the message of the kingdom: as to their nature they are the organism of the kingdom: as to their task they are the ambassadors of the kingdom.[159]

Therefore, while the church is not the kingdom, she nevertheless plays a very vital role in relation to the kingdom.

Never designated as Israel

Growing out of the view that the kingdom and the *ekklesia* are identical is the commonly accepted position that the *ekklesia* is the new Israel or the spiritual Israel, the successor of the Israel of the Old Testament.## Frequent reference is made to Hort's statement that the probable sense of Matthew 16:18 would be seen by substituting the name Israel as follows: "On this rock I will build my Israel."[160] A more recent advocate of this position is T. F. Torrance, who believes that Israel is the root and stock of the New Testament *ekklesia.*

> Although Israel was like a tree cut down to the stump, it remains to remind the church of its origin and root, for the church of the Gentiles is grafted on to the stump of Israel, like branches cut out of a wild olive tree and grafted contrary to

159. Sauer, *From Eternity to Eternity,* pp. 92-93.

##Cf. Campbell, 49:130: "How was it that the early Christians came to choose the Greek word *ekklesia* as the specific name of their new religious community, and what meaning did they attach to the word in this use of it?... There is one answer to the question so generally accepted that it is to be found stated as a securely established result of investigation in almost any recent work which has occasion to refer to the subject.... The source of the name *ekklesia* for the Christian community is the Greek Old Testament. There *ekklesia* translates the Hebrew word *qahal,* which in the Old Testament is the usual term for Israel as the people of God. The full phrase is *qehal Jhvh,* in Greek *ekklesia kuriou,* which in the New Testament becomes *ekklesia Theou.* So in calling themselves the *ekklesia Theou,* the early Christians were claiming to be the true people of God, the true successor of the ancient Israel. But though this view has found such general acceptance that it is difficult to find any recent authority who questions it, *no adequate evidence to support it can be found either in the Old Testament or in the New*" [italics not in the original].

160. Hort, pp. 10-11.

> nature into a good olive tree (Rom. 11:16-24). Here is a fact of such supreme importance that the Christian church inevitably goes astray when it forgets it: that the Christian church has no independent existence over against Israel.***

This view is based on the supposed unmistakable continuity between the Old and New Testaments, according to Hanke, who further states that when one is saved, be he Jew or Gentile, he becomes a spiritual Jew-member in this church.[161]

Other recent writers who have been zealous to confine the biblical unity almost entirely to a redemptive program of God have insisted that there must be a continuity rather than discontinuity between Israel and the *ekklesia.*††† At the same time, they do recognize that the Scriptures make an obvious distinction between Israel and the *ekklesia.* Speaking for this point of view in a book review, Ladd explains:

> It is obvious that the *ekklesia* acquires new depths of meaning in the New Testament, and the present reviewer does not believe Israel in the Old Testament is to be identified with the New Testament church. While there is one people of God, the church, strictly speaking, is a "dispensational" truth and came into existence at Pentecost. However, Israel and the church constitute the one people of God.[162]

***T. F. Torrance, "The Israel of God," *Interpretation,* 10:316. Cf. also Davidson, 38:54: "I believe that Jesus, like the prophets in their time, *intended a new Israel,* not indeed another Israel alongside the old, but the old Israel renewed." Cf. also William Childs Robinson, "Church," in *Baker's Dictionary of Theology,* ed. Everett F. Harrison, pp. 123-24: "The Messianic expectation of the Old Testament includes the formation of a faithful new Israel. In Christ the God of the Old Testament speaks so that the New Testament church is the fulfillment of the Old Testament congregation."

161. Hanke, p. 113.

†††Cf. Ladd, *The Gospel of the Kingdom,* p. 120: "The work of God's Spirit in the formation of the Church and the future divine visitation of Israel by which the Natural branches are regrafted into the olive tree ought not to be seen as two separate and unrelated purposes but as two stages of the *single redemptive purpose* [italics not in the original] of God through His Kingdom."

162. George E. Ladd, "The Rapture Question: Walvoord's New Book Supporting Pretribulationism Reviewed by Fuller Seminary Professor," *Eternity* 8:45. Cf. also, Daniel P. Fuller, "The Hermeneutics of Dispensationalism," pp. 361-62.

In keeping with this theory of the continuity of the program with Israel, Fuller thus interprets the present church as fulfilling Israel's prophecies.[163]

But does the Scripture support the position of the New Testament *ekklesia* as the continuation of Israel and her purpose? Does the fact that in the *ekklesia* God is continuing His work of salvation mean that God is also continuing His program for Israel in the *ekklesia?* Saucy cogently remarks:

> Why call Israel out as a nation, since, it is evident that spiritual salvation can be carried on without national distinctions? It must be seen that in the very calling out of Israel as a nation, God had a national purpose for that nation which is well spelled out in the covenants made with them. Certainly no one would say that the church is national Israel, fulfilling the national promises of that nation.[164]

In addition to these cogent remarks, however, there are weighty arguments that deny the identification of the *ekklesia* with Israel. The fallacy of this position is first of all seen in its erroneous assumption that *ekklesia* in the Septuagint became a technical term for Israel as the people of God.‡‡‡ A previous examination of the usage in the Septuagint has demonstrated that *ekklesia* was never so used in a technical sense. This fact in itself should be sufficient to raise serious questions in the minds of those who stress the continuity between and identity of Israel, the ancient *ekklesia,* and the New Testament *ekklesia* on the basis of their mutual usage of *ekklesia.*

A second factor that denies this continuity and identity is the unique introduction of the *ekklesia* by Christ, as previously demonstrated. This distinctly Christian *ekklesia* was to have a

163. Fuller, p. 347.
164. Robert Lloyd Saucy, "The Relationship of Dispensationalism to the Eternal Purpose of God," pp. 170-71.

‡‡‡Cf. R. Lansing Hicks, "Jesus and His Church," *Anglican Theological Review,* 34:88. Hicks declares that just as the *ekklesia* of ancient Israel was the assembly of God's chosen people, so in the New Testament the *ekklesia* of God's Messiah is described as the "new Israel."

particular content different from the secular *ekklesia* that met on the next street, and the source of that different content may be exhausted in Jesus Christ—not in any etymological or connotational elements. When Jesus established "my *ekklesia,*" it was as different from the Old Testament *ekklesiai* as it was from the numerous *ekklesiai* that existed in every city. The distinctiveness was not in the word *ekklesia,* but in the content of the *ekklesia.* Thus, the term *ekklesia* is used in a specific and technical sense to designate a new entity. This new entity is Christ's assembly, which Christ Himself was to build in the future. The technical New Testament *ekklesia* was to be the Jesus *ekklesia* as compared with the Jewish *ekklesia,* the Greek *ekklesia,* and so forth.

A third factor that denies this supposed continuity is the obvious change of emphasis that may be noted in the teaching of Christ in Matthew. In the light of Israel's rejection of the offered kingdom in the Person of the King, another program was introduced. Christ Himself, after it was evident that He was rejected as the Messiah and consequently that His Messianic kingdom was rejected, taught His disciples in many parables that this age is a postponement of God's work with Israel (Mark 13:34-37; Luke 12:36-40, 42-48; 19:11-27; 21:29-33). Thus, *ekklesia* refers to that new entity Christ was to build in view of the rejection of the Messianic kingdom. The *ekklesia,* therefore, is seen not as a continuation of God's dealings with Israel, but as God's new divine purpose in contrast to the suspension of His covenant promises to Israel.

This latter fact leads to another reason for not equating Israel and the *ekklesia.* Certainly no one would say that the church is national Israel fulfilling the national promises of that nation. Thus, Saucy notes:

> Because God does have a purpose in the nation of Israel and the church is not that nation, the Jews remain distinct

> from the Gentiles as a national people after the inception of the church.[165]

Abundant evidence of this is seen in Scripture. Israel is often addressed as a nation after Pentecost in contrast to Gentiles (Acts 3:12; 4:8, 10; 5:21, 31, 35; 21:28). Furthermore, Paul's prayer for natural Israel (Rom 10:1) is a clear reference to Israel outside the church as a national people. Also, it should be noted that the natural Israel's§§§ privileges continue (Rom 9:3-5) and the Gentiles continue to be excluded from Israel's privileges (Eph 2:12).[166] The strange and miraculous preservation of a distinct Jewish people today after almost two millennia of dispersion among the nations of the world and especially the relatively recent reestablishment of the nation of Israel confirms the scriptural teaching that Israel and her covenant promises have not been absorbed in the *ekklesia* of the New Testament.

Last, but certainly not least, is the fact that Jewish believers and Gentile believers are distinguished in the New Testament. Here is the real crux of the argument: namely, is the word *Israel* ever used of the *ekklesia* in the New Testament. Walvoord phrases the problem: "Is the church ever identified with true or spiritual Israel,|| || || that is, are Gentile Christians ever included in the designation *Israel*?"[167]

It is the thesis of this writer that the word *Israel,* whether natural or spiritual, always refers to the physical descendants of Abraham. Thus, spiritual Israel and believing Gentiles, who together make up the church during this age (cf. Eph 2:11-22),

165. Saucy, p. 171.

§§§This term is used to denote the natural, physical descendants of Abraham through Jacob. Recorded in the Old Testament are the records of God's dealing in a special way with this nation.

166. For an expanded discussion of this cf. John F. Walvoord, *The Millennial Kingdom,* pp. 164-88.

|| || ||This term is used to designate the members of natural Israel who are rightly related to God. They are the faithful remnant that always exists among natural Israelites.

167. Walvoord, p. 168.

are yet distinguished, proving that Israel still means the physical descendants of Abraham. Two principal passages are foundational to this discussion. The first of these is Romans 9:6: "For they are not all Israel which are of Israel." This statement has caused some to argue that the true meaning of Israel is shown to be not that of physical descendants of Abraham, but those of his spiritual seed, thus the church.[168] But this verse does not teach an equation of spiritual Israel and the *ekklesia.* Rather, the distinction is between the nation as a whole and the believing remnant within that nation. Walvoord states:

> The real contrast is not between those who inherit Abraham's promises and those who do not. It is rather that the promises to Abraham are classified as belonging either to Israel according to the flesh or Israel which enters into the spiritual promises by faith—which are given also to Gentile believers (Gal. 3:6-9, 14). It is not, therefore, a contrast between those who are excluded and those who are included, but rather a contrast between those who inherit only the national promises and those who inherit the spiritual promises also. The line of national promises is narrowed to Isaac and his seed (Rom. 9:7), and the line of spiritual promises is narrowed to those who believe. . . . Both Israelites in the flesh (unbelievers) and Israelites who believe are genuine Israelites. . . . [But] unbelieving Israelites are lost and blinded, while believing Israelites come into all the present blessings of the church.[169]

This type of contrast is not unique with Paul, for the same distinction is made within the nation in the Old Testament. Bright explains these two concepts in Isaiah's figure of the servant.

> In many places throughout the book the Servant is merely Israel (e.g. 41:8; 43:10; 44:21; 45:40), so much that the prophet can call the Servant blind and deaf (43:19). . . . **In** other places, *although the Servant is still identified with Israel*

168. Berkhof, p. 161.
169. Walvoord, pp. 168-69.

> (e.g. 49:3), it is clear that he is something other than the visible peoples, because his first duty (49:5) is to lead Israel itself back to its destiny under God. *Here it is plain that the Servant is not Israel itself but the righteous remnant* in Israel (e.g. 44:1; 51:1, 7), the true Israel which is obedient to God's calling and is a witness to his power in the world (49:1-6, 8-13; 42:1-7) [italics not in the original].[170]

In like manner, in Paul's terminology the true Israel is a part of the physical descendants of Abraham, and there is no justification for equating it with the *ekklesia,* which is composed of both believing Jews and Gentiles.

A second important passage set forth in an attempt to prove that the *ekklesia* of the New Testament is in fact the new Israel is Galatians 6:15-16:

> For in Christ Jesus neither circumcision availeth any thing nor uncircumcision, but a new creature. And as many as walk according to this rule, peace be on them and mercy, and upon the Israel of God.

The crux of the issue rests primarily in the grammatical possibilities inherent in the conjunction *kai* (and). It is easy to comprehend that "as many as walk by this rule" refers to the *ekklesia,* the "new creation" of believers in Christ. The problem then is the relation between these and the "Israel of God." Either Paul is making this new creation equal to an Israelite of God or he is making a distinction within the new creation between the spiritual Israelite and the Gentile believer.

In an attempt to solve this problem, appeal has been made to three grammatical possibilities of *kai.* Some take *kai* in an explicative force. For example, Lightfoot writes:

> It stands here not for the faithful converts from the circumcision alone, but for the Spiritual Israel generally, the whole body of believers whether Jew or Gentile; and thus *kai* is

170. John Bright, *The Kingdom of God: The Biblical Concept and Its Meaning for the Church,* p. 150.

> epexegetic, i.e. it introduces the same thing under a new aspect.[171]

Lenski, anxious to equate Israel and the *ekklesia,* utilizes the explicative meaning in his translation: " 'As many as will keep in line with the rule,' constitute 'the Israel of God.' "[172] Ellicott, on the other hand, sees the *kai* used as a simple copulative linking coordinate parts of a sentence. He writes:

> Still it is doubtful whether *kai* is ever used by St. Paul in so marked an explicative force as must here be assigned . . . and as it seems still more doubtful whether Christians generally could be called "the *Israel* of God" . . . the simple copulative meaning seems most probable.[173]

Accepting this usage, Walvoord explains that "God's blessing is declared on those who walk according to this rule (among the Galatians who were Gentiles) and also 'upon the Israel of God.' "[174] When one reads further in Ellicott's explanation of his usage, however, he finds that Ellicott really utilized a third possibility—a refinement of the copulative use. He explains:

> St. Paul includes all in his blessing, of whatever stock and kindred; and then, with his thoughts turning (as they ever did) to his own brethren after the flesh (Rom. 9:3), he pauses to specify those who were once Israelites according to the flesh (1 Cor. 19:18), but now are the Israel of God . . . true spiritual children of Abraham.[175]

Smyth explains that the "copulative *kai* often has an intensive or heightening force; as where it joins a part and the whole, the universal and the particular."[176] The example given for this is

171. J. B. Lightfoot, *The Epistle of St. Paul to the Galatians,* pp. 224-25.
172. R. C. H. Lenski, *The Interpretation of St. Paul's Epistles to the Galatians, to the Ephesians, and to the Philippians,* p. 321.
173. Charles J. Ellicott, *A Critical and Grammatical Commentary on St. Paul's Epistle to the Galatians,* p. 139.
174. Walvoord, p. 170.
175. Ellicott, p. 139.
176. Herbert Weir Smyth, *Greek Grammar,* p. 650.

"Theoi Kai Zeus—the gods and above all Zeus."[177] Arndt and Gingrich suggest this use of *kai* when "adding a (specially important) part to the whole," at which times it means *"and especially"*[178] (cf. Mark 16:7; Acts 1:14).

Whether the *kai* is taken as a simple copulative joining two different groups or whether the "Israel of God" is singled out from the total group (which interpretation seems more likely) it nevertheless distinguishes between Jewish believers and Gentile believers in the church.###

Thus, the grammar alone presents a strong argument for the distinction. There are other arguments, however, which add great strength to this interpretation. The context of Galatians is favorable to the idea of singling out the true Jews for special mention. The apostle's argument is with the Judaizers and verses 12 and 13 give the true character and motives of this group. The motives are twofold. They not only wanted to escape persecution, but also they expected to receive glory for themselves.

> The two reasons suggested by the Apostle for this advocacy of circumcision which he so strenuously opposed are complementary. The first is negative, they thus avoided persecution at the hands of the bigoted Jews; the second is positive, they could boast of their success in proselytising the Gentiles.[179]

The characterization of these false teachers is given as "those who desire to make a fair show in the flesh" (v. 12).

After attacking these Jews, who would be considered Israel after the flesh, it is perfectly logical for Paul, when extending his blessing, to recognize those Jews who had left this legalism

177. Ibid.
178. William F. Arndt and F. Wilbur Gingrich, *A Greek-English Lexicon of the New Testament and Other Early Christian Literature*, p. 392.
###In fact, even Lightfoot, who takes the explicative force, does not believe that this verse in any way equates the church with Israel or her promises. Cf. Lightfoot, pp. 224-25.
179. C. F. Hogg and W. E. Vine, *The Epistle of Paul the Apostle to the Galatians*, p. 335.

and were following the rule of the new creation, the *ekklesia*. Thus, he clarified to the Gentiles that he was not attacking Jews as such, and, likewise, he expressed his love for his "brethren according to the flesh."

Finally, in further support of this distinction is the fact that "everywhere else in the Scripture the term Israel is applied only to those who are the natural seed of Abraham and Isaac, never to Gentiles."[180] Surely, if the New Testament wanted to equate the *ekklesia* and Israel, it would have done so plainly, and in many places, for the term *Israel* is used frequently throughout. Thus, in the face of the evidence that Israel continues as a nation with her special promises and that the church is never equated with a so-called new Israel but is constantly distinguished, it must be concluded that the *ekklesia* is a new dispensational work of God distinct from that of Israel as a nation.

By way of summary, it has been the purpose of this chapter to define the *ekklesia*. To achieve this, the meaning of *ekklesia* has been explained both positively and negatively. Positively stated, it has been seen that the word *ekklesia* experienced a development in meaning from the earlier nontechnical meaning to the technical meaning and to the metaphorical meaning. The great majority of occurrences are technical in meaning, thus stressing both physical unity and spiritual unity. The latter of these was found to be the essence of the metaphorical usage. Furthermore, it has been seen that ecclesiastical organization does not extend beyond the technical usage, which is the local *ekklesia* of Jesus Christ. The emphasis in the metaphorical usage concerns a spiritual relation to Christ and between His saints, while the local *ekklesia* is an active, organized agency of God's kingdom.

Negatively stated, it has been seen that it is improper to speak of the *ekklesia* as a building, a denomination, or a state or national church. Also, it is imperative that it be recognized that

180. Walvoord, p. 169.

the *ekklesia* is not to be confused with Israel or the kingdom of God. The *ekklesia* is a unique dispensational work of God in this age.

Having arrived at these meanings of *ekklesia,* it now remains to develop them theologically in the following chapters.

5

INTRODUCTORY CONSIDERATIONS TO THE DOCTRINE OF THE UNIVERSAL CHURCH

The doctrine of the universal church arises out of an inductive study and systematization of the metaphorical usages of *ekklesia* in the New Testament. When the apostle Paul comes to the metaphorical use of the *ekklesia* (predominately in Ephesians and Colossians), he conceives of an entire world of individual Christians immediately related to Christ apart from local *ekklesiai,* and he terms them simply the (only) *ekklesia.* Thus, the concept of the physical assembly gives way to the spiritual assembly. The locative of place yields to the locative of sphere *(en Christo).*

I. The Unfavorable Extremes

It is to be admitted that the doctrine of the universal church has, through careless application, led to unfavorable extremes. These unbiblical emphases have caused some conservative groups of the present day to reject the idea of a universal church. In their attempt to correct one error, they have cultivated another error. What, then, are these errors that cause radical reaction?

Neglect of the local church

There are those who lay such stress on their association with the body of Christ that their association with a local church is considered of little importance. They may, therefore, be associated with a local church that is essentially nonbiblical in its beliefs and practices. This attitude has kept them from being greatly concerned about the subtle infiltration of modernism into their local assembly. In some cases this lackadaisical spirit has allowed them to remain in apostate denominations with an untroubled conscience. Thus, Tulga complains:

> The doctrine of the invisible church involves its members in corrupt and apostate churches, in innumerable compromises and even betrayal of true Christian doctrines when these members support a visible church which in its nature and ministry contradicts the true local church of the New Testament.[1]

In these days of compromise and doctrinal laxity, one can certainly sympathize with Tulga's complaint, although one cannot condone his denial of the universal church.

The neglect of the local church is further emphasized by the fact that some see no need of joining a local assembly at all. A noted fundamentalist church leader writes:

> Many believers see no need of the local church, are opposed to the local church and teach that local churches are not of God and should not be joined. One theologian in a "fundamental" Bible school stated in a radio address that local churches were man-made and not of God.[2]

Such a de-emphasis of the local church displays ignorance of the biblical teaching that repeatedly attributes the existence of the local churches to the Godhead (cf. 1 Cor 11:16; Gal 1:22; 1 Thess 2:14; 2 Thess 1:4; etc.). It will be seen later that the biblical emphasis makes the local church responsible for being a true, visible, local representation of the universal, invisible church. Any relationship or responsibility encumbent upon the

1. Chester E. Tulga, *New Testament Baptists and the Nature of the Church*, p. 13.
2. B. Myron Cedarholm, *The Witness of the Local Church*, p. 2.

universal church must eventually find its outworking through the localized counterpart.

GROWTH OF NONRECIPROCAL INTERDENOMINATIONAL GROUPS

Another unhappy result of an inaccurate application of this doctrine is the appearance of numerous interdenominational organizations, many of which are necessary and good, working through local churches and supplementing their ministry; but some of these organizations are usurping the responsibilities and functions that God intended for the local church to perform. Many of these groups began as a result of the failure of the local church in certain areas. They were supported by people of vision within the local churches. Some of these groups became nonreciprocal in that while they received their support from the local churches, they themselves failed to work together with the local churches. As a result, oftentimes there is needless duplication of ministries. Furthermore, the support of these organizations interferes with the necessary financial backing for the local church, necessitates the redirecting of valuable time that should be spent in Christian service through the local church, and destroys a proper loyalty to the local church.

STRESS ON ORGANIZATIONAL UNITY

An inaccurate understanding of the doctrine of the universal church is at the heart of the modern ecumenical movement, which sees a true universal church only in the organizational unity of all existing local churches. They have become overwhelmed by the big church concept. Purity of doctrine is secondary to a well oiled and smoothly running ecclesiastical machine.[3] Furthermore, it is this problem that underlies the Roman

3. Ample support of this fact is given by Hermann Sasse, who has been active in the World Conference on Faith and Order for ten years. Cf. "Facing New Delhi: Crisis of the Ecumenical Movement," *Christianity Today* 5:579-82. Cf. also Stanley Lowell, "What Is the Church's Real Task?", *Christianity Today* 5:515-16; and Addison H. Leitch, "Review of Current Religious Thought," *Christianity Today* 5:340.

Catholic Church's claims of being the one universal church with an earthly head.

It is desirable, then, in the development of this biblical doctrine to avoid these nonbiblical extremes that do not give the proper emphasis to the local church. At the same time, however, it is not necessary to let reactionism drive one to the equally untenable position that "The doctrine of the invisible, universal church of Reformed Protestantism is to be rejected."[4] There is a need to find the balanced biblical approach. The fact that a doctrine has been wrongly applied, resulting in extremes and errors in practice, is not reason in itself for abandoning the doctrine.

II. THE TERMINOLOGY INVOLVED

Very often misunderstandings in the study of theology are the result of poor semantics. The choice of the wrong literary vehicle results in a lack of communication. Such has certainly been the case with the subject presently under discussion. Something of the magnitude of the difficulty is expressed by Baker:

> There has been a difference of terms in describing this usage of *ekklesia.* Dana calls it a "spiritual and ideal" usage; Salmond in the *Expositor's Greek Testament* calls it a "spiritual fellowship"; Hort calls it a "unity" and a "new society"; Dargan calls it the "universal *ekklesia*"; Broadus calls it the "ideal congregation or assembly"; Sampey calls it a figurative use "of all who are Spiritually united to Christ as his body"; Robertson calls it a "general body never actually assembled" and "the universal spiritual church or kingdom"; Westcott calls it a "unity"; Hodge says that it is "the company of the redeemed here and in heaven, which constitutes one body."[5]

The list could be extended, but let this suffice to set forth the problem. There are at least four terms that demand some ex-

4. Tulga, p. 14.
5. Robert A. Baker, "An Introduction to the Study of the Development of Ecclesiology," pp. 215-16.

planation. In each case the nomenclature used is an attempt to express the nature of that body of saints regenerated during this age and being intimately related to Jesus Christ, the Head of the body.

INVISIBLE

This is perhaps the most controversial term of them all. Schmidt charges: "Protestantism is also under the influence of this unrealistic Platonism when it differentiates between the Church visible and the Church invisible."[6] He states further:

> Nor is the Assembly of God in Christ to be described as on the one hand visible and on the other invisible. The Christian community in any particular place represents the whole body, and is precisely as visible and temporal as the Christian man.[7]

If a person uses the term *invisible* to speak of the church as an abstraction and to deny its present reality, the usage is ill-advised. This misunderstanding is apparently in the background of Shank's mind, when, in another area of theology, he writes:

> The certainty of election and perseverance is with respect not to particular individual men unconditionally, but rather with respect to the *ekklesia,* the corporate body of all who, through living faith, are in union with Christ, the true Elect and Living Covenant between God and all who trust in His righteous Servant.[8]

McClain answers this mistaken concept:

> Mr. Shank seems to forget that the Church is not an abstraction: it exists only through its members. If the final salvation of the individual members is not certain, then the ultimate fate of the Church must also be uncertain. It can hardly be

6. Karl Ludwig Schmidt, "The Church," in *Bible Key Words from Gerhard Kittel's Theologisches Wörterbuch zum Nuen Testament,* ed. and trans. J. R. Coates and H. P. Kingdon, 1.2:65.
7. Ibid., 1.2:66.
8. Robert Shank, *Life in the Son,* p. 366.

argued that God elects some persons to compose the Church, but not *who* they are to be.[9]

There is a sense, however, in which the term *invisible* may very properly be used of the church. The New Testament knows of no Christian who is not a church member; that is, every regenerate person in this age is a member of the church, the body of Christ. As the pastor of the local church, however, looks out over his flock, he is not able to discern by sight those who are truly regenerate. Only God omniscient is able to do that. It would be sheer arrogance to presume otherwise. Berkhof states:

> The union of believers with Christ is a mystical union; the Spirit that unites them constitutes an invisible tie; and the blessings of salvation, such as regeneration, genuine conversion, true faith, and spiritual communion with Christ, are all invisible to the natural eye;—and yet these things constitute the real *forma* (ideal character) of the Church.[10]

Two factors are included, then, in a proper understanding of this terminology. The union with Christ is invisible, but the church is always composed of people. Even in Ephesians when Paul deals in universal concepts he has definite people in mind, Jews and Gentiles. It should be stated even more emphatically: the New Testament assumes that every Christian will take the necessary steps to give outward evidence of his relationship to Christ and His body. The New Testament knows of no believer who does not submit himself for baptism and join the local church.

IDEAL

There are those who choose to speak of this spiritual institution composed of all true believers in Christ as the ideal church. Dana defends this terminology:

9. Alva J. McClain, review of *Life in the Son,* by Robert Shank, *Grace Journal* 1:35.
10. Louis Berkhof, *Systematic Theology,* p. 566.

> In the earlier epistles of Paul the *ekklesia* is viewed in its functional relation to the work of the kingdom; in Ephesians and Colossians it is viewed in its spiritual relation to the person of Christ. In the earlier epistles Paul is dealing with the problem of the churches as practical agencies of redemption; here he is dealing in the abstract with the church idea in relation to the great metaphysical problem of the person of Christ. There he is dealing with the churches on the side of their active ministry; here he is dealing with the church on the side of its divine relationship . . . an ideal, spiritual body in sacred and vital connection with Christ its divine founder as its head.[11]

To speak of the church as an ideal institution tends to give the impression of something that is a mere mental image existing only in fancy or imagination. Barker remarks: "Too many have been willing to transfer the duties, privileges, and what is more serious, life in the Holy Spirit, to some 'ideal' church whose only existence is in heaven."[12] There is a sense, however, in which the church may be spoken of as the ideal church. Webster defines *ideal* in its primary meaning as that which is "existing as a patterning or archetypal idea."[13] This is true of the church that is the body of Christ. Marsh explains:

> The church invisible, while comprehended in its totality by no period in time, nevertheless does exist in time. There is an obvious sense, therefore, in which it always synchronizes with the existence of the visible church. We term, for this reason, the former the archetype of the latter. . . . As such it [the visible church] is designed to be not merely the embodiment of an ideal, it is to be the nearest possible realization of an invisible fact; the work of saving grace . . . in the hearts of men and women.[14]

11. H. E. Dana, *A Manual of Ecclesiology*, p. 53.
12. Glenn W. Barker, "The Church of God," in *The Word for This Century*, ed. Merrill C. Tenney, p. 113.
13. *Webster's New International Dictionary of the English Language*, s.v. "ideal."
14. W. H. H. Marsh, *The New Testament Church*, p. 129.

SPIRITUAL

DeWolf feels that the relationship of the church and the churches can best be expressed by contrasting the "spiritual church" and the "organized church." Emphasizing the human experience aspect, he explains:

> The spiritual church is not the ideal of what the church ought to be. Neither is it the mere aggregate number of all the individuals known to God as "saved" or destined to salvation.
>
> By the spiritual church is meant that unique and powerful fellowship of sharing created by the power of the Holy Spirit and spoken of hitherto as the *koinonia*. Far from being only an ideal or, on the other hand, a mere aggregation of individuals, it is a living community overreaching all others in extent, surpassing all others in depth of meaning, and richest of all values in the experience of its members.[15]

The word *spiritual* also needs clarification, however, because of its breadth of meaning. It is commonly used in contrast to that which is carnal. When applied to the relation of the church and the churches, therefore, it may imply a disparaging contrast. There are some who, looking with disdain on the local church, affirm that they belong to the spiritual church. The New Testament gives no warrant, however, for substituting a "spiritual" church relation for relation to a particular church, usually designated as a local church. The word *spiritual* is properly used of the church, however, when it is contrasted to that which is the external manifestation of the internal spiritual relationship.

UNIVERSAL

Probably the most popular designation of the church, when speaking of its nature, is the word universal. This seems to do justice to the repeated affirmation of Scripture that the church is *one* body. Calvin stated: "The church is called 'catholic,' or

15. L. Harold DeWolf, *A Theology of the Living Church*, p. 318.

'universal,' because there could not be two or three churches unless Christ be torn asunder [cf. I Cor. 1:13]—which cannot happen!"[16] Thus, the church is universal in that it is a people united to each other because each is united to the risen Lord from whom each receives His divine life. It is impossible that a person could be joined to Christ, the Head, without being joined to His church, His body, which is *one*.

Again, this word is not without semantical problems. The church is not universal in the sense of embracing all churches throughout the world in some form of organization, such as is true of Roman Catholic ecclesiology. Rather, it emphasizes the inclusion of "all those who, in this dispensation, have been born of the Spirit of God and have by that same Spirit been baptized into the body of Christ (1 Pet 1:3, 22-25; 1 Cor 12:13)."[17] There is then only one church, but it may be viewed universally because viewed from union with its Head, or it may be viewed locally because viewed from the membership in a particular place.

It has been seen, then, that each of these terms has a certain legitimacy. In a very real sense the church may be designated an invisible, ideal, spiritual, universal organism. To aid in the facility of expression for the purpose of this book, it shall hereafter be called the universal church.

III. THE HISTORICAL BEGINNING OF THE CHURCH

There is no debate among most theologians as to the origin of the church.* The idea of the church began in the counsel of

16. John Calvin *Institutes of the Christian Religion* 4.1.2.
17. Henry Clarence Thiessen, *Introductory Lectures in Systematic Theology*, p. 407.

*There are some who doubt that it was ever the intention of Jesus to found a church. Rudolf Bultmann is among these. Cf. Gosta Lindeskog, "The Kingdom of God and the Church in the New Testament," in *This is the Church*, ed. Anders Nygren with Gustaf Aulen, trans. Carl C. Rassmussen, p. 141: "It is his [Bultmann's] thought that even if Jesus regarded himself as Son of man and Messiah, one cannot conclude from that fact that he thought himself called upon to establish a church. He holds rather that it was the preaching of the disciples which gave birth to the church. He asks whether Jesus himself intended any such result. For Bultmann that question is decisive; and to it he gives a negative answer." Cf. also DeWolf, p. 321.

God before the foundation of the world. It is, with all components of the plan of God, in a sense, suprahistorical. God has related Himself to time, however, and the points where this plan is tangent with history constitute the present subject matter for investigation.

As to the historical beginning of the church, however, there is no such unanimity of opinion. There are far more suggestions than would be possible to discuss in this study; however, it is necessary to set forth the major viewpoints. The refutation of the inadequate suggestions will be included as a part of the defense of what this writer considers to be the correct, scriptural view.

SURVEY OF INADEQUATE SUGGESTIONS

Adam

The question of the antiquity of the church is of necessity closely related to one's definition of the church. A large host of Christian believers simply see it as the natural result of belief. Hanke says:

> The Church is the natural result of individual religion in several persons who have the opportunity of personal association. Religion makes the Church an unavoidable necessity.... When they come together thus religiously for worship, for mutual religious enjoyment, it is impossible to conduct the worship without regularity, order, rules—and so you have a church.[18]

Holding substantially the same view, Kuiper relates it more specifically to faith in Christ when he explains:

> As New Testament saints are saved through faith in the Christ of history, so Old Testament saints were saved through faith in the Christ of prophecy. . . . And so Isaiah, David, Abraham, Abel and a host of others were members of the one body of Christ, His church. And if we assume, as undoubtedly

18. Howard A. Hanke, *From Eden to Eternity*, p. 100.

we may, that Adam and Eve believed the promise of God that the seed of the serpent would indeed bruise the heel of the seed of the woman, but that the woman's seed would bruise the serpent's head . . . then it may be asserted that they constituted the first Christian church.[19]

Hanke pins this beginning down to a specific verse of Scripture:

> In Genesis 4:26 we read, "then men began to call on the name of the Lord. . . ." This, in substance, is the first instance of what we now call the church. It was on an open public withdrawing of religious people to themselves for religious association and the open assumption of the name of the Lord.[20]

It is plain, then, that those who hold this viewpoint understand the church as simply God's redemptive provision. It is a technical term only in the sense that it is an assembly for worship, but not in any specific content that may vary with the progress of revelation. Actually, the church is soteriologically oriented rather than theologically oriented. It is concerned almost entirely with the plan of salvation rather than with its purpose in the development of the program of God.

Abraham

Most covenant theologians see the beginning of the church with the promises covenanted to Abraham and his seed. A strong exponent of covenant theology who believed that ecclesiastical history had its true beginning in God's promise to Abraham, D. Douglas Bannerman, states:

> In the history of Abraham we see the Church of God visibly set up, built upon the Gospel declared to him, and the covenant made with him and his seed.
>
> There have been believing men and "preachers of righteous-

19. R. B. Kuiper, *The Glorious Body of Christ*, pp. 21-22.
20. Hanke, p. 19.

> ness" before Abraham. . . . But now, for the first time in the record of revelation, we find God by His word and providence distinctly separating to Himself a little company of men "called and chosen, and faithful."[21]

Thus, true to the interpretation set forth by covenant theologians, he understands the Abrahamic covenant as primarily a soteriological covenant. It finds its complete explanation in the plan of redemption and the redeemed community, who exercise faith in Christ. Both of these views, Adam and Abraham, see the New Testament church as a continuation and development of Judaism, the Old Testament church.[22] Indeed, they admit that the church did not come to maturity until the Holy Spirit was poured out upon it at Pentecost and that the New Testament church has a fuller revelation, but it is essentially the same church. The eminent theologian, Charles Hodge, states:

> The church under the new dispensation is identical with that of the old. It is not a new church, but one and the same. It is the same olive tree (Rom. 11:17, 24). It is founded in the same covenant, the covenant made with Abraham.[23]

It should be noted briefly at this point that these viewpoints give scant attention to the historical development of *ekklesia* and to the statement of Christ that the church was still future.[24] In fact, instead of recognizing a true progress of revelation, the concept of *ekklesia* is arbitrarily forced into the stereotyped mold of covenant theology.[25]

Christ

In recent discussions there has been an effort to prove that the *ekklesia* was not only in the mind of Jesus, but also that it

21. D. Douglas Bannerman, *The Scripture Doctrine of the Church*, p. 43.
22. Kuiper, p. 23.
23. Charles Hodge, *Systematic Theology*, 3:549.
24. Cf. Matt 16:18: "I will build my Church."
25. Cf. James Orr, *The Progress of Dogma*, p. 303.

was in a true sense founded by Him.[26] As to the actual stage in the career of Jesus when this "new Israel" was begun, there are several suggestions. Johnston itemizes them:

> (1) The call of the first disciples; (2) The confession of Peter as representative of the Twelve; (3) The Last Supper, which established a New Covenant, to be sealed by Christ's death; (4) The union of the disciples in the Resurrection faith, that is, either at Easter itself with the appearances to Peter, the other Apostles, or the five hundred brethren; or at the Pentecostal gift of the promised Spirit.[27]

Most generally, however, the interpretations seem to center on the declaration of Christ in Matthew 16:18: "I will build my church." The view of Clearwaters is representative of those who see the church established previous to Matthew 16:18:

> The church, therefore, was established in the days of Jesus' sojourn in the flesh and the work of its construction was begun with the material prepared by John the Baptist, later the twelve apostles of our Lord.[28]

Those who adopt this view are forced to make some explanation concerning the future tense of the word 'build" *(oikodomeso)* in Matthew 16:18. Thus, Hodges, defending the view, states:

> The mere future form of the verb itself, however, certainly does not require us to say that the building process had not already begun. As a matter of fact, the verb translated "I will build" also means to *edify, build up, amplify,* or *enlarge.* Jesus could easily have meant . . . that He would *in the future* edify and enlarge His already existing Church.[29]

Another school of thought accepts a more realistic view of the future tense and says:

26. George Johnston, *The Doctrine of the Church in the New Testament,* p. 46.
27. Ibid., pp. 46-47.
28. Richard V. Clearwaters, *The Local Church of the New Testament,* p. 26.
29. Jesse Wilson Hodges, *Christ's Kingdom and Coming,* p. 167.

> In Matthew 16 the Lord had spoken of the church as future; in Matthew 18 he referred to it as a present reality. Somewhere between these two instances he must have begun to build his church.[30]

Although these views, which see the church as a distinctly New Testament institution, give evidence of awareness of the unique contribution of Christ to the concept of *ekklesia,* yet they fail to see the relationship of the ministry of the Holy Spirit to the historical beginning of the church. More will be said of this later in the defense of what this writer considers the biblical viewpoint.

Paul

In recent years there has been a move on the part of some, known as ultradispensationalists, to see two churches in the New Testament. Basically, they understand the church found in the gospels and Acts to be different from the church found in the epistles of Paul. A representative contemporary spokesman, Charles F. Baker, states:

> Perhaps the most evident distinction . . . is the fact that the church of Matthew and of Pentecost is one which was prophesied or predicted by the Old Testament prophets, whereas the church of Paul's epistle is specifically declared to be part of a great body of truth which in former ages had been hidden in God and never before revealed to the sons of men. Eph. 3:5, 9; Col. 1:24-26. Ps. 22:22 as quoted in Heb. 2:12 is evidence that there was a church predicted in the Old Testament scripture.[31]

Full treatment of the passages in Ephesians and Colossians, as mentioned by Baker, will be given among the following arguments in support of Pentecost as the historical day of the founding of the church.

30. Walter F. Bense, "Christ's Ekklesia," p. 3.
31. Charles F. Baker, *Bible Truth—What We Believe and Why We Believe It,* p. 69.

BEGINNING AT PENTECOST DEFENDED

Although the Lord Jesus Christ is the founder of the church and the one who laid the groundwork during His earthly life, the church did not come into functional existence until the day of Pentecost. There are a number of considerations that prove this.

Proved by the concept of the church as a mystery

Covenant theologians claim "that the Church existed in the old dispensation as well as in the new, and was *essentially* the same in both."[32] Such a statement demands investigation in the light of the fact that Paul teaches that the church is a mystery.

> For this cause I Paul, the prisoner of Jesus Christ for you Gentiles, if ye have heard of the dispensation of the grace of God which is given me to you-ward: how that by revelation he made known unto me the mystery; (as I wrote afore in few words, whereby, when ye read, ye may understand my knowledge in the mystery of Christ) which in other ages was not made known unto the sons of men, as it is now revealed unto his holy apostles and prophets by the Spirit; that the Gentiles should be fellowheirs, and of the same body, and partakers of his promise in Christ by the gospel: whereof I am made a minister, according to the gift of the grace of God given unto me by the effectual working of his power. Unto me, who am less than the least of all saints, is this grace given, that I should preach among the Gentiles the unsearchable riches of Christ; and to make all men see what is the fellowship of the mystery which from the beginning of the world hath been hid in God who created all things by Jesus Christ: to the intent that now unto the principalities and powers in heavenly places might be known by the church the manifold wisdom of God (Eph 3:1-10).

The first question to answer from this central passage is, What is a mystery? The word *mystery* of course does not mean some-

32. Berkhof, p. 571.

thing difficult to understand; rather, it means something imparted to the initiated only.[33] Arndt and Gingrich state:

> Our lit. uses it to mean the secret thoughts, plans, and dispensations of God which are hidden fr. the human reason, as well as fr. all other comprehension below the divine level, and hence must be revealed to those for whom they are intended.[34]

"By far the most common meaning in the N. T. is that which is so characteristic of Paul, viz. a Divine truth once hidden but now revealed in the gospel."[35] This is directly stated by the apostle in 3:9, where he refers to "the mystery, which from the beginning of the world hath been hid in God." This statement is so explicit that there remains no excuse for the statement of Allis, who says:

> It was a mystery in the sense that, like other teachings which are spoken of as such, it was not fully revealed in the Old Testament and was completely hidden from the carnal minded.[36]

Paul did not say that it was a mystery hid in the Old Testament or that it was a mystery hid from the carnal minded, but that it was a mystery hid from or unknown by any except God Himself. It was "hid in God" and it had been hid there "from the beginning of the ages *(aionon).*" By this reference to ages he is speaking of eternity past.

The second question to answer, then, is, What is the specific mystery of Ephesians 3? Paul defined it as follows: "That the Gentiles should be fellowheirs, and of the same body, and partakers of his promise in Christ by the gospel" (v. 6). The mystery centers in Gentiles, and consists of their equal position and privilege in Christ by means of the gospel. This equality is

33. D. Miall Edwards, "Mystery," in *The International Standard Bible Encyclopaedia,* ed. James Orr, 3:2104.
34. William F. Arndt and F. Wilbur Gingrich, *A Greek-English Lexicon of the New Testament and Other Early Christian Literature,* p. 532.
35. Edwards, p. 2105.
36. Oswald T. Allis, *Prophecy and the Church,* p. 92.

pictured by three descriptive nouns, each beginning with *sun* (together), giving the elements of the mystery.

The first word, *sugkleronoma,* speaks of equal inheritance.[37] In God's present age program (i.e., "the dispensation of the grace of God" [v. 2] the Gentiles inherit equally with the Jews. This was never true in the previous dispensation. There was blessing for Gentiles, but it was blessing as servants—never on an equality. The second word, *sussoma,* means 'to belong to the same body."[38] It affirms the fact that the Gentiles not only have an equal inheritance, but that they are in the same identical body—the body of Christ. Gentiles were not simply something added that did not belong—like a wart on the nose; they were equal participants in this new body. Some writers, attempting to harmonize this verse with their position, insist that the way is now open for the Gentiles to become members of an already existing body. This problem seems to have been anticipated by Paul, for he has already clearly answered it in the preceding chapter: "for to make in himself of twain *one new man,* so making peace" (2:15). There is no existing group into which Gentiles are brought, but most definitely a new body has been created into which Jew and Gentile alike are introduced.

The third word expressive of equality, *summetocha,* means "a joint partaker."[39] They are joint partakers of the promise of the coming Saviour. Jew and Gentile alike in this present dispensation have received the fulfillment of the promise of the coming Saviour. This is something the Gentiles did not have in the Old Testament. Pentecost notes significantly that when Paul is viewing the coming of the Saviour (v. 6), he adds *Iesou,* which relates it to Gentiles as well.[40] This phrase, "in Christ Jesus," gives the inner sphere of union that is in Christ. Pentecost very adequately summarizes the nature of this mystery. In

37. Arndt and Gingrich, p. 781.
38. Ibid., p. 802.
39. G. Abbott-Smith, *A Manual Greek Lexicon of the New Testament,* p. 431.
40. J. Dwight Pentecost, class lecture notes on Ephesians.

substance he says that these words beginning with *sun* emphasize the equality of Jew and Gentile, and this equality in these three spheres constitutes the mystery: *The union of the two in one body*. In taking these three words, each one adds to and supersedes the previous one. Jew and Gentile are fellow heirs, but could they be fellow heirs, yet on a different level? So the second word is added, showing not only that they have the same inheritance, but also that they have been made in the same body. There is the equality of position—the closest possible union. But if they have been made fellow heirs and in the same body, is it possible that one might receive a greater portion of the blessing than the other? No, the Gentiles are fellow partakers of the one promise. There are not two promises. He is guarding against any possible interpretation that would allow the Gentile to be put in an inferior position.[41] Thus, this truth concerning the body of Christ, the church, the new people of God, Paul considered a mystery unknown in the previous dispensation.

A third question now arises: Could this mystery possibly have been revealed in the Old Testament? Or, to put it another way: Does this mean that Paul actually believed that the church was completely hidden in the Old Testament? An erroneous interpretation of the mystery in Ephesians 3 leads Allis, and other covenant theologians, to the conclusion that the mystery of the one body, the church, was "an old truth which was taught at least in germ in the Abrahamic covenant."[42] The problem centers in the *hos* clause: "as it hath now been revealed" (v. 5). What is the grammatical sense of *hos?*

A study of syntax only determines the grammatical *possibilities* of a word. The context itself must determine which possibility is the correct one. Too often Bible students search until they find the meaning that substantiates their previously determined interpretation. The present problem is a case in point.

41. Ibid.
42. Allis, p. 95.

Allis makes an assumption apparently without considering other grammatical possibilities. Concerning the *hos* clause he states:

> It at once changes an absolute into a relative statement. If the words, "which in other generations was not made known to the sons of men," imply that the mystery was utterly unknown in the past, the words, "as it hath now been revealed," definitely deny that such was the case and as definitely assert that it was previously known, only not with the same clearness and fulness.[43]

In this statement Allis has assumed that the only possible interpretation is as a comparative clause. This takes *hos* as emphasizing the degree of revelation. It was not revealed to the same extent in the Old Testament as it is now revealed. Thus, the difference is not in content but in degree of revelation. However, A. T. Robertson in one of his many discussions of this word lists various other uses, such as exclamatory, declarative, causal, temporal, with the infinitive and participles, and with superlatives.[44] Thus Robertson cautions:

> The relative clause may indeed have the resultant effect of cause, condition, purpose, or result, but in itself it expresses none of these things. It is like the participle in this respect. *One must not read into it more than is there* [italics not in the original].[45]

Even a cursory examination of the contextual argument reveals that the comparative usage of *hos* is inadequate, for the author is not making a comparison to show similarities; he is setting up a distinct contrast. The contrast between the other ages and "now" (*nun*).† The most adequate discussion of this problem is by Stifler, who writes:

43. Ibid., pp. 94-95.
44. A. T. Robertson, *A Grammar of the Greek New Testament in the Light of Historical Research*, pp. 967-69.
45. Ibid., p. 956.

†This adverb of time means "at the present time as opposed to the past." Cf. Abbott-Smith, p. 306.

> The "as" does not give a comparison between degrees of revelation in the former time and "now." It denies that there was any revelation at all of the mystery in that former time; just as if one should tell a man born blind that the sun does not shine in the night as it does in the daytime. It does not shine at all by night.[46]

After mentioning other occurrences of *hos* where there is certainly no comparative element,‡ he significantly states: " 'As' with a negative in the preceding clause has not received the attention which it deserves. It is sometimes almost equivalent to 'but' (1 Cor 7:31)."[47] Such a usage definitely clarifies the relation of *hos* in Ephesians 3:5 to the obvious contrasts set forth in the context. It may then be translated: "Which in other ages was not made known unto the sons of men, *but* it is now revealed unto his holy apostles and prophets."§

The accuracy of this translation is further substantiated by the usage of *apekaluphthe* (to uncover or unveil). When Paul used this word, it signified making something known that previously had not been known, unveiling what was previously veiled.

Finally, one of the most powerful arguments against the comparative view is found in the parallel passages. For example, note Romans 16:25-26: "Now to him that is powerful to stablish you . . . according to the revelation of the mystery, which was kept secret since the world began, but now is made manifest." Even more significant, however, is Colossians 1:26, where he defines the church as "the mystery which hath been hid from ages and from generations, but now is made manifest

46. James M. Stifler, *The Epistle to the Romans—A Commentary Logical and Historical,* p. 254.

‡Acts 2:15: "For these are not drunken, as ye suppose, seeing it is but the third hour of the day." Acts 20:24: "But none of these things move me, neither count I my life dear unto myself, so that [*hos*] I might finish my course with joy."

47. Stifler, p. 254.

§Cf. the translation in the *New English Bible:* "In former generations this was not disclosed to the human race; but now it has been revealed by inspiration to his dedicated apostles and prophets."

to his saints." To the Colossians Paul is teaching the same truth as to the Ephesians, but in slightly different words, allowing no degree of this revelation in past ages. Interestingly enough, Allis does not reckon with this verse where the mystery is stated in absolute terms as completely hidden in previous ages.

It has been seen, then, that the grammatical usage allows for the possibility of such an interpretation and that the argument of the passage and the study of parallel passages demand this interpretation. With this evidence in view, it may be definitely concluded that, although Gentile blessing was predicted in the Old Testament,[48] the mystery of Jew and Gentile in one body, the church, was not made known. The church, the body of Christ, must be confined, then, to this present dispensation.

Before moving on, there is one further question that must be answered because of the confusion that it has injected into contemporary ecclesiological discussion. Does Paul claim to be the sole recipient of the revelation of the mystery? Ultradispensationalists answer with a dogmatic affirmative. The Bullingerites or more extreme type of ultradispensationalists usually place the church entirely after the book of Acts, while the more moderate ones, represented by O'Hair, place it within the book of Acts either at 18:6 or 13:46; or sometimes, more rarely, with the conversion of Paul in chapter 9.[49] In any case they all hold that the church could not have begun at Pentecost, for the revelation of it was exclusively Pauline. Baker contends that a new dispensation began with Paul. The Pauline revelation results in the joining together of Jews and Gentiles as joint members of a joint body; whereas at Pentecost the message was to Jews only and it continued that way for several years. Thus, they see a different church in the latter part of Acts from that Jewish church established at Pentecost.[50]

48. Cf. Gen 9:27; Psalm 67:1-2; Isa 2:2.
49. Cf. Ethelbert W. Bullinger, *The Mystery,* p. 40; J. C. O'Hair, *A Dispensational Study of the Bible,* p. 32.
50. Baker, *Bible Truth,* pp. 42, 62.

Such a view is refuted both by statements previous to Paul's writings and on the basis of Paul's own testimony in the principal passage on the matter. First of all, one must understand that between the major developments in God's plan of the ages there are periods of transition. This is essential to the human comprehension of the progress of revelation. Thus, although the full and complete revelation was given to the apostle Paul by the Holy Spirit, there were precursors to it beginning shortly after Pentecost.|| It was a startling truth to the Jews to realize that Gentiles were to be coparticipants with Jews in one body. McClain sheds light at this point:

> The historical question now is: How did the early disciples interpret *ekklesia?* In reply we may observe that the record provides no evidence that in the early days of the Church's existence its members were fully acquainted with its distinctive character as later revealed in the New Testament epistles. The early Church was wholly Jewish in membership. . . . Furthermore, in our Lord's original prediction concerning *His "ekklesia,"* He reveals only one general feature, i.e. its place of authority in relation to the future "kingdom of heaven" (Matt. 16:18-19). And since the disciples were looking for an early restoration of that Kingdom "to Israel," it should be clear that their hopes were centered on the Kingdom rather than on the *ekklesia.*[51]

This early emphasis on the kingdom helps to explain the misunderstanding concerning the nature of the church and the rise of the Jewish-Gentile hostility in the early assemblies. Concerning the Jewish-Gentile problem, McClain says:

> The proposed explanations range widely, from Baur's theory

||Dispensationalists are misrepresented at this point. For example, Allis states: "Despite the fact that they date the Church from Pentecost, Dispensationalists insist that it was a mystery first revealed to Paul some twenty to thirty years later. . . . And they proceed to draw a sharp distinction between the Pauline mystery Church and the Petrine professing church" (p. 102).

51. Alva J. McClain, *The Greatness of the Kingdom*, p. 427.

> of two versions of Christianity, the one Petrine and the other Pauline, down to the recent theory of two Churches, the one in Acts being Jewish and the other the universal body of Christ in the present age. The true explanation must be found in the transitional character of the period covered in the Book of Acts.... The period begins with the Kingdom in the forefront. And while the prophets had made clear that the Gentile nations were to share in its benefits, the nation of Israel always held the place of priority. Therefore, it becomes understandable that the admission of Gentiles to the *ekklesia* raised the problem of *how* they were to be received, if at all.[52]

Thus, the Lord begins teaching them the true nature of the church by means of life situations and visions. First, it was the branching out to the hated Samaritans with the message. The next step was the Gentiles. Repeated visions were necessary to lead Peter to an acceptance of this move (Acts 10-11). Finally, he admits, "Of a truth I perceive that God is no respecter of persons." The word perceive *(katalambanomai)*, which is in the present tense, may more literally be translated, "I am just now beginning to get a grasp on" the fact that God is no respecter of persons. Peter reveals further comprehension of this truth in Acts 15:7-9.

> Men and brethren, ye know that a good while ago God made choice among us, that the Gentiles by my mouth should hear the gospel, and believe. And God, which knoweth the hearts, bare them witness, giving them the Holy Ghost, even as he did unto us; and put no difference between us and them, purifying their hearts by faith.#

Thus, it is seen that in this transitional period the Lord was

52. Ibid., p. 428.

#Other early intimations of this distinctive truth are found in John 10:16: "And other sheep I have which are not of this fold: them also I must bring, and they shall hear my voice; and there shall be one fold [flock] and one shepherd"; and John 14:20: "At that day ye shall know that I am in the Father, and ye in me, and I in you."

teaching in general ways that which later He specifically revealed to Paul.**

This fact is further substantiated by Paul's own testimony. It is true that this mystery was made known to him by revelation and that he "wrote" about it in "few words" (Eph 3:3). But he does not say "to me exclusively." In fact he makes it quite clear that God had revealed it to the other apostles and prophets as well as to himself (v. 5). Ryrie notes: "This was done by the Holy Spirit, not by Paul, thus making it clear that Paul was not the first nor the only agency of this revelation."[53] He concludes:

> To say, as Paul does in this passage, that he had received something from God is not to say that God had not also given it to others, as indeed He had to the apostles and prophets. It is nevertheless true that although it cannot be said that Paul was the sole recipient of the revelation of the mystery, he was the principal agent of the revelation of it to others, for it is to his theology largely that we owe our knowledge of the Church as a mystery.[54]

In summary, then, this discussion of the mystery of the church as it relates to the church's historical beginning has shown that the very character of the church as a new body composed of Jew and Gentile on a common level must of necessity be limited to the present dispensation because it has been hidden in the mind of God from eternity past. Furthermore, there is only one church since Pentecost, even though it was not fully revealed in the transitional period before the writings of Paul.

**With regard to the problem of ultradispensationalism, it must be kept in mind that "a dispensation is related to what God is doing, not to what he reveals at the time. . . . These are economies of God, not of man, and we determine the limits of a dispensation not by what any one person within that dispensation understood but by what we may understand now from the completed revelation of the Word." Charles C. Ryrie, "The Necessity of Dispensationalism," *Bibliotheca Sacra* 114:253.

53. Charles Caldwell Ryrie, *Biblical Theology of the New Testament,* p. 190.
54. Ibid.

Proved by the promise of Christ in Matthew 16:18

Previous discussion of this passage in chapter 4 has revealed that *ekklesia* in Matthew 16:18 is used in a specific and technical sense to refer to an entirely new entity. Although previously the word always was used of the simple concept of *assembly,* now in Matthew 16:18 it is characterized by the new content that Jesus gave it as over against some other kind of *ekklesia.* Thus, Jesus seems to be saying: "You are familiar with the *ekklesia* of Israel in the Old Testament. But I am going to build an *ekklesia* that will be characterized by the content I shall give it." The contrast, then, would seem to extend to a *spiritual ekklesia* with His content, as over against a *spatial* or *corporeal ekklesia* of the Old Testament. Thus, Robertson says that *ekklesia* came to be applied to an "unassembled assembly."[55]

Among those who admit the fact that the *ekklesia* of Matthew 16:18 is an entirely unique *ekklesia* and is to be differentiated from all others, there are those who insist that it was already in existence at the time Christ spoke these words.[56] In their minds Christ Himself began building the church when He first started calling out disciples to follow Him. A careful study of Matthew 16:18, however, reveals that the inception of the church had to be future to that time.

The key to this particular argument is in the word *oikodomesọ,* which is in the future indicative. Because the future is primarily an indicative tense, the element of time is very pronounced. Thus, the future indicative expresses anticipation of an event in future time. Dana states:

> It is this foretold occurrence of a future event which is its basal significance, and *any qualifying idea is derived from the context* or the nature of the verbal idea [italics not in the original].[57]

55. A. T. Robertson, *Word Pictures in the New Testament,* 1:132-33.
56. Cf. R. Newton Flew, *Jesus and His Church,* p. 135; Clearwaters, p. 27; Roy Mason, *The Church That Jesus Built,* pp. 15-17.
57. H. E. Dana and Julius R. Mantey, *A Manual Grammar of the Greek New Testament,* p. 191.

There are three shades of meaning in the future tense: the volitive, the deliberative, and the futuristic. Robertson lists this usage of *oikodomeso* as possibly a volitive durative future.[58] It would read "I will" rather than "I shall," thus expressing His positive intention of carrying out this undertaking of building an *ekklesia* in the future. It was not to be any *ekklesia* that existed before or during Christ's previous ministry, but an *ekklesia* that was to be built in the future. Concerning this future building, Sanford says:

> The *ekklesia* is represented as a building of which Christ is the Builder. There is no indication that Chirst merely meant that He would make a new beginning in the development of any existing *ekklesia,* for He is dealing here with the founding of an *ekklesia,* not the rebuilding of one.[59]

The grammatical argument gives conclusive evidence that this building was to be a future undertaking.

This is also supported, however, by the contextual argument. Matthew is predominantly the gospel addressed to the Jews, presenting to them their promised King. Matthew 1-10 presents Christ's legal, moral, judicial, and prophetical right to the throne of David as King of Israel. His credentials as King are carefully set forth in relationship to His birth, His baptism, His temptation, His righteous doctrine, and His supernatural power. The message of the nearness of the kingdom and the call to repentance are proclaimed to Israel by John the Baptist, the King himself, and His disciples. In chapters 11-12 the response of Israel is manifest in opposition and rejection of Christ as King. Since the kingdom could not be set up on earth because of the opposition, instruction is given by the King in chapter 13 by means of parables about the postponement of the kingdom and the development of the kingdom program during the time of the King's absence from the earth. From Matthew 13:54

58. Robertson, *A Grammar of the Greek New Testament,* p. 889.
59. Carlisle J. Sanford, "'The Concept of *Ekklesia* in Matthew," p. 24.

through 16:12 the continued course of opposition to the King is traced. Finally, the hatred of Israel's leaders becomes so great that the King simply abandons them and begins to instruct His disciples. It is at this time that Christ makes several great revelations concerning His person, His program, and the principles of His kingdom. In the midst of these great revelations is the revelation in Matthew 16:18-20 of Christ's plan to build an *ekklesia.* Having been spurned and rejected by Israel, Christ reveals that He is going to do something new, namely, build an *ekklesia.*††

In the light of the Jewish background of the book, some would contend that such a specific and unique use of *ekklesia* would not be intelligible to Matthew's readers. Allis attempts to point out the inconsistencies in the claims of dispensationalists:

> According to Darby and Scofield the church of which Jesus was speaking when He said, "Upon this rock I will build my church" was the Christian Church, the mystery Church of Paul. This is the common belief of nearly all Christians. But from the Dispensational viewpoint it is open to serious difficulties. If Matthew's Gospel is Jewish, as Dispensationalists have been insisting for a hundred years and more . . . is it possible to hold that the Church of which He spoke to them was an institution which did not concern them as Jewish believers at all, but was an utter mystery to them?[60]

††Dispensationalists have been greatly misrepresented at this point. A typical misrepresentation is that by Kraus: "He (Christ) did not intend in the first instance to establish the Church, but when it became clear that the Jews would not accept Him as their Messiah he began to prepare His disciples for this new thing which would be brought into being." Cf. Norman Kraus, *Dispensationalism in America,* p. 129. Cf. also Hodges, p. 31; Clarence B. Bass, *Backgrounds to Dispensationalism,* p. 25.

Actually, it is quite naive to imply that dispensationalists believe that Jesus was taken by surprise when the Jews did not accept His offer of the kingdom and to infer that the church was just some kind of a stopgap measure to meet the emergency. Dispensationalists are quite aware that the church has always been in the eternal purpose of God, but they are also cognizant of the fact that in the progress of revelation God did not choose to reveal it to man until after the Jews' rejection of their Messiah. Then God revealed the next step in His eternal program.

60. Allis, p. 160.

The answer to this criticism is quite obvious. First, that a book is primarily concerned with the development of God's program as it concerns the Jews does not mean that all truth in the book must be exclusively Jewish. The death of Christ is certainly not exclusively Jewish, although Matthew certainly emphasizes the part that the Jews had in it. Second, if that which is a mystery is to be revealed, there must be an occasion when for the first time the new program is announced to those who are to be the nucleus of the membership. This is simply the nature of revelation. Third, it is to be noted that the declaration of Christ's purpose in a prophetic context does not necessitate full comprehension on the part of the recipients. Sanford explains:

> Christ often revealed truth to his disciples which they could not comprehend at the time, although they did come to understand later (compare John 2:18-22; 8:27; 10:6; 12:16). Christ had just ended His public ministry in Galilee, had taken the disciples a long journey alone, and was about to go to Jerusalem with the avowed intention of being killed; no moment was more suitable for Him to utter the statement concerning this *ekklesia.*[61]

Thus, the promise of Christ in Matthew 16:18 reveals that it was His purpose to build in the future a new *ekklesia* that would be entirely distinct from the Old Testament *ekklesia* with which the Jews were so familiar. A study of the content of Matthew has revealed that in the light of the previous rejection of Christ by the Jews it was altogether fitting that this announcement of a new development in His program should be made in this "Jewish" book.

One final problem must be dealt with in this passage. It concerns the meaning of *oikodomeso.* There are those who agree that this is a simple future, but they argue that Christ, in the future, would *build up* His church, which had already come into existence sometime before—perhaps with the calling of the

61. Sanford, p. 27.

first disciples. They find the material for their argument in the variety of meaning enclosed by the word *oikodomeo*. Although in the large majority of cases it simply means "to build," it can also mean "to rebuild" or "to build up." Furthermore, it is also used in quite a nonliteral sense, often without any consciousness of its basic meaning, as "benefit, strengthen, establish, or edify."[62] Capitalizing upon the possible meaning "to build up," Bogard states:

> When our Lord established His church He declared He would build it up, edify it, enlarge it, and the gates of hell should not prevail against it. (Matt. 16:18) The Greek word "oikodomeso," in Matt. 16:18, translated "will build" means "will build up," "enlarge," "edify." His church was already in existence when He uttered these words.[63]

Several important factors are overlooked, however, by such a translation of *oikodomeso*. First is the broad contextual argument. The Messiah, having just been rejected, speaks in Matthew 16:17-20 of His future program. Second, in the immediate context Christ speaks of His personal *ekklesia* in terms of the future and the word is not "I am building" but "I will build." Thus, *oikodomeso* expresses a prophetic aspect. Third, the use of *oikodomeo* by Matthew in his gospel is very significant. Bowman has summarized the usages:

> All the occurrences of the verb before Matthew 16:18 are *aorists* (Matt. 7:24, 26) and not *presents*. The houses are seen as being fully constructed and not in the process of being built. Then, in Matthew 16:18, he uses a simple future. The aorist is used after Matthew 16:18 (Matt. 21:33; 26:61). The first occurrence of the verb used in the present tense is Matthew 23:29. Christ uses the present tense to describe that the scribes and pharisees were incessantly building the tombs of the prophets. His denunciation of them required the use of

62. Arndt and Gingrich, pp. 560-61.
63. Ben M. Bogard, *The Baptist Way Book*, p. 30.

> the present. Therefore, in the main, Matthew uses the aorist tense of *oikodomeo* with the exception of Matthew 16:18 and Matthew 23:29. One should note that Peter uses *oikodomeo* to express the idea of "building up" but the word is used only after the church had started at Pentecost (1 Pet. 2:5). Therefore, it cannot be held that *oikodomeo* in Matthew 16:18 has the idea of enlargement. Why use a future tense for a finished fact?[64]

Darby states that in Matthew 16:18 Christ announces His intention to *build* the church, that Paul in Ephesians 2:20-22 says the building *grows,* and that Peter in 1 Peter 2:4-5 says *living stones come* and are built into the spiritual house of God's building.[65]

Having now established that the church is an absolutely new development in this dispensation and that its inception was future to the time of Christ's words in Matthew 16:18, it remains to determine more specifically the precise time of its beginning.

Proved by the necessity of the death, resurrection, and ascension of Christ

Although some of the teaching of Christ was in anticipation of and preparation for the formation of the church, yet His death, resurrection, ascension, and exaltation were the necessary foundation on which the church was to be built. The formation of His body is therefore dependent upon the shedding of His blood on Calvary, by which act forgiveness of sins has been provided. This conclusion is clearly substantiated by Acts 20:28, for there Paul taught the Ephesian elders that the church was purchased with Christ's own blood. Chafer states:

> There could be no Church in the world—constituted as she is and distinctive in all her features—until Christ's death; for

64. Hoyle Eugene Bowman, "The Doctrine of the Church in the North American Baptist Association," p. 21.
65. John Nelson Darby, *Synopsis of the Books of the Bible,* 5:286.

> her relation to that death is not a mere anticipation, but is based wholly on His finished work and she must be purified by His precious blood.[66]

Neither could there be any church until the resurrection, ascension, and exaltation of Christ had occurred. Ephesians 1:22-23 declares that God gave Christ to be Head over all the church, which is His body. The previous verses indicate two very important events, however, which necessarily precede this headship. First, God raised Christ from the dead. Because of this marvelous display of power in resurrection, the church also is raised unto newness of life, which act is absolutely essential to its existence (Eph 1:19-20; Col 3:1). Second, God exalted Christ to a place of honor at His own right hand. Thus, the body of Christ has the necessary Head to whom it is intimately united and from whom it receives its direction.

> There could be no Church until Christ arose from the dead to provide her with resurrection life. . . . There could be no Church until He had ascended up on high to become her Head; for she is a New Creation with a new federal headship in the resurrected Christ.[67]

In Ephesians 4:8-11 it is revealed that Christ had first to ascend in order to give gifts to the body. A body without gifts would be incapable of growth and would therefore lack the ability to accomplish one of its primary responsibilities. Ryrie explains that "its functioning is dependent upon the giving of gifts to individual members, which gifts in turn are dependent upon the ascension of Christ (Eph 4:7-12)."[68]

Proved by the necessity of the baptism of the Holy Spirit

The chief argument for the beginning of the church on the day of Pentecost relates to the baptism of the Holy Spirit. "It dates from the first Christian Pentecost," declares Van Ooster-

66. Lewis Sperry Chafer, *Systematic Theology*, 4:45.
67. Ibid.
68. Ryrie, *Biblical Theology*, p. 190.

zee, "and is in the full sense of the word a creation of the Holy Ghost."[69] With this, interestingly enough, Brunner agrees: "The outpouring of the Holy Ghost and the existence of the *Ecclesia* are so closely connected that they may be actually identified."[70] In 1 Corinthians 12:13 Paul explains that entrance into the body of Christ‡‡ is dependent upon the baptism of the Holy Spirit. This event had not yet occurred in John 7:39: "for the Holy Ghost was not yet given; because that Jesus was not yet glorified." In John 14:17 Christ declares that the disciples will experience a new and distinct relationship to the Holy Spirit, "for he dwelleth with you and shall be in you." In Acts 1:4 Christ commanded the disciples that they should not depart from Jerusalem, but should wait for the promise of the Father. That promise, the baptism of the Holy Spirit, was to occur not many days later. But Peter says in Acts 11:15 that this had already taken place "at the beginning." To discover when it happened, therefore, is to discover the commencement of the body of Christ, and the only possible occasion between Acts 1 and Acts 11 is found on the day of Pentecost (Acts 2). Nash states that verse 2 pinpoints the actual founding of the church at the time when the Holy Spirit sat *(kathidzo)* upon each one of them.[71] Thayer defines this term *kathidzo* as "to have fixed one's abode, i.e. *to sojourn* [cf. our settle, settle down]."[72] Since the church is the body of Christ (Col 1:18, 24), the church could not have begun until Pentecost and it had to begin on that day.

A brief summary of the foregoing evidence should now be noted. The church is not a continuation of Judaism; nor is it to be identified with Israel, for Paul claims that the church, the

69. J. J. Van Oosterzee, *Christian Dogmatics,* trans. John Watson and Maurice J. Evans, 1:295.
70. Emil Brunner, *The Misunderstanding of the Church,* p. 161.
‡‡Cf. Eph 1:22-23, and Col 1:18, 24 for proof that the church is synonymous with the body of Christ.
71. Charles Ashworth Nash, class lecture notes on Acts.
72. Joseph Henry Thayer, *A Greek-English Lexicon of the New Testament,* p. 314.

body of Christ, was a mystery that was hidden from eternity past in the mind of God and is only now, in this age, revealed to His holy apostles and prophets. Not only was the church unknown in the Old Testament, but it had not yet come into being when Christ was living on the earth. Jesus Christ stated that in the future He was going to establish an *ekklesia* that would be a completely new and distinct *ekklesia* from anything the Jews knew. Christ was to be the architect of His *ekklesia,* which would be established in the future upon the foundation of His death, resurrection, and ascension. The precise event that inaugurated the church was the advent of the Holy Spirit on the day of Pentecost, at which time those persons who were tarrying in the upper chamber at Jerusalem, waiting for the promise of the Father, were baptized by the Holy Spirit and became members of the church.

6

THE DOCTRINE OF THE NATURE OF THE UNIVERSAL CHURCH

The most profound truths concerning the nature of the church are pictured by Paul through the literary vehicle of the figure of speech. From these figures one can learn more of Paul's conception of the church than from any other source.* Not only do they communicate profound doctrinal concepts, but also they add color, life, and emphasis to the truth. There are those who are of the opinion that figurative language lacks clarity; however, the serious student of Scripture concurs with the opinion of Barrows, who assures:

> Figurative language is no less *certain and truthful* than its plain and literal declarations. The figures of the Bible are employed not simply to please the imagination and excite the feelings, but to teach *eternal verities*.[1]

It is not correct, then, to imply that figurative language is synonymous with nonclear language. Often it is clearer. For example, the statement "He fights like a lion" says more than one could express in an entire paragraph of propositional declarations. Likewise, to the biblically oriented mind, the phrase

*Cf. Otto Pfleiderer, *Paulinism: A Contribution to the History of Primitive Christian Theology,* trans. Edward Peters, 1:229: "The nature of this community [the church] is only indicated by figurative comparisons, as Jesus only described the nature of the kingdom of heaven in parables."

1. E. P. Barrows, *Companion to the Bible,* p. 557.

"the wrath of the Lamb" speaks volumes. Thus, "figurative language is . . . to be thought of as an ally and not an enemy of literal interpretation," writes Unger, "and as a help to it and not a hindrance."[2]

There is always the danger, however, that one may read too much into a figure of speech. Thus, Ramm presents some helpful guides to curb the excessive imagination of the interpreter.

> The literal meaning of the figurative expression is the proper or natural meaning as understood by students of language. Whenever a figure is used its literal meaning is precisely that meaning determined by grammatical studies of figures. Hence figurative interpretation does not pertain to the spiritual or mystical sense of Scripture, but to the literal sense.[3]

One further introductory matter should be considered relative to the figures that are to be examined. There is not unanimity of opinion as to the number of figures that are used of the church in the New Testament. Chafer declares:

> The all-important revelation respecting the true Church is contained in the seven relationships which she sustains to Christ, which are: (a) the Shepherd and the sheep, (b) the Vine and the branches, (c) the Cornerstone and the stones of the building, (d) the High Priest and the kingdom of priests, (e) the Head and the Body with its many members, (f) the Last Adam and the New Creation, and (g) the Bridegroom and the Bride.[4]

McClain has quite a different list, however, for he finds twelve figures.[5] Among covenant theologians it is popular to see the olive tree (Rom 11:16-24) and the lump of dough (1 Cor 5:6-7) as metaphors of the church.[6] In the present study the criterion for the inclusion of a particular figure was its specific

2. Merrill F. Unger, *Principles of Expository Preaching,* pp. 176-77.
3. Bernard Ramm, *Protestant Biblical Interpretation: A Textbook of Hermeneutics for Conservative Protestants,* p. 141.
4. Lewis Sperry Chafer, *Systematic Theology,* 4:56.
5. Alva J. McClain, "The Church."
6. Russell Philip Shedd, *Man in Community,* pp. 176-77.

contribution to and elucidation of the New Testament doctrine of the corporate, universal church. Therefore, those listed by Chafer are the ones herein investigated with the exception of "the Last Adam and the New Creation," which this writer feels has more individual and cosmic significance than contribution to the explanation of the corporate church.

With these factors in mind, the study will then begin with the greatest of the pictures, the picture of the church as a living body.

I. THE CHURCH AS THE BODY

Although the New Testament term *soma* is used in connection with various doctrines, its most prominent theological use is in relation to the doctrine of the church (cf. Rom 12:15; 1 Cor 10:16-17; 12:12-27; Eph 1:23; 2:16; 4:4, 12, 16; 5:23, 30; Col 1:18, 24; 2:19; 3:15). The Pauline use of the phrase is crucial, having most significant implications, and one can well agree with MacGregor, who claims that:

> Modern scholars have rightly considered the phrase to require the most careful analysis, for the theological and ecclesiological consequences of its interpretation are far-reaching.[7]

INTERPRETATIONS OF THE FIGURE

Scholars are by no means in agreement as to how the phrase "the body of Christ" is to be interpreted. Thus, the question is often raised, Is the phrase to be taken in a plain-literal sense or in a figurative-literal sense?

Plain-literal interpretation

In the plain-literal view the church is "the extension of the incarnation." As once Christ manifested himself through a human body (i.e., in his incarnate life), so now he manifests himself through his body the church, and especially in the sacra-

7. Geddes MacGregor, *Corpus Christi: The Nature of the Church According to the Reformed Tradition,* p. 157.

ments."[8] Thus, the church is identified with Christ. In the main, this is the view of most Roman Catholic writers; however, it is gaining a definite popularity among liberal Protestantism, neo-orthodoxy, and even neoevangelicalism.[9] Because of the widespread adherence to this view, it demands an extensive examination.

Berkouwer has done extensive research in the Roman Catholic viewpoint of the body of Christ. In so doing, he has found that this concept is the very heart and essence of Roman Catholicism.

> In the Roman Catholic church and theology various expressions refer to the *actuality, stability,* and *continuity* of the *corpus mysticum.* According to Brom here is the secret of Roman Catholicism.
>
> Continual appeal is made to Paul's epistles to show that the divine truth has been embodied in the church, and that wisdom has built its house here. The characterization of the church as the mystical body of Christ expresses the deepest essence of the church. The communion between Christ and his church is pictured in such a way that we need not be surprised when the identity between Christ and the church is spoken of without hesitation. . . . The Church "as the flesh of Christ, is one with Him, and necessarily fed and cherished by Him." It is like "the continued incarnation of the heavenly Lord."[10]

Reasoning from the fact that Christ is still man and will forever remain so, it follows that the incarnation is as actual as it is historical. Thus, Grossouw can state that "the continued incarnation of the heavenly Lord" so permeates the universal church

8. Owen R. Brandon, "Body," in *Baker's Dictionary of Theology,* ed. Everett F. Harrison, p. 102.
9. Cf. John A. F. Gregg, "One, Holy, Catholic, Apostolic Church," in *Man's Disorder and God's Design,* by the World Council of Churches, 1:59; John Seldon Whale, *Christian Doctrine,* p. 140; Walter Marshall Horton, *Realistic Theology,* pp. 142-43; William Robinson, *The Biblical Doctrine of the Church,* pp. 115-24; Culbert Gerow Rutenbar, *The Dagger and the Cross,* p. 61.
10. Gerrit Cornelius Berkouwer, *The Conflict With Rome,* trans. H. De Yongste under the supervision of David H. Freeman, p. 23.

that the church itself is like a continued incarnation.[11] "More than once in the New Testament," declares Brom, "the church is identified with Christ, and simply called Christ."[12] Especially 1 Corinthians 12:12 plays an important part in this view: "For as the body is one, and hath many members, and all the members of that one body, being many, are one body; so also Christ."

Now this view may seem quite harmless at first, until one reflects upon the very serious implications of identifying Christ and the church. Brom goes on to draw the conclusion: "The church has the same mission and the *same authority*" [italics not in the original].[13] And certainly this is a logical conclusion if the church is identified with Christ and is the extension of His incarnation. Berkouwer states:

> It is certainly not doing the Roman Catholics an injustice if this idea of identity is considered to be very important to their total view, or even to be the essence of all other views of the church. Even when the dogma about the church is not explicitly formulated—as at the Council of Trent—this insight forms the silent background of all considerations. The existence of the *Catholica* is at stake here. The pretention of the Roman Catholic church, *its ultimate doctrinal authority,* and its claim to be the light of the world, stand and fall with this view of identity [italics not in the original].†

Now it is not difficult to understand why Roman Catholicism emphasizes the "extension of the incarnation." It is absolutely essential to the Roman Catholic system. All will admit that

11. W. Grossouw in Berkouwer, p. 23.
12. G. Brom in Berkouwer, p. 23.
13. Ibid.

†Berkouwer, p. 23. This is confirmed by a leading Roman Catholic professor of ecclesiology, Gustave Weigel, in *Catholic Theology in Dialogue,* p. 76: "The Roman Catholic Church believes that this Church is exclusively the Church of Christ. By that fact she believes that she is Christ continued in space and time, with His mission to save, to teach, to judge, to comfort, to guide, to sanctify, and all this she will do because Christ and Catholicism are fused into one life with Him as head and she as the body."

Christ is ultimate authority. If Christ is made synonymous with His church, that church also shares His infallible authority. Thus, the Roman Catholic regards obedience to the authority of the church as identical with obedience to the authority of Christ. The logic is invincible. This identity view is the foundation of the authority of the church. Pelikan observes: "Failure to understand this identification will make it utterly impossible to fathom the riddle of Roman Catholicism."[14] Berkouwer summarizes:

> With respect to this question of identity, the very existence of the Roman Catholic church is at stake; it is really a matter of "to be or not to be" for Rome. But it is no less a matter of "to be or not to be" for the Reformation to protest against such a view.[15]

It is almost beyond belief, however, to see, rather than a protest, a trend toward this identity view in Protestantism. This identification of Christ and the church, which view was at the very core of the protest of the Reformers, is now actually being espoused by Protestantism. In fact, Berkouwer notes that "Anglicanism and Catholicism tend to be one in this."[16]

One noted Protestant exponent of this view today is William Robinson, professor of Christian doctrine and theology in the school of religion at Butler University. Because of his prominence in the contemporary ecumenical discussion, his presentation may be accepted as representative. Concerning the phrase "the body of Christ," he explains:

> It is no mere figure of speech when Paul names the church the "body of Christ"—it is a mystical reality. . . . Wherever the church of Christ is, at that point the eternal penetrates (shoots down into) the temporal. . . . More than once he [Paul] suggests that "the Christ" is not simply the historic Jesus, nor

14. Jaroslav Pelikan, *The Riddle of Roman Catholicism*, p. 80.
15. Berkouwer, p. 24.
16. Ibid., p. 210.

> even the glorified Christ, but the glorified Christ plus the church.[17]

As proof of this identity, appeal is made to the same biblical texts that are used as proof texts by the Roman Catholics. Robinson continues:

> It is this daring identification of the Christ and the church which underlies his discourses on Christian marriage in Ephesians. . . . It involves that interpenetration of personality which is the hidden secret of reality. We have also seen that this was understood by Paul in his earlier Corinthian correspondence, where we have explicitly the boldest of all his assertions about the Christ (1 Cor. 12:12). There he definitely calls the church the Christ: "For just as the body (the physical body) is one and has many members, and all the members of the body, though many, are one body, *so it is with Christ.*" Here, following his argument, we should expect to find, "so it is with the church"; and indeed, that is what he means, as the subsequent argument shows. His substitution of "the Christ" for "the church" is not accidental. It is intentional—Christ and the church are, in some sense, identified.[18]

Not only does Robinson defend the identity of Christ and the church, but he sees a historical continuity. Appealing to John's gospel he says:

> The church is set forth as the universalizing of "the Word made flesh." It is expedient that Jesus should go away, so that the Paraclete may come (John 16:7). But the Paraclete is, in a way, Jesus' "other self": " 'A little while, and you will see me no more; again a little while, and you will see me' " (John 16:16). He is going away a little while only that his witness, which had been necessarily circumscribed by temporality and locality, might be universalized in the church, which was to be

17. Robinson, p. 70.
18. Ibid., pp. 115-16.

> catholic—in all ages and in all places. The church is the continuation of the incarnation.[19]

The truth of this continuation, according to Robinson, is seen in the primitive church. The earthly life of Jesus was only the *beginning* of His doing and teaching; "The former treatise have I made, O Theophilus, of all that Jesus began both to do and teach" (Acts 1:1). But the following is all that Jesus *continued* to do and teach.[20]

Finally, not only is this church, which is identified with Christ, seen to have a historical continuity from the time of Christ's earthly life, but it also is divine. Robinson affirms:

> The church is not of human contriving—it is divine. It has ontological reality. . . . If the church is the perpetuation of the Incarnation, it will have about it those paradoxical qualities in duality which he, our Lord had. Like him, it is both human and divine. . . . In the church, there are two natures in one body.[21]

Because of this development in his thinking regarding the church, it is not surprising that Robinson and others who follow him reject the principle of *sola Scriptura* in matters of authority. He feels that "Protestants have . . . erred in denying the infallibility of the church. The church is *both* fallible and infallible."[22] He denies an either/or solution and falls back on a "paradoxical duality." He explains:

> This emphasis on "church *and* New Testament," over against "church *or* New Testament," as well as over against the doctrine of *sola Scriptura,* is surely sound wisdom, for if we put reliance on the New Testament as conveying to us a sure word of God, we must remember that it is the church which gives it its sanction; and if we put reliance on the authority of the church, we must remember that it was the word

19. Ibid., pp. 116-17.
20. Ibid., p. 118.
21. Ibid., p. 119.
22. Ibid., p. 121.

> of God which called it into being and which forever preserves it from becoming a mere human society.[23]

It is not difficult to understand why Tulga has referred to this viewpoint as "the developing catholicism of liberal ecumenicity."[24] The implications are extremely significant and far-reaching. Horton, who feels that his theology is realistic, draws out some of these:

> All that we have said of the work of Christ applies, therefore, to the work of the church—except that the church can have only one founder, one "chief cornerstone." (1) The church continues Christ's work of mediation between God and man; it makes the life of God more and more immanent and actual in human life. (2) The church continues the work which was so important a part of his Galilean ministry, that of bringing new power and forgiveness to individuals who are bound in fetters of evil habit. (3) The church continues the work which led him to the Cross, that of defying and breaking the power of evil social customs and institutions. One might go on, indeed, to note that all theological concepts which apply to Christ so also apply to the church. If God becomes manifest and incarnate in Christ, so also in the church; if Christ has two natures, divine and human, so has the church, if he has power to forgive sin, make atonement, and bestow saving grace, so has the church. . . . The view just defined undoubtedly has more affinity with medieval Catholic realism than with Protestant individualism and nominalism.[25]

This is a strange doctrine, indeed, for those who trace their ancestry back to the Reformation. It is another in the long line of evidences that Christendom is well on its way to the great apostasy, embracing the heresies of Roman Catholicism while rejecting its orthodoxy. The ultimate merger of Roman Catholicism and Protestantism is becoming more and more plausible.

23. Ibid., p. 150.
24. Chester E. Tulga, *The Doctrine of the Church in These Times*, p. 53.
25. Horton, pp. 142-43.

Significantly, the changes of doctrine are taking place in Protestantism, not in Roman Catholicism.

Unfortunately, very few writers of orthodox persuasion have spoken out against this new catholicism. This surely is a subtlety of Satan, for it is not just a minor ecclesiological point that is at stake. With one stroke both orthodox ecclesiology and soteriology are infected at their heart. Best declares:

> Atonement and incarnation cannot be separated— every book on either the person or work of Christ witnesses to that. Christians in the Church suffer, but we have seen that their sufferings cannot be regarded as possessing any atoning value; they may serve to build up the Church or to bring nearer the End but they do not serve to reconcile man to God. If the Church does not continue the atonement, it does not continue the incarnation. The agreement of some with the Catholic emphasis is best understood from this angle. For the former, Christ's sufferings have an exemplary value but do not atone; thus, Christ's work can be continued by Christians, and so the Church can be called the extension of his incarnation.[26]

This view is exceedingly attractive for liberals. It robs the events under Pontius Pilate of part of their uniqueness; they become only the beginning of the still continuing incarnation of Christ. They destroy the once-for-allness of the events that happened under Pontius Pilate. The church becomes simply a "social Organism of His Incarnation, as this seeks to spread outward, re-creating and re-ordering the disorder of the fallen world."[27]

Most of the objection has come from neoorthodox theologians. In Barth's earlier writings he seemed to agree with the identity view, for he wrote that the incarnation of the Word of God in Jesus Christ is given through the Spirit a "repetition" (*wiederholung*) in the historical existence of the church.[28] In

26. Ernest Best, *One Body in Christ,* p. 196.
27. F. H. Smyth, *Manhood into God,* p. 120.
28. Karl Barth, *Die Kirchliche Dogmatik,* 1. 2:135-36.

his latest volume, however, he rejects the concept of "repetition" and falls back upon a careful use of "reflection" or "analogy."[29] Torrance observes that what has led him to make this change is the "astonishing likeness he finds between Bultmann's conception of the existential repetition of Christ's work in the subjectivity of faith, and the Romanist conception of the Mass."[30] Thus, Barth carefully expresses the relationship, presenting Jesus Christ as the heavenly Head of the church; but the church is

> as His earthly body, bound to Him as such, and yet as distinct from Him in herself, between whom and her there is no reversible, interchangeable relationship, as certainly as the relationship between master and servant is not reversible.[31]

This new catholicism would make the experience of being "in Christ" a church relationship rather than a personal relationship between Christ and the individual. Commenting on this development of ecclesiastical thought, J. Robert Nelson observes:

> Instead of a union between the individual and Christ, we now see the individual in relation to the community, which is the body of Christ. In short, Paul's phrase, "in Christ", is said by many to be equivalent of "in the church."[32]

Refuting this position, he continues:

> As Head of the Body, then, Christ is both distinct from the Body and inseparable from it. He unites the body in Himself, and is yet not to be identified with it. His Spirit gives the church life and direction, but He is not the soul of the church. Again, the paradoxical relationship of Christ to the church, the Head of the Body, becomes manifest. . . . However much Christ may need the church as the instrument of His redemptive work in the world, therefore, it remains subordinate to Him in nature, drawing whatever meaning and value it has

29. Ibid., 4. 1:857-59.
30. T. F. Torrance, *Royal Priesthood*, p. 25n.
31. Karl Barth, *The Doctrine of the Word of God*, trans. G. T. Thomson, p. 113.
32. J. Robert Nelson, *The Realm of Redemption*, p. 86.

> from its relation to Him. The Body lives only because it draws power from the Head, but it is not identical with the Head.[33]

The correct perspective of this doctrine is given by Markus Barth.

> The name "body of Christ," when given to the church, praises Christ. It is a Christological statement about what Christ is and does; it is not an ecclesiastical self-glorification. . . . It is and remains *his* glory, of and in which the church lives. That the risen Christ identifies himself with the persecuted church (Acts 9:4, 22:7, 26:14) is one thing. . . . That the church extols herself to almost divine rank by considering herself identical with Christ is another thing. . . . We are never Christ himself, but we are his body. This term calls for humility and decency precisely within the union with Christ. . . . There is a world of difference between the self-assertive statement that we, the church, are Christ, and the bashful amazement of those who are told that they are the body, the members of Jesus Christ.[34]

The acceptance of this identity view of Christ and the church paves an open road to Roman Catholicism. The logic of the Roman Church is invincible at this point. Once one gets on the road there is no turning-off point short of an infallible, authoritative church that can trace its historical continuity right back to Christ Himself. The very existence of the Roman Church is at stake in preserving this central doctrine, and the elimination of all other churches will eventuate if the doctrine is not protested. The words of Markus Barth may well serve as a summary and warning.

> Individual Protestant writers are recommending submission to some form of episcopacy as one of the steps toward the recovery of the "Great Church." Others counsel a rethinking of the relation of tradition and Scripture, of priesthood and sacrament, of institution and event in the church. . . . Despite all,

33. Ibid., pp. 93-95.
34. Markus Barth, "A Chapter on the Church—The Body of Christ," *Interpretation* 12:145-46.

> *Rome will not choose the way to Wittenberg.* But it seems, whether consciously or not, that much current Protestant thinking knows nothing better than to lead and pave the way to Rome.[35]

Figurative-literal interpretation

Among most evangelical writers the phrase "the body of Christ" is interpreted less strictly. The church is the body of Christ analogically or metaphorically but *not by strict equation.* "There is no need to look for literal realities in the presentation of the doctrine," writes Johnston. "If only dimly, we perceive the adorning wonder of the thought."[36] Continuing, he explains:

> There is a new spiritual personality, Christ the soul, the Church the body. The body is His. He is the self. In our modern categories His are the head and the heart. For He is not only controller and director, but the vital centre too. To be Christ's is to be part of this personality, to belong to His Body. . . . It is well not to exaggerate the *union* between Christ and the mystical Body, His Church. Christians are not absorbed in the Lord or identified with Him.[37]

More abruptly, MacGregor states that "it would . . . be absurd to suggest that the 'Head and Body' figure is to be taken 'literally.' "[38] It should be noted, however, that these men are not objecting to the reality of the union pictured by the figure, but against the mechanistic letterism that is out of accord with literal interpretation.[39]

The matter is not settled, however, by determining that this is a figure of speech. "The exegesis is difficult," explains MacGregor. "While the phrase is plainly figurative, it is not at all clear precisely what kind of figure it is."[40] According to its

35. Ibid., 12:155.
36. George Johnston, *The Doctrine of the Church in the New Testament*, p. 93.
37. Ibid.
38. MacGregor, p. 167.
39. Ramm, pp. 89-96, 141-42.
40. MacGregor, p. 157.

literary classification, "the body of Christ" is regularly used as a metaphor. In this discussion of figures of speech, Perrin has written:

> A metaphor is the shortest, most compact of these comparisons; in it the likeness is implied rather than stated explicitly. Typically the writer asserts that one thing is another (in some respect), or suggests that it acts like or has some of the qualities of something else.[41]

These metaphors, which Perrin has defined, abound in ordinary literature. One may refer to a virtuous woman as a house of gold or tower of ivory. But when the comparison passes from concrete reality to ontological reality,‡ the matter of interpretation becomes complicated. MacGregor explains:

> Metaphysical and theological concepts, if they are to be expressed at all, must be expressed in metaphorical language; but the metaphors become what have been called "root" metaphors; they are to be distinguished from the more ephemeral figures of speech that every poetic imagination is continually creating.[42]

This is the factor that has caused some interpreters to go into the realm of "Beyond-Metaphor."[43] They have attempted to find some higher and richer and more adequate form of speech than metaphor when referring to divine realities. This led to the identity view, which was mentioned above. A safe assumption in the use of the metaphor, however, would be to remember that the reality itself must always be greater than the word that describes it. No metaphor can ever fully represent the entity to which it is applied.[44] This is precisely why Paul uses

41. Porter Gale Perrin, *Writer's Guide and Index to English,* p. 235.
‡Cf. Torrance, p. 29; "When we speak of the Church as Christ's Body we are certainly using analogical language, but we are speaking nevertheless of an ontological fact, that is, of a relation of *being* between the Church and Christ."
42. MacGregor, p. 168.
43. Cf. F. W. Dillistone, "How Is the Church Christ's Body?," *Theology Today* 2:57-59.
44. Ibid., 2:59.

several metaphors to describe the church. The metaphor of the body, however, is the only one with which he actually equates the church (Eph 1:22-23). A comparison to the human body becomes for Paul the most descriptive and most accurate way to picture this corporate body of believers. When, therefore, the apostle Paul refers to the "church, which is his body" (Eph 1:22-23), he is clearly likening one thing that has real ontological reality to another concrete reality, with a view to clarifying and pictorially describing the first.

One final matter must be considered with respect to the interpretation of this metaphor. To some extent the variety of suggestions as to interpretation have been somewhat dependent upon various ideas as to the origin of Paul's use of the phrase, "the body of Christ." For example, some see the origin of the phrase in the transference by Paul from contemporary Greek literature. They say that the church as a body, of which the individuals were members, was derived from the common Stoic conception of the state as a body in which each member had his part to play. But that is not adequate, for Paul does not compare the church to a "body," but to the "body of Christ" (1 Cor 12:27). Between these there is a great difference. When the church is called "a body," attention is focused solely upon the community; when it is called "the body of Christ," Christ becomes the center of attention.

Others have attempted to find the origin of the Pauline phrase in Gnosticism, cult meals, Rabbinism, and Apocalypticism, or else through the "bride," "in Christ," and other Pauline phrases. After an examination of all these theories, Best summarizes certain facts of which any theory must take account if it is to win acceptance.

> (i) The phrase is interlocked with other Pauline phrases concerning the relationship of believers to Christ.
>
> (ii) The primary emphasis of the phrase is on the unity of believers with Christ rather than on their mutual interdepend-

ence. Thus it is used in 1 Corinthians to describe the Church *before* the lesson of mutual interdependence is drawn from it.

(iii) At about the time Paul was writing [*soma*] was being used more and more to describe both the corporateness of a group of people and the unity of the whole of nature with the supreme god, and after Paul's time this new use of the word increased. Consequently this usage was "in the air."

(iv) Though never set down in explicit terms the idea of corporate personality was widespread in the thought of the ancient world, especially in Judaism.

(v) Paul believed in the "togetherness" of Christians with Christ; no man was connected to Christ by himself but only with others.[45]

It should certainly be remembered that, although he probably knew of the use of the word *body* in Stoicism and Gnosticism and elsewhere, Paul may have come upon the use of the term apart from those sources. Best sets forth a rational process that may have occurred quite unconsciously in the mind of Paul.

> Convinced that Christians co-exist with Christ he has been using various picture-phrases to seek to bring this home to the minds of his converts, believers are "in Christ"; they are dead and risen "with Christ"; Christ . . . is the source of new life and righteousness. But none of these phrases will quite describe the togetherness of Christians as a whole with Christ; to make any one of them do it strains it unnecessarily. Eventually he used the phrase "members of Christ" (1 Cor. 6:15). By itself this had dangerous possibilities, and might suggest too close an identification between Christ and Christians; his Lordship over them must be preserved. But "members" suggests "body"; Christians are then "members of the Body of Christ." Thus they are not identified with Christ though they are linked to him.[46]

What Best has set forth here may very well have been part of the

45. Best, pp. 93-94.
46. Ibid., p. 95.

rational process of Paul. It should be remembered, however, that behind this entire process was the supernatural superintendence of the Holy Spirit. The origination of the truth was in the mind of God, and man recorded it as he was borne along by the Holy Spirit (2 Pet 1:20-21).

It now becomes necessary to relate the metaphor to the reality that it describes, bearing in mind the caution against reading into the body concept more than it can legitimately bear. Previous discussion has shown that it is exceedingly easy to read into the minds of the biblical writers ideas that they could hardly have entertained. The metaphor is designed simply to show certain likenesses to the human body and no more.

IMPLICATIONS OF THE FIGURE

Most significant of the teachings inherent in this metaphor is the relation of the Head to the body. The idea of Christ as the Head of the church is a frequently recurring idea in Ephesians and Colossians. God has given Christ to be Head over all things to the church (Eph 1:22). The members of the church must grow up into Him who is the Head, that is, Christ (Eph 4:15). As the husband is the head of the wife, so Christ is the Head of the church (Eph 5:23). Christ is the Head of the body, that is, the church (Col 1:18). He is the Head by which all the body is nourished and administered and knit together (Col 2:19).

These several references raise the question, What is the significance of Headship? Negatively stated, it is a direct refutation of the view that would equate Christ and the church, for in this case there is obviously a clear and definite distinction between Christ and the church. At the same time, however, there is a wonderful unity implied. Lightfoot summarizes the teaching in the following concatenation:

> *He kephale "the head,"* the inspiring, ruling, guiding, com-

> bining, sustaining power, the mainspring of its activity, the centre of its unity, and the seat of its life.[47]

The preeminence of the Head

Primary among these significances is certainly the fact of the preeminence of Christ, the Head.§ This is particularly displayed in Colossians 1:15-19. The fact of this preeminence is strikingly felt by a comparison with Christ's position as sovereign Lord of all creation (cf. vv. 15-17). He in whom was created the universe, and in whom it consists, is the Head of His body, the church. Nicholson declares:

> His relation to the Church is the exact parallel of that which He sustains to the universe. It is the parallel; a relation distinct from that other, but of equal creative power, and an equal sovereign Lordship.[48]

Hence, Paul projects boldly the idea that Christ is supreme. He has lordship and dominion over His church, precisely as the head rules the body. Robertson remarks: "The body . . . does not give orders to the head. It may give pain, and often does, but it is under the control of the head and subordinate to the head."[49] It is only reasonable that Christ should be preeminent in the church, for "He loved the church and gave himself for it" (Eph 5:25). The incredible fact of the gospel is that "He who knew no sin was made sin for us that we might be made the righteousness of God in him" (2 Cor 5:21), that "though he was rich yet for your sakes he became poor, that ye through his poverty might become rich" (2 Cor 8:9). Finally, Colossians 1:18 indicates that the very reason the Father gave the Son to

47. J. B. Lightfoot, *Saint Paul's Epistles to the Colossians and to Philemon*, p. 157.

§If Christ is the head of the church in the sense of being its Sovereign or Ruler, it is blasphemous to call anybody else the head of the church. Thus, the churches should recognize no supreme earthly ruler of the faithful, no human vicar, no special representative of God on earth; their Head is in heaven.

48. W. R. Nicholson, *Oneness with Christ: Popular Studies in the Epistle to the Colossians*, ed. James M. Gray, p. 81.

49. A. T. Robertson, *Paul and the Intellectuals: The Epistle to the Colossians*, ed. and rev. W. C. Strickland, p. 50.

be Head over the church was "that in all things he might have the pre-eminence." The emphasis here is on Christ Himself (*autos*). So eloquently has Nicholson put it:

> He should be *pre-eminent.* That first rank, that chiefest place, that brightest splendor, that everlasting and universally conceded divine Supremacy; how much does it all mean? Nothing shall there ever be to obscure Him. In creation, in providence, in redemption, in personal dignity, in excellence, in majesty, in love, in sweetness, in wisdom, in power, in preciousness; through "all the generations of the ages of the ages," always and everywhere, pre-eminent, supreme, first, chiefest, absolute, ineffable. And to such a one, even to Him, His saved ones shall be forever and forever united, even as a body is *livingly* one with its head.[50]

This headship of Christ as preeminent Lord of the church "is intended to convey the idea of the subordination of the church to the directions of Christ" (Eph 5:24).[51] Metzger writes of this subordination:

> Insofar as the members of the body are in subjection to and respond to orders from the head, the body is healthful and efficient; when such harmony does not prevail, there is discord and anarchy.[52]

It should be noted, however, that this is a subjection of willing and enjoyable response to the infinite love of Christ for His church.

The unity with the Head

Christ is not merely the sovereign, ruling Head, "head over all things to the church" (Eph 1:22), but the *vital* Head as well, since that of which He is the Head is His body, which, "by joints and bonds having nourishment ministered, knit together, in-

50. Nicholson, pp. 81-82.
51. Charles Caldwell Ryrie, *Biblical Theology of the New Testament*, p. 192.
52. Bruce M. Metzger, "Paul's Vision of the Church: A Study of the Ephesian Letters," *Theology Today* 6:55.

creaseth with the increase of God" (Col 2:19). Not only does the sovereign Lord of all creation govern for the benefit of His church, but, in addition, He is the seat of its life. The church is one with Him in life. Thus, Eadie observes: "There is first a connection of life: if the head be dissevered, the body dies."[53] Christ is the first who rose from the dead without dying again. Thus, Colossians 1:18 reads: "He is the head of the body, the church: *who is the beginning, the firstborn from the dead* [italics not in the original]." His resurrection from the dead is His title to the Headship of the church. Best writes concerning Christ's position:

> *Prototokos* suggests the opening of a new sequence of life, which the first-born can be both said to bring and over which he will exercise a measure of sovereignty; Christ as first-born not only comes first, but is the underlying principle of resurrection. He is first, but first of a sequence; because he comes first, the sequence will follow. Christ is consequently both the source of the life of the Christian community and sovereign over it.[54]

Thus, Christ is the vital Head of a community that has passed from death unto life. Apart from Him there would be no church, for He is its originating cause.|| The very nature of the life Christ gives to His church, then, is the cause of an inseparable union, for they possess the same life. Thornton feels that this is the major teaching of this figure.

> Thus whatever developments may be traced in the doctrine of the Body of Christ . . . these are subsidiary to the main conception, namely, that Christ and his people share one single life together after a manner which can be fitly symbolized by the idea of a single human organism.[55]

53. John Eadie, *Commentary on the Epistle to the Ephesians,* ed. W. Young, p. 107.
54. Best, p. 129.
||This is a significant proof that the church could not have existed until Christ had risen from the dead and had been exalted by the Father to become Head over the church.
55. Lionel S. Thornton, *The Common Life in the Body of Christ,* p. 48.

The possession of the resurrection life of Christ and the inseparable union of the body with the Head make it quite obvious that the body of Christ could not possibly be a visible organization, whether local or universal, for historical and contemporary evidence demonstrates that some not possessing this resurrection life are within the boundaries of the visible organization. Furthermore, the visible organization is not beyond the powers of death. Only those who are "in Christ" belong to this body, which is inseparably united to the Head and shares Christ's resurrection life.

Again, the ecumenicists' long, loud cries about the division of the church are fruitless, for *the* church cannot be divided. The members *cannot* be divided into two or more bodies. They are connected with each other and with Christ the Head in an inseparable union.

The sustenance from the Head

A third feature of this Headship is the matter of nourishment and growth. The head nourishes and unifies the body so that it increases. The following parallel passages are particularly pertinent to this teaching.

> The Head, from which all the body by joints and bonds having nourishment ministered, and knit together, increaseth with the increase of God (Col 2:19).
>
> The head, even Christ: from whom the whole body fitly joined together and compacted by that which every joint supplieth, according to the effectual working in the measure of every part, maketh increase of the body unto the edifying of itself in love (Eph 4:15-16).

In the Ephesians passage there is an evident emphasis on the internal workings of the body. Lightfoot says of this distinct emphasis:

> The difference corresponds to the different aims of the two

> epistles. In the Colossian letter the vital connexion with the Head is the main theme; in the Ephesian, the unity in diversity among the members.[56]

These two emphases—the nourishment from the Head and the unification and interdependence of the members—are brought out in these passages. "The head is thus both the source of the sustenance by which the body lives and the source of the unity by which it is enabled to be an organic whole."[57]

The emphasis on the Head as the source of the sustenance of the body is basically pictured in the phrase "having nourishment ministered," which translates the present passive participle *epichoregoumenon.* The emphasis here is on that which the Head *continuously* supplies to the body. This is an intensely interesting and meaningful verb that Paul has here used. Lightfoot relates that "even the simple word implies more or less of *liberality,* and the compound *epichoregein* expresses this idea more strongly."[58] Actually, the word *choregia* goes back to the greatest days of Athens, when the greatest of all the glories of Athens was the plays that great writers such as Sophocles, Euripides, and Aristophanes wrote. The chorus was an integral actor in the play and the cost involved in dressing, maintaining, and training a chorus was great. It was the custom for public-spirited and generous Athenian citizens to underwrite the cost. Clearly the undertaking of a *choregia* was the action of a man who loved his city and was prepared to be lavishly generous to it.[59] From this initial concept of loving generosity, the meaning of the word has widened. Barclay summarizes these usages:

> (a) It is regular in marriage contracts. "Let the husband supply (choregein) the wife with all necessaries according to his means." It is the word for the support which a man in honour and in love was bound to give his wife. (b) It is reg-

56. Lightfoot, p. 200.
57. Best, p. 127.
58. J. B. Lightfoot, *The Epistle of St. Paul to the Galatians,* p. 136.
59. William Barclay, *The Promise of the Spirit,* p. 64.

> ularly used of equipping an army for war. It is used of sending into battle men who are fully and generously equipped for the struggle which lies ahead of them. (c) It is used of a man's natural endowment for life. For instance, it is used of the physical strength and bodily fitness of a gymnast or an athlete.[60]

Thus, the body of Christ is fully and lavishly equipped by its Head to play its part in the great action of the drama of life.

The emphasis on the Head as the source of unity by which the body is enabled to be an organic whole is seen in the second present passive participle, *sunbibazomenon.* Here again is the continuous action of the Head in knitting together the members of the body into an organic unity. Speaking of the two participles (*sunarmologoumenon kai sunbibazomenon*) used to express this unifying action in Ephesians, Pentecost states:

> These together express that the Body, made up of many parts, is a mutual adaptation and relationship to one another, so that a firm structure is built out of the parts. That work of uniting and forming a solid structure is the thought that seems to be in Paul's mind here.[61]

The instrumentality by which the supply is administered and the compactness is achieved is the joints and ligaments (*dia ton aphon kai sundesmon*). Lightfoot states:

> Galen, when describing the structure of the human frame, more than once specifies the elements of union as twofold: the body owes its compactness partly to the *articulation,* partly to the *attachment.*[62]

Thus, contact and attachment are the primary ideas in *aphai* and *sundesmai* respectively. "The relation of contiguous surfaces and the connexion of different parts together effect struc-

60. Ibid.
61. J. Dwight Pentecost, class lecture notes on Ephesians.
62. Lightfoot, *Colossians,* p. 198.

tural unity."[63] In the physical body, there is a constant secretion of fluid in the joints so that there can be harmony in this union of joint to joint. If this fluid dries up, movement is impossible. But the apostle Paul is here picturing that action of the joints in supplying that which promotes perfection of the body and movement of the body together in harmony.

Finally, the apostle stresses the end process in view: the maturity or building up or completion of the whole. Through the twofold means of contact and attachment, nourishment has been diffused and organic, structural unity has been attained, but these are not the ultimate result; they are only the intermediate processes. The end in view is *growth*. Colossians 2:19 speaks of increasing "with the increase of God," and again, in Ephesians 4:16 the goal is "the increase of the body unto the edifying of itself in love." Robertson observes:

> Modern knowledge of cell life in the human body greatly strengthens the force of Paul's metaphor. This is the way the body grows by cooperation under the control of the head and all "in love" (*en agapei*).[64]

This divine growth of the whole body is the ultimate result of the body's union with the Head. Each part contributes that for which it was placed in the body with a view to the maturity of the whole body so that the fullness of Christ may be made up (Eph 1:23). Each member of the body has been given a special gift of grace (Eph 4:7). But this individual gift has its relation to the whole. Each member, in proportion to the gift he has received, gives to the whole in due measure. Each is able to give his gift to the whole because the body is a unity, fitly framed and knit together; thus, the body is built up.

By way of summary of this figure of the church as the body of Christ, the teaching of the Headship relationship is set forth as predominant. It is clear that the *source* of all—both unity

63. Ibid.
64. A. T. Robertson, *Word Pictures in the New Testament*, 4:539.

and nourishment—is Christ Himself. The *channels* of the communication, however, are the different members of the body of Christ, in their relation one to another.#

It should be noted that some feel that the main emphasis of this figure is on the function of the church as the instrument and agent of Jesus Christ, the essential complement through which Christ makes known to all men that which He has already done. Thus, they reason that the body is that without which the Head is practically helpless.[65] Although there is certainly an element of truth here, it seems to miss the basic point. The emphasis, as far as increase is concerned, is aimed at internal maturity and growth. Best concludes:

> As we have seen he [the Head] creates and maintains the Body; he is thus distinct from every other member of the Body. The whole unity is Head and Body. The Body depends on the Head; but the Head does not depend on the Body; this would only be so if the Body were regarded as the instrument of the Head, and there is no suggestion of that in Colossians. The metaphor looks inward and not outward.[66]

Thus, although what has been set forth does not exhaust the meaning of this key figure of the apostle Paul, yet it has emphasized the strategic points. As the governmental Head, Christ is preeminent. As the vital Head, He is the originating cause of the church's life. Furthermore, He is the continually active source of both sustenance and unity, which He communicates through the members of the body.

II. THE CHURCH AS THE BRIDE

The church is commonly called "the bride of Christ." Scriptural references are not numerous, yet the figure is well established in the Christian mind. "Come hither, I will shew thee the

#These clear and definite distinctions between the Head and the body make it evident that the body cannot be equated with the Head, as is taught by those who view the body of Christ as the "extension of the incarnation."

65. William Barclay, *The Mind of St. Paul*, pp. 247-51.

66. Best, p. 137.

bride, the Lamb's wife" (Rev 21:9). "I have espoused you to one husband," says Paul to the Corinthian Christians, "that I may present you as a chaste virgin to Christ" (2 Cor 11:2). The most beautiful picture is undoubtedly that painted by Paul in Ephesians 5:23-32:

> The husband is head of the wife, even as Christ is head of the church: and he is the saviour of the body. Therefore, as the church is subject unto Christ, so let the wives be to their own husbands in every thing. Husbands, love your wives, even as Christ also loved the church, and gave himself for it; that he might sanctify and cleanse it with the washing of water by the word, that he might present it to himself a glorious church, not having spot, or wrinkle, or any such thing; but that it should be holy and without blemish. So ought men to love their wives as their own bodies. He that loveth his wife loveth himself. For no man ever yet hated his own flesh; but nourisheth and cherisheth it, even as the Lord the church: For we are members of his body, of his flesh, and of his bones. For this cause shall a man leave his father and mother, and shall be joined unto his wife, and they two shall be one flesh. This is a great mystery: but I speak concerning Christ and the church.

INTERPRETATIONS OF THE FIGURE

Among the various interpretations of the phrase "the bride of Christ" are three that should be noted at this point.

The triumphant church of the future

First, there are those who say that "the bride" could not possibly be a present reality, but, rather, that it refers to the future church in glory.[67] In an exposition of Ephesians 5:22-33, Carroll states:

> The reader will readily see that the church in this mystical sense has no real existence now except in the continuous prep-

67. Benejah Harvey Carroll, *An Interpretation of the English Bible,* ed. J. B. Cranfill and J. W. Crowder, 15:102.

> aration of tis members. It is not yet a church except in purpose, plan, and prospect. It is called a church by anticipation. . . . To be a church they must be assembled and organized. What is called the "presentation and marriage" is a definite transaction yet for the future.[68]

Some have objected to Carroll's viewpoint on the basis of Ephesians 5:29, which declares that Christ nourishes and cherishes the church, as a husband does his wife. The present tense of these verbs would seem to imply the present existence of "the bride." But Carroll replies: "The nourishing and cherishing of verse 29 refer to after-marriage conduct, as the context shows, and Christ's marriage with the church is far away in the future."[69] He argues that all the verbs employed of the figure must be considered as a unit:

> When we come to the historical facts we find:
>
> (1) That the love, in eternity, preceded the existence of any part of the church.
>
> (2) The giving himself preceded the existence of the greater part of the church.
>
> (3) The cleansing . . . applies to the process of preparing the members, as each one in turn comes upon the stage of being throughout the gospel dispensation from Adam to the second advent.
>
> (4) The presentation of the completed and perfected church, as a bride, follows the second advent.
>
> (5) The nourishing and cherishing . . . of the perfected church, as a wife, follows the presentation.
>
> Now if the present tense of the nourishing proves present existence of the general assembly, does not the past tense of "loved" prove past existence of the general assembly before man was created?[70]

Apparently Carroll has completely missed the argument of the

68. Ibid., 15:163.
69. B. H. Carroll, *Ecclesia—The Church,* p. 63.
70. Ibid., pp. 63-64.

tenses. The aorist tense expresses punctiliar action, that is, action is simply presented as a point by the tense; whereas, the present tense expresses durative or continuous action. The time element is always subordinate to the kind of action expressed.[71] Thus, in the Ephesians passage the phrase "as Christ loved the church" (aorist) is followed by the explicative *kai:* "and gave himself for her" (aorist). Both usages of the aorist tense refer to the supreme act (punctiliar action) of Christ's love, his death for sinners on the cross. The formation of the church was dependent upon the shedding of His blood on Calvary (cf. Eph 1:7; Acts 20:28). This action is to be distinguished from the present, continuous work of nourishing and cherishing. This same ministry has been previously discussed under the figure of the body, in which the Head is seen as the source of sustenance.

Furthermore, Carroll is inconsistent in the development of his viewpoint. Whereas in some places he denies the present existence of the church as "the bride," in other places he affirms that the local congregation is "the bride." He declares:

> Each particular assembly is *a representation or type* of the general assembly, and therefore the broadest figures of the antitype may be applied to all its types without being obnoxious to the criticism. There may well be many representations of the body or the bride of Christ.[72]

The words of W. O. Carver on the figures of the church as they are seen in Ephesians serve admirably to answer this argument.

> In view of the Biblical figure of the church as Christ's bride, the insistence of some that all uses of the term "church" in the New Testament refer only to local organizations becomes absurd almost to the point of sacrilege, attributing to Christ a bride in every locality where a church is found. Likewise the term "body of Christ" in Ephesians 1 and 2 cannot be restricted to local organized bodies. How can one conceive of

71. A. T. Robertson, *A Grammar of the Greek New Testament in the Light of Historical Research,* pp. 823-25.
72. Carroll, *Ecclesia—The Church,* p. 22.

> any one local church as being "the full expression of Him who is fulfilling all things in all respects"? How can one conceive of independent local bodies as growing into "one holy temple of God in the Holy Spirit," especially when the whole context of the paragraph emphasizes the unity of all members of the new human race produced by the cross of Christ?[73]

Finally, Carroll has been previously quoted as stating that the "presentation and marriage" of the church is still future. It should be noted, however, that the bride has been betrothed to Christ (cf. 2 Cor 11:3). Not only does this demand the present existence of the bride, but, according to Oriental marriage customs, this legal contract cements the relationship. Edersheim explains:

> From the moment of her betrothal a woman was treated as if she were actually married. The union could not be dissolved, except by regular divorce; breach of faithfulness was regarded as adultery; and the property of the woman became virtually that of her betrothed, unless he had expressly renounced it. . . . But even in that case he was her natural heir.[74]

Thus, the universal church is presently the bride of Christ awaiting the future presentation to the Bridegroom and the consummation of the marriage ceremonies. This position is also defended by Best:

> In Eph. 5:22-23 the marriage is conceived as already existing; it is because of the known existing marriage between Christ and his Church that Paul can instruct his readers on the relationships of husbands and wives. The husband is to treat the wife as Christ now treats his Bride, the Church; there is now before their eyes an example of marital relationships. The Church is already the Bride, and it is no idealized example of marital relationships.[75]

73. W. O. Carver, "Introduction," in *What Is the Church?*, ed. Duke McCall, p. 9.
74. Alfred Edersheim, *Sketches of Jewish Social Life in the Days of Christ*, p. 148.
75. Best, p. 175.

Undoubtedly, the responsible factor in Carroll's rejection of the present reality of the bride was his overruling persuasion that the *ekklesia* could never be anything but a physically assembled group. The error of this persuasion has been demonstrated by the presentation of the metaphorical usage of *ekklesia* in chapter 4.

The Jewish church of the past

A second inadequate interpretation of the figure of the bride is that advocated by ultradispensationalism. This school of thought holds that there are two churches in the New Testament—a Jewish church and a Gentile church. The leader of this thinking, E. W. Bullinger, attempted to distinguish between the Pentecostal Apostolic Church of the book of Acts and the Mystery Pauline Church of the prison epistles. He called the one the "bride church" and the other the "body church."[76] His reason for this interpretation was that it is inconsistent for the church to be, at one time, both a body and a bride. This should not have confused him, however, for the Scriptures use numerous symbols with wide distinctions. The very purpose of the many symbols, in fact, was due to the inability of any one symbol to express all that the Lord had to say about His relationship to the church. It has been urged by some authorities that because in the metaphor of the body the church is a part of Christ, it cannot be intended to represent the church as His bride, since the bride is not a part of the husband, but is separate from him.[77] In answer Griffith Thomas states:

> It is more likely that we are to regard these metaphors as two aspects of the same relationship between Christ and the Church, the one a relationship of life, the other a relationship of love.[78]

76. Ethelbert W. Bullinger, *How to Enjoy the Bible,* pp. 94-96, 145-49.
77. Cf. Robert Anderson, *The Coming Prince: The Marvelous Prophecy of Daniel's Seventy Weeks Concerning the Antichrist,* p. 200n.
78. W. H. Griffith Thomas, "The Doctrine of the Church in the Epistle to the Ephesians," *The Expositor,* 7th series, 2:331.

Thus, each symbol has its place in expressing the many facets of the vital relationship that exists between Christ and the church.

Much of the reason for confusion regarding the symbol of the bride is due to the replaced usage of the nuptial metaphor in the Bible. Furthermore, different aspects of the nuptial metaphor are used of both Israel and the church. In the Old Testament Israel is declared to be the wife of Jehovah. In referring to Israel, and rebuking her, God says, "for more are the children of the desolate than the children of the married wife" (Isa 54:1). In a passage of extreme rebuke, God says of her, "She is not my wife" (Hos 2:2). Old Testament Israel is pictured first as the wife of Jehovah, and then as a wife rejected.** By contrast the church in figure is described as a pure virgin being prepared for future marriage.†† It is quite evident that even a forgiven and restored *wife* could not be called either a *virgin* or a *bride*. This teaching is summarized by Unger:

> The figure of marriage is used also in the O. T. to denote the relationship between Jehovah and the Jewish nation, however, with this important contrast. Israel is portrayed as the *wife* of Jehovah (Hos. 2:2, 16:23) now because of unbelief and apostasy, disowned and dishonored, but yet to be restored (Hos. 2:14-23). The church, on the other hand is a pure virgin, espoused to Christ (II Cor. 11:1, 2), which could never be true of an adulterous wife, although she is eventually to be restored in grace. In the mystery of the Divine-triunity it can be true that Israel is the adulterous wife of Jehovah (to be forgiven and re-instated), while the church is the virgin wife of the Lamb (John 3:29; Rev. 19:6-8). To break down this distinction between Israel, God's elect nation with a unique

**Whenever the figure of the bride is used in connection with Israel in the Old Testament, it is always as an illustration and never as a formal type or figure (cf. Isa 49:18; 61:10; 62:5; Jer 2:32; 7:34; 13:11; 16:9; 25:10; Joel 2:16).

††In his exhaustive study of *numphe,* Jeremias maintains that there was no identification of the Messiah with the Bridegroom in either the Old Testament or Judaism of the time of Jesus; Jahweh himself was always the Husband of Israel. Cf. Joachim Jeremias, *"Numphe, Numphios,"* in *Theologisches Wörterbuch zum Neuen Testament, herausgegeben von Gerhard Kittel,* 4:1092-99.

> future when restored (Rom. 11:1-25), and the Church, the body (1 Cor. 12:13) and bride of Christ (Eph. 5:25-27), formed by the baptizing work of the Holy Spirit during the period of Israel's national unbelief and setting aside, is to plunge Biblical prophecy into confusion.[79]

The ultradispensational viewpoint that the early church was the bride can be refuted by two principal arguments. First, it is not possible to distinguish the body and the bride in Ephesians 5. The bride, wife, and body are all put together in the description of the vital relation between Christ and the church. Second, it has been demonstrated previously that the church, the body of Christ, began with the baptizing work of the Holy Spirit on the day of Pentecost.

The mystery church of the present

Having rejected the theory that the church as the bride is entirely future and the theory that the church as the bride is the past Jewish church, there is a third alternative, which this writer believes to be the correct one. The church, the bride of Christ, includes all those who have put their faith in Christ in this age of grace, which had its beginning at Pentecost and will continue until the Bridegroom comes to receive His bride unto himself to consummate the marriage. Although the bride of Christ is the same group as the body of Christ, this figure brings out certain distinctive ideas that are not displayed by the body metaphor.

IMPLICATIONS OF THE FIGURE

The infinite love of the Bridegroom

Both the body metaphor and the bride metaphor speak of the inseparable and vital union that exists between Christ and the church, but each has its own facet of this relationship to express. The former is a relationship of life and the latter a relationship

79. Merrill F. Unger, *Unger's Bible Dictionary,* p. 156.

of love. Twice in Ephesians 5, the apostle cites the infinite sacrifice of Christ as the expression of infinite love:

> And walk in love, as Christ also hath loved us, and hath given himself for us an offering and a sacrifice to God for a sweetsmelling savour (v. 2).
>
> Husbands, love your wives, even as Christ loved the church, and gave himself for it; that he might sanctify and cleanse it with the washing of water by the word, that he might present it to himself a glorious church, not having spot, or wrinkle, or any such thing; but that it should be holy and without blemish (vv. 25-27).

In the third chapter the apostle Paul prayed that the Ephesian saints might "be able to comprehend with all saints what is the breadth, and length, and depth, and height; and to know the love of Christ, which passeth knowledge" (Eph 3:18-19). This is the major point of the bride metaphor—the knowledge-surpassing love of the Bridegroom for the bride.

There is no earthly relation that could picture Christ's love for the church as can the relation of marriage. It is a relation that supposes love—strong, mutual love. Spilman hits right at the heart of its meaning when he says:

> Love grows out of some relations, but this relation grows out of love. The mother loves her child because it *is* her child; a brother loves his sister because she *is* his sister. But the bride and bridegroom enter into a life-long covenant through a love which springs from no natural relations. It is free and unconstrained.[80]

This love (*agape*) that Christ displayed is far different from ordinary emotional love. Speaking of the ordinary words for love, Barclay states:

> They express an experience which comes to us unsought, and, in a way, inevitably. We cannot help loving our kith and

80. T. E. Spilman, *Scripture Emblems of God's People*, pp. 149-50.

> kin; blood is thicker than water. We speak about *falling in love.* That kind of love is not an achievement; it is something which happens to us and which we cannot help. There is no particular virtue in falling in love. It is something with which we have little or nothing consciously to do; it simply happens. But agape is far more than that.[81]

Agape is the "spiritual affection which follows the direction of the will, and which, therefore, unlike the feeling that is instinctive and unreasoned, can be commanded as a duty."[82] This is a thought-out and reasoned love. It is a determination of the will, the exercise of which is not dependent on the loveliness of the object loved. Griffith Thomas writes:

> Love in our Lord's case is no sentiment, but a sacrifice, and it does not even cease with His sacrifice of Himself; it is maintained and continued in service. "Loving and cherishing it" (v. 29).[83]

Recognition of this utterly selfless and self-sacrificing love caused Westcott to write that "Christ loved the church, not because it was perfectly lovable, but in order to make it such."[84] In this inscrutable, knowledge-surpassing love, Christ gave Himself unstintingly, even unto death—"even as Christ also loved the church, and gave himself for it." Lenski states: " 'And' is explicative: 'he gave himself' expounds 'he loved.' "[85] Speaking of the parallel phrase in verse 2, he says:

> Jesus delivered himself into the hands of his enemies at the gate of Gethsemane and thereby gave himself to God as the sacrifice to be slain according to God's determinate counsel and foreknowledge (Acts 2:23). Here there is the voluntariness of Christ's sacrifice, and it was this that made it such a

81. William Barclay, *More New Testament Words,* p. 15.
82. G. Abbott-Smith, *A Manual Greek Lexicon of the New Testament,* p. 3.
83. Thomas, p. 332.
84. Brooke Foss Westcott, *Saint Paul's Epistle to the Ephesians: The Greek Text with Notes and Addenda,* p. 84.
85. R. C. H. Lenski, *The Interpretation of St. Paul's Epistles to the Galatians, to the Ephesians, and to the Philippians,* p. 593.

> sweet odor. Here there is the supreme evidence of Christ's love for us; greater love is impossible.[86]

This love is even more amazing in the light of the infinite distance of nature between the lover and the beloved. Never was there love that fixed itself upon an object so much below the lover. Nor has there ever been an instance of such love to those so far from being capable of benefiting the lover. Among men the lover looks upon the beloved as one capable and fitted to complement or benefit the lover. But Jesus Christ is above want. Again, never was there any that set his love upon those in whom he saw so much filthiness and deformity. Men may set their love upon those who are inwardly very hateful because they are ignorant of them. They do not know what is in them. But Christ knew perfectly all man's filthiness (Heb 4:13). Again, never was there a lover who set his love upon those who were so far from loving him. Every natural man has a mortal enmity against Christ. And this enmity is infinitely unreasonable, for Christ has never done him any wrong. Yet, knowing of this contempt beforehand, Christ was pleased to set His love upon them. Finally, never was there any love so beneficial to the beloved. By means of Christ's dying love, the beloved is rescued from eternal destruction to enjoy Him fully for all eternity. All this is just a mere glimpse at the knowledge-surpassing love that the apostle speaks of and that is pictured in the beautiful bride metaphor. The following word-picture captures something of its nature.

> For Christ's love to His elect passes knowledge; its depths are beyond the plumblines of created intelligences, its flame self-fed, self-kindled, aglow with an incandescence that many waters could not quench; a purpose to redeem which nothing could divert from its resolve, nor any obstacle, however tremendous, deter from achieving it once for all. The king of terrors, armed with his fellest sting, had no power to withhold

86. Ibid.

> this unblenching Lover from standing proxy for the bride of His choice. What an amazing spectacle this, of Life essential plunging into a dread abyss of dereliction that His bride might partake with Him of everlasting bliss and joy! Is He not the mirror of chivalry no less than of devotion? No human suitor has ever loved, or ever will, on such a scale as that.[87]

The exalted position of the bride

Another major teaching of the figure of the church as the bride of Christ is her exalted position. This teaching primarily concerns the future of the church and, perhaps, may best be understood by relating it to the Oriental marriage customs. There were three tenses of Oriental marriage. The first was the betrothal, in which the pair entered into a legal contract. This was sealed with a bridal present, which, in most cases, was the purchase price.‡‡ Edersheim writes:

> At the betrothal, the bridegroom, personally or by deputy, handed to the bride a piece of money or a letter, it being expressly stated in each case that the man thereby espoused the woman.[88]

This is the past tense of the ceremony for the church. Christ, the Bridegroom, has purchased the church with His own blood (Acts 20:28) and the church has been espoused to Him as His bride (2 Cor 11:2).§§ Speaking of this relationship, Edersheim continues:

> From the moment of the betrothal both parties were regarded, and treated in law (as to inheritance, adultery, need of

87. E. K. Simpson and F. F. Bruce, *Commentary on the Epistles to the Ephesians and the Colossians*, p. 132.

‡‡Cf. Alfred Plummer, "Bride," in *A Dictionary of the Bible*, ed. James Hastings, 1:326: "The bride was commonly paid for; *i.e.* her father received money or service in return for his consent to part with her (Gn. 31^{15}, 34^{12}, 1 S $18^{25, 27}$ etc.)." Cf. also E. Neufeld, *Ancient Hebrew Marriage Laws*, pp. 94-117; Millar Burrows, *The Basis of Israelite Marriage*, pp. 1-72.

88. Alfred Edersheim, *The Life and Times of Jesus the Messiah*, 1:354.

§§Although the betrothal in this passage refers specifically to the Corinthian Christians, it may, by extension, be applied to the entire church.

> formal divorce), as if they had been actually married, except as regarded their living together.[89]

M. Mielziner, the former professor of the Talmud and of the rabbinical disciplines at the Hebrew Union College states that "a betrothal is not a mere promise to marry, but it is the very initiation of the marriage."[90] After this initial step, there was no set time as to when the next step of the marriage—the presentation of the bride to the bridegroom—must be consummated. It may be a month, a year, or longer.|| ||

Some have objected, not understanding the Oriental marriage customs, that the church could not be the bride because "the marriage of the Lamb" has not yet come. Others have objected, as previously noted, that the church could not be both the body and the bride. In the following illuminating statements, Van Gilder sheds light on both these arguments.

> Paul points to a most illuminating parallel by quoting (v. 31) from Genesis 2:24: "For this cause shall a man leave his father and his mother, and shall be joined unto his wife, and they two shall be one flesh." The words were spoken by the Lord God to Adam and Eve in instituting the marriage relationship. Eve was the only bride in the history of mankind of whom it could be said that she was of her husband's body before she became his bride. When she was presented to Adam, he said: "This is now bone of my bones, and flesh of my flesh: she shall be called *Woman,* because she was taken from Man" (Heb. *Isha* because she was taken from *Ish*).
>
> The Last Adam, too, was put to sleep in a garden; there His side was wounded (John 19:34, 41) and from that wounding

89. Edersheim, *The Life and Times of Jesus the Messiah,* 1:354.
90. M. Mielziner, *The Jewish Law of Marriage and Divorce in Ancient and Modern Times, and Its Relation to the Law of the State,* p. 76.

|| ||Cf. Alfred Plummer, "Bridegroom," in *A Dictionary of the Bible,* ed. James Hastings, 1:327: "The interval between betrothal and marraige might be of any duration, for the espousal of children to one another has always been common in the East; but a year for maidens and a month for widows seems to have been customary."

> has come one who is bone of His bone, and flesh of His flesh, and who shall, in some future day, be presented to Him to be His holy Wife.[91]

The church today, then, is an espoused bride. It is awaiting that which is the second step of the Oriental marriage—the presentation of the bride to the Bridegroom. This presentation, which was generally a night procession, was the principal feature of the marriage.[92] Neufeld has picturesquely described the bridegroom going to fetch his bride.

> Among the wealthy the bridegroom was dressed in specially sumptuous clothes (Isa. 61, 10) and wore a matrimonial crown (Cant. 3, 11). He came with a company of his family and friends (Jdg. 14, 11; Matt. 9, 15) to meet his bride who was accompanied by her family and friends (Jer. 2, 32). The bride met her bridegroom with her face covered by a veil (Gen. 29, 25. Cf. also Gen. 39, 14; Jer. 2, 31). He brought her to his house, where all the proceedings took place by the light of lanterns to the accompaniment of music and songs (Jer. 24, 8; 7, 34; 16, 9; 25, 10). When both companies met, they sang to the young couple (Jer. 7, 34; 16, 9; 25, 10; Ps. 45, 16).[93]

All this background is very pertinent to the understanding of the bride metaphor. The church, the bride, has the promise of the Bridegroom that He will come again and take His bride unto himself (John 14:3). Speaking of this same occasion, Paul rejoices:

> For the Lord himself shall descend from heaven with a shout, with the voice of the archangel, and with the trump of God: and the dead in Christ shall rise first: Then we which are alive and remain shall be caught up together with them in the clouds, to meet the Lord in the air: and so shall we ever be with the Lord (1 Thess 4:16-17).

91. H. O. Van Gilder, *The Church Which Is His Body*, pp. 12-13.
92. A. J. Maclean, "Marriage," in *Dictionary of the Apostolic Church*, ed. James Hastings, 2:13.
93. Neufeld, p. 149.

With more specific reference to the bride metaphor Paul states concerning the bride that the Bridegroom is going to "present it to himself a glorious church, not having spot, or wrinkle, or any such thing; but that it should be holy and without blemish" (Eph 5:27). There is an important contrast to note here. In Judea there were at every marriage two groomsmen, or "friends of the bridegroom"—one for the bridegroom and the other for his bride. Before marriage they acted as a kind of intermediary between the couple. Furthermore, Edersheim writes: "we know that it was specially the duty of the friend of the bridegroom so to present to him his bride."[94] But in the case of the bride, the church, the Bridegroom reserves the privilege of presentation for Himself. Paul emphatically demonstrates this in the double usage of the reflective pronoun (*autos heautoi*). Ellicott translates it: "Himself to Himself."[95] He goes on to state that "Christ permits neither attendants nor paranymphs to present the Bride: He alone presents, He receives."##

The condition in which Christ presents the bride to himself is exceedingly remarkable. His purpose is to "present a church, glorious" without any fault or blemish whatsoever. Hodge states:

> That is glorious which excites admiration. The church is to be an object of admiration to all intelligent beings, because of its freedom from all defect, and because of its absolute perfection. It is to be conformed to the glorified humanity of the Son of God, in the presence of which the disciples on the mount became as dead men, and from the clear manifestation of which, when Christ comes the second time, the heavens and

94. Edersheim, *Sketches of Jewish Social Life*, p. 153.
95. Charles J. Ellicott, *A Critical and Grammatical Commentary on St. Paul's Epistle to the Ephesians*, p. 135.
##Ibid.; cf. also Eadie, p. 421: "*Autòs—eautō*—He and none other presents the bride, and He and none other receives her to HIMSELF. No inferior agency is permitted; a proof in itself, as well as His death, of His love to the church"; cf. also Lenski, p. 635: "Paul sees a grand vision: the church at the last day, Christ himself presenting her to himself, making her stand forth by his side (*pará*) enfolded in glory, beautiful in sanctity, the spotless Bride of the Lamb."

> the earth are to flee away. God has predestined his people to be conformed to the image of his Son. And when he shall appear, we shall be like him, for we shall see him as he is, 1 John 3:2. The figure is preserved in the description here given of the glory of the consummated church. It is to be as a faultless bride; perfect in beauty and splendidly adorned.[96]

These words shed light on Paul's benediction: "Unto him be glory in the church by Christ throughout all ages, world without end." The glory that belongs to the Bridegroom shines in the bride. The bride will be the everlasting manifestation of the glory of the Bridegroom. That this should be true is even more amazing in the light of the depths to which the Bridegroom had to stoop to reach His bride. Simpson finds a parallel application in the mystery of love exhibited in Ezekiel 16.

> The prophet describes the foundling child lying in her blood, repulsive and utterly wretched; but as the Lord passed by he saw her in her blood, and it was the time of love; and so He spread His skirt over her and gently took her, washed her, robed her, educated her, trained her, crowned her with a crown of glory, and then wedded her and made her all His own. So He has loved us, saved us, quickened us together with Him, and now He takes us into this intimate and unspeakable relationship which all earthly figures fail fully to express—the marriage of the Lamb.[97]

Thus, the ultimate object of the death of Christ, according to Paul, was "that He might himself present to himself the church glorious." "He is at once the Agent and the End or Object of the presentation."[98] Salmond concludes:

> The presentation in view, which is given here as the *final* object of Christ's surrendering of Himself to death, and is ex-

96. Charles Hodge, *A Commentary on the Epistle to the Ephesians*, pp. 330-31.
97. A. B. Simpson, *The Highest Christian Life: Exposition of the Epistle to the Ephesians*, p. 147.
98. S. D. F. Salmond, "The Epistle to the Ephesians," in *The Expositor's Greek Testament*, ed. W. Robertson Nicoll, 3:369.

hibited (by use of the aor.) as a single def. act, cannot be anything done in the world that now is . . . but must be referred . . . to the future consummation, the event of the *Parousia.*[99]

The exaltation of the bride is not exhausted, however, in the presentation. After the bridegroom has gone to receive his bride to himself, the final step, according to Oriental custom, is the marriage feast, in which case the wife would accompany the bridegroom.

> Having reached the house of the bride, who with her maidens anxiously expected his arrival (Matt. 25:6), he conducted the whole party back to his own or his father's house, with every demonstration of gladness (Psa. 45:15). On their way back they were joined by a party of maidens, friends of the bride and bridegroom, who were in waiting to catch the procession as it passed (Matt. 25:6). . . . At the house a feast was prepared, to which all the friends and neighbors were invited (Gen. 29:22; Matt. 22:1-10; Luke 14:8; John 2:2), and the festivities were protracted for seven, or even fourteen days (Judg. 14:12; Tob. 8:19). The guests were provided by the host with fitting robes (Matt. 22:11). . . . The bridegroom now entered into direct communication with the bride. . . . The last act in the ceremonial was the conducting of the bride to the bridal chamber, (Heb. *hĕdĕr,* Judg. 15:1; Joel 2:16), where a canopy, named *hŭppäh,* was prepared (Psa. 19:5; Joel 2:16).[100]

The key passage of Scripture bearing on this subject is Revelation 19:7-9:

> Let us be glad and rejoice, and give honour to him: for the marriage of the Lamb is come, and his wife hath made herself ready. And to her was granted that she should be arrayed in fine linen, clean and white: for the fine linen is the righteousness of the saints. And he saith unto me, Write, Blessed are they which are called unto the marriage supper of the Lamb.

99. Ibid., 3:370.
100. Unger, *Unger's Bible Dictionary,* pp. 698-99.

According to John's words here, this marriage has already taken place at the time of the second advent, for the declaration is: "the marriage of the Lamb is come." The aorist tense, *elthen,* translated "is come," signifies a completed act, showing us that the marriage has been consummated.[101] Pentecost places the event in its eschatological setting:

> This marriage is seen to follow the events of the bema of Christ, inasmuch as when the wife appears she appears in the "righteousness of the saints" (Rev. 19:8), which can only refer to those things that have been accepted at the judgment seat of Christ. Thus the marriage itself must be placed between the judgment seat of Christ and the second advent.[102]

The clause "his wife hath made herself ready" indicates that there is something for the bride to do in preparation for this ceremony (cf. 2 Cor 7:1; 1 John 3:3; Jude 21). In harmony with this teaching is the phrase "the righteousness of saints," which might be better rendered "the righteous awards of the saints."[103] These are the rewards she received at the bema of Christ (cf. 1 Cor 3:8; 4:5; 2 Cor 5:10). This explains why there is work for the bride as well as for Christ (cf. Phil 2:12-13). The chief work, however, is still the act of Christ in death (cf. Eph 5:25).[104] The bridal dress with which she arrays herself is a gift from Christ in return for her righteous acts. As Johnson says, "This garment is what she has spun out on earth in the power of the Lamb."[105] Scott declares:

> She can now enter on the enjoyment of eternal companionship and union of the closest nature (that of wife) with her husband, the Lamb. Her deeds on *earth* have been appraised at their true value in *Heaven.* She is arrayed in them, or in the

101. J. Dwight Pentecost, *Things to Come: A Study in Biblical Eschatology,* p. 226.
102. Ibid., pp. 226-27.
103. S. Lewis Johnson, class lecture notes on Revelation.
104. Robertson, *Word Pictures,* 6:449-50.
105. Johnson.

> expressive words of the text, "has made herself ready." She passes from the bema to the marriage, and from thence to the kingdom.[106]

The grand consummating event is the marriage itself, the entire scene of which is set by John "in heaven" (Rev 19:1), not upon the earth. Pentecost writes:

> Inasmuch as this follows the judgment seat of Christ, which has been shown to be in the heavenlies, and it is from the air the church comes when the Lord returns (Rev. 19:4), the marriage must take place in heaven. No other location would fit a heavenly people.[107]

Thus, John puts the church in heaven before the glorious coming of Christ.

After the marriage ceremony comes the marriage feast. John writes: "Blessed are they which are called unto the marriage supper of the Lamb." The guests at the marriage feast always felt highly privileged; thus, here the guests are pronounced "Blessed." There is not complete agreement as to the identity of the guests here,*** but that is not necessary to know. What is significant is this glorious event in which the church takes her place as the bride of Christ. Enthralled with the splendor of it, Spilman writes:

106. Walter Scott, *Exposition of the Revelation of Jesus Christ,* p. 382.
107. Pentecost, *Things to Come,* p. 227.
***Cf. Scott, pp. 382-83: "The Baptist was martyred before the Church was formed, hence he comes in as perhaps the most honoured of the guests at the marriage supper. Old Testament saints constitute the large company of called guests, each one being a friend of the Bridegroom and rejoicing in His presence and voice. The apocalyptic martyrs are not raised till *after* the marriage, hence cannot be numbered amongst the guests." Pentecost differs from this view. Cf. Pentecost, *Things to Come,* pp. 227-28: "The marriage supper is an event that involves Israel and takes place on the earth. In Matthew 22:1-14; Luke 14:16-24; and Matthew 25:1-13, where Israel is awaiting the return of the bridegroom and the bride, the wedding feast is located on the earth and has particular reference to Israel. The wedding supper, then, becomes the parabolic picture of the entire millennial age, to which Israel will be invited during the tribulation period, which invitation many will reject and so will be cast out, and many will accept and they will be received in. Because of the rejection the invitation will likewise go to the Gentiles so that many of them will be included."

> If it would be enrapturing to hear the mighty throng saying, "Blessing, and honor, and glory, and power, be unto him that sitteth upon the throne, and unto the Lamb for ever and ever,"—if it would be a joy to be a spectator at the marriage supper of the Lamb, what would it be to be one in that church which shall constitute the bride of Christ . . . leaning upon his arm as upon the arm of a strong and loving bridegroom and hear him say as to a bride, "I have loved thee with an everlasting love?"[108]

It will be the bride's exalted privilege to reign with the King of kings. "In that sense in which other citizens are subjects," writes Chafer, "the wife of the king is not a subject of the king. As the word *consort* suggests, she is a co-sharer in his reign."[109]

Finally, after the celebration of the marriage, the bridegroom takes his bride to their new home. He usually prepares a place for her before the marriage supper takes place. So while the church, the bride of Christ, makes herself ready for the marriage supper, Christ, the Bridegroom, prepares a place for her. When He was on earth making offers of love to His future bride, He said,

> In my Father's house are many mansions [abiding places]: if it were not so, I would have told you. I go to prepare a place for you. And if I go and prepare a place for you, I will come again, and receive you unto myself; that where I am, there ye may be also" (John 14:2-3).

In his intercessory prayer, Christ said, "Father I will that they whom thou hast given me be with me where I am" (John 17:24). Thus,. the Bridegroom shall lead His bride into His own glorious home.

These truths, then, are something of the splendor and glory manifested in the bride metaphor of Scripture. Basically, it is a manifestation of the knowledge-surpassing love of Christ for the

108. Spilman, pp. 159-60.
109. Chafer, 4:135.

church. In addition, however, it sets forth a marvelous panoramic view of the exalted position of the church, both now and for all eternity. In response, Simpson utters these challenging words:

> Beloved, Christ has betrothed you to Him. You are to spend eternity in His palaces and on His throne. You are to be the companion and partner of His mightiest enterprises in the ages to come. Perhaps with Him you are to colonize a constellation of space, and govern the boundless universe of God. Do you know that He is educating you now to be a fit companion for such a kingdom? Will you let Him love you all He wants to, and fit you for such a destiny as will some day fill you with everlasting wonder and adoring love?[110]

III. THE CHURCH AS THE BUILDING

Another favorite metaphor that appears repeatedly throughout the New Testament is that of the building. Already it has been seen to be applied to, and used side by side with, the metaphor of the body. In that case, however, its emphasis was primarily on the process of the building up or edifying of the body of Christ; whereas in the present usage attention is drawn to the actual building itself. The whole church is regarded as a great structure, and several aspects of truth are brought out by means of this symbol. Two central passages for the building metaphor are Ephesians 2:19-22 and 1 Peter 2:4-7.

THE FOUNDATION OF THE BUILDING

In summarizing his argument of the equal privileges of the Gentiles with Jews in one new body, Paul utilizes two figures:

> Now therefore ye are no more strangers and foreigners, but fellowcitizens with the saints, and of the household of God; and are built upon the foundation of the apostles and prophets (Eph 2:19-20).

110. Simpson, pp. 150-51.

In the first instance, Paul explains that both are fellow members in the household (*oikeioi*) of God; that is, they have family privileges. Then in verse 20 his thoughts move from that of Christians dwelling in the house, and he now views them as constituting the house. These are the living stones Peter says "are built up a spiritual house" (1 Pet 2:5). Thus, Paul speaks of the universal, invisible church, a great temple in the process of construction, rising on its foundation and its Cornerstone.††† The first feature to be discussed about this building is its foundation, of which the text says, "and are built upon the foundation of the apostles and the prophets."

The nature of the foundation

Much discussion has centered on the words of the text. In the first place, does this contradict 1 Corinthians 3:11, which says that "other foundation can no man lay than that is laid, which is Jesus Christ"? The answer to this comes by understanding the differing usages of the building metaphor. In the Corinthian passage, Paul speaks of the local church and the doctrine of Christ upon which Paul, "the wise master-builder," founded it.‡‡‡ In the Ephesians passage, however, he speaks of the universal church, which is built up of people, not doctrines. Speaking of the Corinthians' "foundation," Robinson states:

> He is not speaking of persons who are builded in, but of

†††Cf. Robertson, *Word Pictures,* 6:96: "This 'spiritual house' includes believers in the five Roman provinces of 1:1 and shows clearly how Peter understood the metaphor of Christ in Matt. 16:18 to be not a local church, but the church general."

‡‡‡The expanded translation by Robertson and Plummer brings out clearly this local emphasis. Cf. Archibald Robertson and Alfred Plummer, *A Critical and Exegetical Commentary on the First Epistle of St. Paul to the Corinthians,* pp. 59-60: "As to the grace which God gave me to found Churches, I have with the aims of an expert master-builder, laid a foundation for the edifice; it is for some one else to build upon it. But whoever he may be, let him be careful as to the materials with which he builds thereon. For, as regards the foundation, there is no room for question: no one can lay any other beside the one which is already laid, which is of course Jesus Christ."

> persons who build. He himself, for example, is not a stone of the building, but "a wise master-builder": those of whom he speaks are builders also, and their work will come to the testing. The foundation he has himself laid in the proclamation of Christ Jesus: it is not possible that any of them should lay any other foundation: but it is only too possible that the superstructure which they raise should be worthless, and that instead of wages for good work done they should come in for the fine which attached to careless or fraudulent work.[111]

The application of the metaphor in Ephesians is different, however, and by way of contrast he observes that "the stones are persons: the foundation stones are the apostles and prophets, the most important stone of all being *'Christ Jesus Himself.'* "[112] Answering the view that sees this as doctrine, Hort cogently remarks that "it remains difficult to see what foundation they [the apostles] can be said to have laid, in connexion with which Christ could be called a cornerstone."[113]

Remembering, therefore, that the apostle is speaking of persons and not doctrines as the foundation of this building should help to solve the grammatical problem that Gerstner sets forth.

> Describing it as a foundation "of the apostles and prophets" he may mean to say that it is a foundation consisting of, belonging to, or proceeding from the apostles and prophets, so far as the genitive employed is concerned.[114]

Because he is referring to persons in the context, the first grammatical possibility, the genitive of apposition (foundation consisting of) seems most probable.

The identification of the foundation

A second problem is the identity of "the apostles and prophets." Basically the question is, Are they Old Testament or New

111. J. Armitage Robinson, *St. Paul's Epistle to the Ephesians,* pp. 67-68.
112. Ibid, p. 68.
113. Fenton John Anthony Hort, *The Christian Ecclesia,* p. 167.
114. John H. Gerstner, *The Epistle to the Ephesians: A Study Manual,* p. 39.

Testament prophets? There are some who teach that the reference here is to the Old Testament prophetic order in that the Old Testament prophets anticipated the coming of Christ and proclaimed Him. One would think that the order should be reversed, however, if the Old Testament prophets are in view. "It all depends," writes Lenski:

> The apostles added the testimonies of the prophets to the revelation they transmitted. Their constant refrain is: "As it has been written." The apostles brought Christ and then the prophecies; they did not present the prophecies and then offer Christ.[115]

This seems to be a strained interpretation, especially in light of the fact that persons, and not their messages, are in view. Calvin, who held this same view, made no attempt to explain the order but, rather, arbitrarily reversed it. Writing of Paul, he says: "He testifies that the church is 'built upon the foundation of the prophets and apostles.' "[116] Surely, this is playing quite loose with the text.

There seem to be a number of considerations that lead to the conclusion that these are New Testament prophets. First, the fact that the apostles are put first in the order followed by the prophets seems to carry most naturally a chronological implication.[117] These must be New Testament prophets who arose after the apostles. Second, the Christian *ekklesia,* the body of Christ, of the new dispensation may more appropriately be said to rest on the foundation of the New Testament prophets than on Old Testament ones.[118] This is further supported by the use of the one article with the two nouns, apostles and prophets, which use shows that they are viewed as being one class.[119] This does not mean that the apostles are also the prophets, though

115. Lenski, p. 453.
116. John Calvin *Institutes of the Christian Religion* 1. 7. 2.
117. Hodge, p. 148.
118. Ibid., p. 149.
119. Robertson, *A Grammar of the Greek New Testament,* p. 787.

some support this,§§§ but that they are two different groups, yet viewed as one class in their relationship to the church. Third, the passage in Ephesians 3:5 that says that the mystery of Christ, not revealed in other ages, is now revealed unto His holy apostles and prophets by the Spirit is unquestionably speaking totally of a New Testament work, and thus, New Testament prophets. Fourth, Gerstner declares that "such prophets would be more immediately and easily understood by Gentile converts not so familiar with Old Testament institutions as with New Testament ones."[120] Since the Ephesians were a Gentile church and since the Gentiles had previously not heard of the Old Testament prophets, it would be strange to introduce them here. Finally, the New Testament prophets are named in this same epistle (4:11) among the ascended Lord's gifts to His church and assigned a prominent place second only to the apostles.

The foundation of the building, the universal church, consists of persons, namely, the apostles and prophets of the present dispensation in its initial stages. It is significant to note that the foundation is not Peter; he is only a part with the others of the foundation. Thus, this verse as well as Peter's own discussion in 1 Peter 2:4-7 should be helpful commentaries on Matthew 16:18.

THE CHIEF CORNERSTONE OF THE BUILDING

"Corner stone" is one word in the Greek (*akrogoniaios*), a purely biblical term,[121] found in Ephesians 2:20 and 1 Peter 2:6. The latter reference appears in a quotation from Isaiah 28:16. There appears to be little justification for the rendering "chief corner stone," which follows the late Latin translation

§§§Cf. Hort, p. 165: "It is truly said that we cannot lay much stress on the absence of a second article before 'prophets'; but in iii, 5 the prefixing of *hagíois* and subjoining of *autoû* to *apostólois* is difficult to account for, if the prophets meant were a second set of persons."

120. Gerstner, p. 40.

121. William F. Arndt and F. Wilbur Gingrich, *A Greek-English Lexicon of the New Testament and Other Early Christian Literature*, p. 33.

summmus angularis lapis.[122] It is a combination of *akros,* which means the "high point," the "top," or the "extreme limit, end," and *gonia,* which means "corner, angle." Thus, Thayer translates it "placed at the extreme corner,"[123] and Lenski says "at the tip of the angle."[124]

While it is relatively easy to determine the etymology of the word, it is much more difficult to determine the precise purpose of the cornerstone. Older commentators have generally held that, in Paul's time, it was a stone that was put at the juncture of two walls in order that the two walls might be tied together by this one stone that belonged to both. Thus, the cornerstone would have reference to that which unites the two in itself. In agreement with this view, Moule states:

> On the whole we take the image to be that of a vast stone at an angle of the substructure into which the converging sides are imbedded, "in which" they "consist"; and the spiritual reality to be that which gives coherence and fixity to the foundation doctrines of His Church; with the implied idea that He is the essential to the foundation, being the ultimate Foundation (1 Cor. 3:11).[125]

This meaning seems to gain some weight in the light of the context. In concluding this whole concept of the uniting of Jew and Gentile, Christ is called the Cornerstone, the one "in which" (*en ho*) the two partitions of the building are united.

A somewhat different connotation is seen by Lenski, who explains that this stone is

> set at the corner of a wall so that its outer angle becomes important. This importance is ideal, we may say symbolic: the angle of the cornerstone governs all the lines and all the other angles of the building. This one stone is thus laid with special,

122. Robinson, *St. Paul's Epistle to the Ephesians,* p. 164.
123. Joseph Henry Thayer, *A Greek-English Lexicon of the New Testament,* p. 24.
124. Lenski, p. 454.
125. H. C. G. Moule, *The Epistle to the Ephesians, with Introduction and Notes,* p. 84. Cf. also Thayer, p. 24; J. A. Selbie, "Corner-stone," in *A Dictionary of the Bible,* ed. James Hastings, 1:499.

> sometimes elaborate ceremonies. It supports the building no more than does any other stone. Its entire significance is to be found in its one outer angle. Its size is immaterial and certainly need not be immense. It is thus also placed at the most important corner, in or on the top tier of the foundation, so as to be seen by all.[126]

This idea emphasizes, then, the fact that there is not a single line or an angle in this building that is not determined by this Stone. This has a definite connection, also, with the following words "in whom all the building fitly framed together groweth unto an holy temple in the Lord." Thus, inner harmony, oneness, correspondence, and symmetry pervade all that forms the building, because "what the foundation and its cornerstone demand is carried out in all that is superstructure even to the joining of every stone and timber."[127] In agreement with this view is Lloyd, who states:

> The *akrogoniaios* here is the primary foundation-stone at the angle of the structure by which the architect fixes a standard for the bearings of the walls and cross-walls throughout.[128]

A third view is championed by Jeremias, who explains it in the same sense as "the head of the corner" (1 Pet 2:7), as the capstone (*abschlussstein*) that holds the building together and completes it. He thinks it is the stone that crowns the building, the capstone over the portal, and he maintains that the building is the Temple, that is, the redeemed community of the end time.[129] Thus, the "capstone" is the last stone to be put in position, and it may be the keystone of the arch above the entrance; if so, it is also a locking stone. Selwyn rejects this view on the basis that

126. Lenski, p. 455.
127. Ibid., p. 457.
128. Cited by Robertson, *Word Pictures,* 4:528-29. Cf. also T. K. Abbot, *A Critical and Exegetical Commentary on the Epistles to the Ephesians and Colossians,* p. 71.
129. Joachim Jeremias, "*Gonia, Akrogoniaios, Kephale Gonias,*" in *Theologisches Wörterbuch zum Neuen Testament,* herausgegeben von Gerhard Kittel, 1:792.

> both the *akro-* in *akrogōniaion* [Eph. 2:20; 1 Pet. 2:6] . . . and the *kephalēn* in *kephalēn gōnias* [1 Pet. 2:7] . . . mean no more than the extremity of the angle: extremity and not height is the point connoted. The chief features of a cornerstone are that it controls the design of the edifice and that (unlike a foundation stone) it is visible.[130]

Furthermore, this view does not seem to fit as well in the context, which implies a close connection between the foundation and the cornerstone. Nor does it seem to agree with the following phrase "in whom all the building fitly framed together groweth into an holy temple in the Lord."

What, then, may be concluded as to the meaning of *akrogoniaion?* All three views have considerable support from the commentators; however, the first two views seem to be most agreeable to the context. Perhaps it will be necessary to take both these views in order to get the full force of what the apostle is seeking to teach. In Christ, Jew and Gentile have been united in one as the cornerstone in which the two partitions of the building are united. In Christ, the building has coherence and stability in its structure. In Christ, the rest of the building finds its inner harmony, oneness, correspondence, and design. "The 'Corner Stone' clearly emphasizes the cohesion of believers in the Body of Christ," writes Swete, "as the 'Foundation Stone' (1 Cor. 3:11) implies their dependence on His work and strength."[131] The words of Simpson speak meaningfully:

> Calvary has not inaptly been likened to the golden milestone in the centre of the Roman forum, whence all distances throughout the Empire were computed. The temple here delineated owes all its augustness to the foundationstone at its base, laid in a bedrock of propitiation and identified with it (1 John 2:2), and to its vital intertexture with the whole *shrine;* for Paul so entitles it (*naos*), the sacrosanct adytum innermost of all.[132]

130. Edward Gordon Selwyn, *The First Epistle of St. Peter,* p. 163.
131. Henry Barclay Swete, *The Gospel According to St. Mark,* p. 272.
132. Simpson and Bruce, p. 66.

THE STONES OF THE BUILDING

By implication the individual Christians are regarded as stones, each in his own place, contributing his part to the progress and completeness of the whole. They are the building materials. Peter speaks of them as "living stones" (*lithon zonta* [1 Pet 2:5]). These same words are used of both Christ (v. 4) and the believers (v. 5). There are three words in the New Testament for *stone*.

> *lithos* is the usual word for a worked stone, whether a stone used in a building or a precious stone; and it is to be distinguished from *petros,* a loose stone lying on field or roadside, and from *petra,* a rock.[133]

Even as Christ is spoken of as a stone, prepared and precious, so the believer partakes of His character. He is a worked stone—a prepared stone—for which a special place is made in the spiritual house. Every believer has his niche to fill.

> In the resurrection God took the rejected stone—a living stone indeed (I Pet. 2:4)—and made it the foundation (I Cor. 3:11), the chief corner stone (Luke 20:17; Acts 4:11; Eph. 2:20; I Pet. 2:7) of a new edifice, the church of Christ, in which all believers have their place as living stones (I Pet. 2:5).[134]

Not only are these stones worked stones, but also they possess life. Indeed, this appears to be a contradiction of terms—that a stone could be living. Yet, one is reminded of the words of John: "For I say unto you, that God is able of these stones to raise up children unto Abraham" (Luke 3:8*b*). And that God has done, for men who were as lifeless as stones become partakers of the divine nature (2 Pet 1:4). The living stones of the building partake of the nature of the Living Stone for He is him-

133. Selwyn, p. 158.
134. Everett F. Harrison, "Rock," in *Baker's Dictionary of Theology,* ed. Everett F. Harrison, p. 463.

self "a life-giving spirit" (1 Cor 15:45, RV). Speaking of the nature of this life, Selwyn explains:

> It connotes all that we mean by human vitality—the power of will and feeling and thought, and of entering into relationship with God and with one another. When applied to Christ or to His gifts, it adds to the idea of "living" that of life giving.[135]

Thus, the living stones of the building derive their life from the Living Stone.

THE PROGRESS OF THE BUILDING

Here is another paradox. Just as it is unnatural to think of "living stones," so it seems contradictory to think of a building growing. Yet, that is exactly the teaching of Paul concerning the building. "Unlike dead matter this monumental structure possesses a capacity of growth and interaction."[136] Thus, stress is laid on the gradual upbuilding of this spiritual structure. The tenses of the verbs used are particularly instructive in this connection. The Christians have been placed once for all upon the foundation (aorist [Eph 2:20]). They have been permanently founded (perfect [2:21]). They are being continuously fitted together harmoniously in the process of building (present [2:21; 4:16]). The result is that the whole building is to be one perfect outcome of a continuous increase and growth (2:21; 4:12, 16). Also instructive are the words used to describe this process, for they describe both a qualitative and a quantitative growth of the building.

The qualitative growth

The qualitative aspect is particularly illustrated by the words "fitly framed together" (Eph 2:21), which translate the present participle *sunarmologoumene*. This word is used in the New

135. Selwyn, p. 159.
136. Simpson and Bruce, pp. 67-68.

Testament only here and in Ephesians 4:16, and was apparently coined by Paul as an "architectural metaphor."[137] The word, then, speaks of that continual process of jointing together for which it is necessary to have a bonding union. The building is not made up of unmortared or uncemented stones that are simply laid on one another; such a building would be very weak. Rather, Paul is emphasizing that which has jointed the stones together to form a union—none other than Christ. The text reads: "Christ, in whom all the building fitly framed together groweth unto an holy temple in the Lord." Significantly, the process begins and ends with Christ. He is the Cornerstone from which all the dimensions are measured and upon which the stability of the structure depends. "It is not held in position by artificial clamps or grooves, by mechanisms of pressure or resistance."[138] Rather, Christ himself, the Living Stone, is the bonding union of the living stones. Referring to this qualitative growth, Moule writes:

> The idea is not of a completed but of a progressive work, a "framing together" of the structure even more closely and firmly. The building shrinks into a greater solidity, binds itself into more intense coherence, as it grows.[139]

This matter of qualitative growth, or growth in compactness, is also discussed in connection with the body metaphor. In Ephesians 4 the apostle speaks of the perfecting of the body of Christ, the church. He indicates God's provision for growth, the means by which it is accomplished, and the end result. There is a dual provision. To each individual member of the body "is given grace according to the measure of the gift of Christ" (Eph 4:7). Because of the sovereign distribution of the gifts, every member is absolutely indispensable to the function of the whole. Then, to the church are given specially gifted men (cf. Eph 4:11) as a provision for its spiritual increase. They

137. Robertson, *Word Pictures,* 4:529.
138. Simpson and Bruce, p. 68.
139. Moule, p. 85.

are to equip the members, and the members are to be actively engaged in carrying out the work of the ministry. Metzger declares:

> Thus the whole work of the ministry refers to the saints as a whole and not to a class called "ministers." In other words, each and every Christian (4:7), as a member of Christ's body, has a divinely conferred duty to accomplish in fulfilling his part of "the work of the ministry" (4:12).[140]

The desired result of all this is that the body

> may grow up into him in all things, which is the head, even Christ: from whom the whole body fitly joined together [*sunarmologoumenon*] and compacted by that which every joint supplieth, according to the effectual working in the measure of every part, maketh increase of the body unto the edifying of itself in love (Eph 4:15*b*-16).

Thus, both the body metaphor and the building metaphor stress this responsibility of qualitative growth. There is a contrast, however, to be noted. In the body metaphor the emphasis is on the place and importance of the individual member; whereas, in the building metaphor the emphasis is on Christ, who is the source of the growth.

The quantitative growth

Qualitative growth is not sufficient, however. There must also be quantitative growth. This building, which is being bound together into more intense coherence, is to *grow* (Eph 2:21) with the perpetual addition of new "living stones." "Observe two distinct ideas in harmony," says Moule, "growth in compactness, growth in extension."[141] While one purpose of God is to perfect His church, another is to enlarge it. The latter is as much the responsibility of the individual members as the former. This is brought out particularly in the clause "ye . . .

140. Metzger, 6:56.
141. Moule, p. 85.

are builded together" (Eph 2:22), which translates the present passive indicative verb *sunoikodomeisthe.* Peter uses *oikodomeisthe* for the same process: "Ye also, as lively stones, are built up a spiritual house" (1 Pet 2:5). The obvious implication here is outreach. "It is a process; carried on in new accessions of regenerate souls, and new and deeper 'framing together' of the already regenerate."[142] Thus, the fact of numerical increase is a vital aspect of the teaching of this figure. "The building . . . is not conceived of as static, but alive and increasing as by implication, new stones are fitted into their place."[143]

There is a problem that needs to be examined with respect to the force of *pasa oikodome,* which the King James Version translates as "all the building" (Eph 2:21). Accepting the American Standard Version, Hort renders it "each several building" and says that "the thought of a universal spiritual temple of God is, to say the least, not definitely expressed anywhere by Paul."[144] It seems strange that Hort should be so exacting with this particular figure when he had previously declared that the major contribution of Ephesians is of "the one universal Ecclesia absolutely.[145] In fact, the rendering "each several building" would seem to contradict his statement that "not a word in the Epistle exhibits the One Ecclesia as made up of many Ecclesiae."[146]

The question here is occasioned by the absence of the definite article. The omission of the article had New Testament sanction in other passages (cf. Matt 28:18), and F. F. Bruce maintains that it is "the regular usage in the case of *pasa sarx,* which according to Blass is a distinct Hebraism."|| || || Thus, the con-

142. Ibid., p. 86.
143. Metzger, 6:58-59.
144. Hort, p. 164.
145. Ibid., p. 117.
146. Ibid., p. 168.
|| || ||Simpson and Bruce, p. 67n. Cf. Moule, p. 85: "The law of the definite article . . . is undoubtedly somewhat less exact in the Greek of the Scriptures than in that of the classics."

text must decide the answer. So the question to ask is, Does the context favor the imagery of *detail* or that of *total?* Robinson replies:

> Such a rendering then as 'every building' (that is to say, 'all the buildings') is out of harmony with the general thought of the passage. If the Apostle has in any way referred to parts which go to make up a whole, it has always been to two parts, and only two, viz. the Jew and the Gentile. To introduce the idea of many churches going to make up one Church is to do violence to the spirit of this whole section. . . . For it must logically imply that the 'several buildings' grow into 'several temples': and this is at once inconsistent with the single 'habitation' or 'dwelling-place' of God, which the Apostle mentions in the next verse.[147]

By way of a positive solution, he suggests that "all that is builded" or "all building that is done" might express the sense with sufficient accuracy;[148] however, this hardly differs from "all the building" if one keeps before his mind the thought of the building in process, as opposed to the completed edifice, which thought is the major idea of "building" [*oikodome*].[149]

THE CHARACTER OF THE BUILDING

A striking fact about the character of this building is brought out in Ephesians 2:21. It is a temple. The word *temple* in the English Bible is used to render two Greek words, *hieron* and *naos*. The former is the whole compass of the sacred enclosure, including the outer courts, the porches, porticoes, and the various buildings in which the people gathered for worship. The *naos*, however, denotes the shrine, the actual house of God, which in the Jewish Temple consisted of the holy place and the Holy of Holies. This distinction between the *hieron* and the *naos* was one that existed and was acknowledged in profane

147. Robinson, *St. Paul's Epistle to the Ephesians*, p. 70.
148. Ibid., p. 71.
149. Cf. Arndt and Gingrich, p. 561.

Greek (with reference to heathen temples) quite as much as in sacred Greek (with relation to the temple of the true God).[150]

Entrance to the *naos* was granted to none except the priests. Not even the Lord Jesus Himself could enter. Trench writes:

> Into the *naos* the Lord never entered during his ministry on earth; nor indeed, being "made under the law," could He have so done, the right of such entry being reserved for the priests alone. It need hardly be said that the money-changers . . . whom the Lord drives out, He repels from the *hieron,* and not from the *naos.* Profane as was their intrusion, they yet had not dared to establish themselves in the temple more strictly so called.[151]

Most awesome is the fact that the *naos* (the special place of the presence of God) is used to describe the church as the *permanent* abode of God (*katoiketerion* [Eph 2:21-22]). Gerstner notes that the entire Godhead is implied here.

> The Trinity is again assumed. This building takes place *by Christ* ("in whom") *for* a dwelling place of *God* (the Father, especially), who manifests himself *by means of the (Holy) Spirit.*[152]

The true church, indeed, is already (cf. 1 Cor 3:16; 2 Cor 6:16) "the sanctuary of the living God." "Israel *had* a building in which God dwelt," writes Chafer, "the church *is* a building in which he dwells."[153] But, perhaps someone would raise the question concerning the incompleteness and imperfection of this temple. Moule responds:

> But it is this [*naos*] as a still imperfect thing. . . . The absolute and final in the matter is yet to come; and this will so transcend the partial and actual that it is spoken of *as if* the Indwelling were not yet. We may faintly illustrate by an un-

150. Richard Chenevix Trench, *Synonyms of the New Testament,* p. 12.
151. Ibid. Cf. also W. E. Vine, *An Expository Dictionary of New Testament Words,* 4:115.
152. Gerstner, p. 41.
153. Chafer, 4:64.

> finished cathedral, used already for Divine worship, but not yet ideally prepared for it.[154]

By way of summary it has been seen from the building metaphor that Gentile and Jew share equal family privileges in the household of God. Each one is a part of His house, which is built upon the foundation of the apostles and prophets of the New Testament and is secured by its Cornerstone—that Cornerstone who gives unity to all the superstructure rising from it—so that all such building, being welded into one, is growing into a holy temple, the permanent spiritual dwelling-place of God. Simpson concludes:

> At the end of the vista, seen in the interim through the perspective glass of prophecy, a majestic edifice, absolutely faultless, looms in view; and when the copestone shall be laid atop with anthems of jubilation this house not made with hands, founded on God's own Cornerstone and indwelt by His Holy Spirit, shall be right glorious to behold.[155]

IV. THE CHURCH AS THE PRIESTHOOD

In this present dispensation every believer is a priest unto God, and this entire complex of believer-priests constitutes a holy and royal priesthood under the authority of Christ, who is the true High Priest, of whom all other high priests were but types. The specific statements of the church as a priesthood are limited to 1 Peter 2:5-9, but the truth is greatly elaborated in other books, especially the epistle to the Hebrews. Peter places this figure in juxtaposition with the figure of the spiritual house or temple, and there seems to be a logical relation between the two. "The previous words have defined the nature of the Church," declares Selwyn; "these describe its vocation."[156] Thus, the living stones, when they are built into the house, become also the body of priests who minister in the house. Per-

154. Moule, p. 85.
155. Simpson and Bruce, p. 68.
156. Selwyn, p. 160.

haps this close connection accounts for the translation by Hart—"a spiritual house for### an holy priesthood"—for he explains that "the connection with *priesthood* (Heb. x. 21) and the offering of sacrifices points to the special sense of the House of God, i.e., the Temple."[157]

THE PROBLEM OF THE RELATIONSHIP TO ISRAEL

The apostle Peter says of the church that it is "a chosen generation, a royal priesthood, an holy nation, a peculiar people" (1 Pet 2:9). A cursory reading of this statement brings out a striking similarity with Israel, for these appellations seem to be used also of Israel (cf. Exod 19:5-6; Deut 7:6-7; Isa 43:20-21). Recognizing this as almost self-evident, Flew asserts that "all the titles of privilege can be applied to them which were applied to Israel of old."[158] One of the foundational elements of Wyngaarden's book, *The Future of the Kingdom in Prophecy and Fulfillment,* is the defense of the position that Israel is a type of the church. He feels justified in pursuing this thinking because "it is clear that there are certain instances of spiritualization."[159] One such instance, which is a major theme of his book, is the relation of Exodus 19:6 to 1 Peter 2:9. On the basis of Exodus 19:6 he understands Israel to be a theocracy that is typical****

###The words "holy priesthood" in the Greek text are preceded by a preposition showing purpose.

157. J. H. A. Hart, "The First Epistle General of Peter," in *The Expositor's Greek Testament,* ed. W. Robertson Nicoll, 5:55-56.

158. R. Newton Flew, *Jesus and His Church,* p. 220.

159. Martin J. Wyngaarden, *The Future of the Kingdom in Prophecy and Fulfillment: A Study of the Scope of "Spiritualization" in Scripture,* pp. 26-27.

****Wyngaarden uses typical interpretation and spiritualization interchangeably. McClain notes that "just as in any proper interpretation of Old Testament *history* Joseph is always Joseph and not Christ, even so in *prophecy* Israel is always Israel and never the Church. This does not mean that the preacher may never take a *prophecy* concerning Israel and apply it to the Church. But he should always know what he is talking about, and make certain that his hearers know, so that there can be no possible confusion between the history and its typical application, or between a prophecy and any so-called 'typical interpretation.' " Cf. Alva J. McClain, *The Greatness of the Kingdom,* p. 141. Furthermore, the statements of Exodus 19:5-6 are presented in the terms of a covenant (much like a legal contract) and may not properly be spiritualized or regarded as typical. Cf. George N. H. Peters, *The Theocratic Kingdom of Our Lord Jesus, the Christ, as Covenanted in the*

of the church. Thus, he writes:

> This results in the spiritualization of the theocracy, the spiritualization of Jehovah's kingdom of priests,—his holy nation. It gives us the spiritual eschatology of the theocracy, the spiritual future of the kingdom.
>
> And so, even if we should say that prophecies are fulfilled literally, as a rule, we find a series of exceptions to this rule, in the future state of Israel, in the eschatology of the theocracy, in the spiritualization of the kingdom of priests,—the holy nation.[160]

Now, no one who examines the Scripture can legitimately deny that there are similarities between Israel and the church. Chafer states:

> There are similarities between these two groups of elect people. Each, in turn, has its own peculiar relation to God, to righteousness, to sin, to redemption, to salvation, to human responsibility, and to destiny. They are each witnesses to the Word of God; each may claim the same Shepherd; they have doctrines in common; the death of Christ avails in its own way for each; they are alike loved with an everlasting love; and each, as determined by God, will be glorified.[161]

At the same time, however, it should be noted that the New Testament clearly distinguishes between Israel and the church. Thus, while there are definite similarities between them, because of the distinctions the two cannot be equated or identified. A table and chair may be similar in that they have common characteristics, such as being products made of wood and having

Old Testament and Presented in the New Testament, 1:291: "The promises in the covenants are *not typical,* . . . for a typical character is *opposed* to the very nature of a covenant. It would in a great measure make the real truth unrecognizable until the appearance of the antitype, and the result would be to enshroud the covenants themselves in conjecture and mystery, which is opposed to the simple fact that God appeals to the covenants as to promises *well comprehended.* The *partial fulfillment* of them clearly shows that they are not to be regarded as typical."

160. Wyngaarden, p. 28.
161. Chafer, 4:53.

four legs. Yet, one would hardly attempt to say that they are the same.

Recognizing an obvious similarity between Israel and the church with respect to the "kingdom of priests," what can be deduced as the point of similarity? A clear answer to this can be seen only if one goes back to the original statement of Exodus 19:5-6.

> Now, therefore, if ye will obey my voice indeed, and keep my covenant, then ye shall be a peculiar treasure unto me above all people: for all the earth is mine: and ye shall be unto me a kingdom of priests, and an holy nation. These are the words which thou shalt speak unto the children of Israel.

This is the Bible's first direct association of the word *kingdom* with the rule of God upon the earth. This is more than the abstract concept of ruling, for it includes both subjects and a realm. This kingdom was to be given to one nation, "the children of Israel" (v. 6). Although Israel was to be specially related to God as His "peculiar treasure" (v. 5), yet it was to have a ministry to all the nations, for the Lord declares: "all the earth is mine" (v. 6). In the light of this universal relationship the nation Israel was to be constituted a "kingdom of priests" in order that it might be the mediatorial agency in religious matters between the true God and the nations of the earth. McClain states:

> Thus the mediatorial nature of the historical kingdom is broadened: it is not only that God will reign over one nation through a mediatorial ruler, but that through the nation thus ruled there will be mediated the blessings of God to all other nations.[162]

It is most important to note, however, that this was a conditional covenant that was added alongside (cf. Gal 3:17-19) the

162. McClain, p. 62.

unconditional Abrahamic covenant.†††† The introductory clause sets forth the divine condition: "If ye will obey my voice indeed" (Exod 19:5), and the central factor, which is thereby conditional, is stated in the words that follow: "Ye shall be unto me a kingdom of priests" (v. 6). McClain writes:

> As to the conditionality of the kingdom-covenant at Sinai, it is important to remember that this had to do only with the regal and mediatorial activity of Israel in her own land and in relation to Jehovah and the nations. There is no question here of the position of Israel as the elect nation.[163]

Thus, the nation of Israel as the mediatorial agency, functioning as God's "kingdom of priests" among the nations of the earth, could continue to be exercised only as long as the nation obeyed the voice of God as expressed in the Mosaic code of laws (Exod 19:5-6ff). Thus, God reserved the right to cut off Israel as a mediatorial agency—a "kingdom of priests"—if it became disobedient and an unworthy representative.

The New Testament revelation attests the fact that this is precisely what God did. This is seen in the figure of the olive tree of Romans 11. This olive tree has been designated by premillennialists as "the place of blessing"[164] or "the place of privilege."[165] Although these terms are both acceptable, perhaps it could more clearly be designated as "the place of privilege as the mediatorial agency of God upon the earth." Scriptural revelation describes both Israel and the church as earthly mediatorial agencies through which God has worked and is working among the nations of the world. Although each is a distinct entity and is not included in the other, both hold a similar function; that is, both are agencies through which God mediates His blessing to mankind. Israel *is not* the olive tree but is *in* the olive tree; the church *is not* the olive tree but is *in* the olive tree;

††††For an extended defense of the unconditional nature of the Abrahamic covenant, see John F. Walvoord, *The Millennial Kingdom*, pp. 149-58.
163. McClain, p. 63.
164. Pentecost, *Things to Come*, pp. 88, 468.
165. Charles Caldwell Ryrie, *The Basis of the Premillennial Faith*, p. 66.

and each finds its place in the olive tree in this order: first Israel, then the church, then Israel.

This development seems to preserve the biblical emphasis and also explains the reason Israel could be referred to as a "kingdom of priests" and the church can be called a "royal priesthood." Thus, because of Israel's rejection, the church has been constituted the mediatorial agency—the "royal priesthood"—in this present dispensation. This by no means implies that the church is Israel or Israel is the church. The promises of Israel do not transfer to the church, which has specific blessings and privileges of its own. McClain writes:

> Does the mediatorial kingdom exist in any sense during the present era; and if so, what is the relation of the church to this kingdom? . . . The promise of God to all believers of the present era is that we shall "reign with Him" in the coming kingdom. This body of true believers constitutes the royal family, the ruling aristocracy of the kingdom. It would not be improper, therefore, to speak of the kingdom as now existing on earth, but only in the restricted sense that today God is engaged in selecting and preparing a people who are to be the spiritual nucleus of the established kingdom. Thus, as Christian believers, we actually enter the kingdom prior to its establishment on earth, something so remarkable that it is spoken of as a translation (Col. 1:13).[166]

Further support of this position may be gained from the parable of the wicked husbandmen recorded in Matthew 21:33-46. The vineyard in this parable is a picture of the kingdom (v. 43), and the detailed description of the vineyard is given to indicate that the owner of this vineyard has provided for its well-being with utmost care.[167] The sweep of the argument is summarized by Toussaint:

> In verse forty-two the figure is changed from a vineyard to a

166. Alva J. McClain, "The Greatness of the Kingdom" *Bibliotheca Sacra,* 112: 307.
167. Alan Hugh M'Neile, *The Gospel According to St. Matthew,* p. 308.

> stone, but the same thought is carried on. The wicked husbandmen kill the heir, and the parable stops there. In the parable of the stone the heir who is killed is represented by the rejected stone. In this manner the parable of the stone takes the rejected One, who is Christ, from death to glory (verse forty-two) and judgment (verse forty-four). . . . Because Israel rejected its Messiah the King says, "The kingdom of God shall be taken from you and shall be given to a nation bringing forth its fruits" (verse forty-three). This verse looks back to the parable of the wicked husbandmen and especially verse forty-one. Thus, the parable becomes fairly evident. The owner of the vineyard is God. The husbandmen represent Israel. The servants are God's messengers sent to Israel and so shamefully treated by that nation.[168]

This seems to be a picture of that of which Israel was warned in Exodus 19:5-6. Because of disobedience and rejection, the privilege of serving as a "kingdom of priests" was taken from them and given to another nation. After a survey of the various views as to the identity of this nation, Toussaint concludes that the most tenable view is that the nation is the church.

> The church is said to enter into the blessings of the kingdom (Galatians 3:7-9, 29; Romans 11:20-24). . . . Not only does the church inherit the kingdom with Israel, *but the church is also called a nation* (1 Peter 2:9-10; Romans 10:19). The logical conclusion is, therefore, that the church is the nation to whom the kingdom is given in Matthew 21:43 [italics not in the original].[169]

It seems significant that the context of 1 Peter 2:9 follows closely that of Matthew 21:42-43. In verse 7 Peter speaks of the stone that the builders rejected becoming "the head of the corner." Christ is the Cornerstone of the church. Peter then continues by saying of the church: "Ye are a chosen generation, a royal priesthood, an holy nation, a peculiar people" (v. 9*a*).

168. Stanley Dale Toussaint, "The Argument of Matthew," pp. 291-92.
169. Ibid., p. 294.

These factors seem to teach, then, that the church as a "royal priesthood" exercises on the earth a mediatorial agency that was formerly exercised by Israel as a "kingdom of priests." With this teaching, Peters agrees:

> In Ex. 19:5, 6 we have presented God's desire to exalt the Theocratic ordering by making it "a Kingdom of priests," i.e. a Kingdom so permeated by heartfelt allegiance to God, the Ruler, that it would be under the permanent authority of a holy priesthood, thus making *the Divine a controlling element.* A Theocracy in its purity demands *holiness, an entire consecration* to its Ruler. This idea remained unrealized, notwithstanding its tender to the Jewish nation on account of disobedience. But this sinfulness of the nation will *not prevent* God from ultimately realizing in ample fulfilment His purpose as indicated. This will be done when the Theocracy is restored under David's Son. In the mean time, to insure the complete realization, God is constantly raising up those *who are destined* to officiate as Priests in the coming Kingdom. These are specified, and the promise of Ex. 19:5, 6 applied to them, by Peter (1 Pet. 2:9).[170]

It must not be concluded from this that the kingdom is removed forever from Israel. This is impossible due to the unconditional covenant promises addressed to Israel as a nation. That Israel is yet to be restored as a mediatorial agency is asserted by Paul in Romans 11:26-27.

THE PREREQUISITES OF THE OLD TESTAMENT PRIESTHOOD

Priesthood is at the very root of all religion. Every pagan religion, regardless of how corrupt and degenerate it might be, has a priesthood. The human heart cries out for a priest. As Job said concerning God: "For he is not a man, as I am, that I should answer him, and we should come together in judgment. . . . Neither is there any days-man betwixt us, that might lay his hand upon us both" (Job 9:32-33). This need was met for

170. Peters, 2:608.

Israel by a God-appointed and -directed priesthood. The office of priest in Israel was of supreme importance and of high rank. The high priest stood next to the monarch in influence and dignity. As to its significance Moorehead states:

> It was in virtue of the priestly functions that the chosen people were brought into near relations with God and kept therein. Through the ministrations of the priesthood the people of Israel were instructed in the doctrine of sin and its expiation, in forgiveness and worship. In short, the priest was the indispensable source of religious knowledge for the people, and the channel through which spiritual life was communicated.[171]

The essential idea of this exalted office is furnished by Moses in Numbers 16:5. It is seen to consist in three elements—the being chosen or set apart for Jehovah as His own, the being holy, and the being allowed to come or bring near. "The *first* expresses the fundamental condition, the *second* the qualification, the *third* the function of the priesthood."[172] According to Exodus 19:5-6, it was upon these three elements that the character of the whole covenant people is based. With regard to the fundamental condition, that priesthood implies choice, Hebrews states: "For every high priest taken from among men is ordained for men in things *pertaining* to God. . . . And no man taketh the honor unto himself, but when he is called of God, even as was Aaron" (5:1, 4). "The priest was not elected by the people, much less was he self-appointed. Divine selection severed him from those for whom he was to act."[173]

As to the qualification, Israel was to be "a holy nation" reconciled through the "sprinkling of blood." The priesthood, as representative offerers of that blood and mediators of the people, was also to show forth the holiness of Israel. Thus, not only

171. William G. Moorehead, "Priest," in *The International Standard Bible Encyclopaedia,* ed. James Orr, 4:2439.
172. Unger, *Unger's Bible Dictionary,* p. 882.
173. Moorehead, 4:2439.

was the high priest to be physically perfect, but he was to be ceremonially pure and holy as well. As Edersheim writes:

> Everyone knows how this was symbolized by the goldplate which the high-priest wore on his forehead, and which bore the words: "Holiness unto Jehovah." But though the high-priest in this, as in every other respect, was the fullest embodiment of the functions and object of the priesthood, the same truth was also otherwise shown forth. The *bodily qualification* required in the priesthood, the kind of *defilements* which would temporarily or wholly interrupt their functions, their *mode of ordination,* and even every portion, material, and colour of their *distinctive dress* were all intended to express in a symbolical manner this characteristic of holiness.[174]

Hence, being holy formed the indispensable condition of approach to God, the Holy One.

As to the function of the priesthood, it was basically to act for men in things pertaining to God (Heb 5:1). Even the Hebrew term for priest (*Cohen*) denotes in its root the meaning "one who stands up for another, and mediates in his cause."[175] These functions they performed were evidence of the fellowship with Jehovah into which the priests were allowed to enter in the various acts of worship. Access to God was a chief factor of the priesthood. Included in this representation, and basic to it, is the offering of sacrifice. Moorehead writes:

> Nothing is clearer in Scripture than this priestly function. It was the chief duty of a priest to reconcile men to God by making atonement for their sins; and this he effected by means of sacrifice, blood shedding (Heb. 5:1; 8:3). He would be no priest who should have nothing to offer.[176]

174. Alfred Edersheim, *The Temple: Its Ministry and Services as They Were at the Time of Jesus,* pp. 85-86.
175. Samuel Prideaux Tregelles, trans., *Gesenius' Hebrew and Chaldee Lexicon to the Old Testament Scriptures,* p. 385.
176. Moorehead, 4:2440.

Growing out of this is the priestly ministry of intercession, for intercession is grounded in the atonement.

Although this survey, of necessity, is brief, these minimal factors set forth herein are essential to an understanding of the church as a priesthood. But perhaps some would doubt the value of this background, for the Christian church began its career without an official class of priests. As reported in Acts, in the early days of the church the apostles were given a prominent place. They served as pastors and teachers, but they never laid claim to the status of priests. Hence the church had leadership, but it did not have priests. This is especially striking in the light of the common practice of the day. Arndt writes:

> In the Gentile world outside of Palestine . . . the absence of priests in the Christian Church must have attracted attention. The heathen saw that the Christian churches had elders, likewise called bishops (overseers), but if one looked for priests, there was disappointment. The pagan religions had priests. When one thinks of the Greeks, the case of the priest of Jupiter, mentioned in Acts 14 in the story of the experiences of Paul and Barnabas in Lystra, readily comes to mind. Priests played an important role in the religions of the Hellenic world. Similarly the Romans had their priests; the emperors had the title of *pontifex maximus*. The Egyptians, as we know from ancient history, had priests who superintended and conducted the religious worship. How strange it must have seemed to an interested observer that the new religion, that of Christ, was not provided with religious functionaries of this nature.[177]

This observation draws attention to a remarkable fact. While the Christians had no priests, the truth is that in the Scriptures every Christian is called a priest. In the former dispensation, Israel *had* a priesthood, but in the present dispensation, the church *is* a priesthood. Thus, Peter calls the church "an holy priesthood" (1 Pet 2:5) and "a royal priesthood" (1 Pet 2:9).

177. W. Arndt, "A Royal Priesthood, 1 Pet. 2:9," *Concordia Theological Monthly* 19:241-42.

It remains then to examine the significance of this priesthood metaphor as applied to the church.

THE PRIVILEGE OF ACCESS

In contrast to the unbelieving world, which stumbles at the Word while hurrying to its dark destiny, Peter says, *"But ye"* and engages in a burst of inspired eloquence in which he depicts vividly the high station and destiny of the Christian. Central among these epithets of privilege and dignity is the "royal priesthood." As has been observed in the Old Testament pattern, the major idea of the priesthood was access—access to God. In the Old Testament the priests served before God in the tabernacle and the Temple; they had the right to enter the holy place; and one of them, the high priest, although only once a year, went into the Holy of Holies. Their relationship with God was much more holy and intimate and direct than that of the ordinary people.

Now, in the New Testament each member of the church has the privilege of appearing directly before God. No intermediary is required, for their great High Priest, the Lord Jesus Christ, has gone before them once and for all to open up a way of access. He has offered the sacrifice that has put an end to all sacrifice.

> And every priest standeth daily ministering and offering oftentimes the same sacrifices, which can never take away sins: but this man, after he had offered one sacrifice for sins for ever, sat down on the right hand of God (Heb 10:11-12).

And again:

> Nor yet that he should offer himself often, as the high priest entereth into the holy place every year with blood of others . . . but now once [once for all] in the end of the world hath he appeared to put away sin by the sacrifice of himself (Heb 9:25-26).

Because of this finality of the once-for-all offering of the High Priest and the fact that He has passed through the heavens (Heb 4:14) to the very throne of God, the writer of Hebrews is able to exhort the members of the priesthood, the church, "to come boldly unto the throne of grace" (Heb 4:16). And again:

> Having therefore, brethren, boldness to enter into the holiest by the blood of Jesus, by a new and living way, which he hath consecrated for us, through the veil, that is to say, his flesh; and having a high priest over the house of God; let us draw near with a true heart in full assurance of faith (Heb 10:19-22*a*).

This privilege of free access to the throne of grace is not limited to a certain class. The laity as well as the clergy have equal privileges of access. As Arndt states: "With prayers, pleadings, and thanksgiving every believer, let him be ever so humble, can approach God; there is no barrier beyond which some may go, others not."[178] In support of this is the term *priesthood,* which is a collective term and views the Christians as one company.[179] Wherever they are, whoever they may be, however they may rate socially, whatever their denominational connections are, if they are true believers, they belong to this royal priesthood. All together they form a priesthood. The church is not an oligarchy in which a few have authority to dictate to the many, nor is it a sacerdotal religion in which there is a class of priests with special privileges. Stibbs writes:

> What was unthinkable in Judaism is fundamental to Christianity; proselytes became priests. The priesthood and its ministry are a status and a privilege enjoyed by the whole laity. . . . They are no longer restricted to a specially qualified minority, on whose ministries the majority of the people is dependent.[180]

178. Ibid., 19:247.
179. Selwyn, p. 160.
180. Alan M. Stibbs, *The First Epistle General of Peter,* p. 100.

Every member of the church is a priest and entitled to all the privileges and rights indicated by that term.

THE PURPOSE OF ACCESS

Not only privileges but also responsibilities are implied in the priesthood metaphor. As Arndt so aptly states: "The priests in the Old Testament . . . were not supposed to be drones; they were to give their time to the service of Jehovah."[181] A clue to this activity in service is seen in the word *hierateuma* (priesthood) itself, for the *-ma* ending suggests that it is the result of an activity.[182] Chafer apparently understood this as the real significance of the priesthood metaphor, for his entire discussion centers on service: the service of sacrifice, the service of worship, the service of intercession.[183] An understanding of *basileios* (translated "royal") is also significant in this regard. Although there is considerable discussion as to the proper translation of *basileios hierateuma,* the paraphrase by Findlay draws out the meaning clearly—"a priesthood in the service of a King."[184] This paraphrase takes the adjective *basileios* as signifying "being the property of a king." Chamberlain states that adjectives ending in *ios* (*basileios*) express the idea of possession, while those that end in *ikos* (*basilikos*) denote ability or fitness.[185] Thus the paraphrase by Findlay agrees with the meaning of *basileios,* the adjective denoting possession: the priesthood in question belongs to Christ, the exalted Lord. Finally, this agrees with the general concept of a "kingdom of priests" previously defended: that it is God's mediatorial agency on earth. The idea of service is foremost in this figure.

What then is this service the priesthood is to render for its King? In contrast to the Levitical priesthood, the royal priest-

181. Arndt, 19:247.
182. William Douglas Chamberlain, *An Exegetical Grammar of the Greek New Testament,* p. 12.
183. Chafer, 4:65-68.
184. J. Alexander Findlay, *A Portrait of Peter,* p. 174.
185. Chamberlain, p. 13.

hood does not offer a sacrifice in atonement for sin. As Hebrews declares, the sacrificial death of Christ is once and for all and all-sufficient; thus "there is no more offering for sin" (Heb 10:18). But the offering of sacrifice to atone for sin was not the whole of the function of the Levitical priesthood. Other sacrifices signified thanksgiving, consecration, and fellowship with God. The New Testament counterpart is to be found in the various spiritual sacrifices to be offered by the church. Leighton states:

> As the Apostle speaks (Heb. vii. 12) of the high priesthood of Christ, that this *priesthood being changed, there followed of necessity a change of the law;* so, in the priesthood of Christians, there is a change of the kind of sacrifice from the other.[186]

Thus, Peter states that the church is "a spiritual house for a priesthood to offer up spiritual sacrifices through Jesus Christ" (1 Pet 2:5). The word *anaphero* is the usual word for offering sacrifices (cf. Heb 7:27); it speaks of the Old Testament priest's bearing the sacrifice up to the altar. The particular form of the word used here (*anenegkai*) is aorist active infinitive. The most common verbal usage of the infinitive is that of purpose; that is, the infinitive is used to express the aim of the action denoted by the finite verb.[187] Thus, the purpose of believers' (the living stones) being built up (*oikodomeisthe*) a spiritual house for a holy priesthood is that they might offer up spiritual sacrifices acceptable to God through Jesus Christ. Central to the idea of the priesthood, then, is the purpose of offering up spiritual sacrifices. Although Peter does not go on to describe these sacrifices, they are clearly identified elsewhere in Scripture.

A foundational passage in Romans 12:1: "I beseech you therefore, brethren by the mercies of God, that ye present your

186. Robert Leighton, *A Practical Commentary upon the First Epistle General of Peter,* 1:247.
187. H. E. Dana and Julius R. Mantey, *A Manual Grammar of the Greek New Testament,* p. 214.

bodies a living sacrifice, holy, acceptable unto God, which is your reasonable service." The first act of sacrifice that the believer-priest is to make is the presentation, or offering up, of his body (cf. 6:13, 19) to the service of God.‡‡‡‡ Stifler explains:

> "Bodies" is the comprehensive term for the whole man, body, soul, and spirit (1 Thess. 5:23). It is equivalent to "yourselves," but better suited than the latter word to Paul's sacrificial idea.[188]

The word *parastesai,* which Stifler calls a "temple term," was a technical term for offering a sacrifice.§§§§ The aorist tense (punctiliar action) emphasizes that this is a presentation made at a point of time in one's life, not a continual process. As Pentecost has stated: "There is to be a discharging of the office of believer-priest which begins with the presentation of the believer as a living sacrifice."[189] In contrast to the involuntary Old Testament sacrifices in which the animal was slain, this was to be a voluntary, living sacrifice that could therefore be set free by God to live as a sacrificial victim—one completely set apart to God.|| || || || This presentation, says Paul, is "your reasonable service." Robertson translated it: "Your rational (spiritual) service (worship)."[190] The word for service (*latreian*) is also a word from the figure of the priesthood; it speaks of the service or ministry of the priests in the Temple. Thus, it can

‡‡‡‡There is no thought of cleansing here. That has been done previously (Rom 1-11) and forms the basis for the presentation here. Cf. "by means of the mercies of God."

188. James M. Stifler, *The Epistle to the Romans—A Commentary Logical and Historical,* p. 204.

§§§§Robertson, *Word Pictures,* 4:402. It was used of presenting the child Jesus in the Temple (Luke 2:22), of the Christian presenting himself (Rom 6:13), of Christ presenting His church (Eph 5:27), of God presenting the saved (Col 1:28).

189. J. Dwight Pentecost, class lecture notes on Romans.

|| || || ||Isaac is an Old Testament illustration of a sacrificial victim who was a living sacrifice. He became a sacrifice the moment he was placed on the altar. He was freed by God from the altar of sacrifice. Thus, he was a living sacrifice.

190. Robertson, *Word Pictures*, 4:402.

be seen that the priesthood metaphor forms the background for this great passage. As believer-priests, then, the first item of priestly service is to make a voluntary presentation of oneself to God.

Having made this initial offering, the believer-priest is exhorted to offer up other spiritual sacrifices. Certain of these are specified in Hebrews 13:15-16.

> By him therefore let us offer the sacrifice of praise to God continually, that is, the fruit of our lips giving thanks to his name. But to do good and to communicate forget not: for with such sacrifices God is well pleased.

There is a significant contrast between the sacrifice of Romans 12:1 and these sacrifices. The aorist tense in the former case stressed the singularity of the offering, whereas the present tense in the latter case stresses the continual, durative process. Thus, *anaphero* could be translated, "let us keep on offering up." This continual offering to God can be none other than the sacrifice of praise. "As those who partake of the altar of Golgotha," writes Archer, "We N. T. priest-believers have just one kind of sacrifice to offer up to God: the thank-offering."[191] The phrase "sacrifice of thanksgiving" occurs in Leviticus 7:12 and elsewhere as the highest form of peace offering. The thank offering was made not in fulfillment of a vow or in general acknowledgment of God's goodness, but for a favor graciously bestowed.[192] Of this unique offering, Westcott observes: "That which was an exceptional service under the Old Dispensation is the normal service under the New."[193] The sacrifice of praise is further defined as "giving thanks" (*homologeo*), which is usually translated "confess" (cf. 1 John 1:9). Thus, in biblical usage, to confess God's name involves not only uttering it, but also recog-

191. Gleason L. Archer, *The Epistle to the Hebrews: A Study Manual*, p. 104.
192. Gustave Friedrich Oehler, *Theology of the Old Testament*, rev. George E. Day, pp. 287-89.
193. Brooke Foss Westcott, *The Epistle to the Hebrews: The Greek Text with Notes and Essays*, p. 443.

nizing and proclaiming and praising it above all other names and before the people.

The latter thought brings to attention the third aspect of the service of the believer-priest. Spiritual sacrifice must find an outward expression. Two such expressions are given in Hebrews 13:16, where the word for kindly service, *eupoiia,* ("to do good"), is followed by *koinonia* ("to communicate"), which two expressions among other things suggest sharing with a brother in material need (cf. 2 Cor 9:13, where *koinonia* is translated "distribution"). But not only is there the duty of benevolence and generosity. The service of the priesthood also includes the duty of evangelism—a service often overlooked. After he states the epithets of privilege, which include the "royal priesthood," Peter gives a strong purpose clause in verse 9; it might be quite literally rendered, "in order that you should proclaim (or advertise) the excellencies (or grand qualities) of Him who called you out of darkness into His marvelous light." Arndt writes:

> The Christians have been made priests of God for the purposes of a holy propaganda in which the greatness and the goodness of the Lord is to be exalted. The Apostle indirectly indicates one of the lines this effort may take: God has done great things for you; He has taken you out of the desert of darkness and death and brought you into the garden of life and light. Shout this from the housetops, and tell people that what He has done for you He is eager to do for others.[194]

The apostle Paul also uses the metaphor of the priesthood for evangelism in Romans 15:16, where he speaks of the grace given him by God, "that I should be the minister [*leitourgos*] of Jesus Christ to the Gentiles, ministering [*hierourgounta*] the gospel of God, that the offering up [*prosphora*] of the Gentiles might be acceptable, being sanctified by the Holy Ghost." Thus,

194. Arndt, 19:247.

both Paul and Peter regard the work of evangelism as a work of priestly mediation.

Although that which has been presented certainly does not exhaust the teaching of the church as a priesthood, yet it does represent the truths presented in those passages in which the priesthood metaphor is in view. It has been seen that every believer, be he ever so humble, is a priest before God and has free access to the throne of grace. This exalted privilege that is his begets to him certain responsibilities, for the privilege has a purpose. Thus, the believer is to offer spiritual sacrifices, the first of which is a presentation of himself, which presentation inaugurates him into his priestly ministry. Having taken this step, the believer-priest has wide opportunities of service of sacrifice open to him, chief among them being the sacrifice of praise to God. This thank offering, which is his continual responsibility, eventuates in the service of sacrifice to others, including sharing of substance as well as proclamation of the excellencies of the Saviour. With this twofold offering of spoken witness and practical loving-kindness, God is well pleased (Heb 13:16).

V. THE CHURCH AS THE FLOCK

The figure of the flock is one of the broadest in application of any of the figures used of the church. In the Old Testament, Israel is called "the Lord's flock" (Jer 13:17; cf. Zech 10:3). Jesus referred to his small circle of disciples as the "little flock" (Luke 12:32). Again, the term is used of the church on several occasions (cf. Acts 20:28; 1 Pet 5:3). In addition to these are the repeated references to the sheep that compose the flock (cf. John 10:16; 21:15-17) and to the Shepherd of the flock (John 10:2-16; 1 Pet 2:25; 5:4; Heb 13:20). Although this figure is rich with potential for application, there are a few things that deserve special note, for this figure is used to speak of relationships within the church.

THE GATHERING OF THE FLOCK

One of the few instances of parabolic form of discourse in John is the parable of the Good Shepherd, found in John 10:1-6. The teaching that follows (vv. 7-16) is stated in the form of bold metaphor and the action is based on the normal daily procedure of the Oriental shepherd, who in the morning enters into the fold where his sheep are kept, calls to them, and leads them out to pasture for the day.[195] In the teaching, Christ, the Good Shepherd, anticipates not only His forthcoming death for the sheep but also the future gathering of all His sheep into one flock. In the development, the two ideas of the fold (*aulen*) and the flock (*poimne*) are presented distinctly. Judaism was a fold out of which the Shepherd called His own sheep by name and led them out (cf. v. 5). Since the shepherd calls his own sheep, it is implied that there are in the fold other sheep, which are not His. Thus, only the believing Jews within the fold followed Him out. Barrett asserts: "This, then, is the fold of Judaism, which contained the first disciples and also the unbelieving Jews."[196] But Jesus declared that the Jewish sheep were not the only ones He had: "And other sheep I have, which are not of this fold: them also I must bring, and they shall hear my voice; and there shall be one fold [flock], and one shepherd" (John 10:16). Thus, the flock of Christ is not confined to the Jewish fold. "Even before His death," observes Westcott, "while the wall of partition is still standing, He 'has' other sheep, who even if they know Him not are truly His (comp. xi. 52)."[197] Verse 16 forms the complement, then, to verse 5. Barrett states:

> The *aule* is Israel and it contains some who are Christ's own sheep and some (the unbelieving Jews) who are not. The incarnation makes clear the predestined distinction between

195. Edersheim, *Life and Times,* 2:189.
196. C. K. Barrett, *The Gospel According to St. John,* p. 306.
197. Brooke Foss Westcott, *The Gospel According to St. John: The Authorized Version with Introduction and Notes,* p. 155.

> the two groups. Christ then has some sheep in the *aule* of Judaism, but also others who are not of that *aule,* that, is Gentiles.[198]

In the case of the Gentiles there was no fold, for they had no fold, for they had no outward organization as did the Jews. Rather, they were sheep "scattered abroad" (cf. John 11:52; 1 Pet 2:25), but, as Westcott states, "they were Christ's 'sheep' in fact, and not only potentially."[199]

These Jewish believers and Gentile believers together were to form one flock (*poimne*), the church. The King James Version is incorrect at this point in using the word "fold," for Judaism was a fold; but the church is not. Westcott declares:

> The translation "fold" for "flock" (*ovile* for *grex*) has been most disastrous in idea and influence. . . . The obliteration of this essential distinction . . . in many of the later Western versions of this passage indicates, as it appears, a tendency of Roman Christianity, and has served in no small degree to confirm and extend the false claims of the Roman see.[200]

Contrary to the outward organizational unity implied by "fold" (*aulen*), the unity of the flock (*poimne*) is "a unity created in and by Jesus."[201] This unity of Jew and Gentile in the church is later elaborated and elucidated by the apostle Paul in Ephesians.

One further grammatical notation should be made concerning the plural verb *genesontai,* which the King James Version renders "there shall be." The American Standard Version renders it more acceptably "they shall become." The latter part of verse 16 then reads: "They shall become one flock, and one shepherd." Here is a unity, then, that not only goes beyond the bounds of the local church and beyond denominational barriers, but it also transcends all external organizational unity and finds its organic unity in Christ alone. The unity of the flock is

198. Barrett, p. 312.
199. Westcott, *The Gospel According to St. John,* p. 155.
200. Ibid., pp. 155-56.
201. Barrett, p. 313.

determined by a common following of the one Shepherd, not by the erection of a single outward organization. He has one flock, and there is one Shepherd today.

THE TENDING OF THE FLOCK

One of the most significant teachings of the flock metaphor is that the Shepherd of the flock has committed the task of shepherding to undershepherds. This is the essence of the thrice repeated charge given to Peter in John 21:15-17. When Christ charges Peter, "Feed my sheep," in verse 16, He uses the verb *poimaino,* which implies more than simply feeding. Concerning the contrast between *bosko* (vv. 15, 17) and *poimaino,* Trench explains:

> The distinction . . . is very far from fanciful. *Boskein,* the Latin 'pascere,' is simply 'to feed:' but *poimainein* involves much more; the whole office of the shepherd, the guiding, guarding, folding of the flock, as well as the finding of nourishment for it. . . . The wider reach and larger meaning of *poimainein* makes itself felt at Rev. ii. 27; xix. 15; where at once we are conscious how impossible it would be to substitute *Boskein.*[202]

Thus, this verb includes all that is involved in the shepherd's task in looking after the flock. In the spiritual care of God's flock, the process of feeding from the Word of God is the constant and regular necessity; it is to have the foremost place. The tending or shepherding, however, consists of other acts (of discipline, authority, restoration, material assistance of individuals) as well as the feeding.[203]

Writing on a later occasion to the elders of the flock as it was scattered throughout the five provinces of Pontus, Galatia, Cappadocia, Asia, and Bithynia, Peter gives the very same charge: "Feed [*poimaine,* "shepherd"] the flock of God which is among you" (1 Pet 5:2). Thus, the charge of shepherding is

202. Trench, p. 85.
203. Vine, 2:89.

passed on to other undershepherds in harmony with Paul's charge to Timothy: "And the things which thou hast heard of me among many witnesses, the same commit thou to faithful men, who shall be able to teach others also" (2 Tim 2:2). Again, on an earlier occasion, Paul had commissioned the elders at Ephesus in like manner:

> Take heed therefore unto yourselves, and to all the flock, over which the Holy Ghost hath made you overseers, to feed [poimainein] the church of God, which he hath purchased with his own blood (Acts 20:28).

Involved in these charges are the basic factors that ought to be noted concerning the figure of the flock.

In the first place, the ownership of the flock is clearly recognized. Christ had told Peter: "Feed *my* sheep" (John 21:16, italics not in the original), and Peter in turn tells the elders: "Feed the flock *of God* which is among you" (1 Pet 5:2, italics not in the original). The charge from the lips of the Lord undoubtedly lingered in his remembrance. He reminds the shepherds that the flock is God's, not theirs, and that they are only undershepherds. The rights of ownership rest with the "chief Shepherd" (1 Pet 5:4; cf. Heb 3:20), who has purchased the flock, the church of God, with His own blood (cf. Acts 20:28). Thus, Peter reminds the elders that what is committed to them is "God's heritage" (1 Pet 5:3). The American Standard Version more adequately renders this "the charge allotted to you." In Acts 1:17, 25, the word is used in the sense of a charge, or allotment.#### The background of the word is given by Selwyn:

> In classical Greek *kleros* was an allotment of land assigned to a citizen by the civic authorities, . . . the distribution frequently being made by lot. . . . The term was therefore familiar

####Luke says of Judas: "he was numbered with us, and had obtained part [*tou kleron*] of this ministry." Again, of Judas's successor Luke says "that he may take part of this ministry and apostleship."

> to Gentile readers; while Jewish members of the Church would have found in it a still richer meaning owing to its association with *kleronomia,* a word already used in 1:4.[204]

Thus, Arndt defines it: "that which is assigned by lot . . . *esp. what comes to someone by divine grace*" [italics not in the original].[205] Therefore, because they are the recipients of a trust, there is no room for high-handed autocratic rule over the flock. Instead of lording it over those portions of God's flock assigned to them, these local pastors are exhorted to be an example to the entire flock. Undershepherds should be living patterns, or models, of the Chief Shepherd, the Lord Jesus. The first lesson from the figure, then, is a note of instruction concerning the ownership of the flock and the relation of the undershepherd to it.

A second factor Peter learned from the Lord and passed on to the elders is the basic unity of the flock. The Lord had stated that He was going to take believers from Jews and Gentiles and make one flock. Peter conveys this basic unity to the elders when he says, "Feed the flock of God which is among you [*en humin*]." There is only one flock, but individuals all over the world make up that flock. The preposition *en* must be local.[206] "The flock which is among you" may be taken to mean "the flock in your town or village." Thus, the elders are charged with the task of shepherding the part of the flock that is in their area. "The flock is God's," writes Selwyn, "and it is distributed in the different localities where the presbyters live and work (*en humin*)."[207] God has only one flock. It is portioned out among the shepherds, each of whom has a charge allotted (*kleroi* [v. 3]) to him in relation to which he is to fulfill his ministry. Arndt writes: "1 Pet. 5:3 the *kleroi* seem to denote the 'flock' as a whole, i.e., the various parts of the congregation which have

204. Selwyn, p. 231.
205. Arndt and Gingrich, p. 436.
206. Charles Bigg, *A Critical and Exegetical Commentary on the Epistles of St. Peter and St. Jude,* p. 188.
207. Selwyn, p. 230.

been assigned as 'portions' to the individual presbyters or shepherds."[208] It should be noted that the responsibility for shepherding was limited to the "portion" allotted to the individual shepherds, but their manner of carrying out their duties would be an example, or pattern, for the whole flock. This confirms what has been seen several times before, namely, that organization is limited in Scripture to the local level. Speaking of the example of Ephesus, Hort states:

> He [Paul] begins with the actual circumstances of the movement, the local Ephesian community, which was the flock committed to the Ephesian Elders, and then goes on to say that that little flock had a right to believe itself to be the Ecclesia of God which He had purchased to be His own possession at so unspeakable a price. Of course in strictness the words belong only to the one universal Christian Ecclesia: but here they are transferred to the individual Ecclesia of Ephesus, which alone these elders were charged to shepherd. In the Epistles we shall find similar investment of parts of the universal Ecclesia with the high attributes of the whole.[209]

A third factor to be considered is the actual nature of this shepherding as it relates to the sheep. Long lists of specific items could doubtless be given at this point, but it seems that they could all be summarized under provision, particularly the provision of spiritual food. This was emphasized by Christ in that in two of the three charges to Peter He used the word *bosko,* which concerns the provision of food. This is not meant to discount the governing and guiding inherent in shepherding, but these must allow the priority to be given to the provision of food. Perhaps someone would object that the duties of guarding and protecting are also necessary. This certainly is true, but the best means of spiritual protection is a solid grasp on the Word of God. After instructing the Ephesian elders to feed the flock, Paul warns them: "For I know this, that after my departing

208. Arndt and Gingrich, p. 436.
209. Hort, pp. 102-3.

shall grievous wolves enter in among you, not sparing the flock" (Acts 20:29). For this reason, Paul had for three years "ceased not to warn every one night and day with tears" (v. 31). This provision of food ought to be a balanced diet, as Paul tells Timothy, of doctrine, reproof, correction, instruction in righteousness (cf. 2 Tim 3:16; 4:2), but at all costs the shepherd must be able to provide food (cf. 1 Tim 1:3; Titus 1:9). The shepherd must go before, and find the food, and lead the flock into the luxuriant growth.

THE SUBJECTION OF THE FLOCK

Just as the duty of the shepherd can be summed up in one main responsibility—provision for the sheep—so the chief obligation of the flock may be stated as one—subjection to the shepherd. One of the most characteristic facts about sheep is their willingness and need to be subject to their shepherd (cf. Isa 53:7). Christ pictures the sheep without a shepherd as scattered and going astray (1 Pet 2:25; Matt 26:31). Bigg says of this figure: "It brings out the general ignorance and helplessness of man, who, without aid from above, can only go astray like sheep without a shepherd."[210]

When speaking of the church under the figure of the flock, it must be noted that Christ as the Good Shepherd has given His life for the sheep (John 10:11) and is, therefore, the Shepherd to whom the sheep are ultimately in subjection. Authority has been committed to undershepherds, however, who are responsible for the care of the sheep. The office of the shepherd (*poimen,* [pastor]) is one of the gifts to the church (Eph 4:11). Paul states that they have been given the duty of oversight***** by the Holy Spirit (cf. Acts 20:28; 1 Pet 5:2). Thus, Hebrews 13:17 directs:

210. Bigg, p. 149.

*****Cf. Kenneth S. Wuest, *First Peter in the Greek New Testament for the English Reader,* pp. 124-25: "The word 'oversight' is the translation of the same Greek word in another form which in other places is rendered by the words 'overseer,' or 'bishop,' referring to the spiritual care of the flock."

> Obey them that have the rule over you, and submit yourselves: for they watch for your souls, as they that must give account, that they may do it with joy, and not with grief: for that is unprofitable for you.

Thus, when the Chief Shepherd appears (cf. 1 Pet 5:4) the undershepherd must give an account and receive the reward given to faithful shepherds of the flock of God. Selwyn notes that Peter's word *archipoimen* (translated "chief shepherd") relates specifically to pastoral charge in the Christian ministry. He states: "In relation to them Christ is the *chief s*hepherd, set over them yet sharing their function."[211] It is seen then that, although every member of the church is a believer-priest before God, yet, on the organizational side within the local church, he is to submit to those who have been designated as undershepherds by the Holy Spirit.

The study of the figure of the flock has reemphasized certain of the truths, such as the unity and oneness of the church, that are found repeatedly in the other figures. As each figure has had special contributions of its own to make, however, so the flock metaphor has contributions that are unique to itself. This figure seems to come closer than any of the others to showing the relationship of the universal and local churches. There are in various local situations portions of the flock whose charge is allotted to undershepherds, who in turn are responsible to the Chief Shepherd for the care of their souls. This "oversight" on the part of the undershepherd is limited to the specific portion of the flock allotted to him in his local area. As a shepherd he is responsible to provide for the sheep in various areas, such as government, guidance, and protection, but most especially is he to provide a well-balanced diet of spiritual food. On the other hand the sheep are to be in subjection to the shepherd. This figure, then, guards against the possible misuse of the believer-priest teaching, which, if it were taken to an extreme, could

211. Selwyn, p. 232.

eliminate subjection to any local church organization. Here again is evidence, then, of the need of all these biblical figures in order to understand the true nature of the church.

VI. THE CHURCH AS THE BRANCHES

In chapters 13-17 of John's gospel, the Lord Jesus Christ gives His farewell discourse to His disciples. The key statement is "Jesus knowing that his hour was come that he should depart out of this world unto the Father, having loved his own that were in the world, he loved them unto the end" (13:1). Thus, in the privacy of the upper room, Christ gave to the disciples, the true believers,††††† a brief foreview of that which was to take place during the period of His absence. As Henry has put it: "Bearing human nature on high, he will inaugurate new but undefined relationships with His disciples on earth."[212] Thus, the Lord Jesus states: "What I do thou knowest not *now;* but thou shalt know *hereafter*" (John 13:7, italics not in the original). Again, Henry notes:

> His instructions anticipate a decisive transition in relationship with His followers. It is this transition which carried the message of the Fourth Gospel beyond that of the earlier Gospels, and foresees Pentecost in the Acts of the Apostles,

†††††Some have contended that Christ is here speaking of the visible church, both believers and unbelievers. Cf. Frederick Louis Godet, *Commentary on the Gospel of John,* rev. and trans. Timothy Dwight, 2:294: "He is thinking of the future of His Church; He sees beforehand those professors of the Gospel, who, while being outwardly united to Him, will nevertheless live inwardly separated from Him. . . . After having for a time tolerated this dead member in the Church, God . . . severs him externally from the community of believers with which only an apparent bond connected him." This view cannot be accepted, because it is completely out of harmony with the context. Christ was speaking to true believers only. Those addressed are those "in Christ." Cf. Chafer, 8:4: "Christ declares that a *branch in Him*—which terminology connotes the most vital and immutable union that could ever exist—may fail to bear fruit. . . . The branch is not in Christ because it bears fruit; but being in Christ, the branch may or may not bear fruit. Thus it is demonstrated that abiding in Christ is not a matter of maintaining union with Christ, but of maintaining communion with Him."

212. Carl F. H. Henry, "John," in *The Biblical Expositor,* ed. Carl F. H. Henry, 3:177.

> where the Risen Christ participates in the life of His radiant Church.[213]

Thus, long before reunion in a blessed future immortality, believers are to be linked with their Lord in an intimate spiritual union, a union that, in fact, will be no less vital than that between the Father and the incarnate Son, for He says: "In that day you will know that I am in my Father, and you in me, and I in you" (14:20).

In the midst of this upper room discourse, Christ speaks of the relationship that is to exist between Himself and His true followers: "Abide in me, and I in you" (15:4). Again, "I am the vine, ye are the branches. . . . Without me," continues Christ, "ye can do nothing" (15:5). Thus, the relation with Christ, which was then yet future,‡‡‡‡‡ is described with special intimacy in the figure of the vine and the branches. Taylor declares that "a more vital relationship could hardly be described."[214] Although the significance of this figure is deeply profound, it can be handled briefly, because the basic factors of the relationship are not complicated, nor is the figure treated in the New Testament anywhere outside of John 15.

THE ESSENCE OF THE RELATIONSHIP

Christ says, "I am the vine; ye are the branches." The real core of the teaching of this figure is found in the kind of union that exists between the vine and the branches. There is an inseparable, vital conjunction of the two, without which the branches would wither and die. Here is a unity of life, for the sap that is the life of the trunk is also the life of the branch. Thus, Godet states: "The point of comparison between Christ

213. Ibid., 3:179.

‡‡‡‡‡Cf. Chafer, 4:59: "This figure, quite in contrast to that of the Shepherd and the sheep which was spoken to Israelites, is addressed to believers (John 15). It is the peculiar character of the Upper Room Discourse . . . that it looks on to conditions that would obtain after Christ's death, after His resurrection, after His ascension, and after Pentecost."

214. Vincent Taylor, *The Names of Jesus*, p. 104.

and the vine is the organic union by which the life of the trunk becomes that of the branches."[215] There is such a union here that it is difficult to tell where the trunk ends and the branches begin. It may be compared with the difficulty of determining where the ocean ends and the inlet begins.

As profound as these facts are, there is still a greater significance to note. Christ does not say, "I am the root," or "I am the trunk," but "I am the vine; ye are the branches." He presents himself and all believers as one organic whole. To the same point Taylor writes:

> Its communal aspects are even more apparent when it is observed that Christ does not say that He is the stem, but the Vine of which His disciples are the branches. The closeness of this relationship is more completely expressed than it is in the imagery of the body; although here it is true that, while Christ is "the Head," the Church is also His Body, the Body of Christ (1 Cor. xii. 27). In the use of the name "the Vine" no such qualifying phrase is necessary.[216]

Thus, this figure teaches an even closer organic union and identification of the believer with Christ than that taught by the figure of the body. Believers are parts of the whole. It is this precise identification that is repeatedly emphasized in Scripture by the use of the phrase *in Christ.*§§§§§ Apprehension of this truth of identification revolutionized the life of J. Hudson Taylor and caused him to write the following words in a letter to his sister:

> As I thought of the Vine and the Branches, what light the blessed Spirit poured direct into my soul. . . . I saw not only that Jesus would never leave me, but that I was a member of

215. Godet, 2:293.
216. Taylor, p. 105.
§§§§§Cf. Merrill F. Unger, *The Baptizing Work of the Holy Spirit,* p. 9: "There are . . . approximately 150 passages which state or imply the truth that the believer is 'in Christ,' and every one has reference to the Spirit's work in baptism, for that operation alone can put one 'in Christ.'"

> His body, of His flesh, and of His bones. The Vine, now I see, is not the root merely, but all—root, stem, branches, twigs, leaves, flowers, fruit; and Jesus is not only that: He is soil and sunshine, air and showers, and ten thousand times more than we have ever dreamed, wished for or needed.[217]

Such is the vital union that exists between Christ and His church.

THE RESULT OF THE RELATIONSHIP

"Before the seed sends any sprouts up it sends a long root down."[218] The latter part of that statement concerning the "long root down" involves the intimate union of the church with Christ, which union has now been discussed. This fact of *union* with Christ is largely assumed in the development of the figure in John 15, as evidenced by the words, "every branch in me" (v. 2). The central theme of the development, however, concerns the fruit-bearing that results from abiding in Christ. Thus, *karpos* ("fruit") is used eight times and *meno* ("to abide") occurs twelve times. A more appropriate figure could not have been used to teach this truth, for the primary function of a vine is to produce fruit. Outside of this the vine has no value. This is illustrated by McGee, who says:

> Actually, a grape vine is a plant, the wood of which has no value. You cannot make furniture of it. You would not go to a furniture mart and ask to be shown the latest models in "grapevine wood." You would be shown maple, cherry, or walnut, but not grapevine wood. The only value that a grapevine has is to produce fruit.[219]

Within the realm of its intended purpose, however, the vine has tremendous potential productivity. Barnhouse vividly confirms this:

> In Hampton Court near London, there is a grapevine under

217. In F. J. Huegel, *Bone of His Bone*, p. 105.
218. Ibid., p. 43.
219. J. Vernon McGee, *Christ, His Cross, His Church*, p. 19.

> glass; it is about 1,000 years old and has but one root which is at least two feet thick. Some of the branches are 200 feet long. Because of skillful cutting and pruning, the vine produces several tons of grapes each year. Even though some of the smaller branches are 200 feet from the main stem, they bear much fruit because they are joined to the vine and allow the life of the vine to flow through them.[220]

Thus, when Christ refers to the believers, the members of His church, as branches, He is teaching them their major responsibility—fruit-bearing; and their potential productivity is immeasurable because of the infinite resource of life flowing through the Vine. The sole condition for tapping these resources of fruit-bearing is to abide in the Vine.

If it is the chief responsibility of the believer to abide in Christ, the question arises, What does 'abiding' mean? This is anticipated by the Lord in the repeated use of the word *meno*. Having summarized the usage of the word in the writings of John, Arndt and Gingrich state: "The phrase *m. en tini* is a favorite of J to denote an inward, enduring personal communion."[221] Chafer has defined it as "unbroken fellowship with Christ."[222] Not differing from this essentially but elucidating it somewhat, Scofield explains:

> To abide in Christ is, on the one hand, to have no known sin unjudged and unconfessed, no interest into which He is not brought, no life which He cannot share. On the other hand, the abiding one takes all burdens to Him, and draws all wisdom, life and strength from Him. It is not unceasing *consciousness* of these things, and of Him, but that nothing is allowed in the life which separates from Him.[223]

One of the finest definitions of abiding is given by the apostle Paul in Galatians 2:20.

220. Donald Grey Barnhouse, "Chain of Glory," *Eternity* 9:17.
221. Arndt and Gingrich, p. 505.
222. Chafer, 8:4.
223. C. I. Scofield, *The Scofield Reference Bible*, pp. 1136-37.

> I have been crucified with Christ; and it is no longer I that live, but Christ liveth in me: and that life which I now live in the flesh I live in faith, the faith which is in the Son of God, who loved me and gave himself up for me. (Gal 2:20, ASV).

The first part of this verse defines the first teaching of the vine metaphor, namely, identification with Christ. "I have been crucified with Christ." The second part of the verse defines the second teaching, namely, the responsibility of abiding. "It is no longer I that live, but Christ liveth in me." Christ must live His life through the believer. The Lord Jesus said: "Without me ye can do nothing" (John 15:5). In essence He is saying that no Christian can live the Christian life. Furthermore, God never asked anyone to live the Christian life. Rather, He desires that the believer abide, or rest, in Him. Thus, from the vine there comes life, it flows into the branch, and the branch produces fruit. But the branch can never say, "I produced this fruit on my own; I did it of myself." Contrariwise, the branch knows that the fruit it produced came out of the vine to which it was joined. The believer does not produce fruit by attempting to imitate Christ, but by abiding in Christ with whom He is so vitally identified. Speaking to this point, Huegel says:

> We have conceived of the Christian life as an imitation of Christ. It is not an imitation of Christ. It is a participation of Christ. "For we are made partakers of Christ" (Heb. iii. 14). There are good things in Thomas a Kempis' *Imitation of Christ,* but the basic idea is false to the principles that underlie the Christian life. . . . For, what is impossible to me as an imitator of Christ, becomes perfectly natural as a participant of Christ. It is only when Christ nullifies the force of my inherent "selflife," and communicates to me a Divine life, that Christian living in its truest sense, is at all possible for me.[224]

Here then is a basic attitude of life. The branch must always be completely dependent on the vine for the fruit-producing flow

224. Huegel, p. 19.

of life. This does not etherealize the responsibility of the branch. To the contrary, the Lord makes it very concrete: "If ye keep my commandments, ye shall abide in my love; even as I have kept my Father's commandments and abide in his love" (John 15:10). But, lest the emphasis should be wrongly placed, the Lord adds these significant words in verse 16:

> Ye have not chosen me, but I have chosen you and ordained, that [*hina*] ye should go and bring forth fruit, and that your fruit should remain: that [*hina*] whatsoever ye shall ask of the Father in my name, he may give it you.

The two purpose (*hina*) clauses indicate that the "fruit perpetual" and "prayer effectual" are the Lord's doing. It is not the duty of the believer to produce fruit, but to abide in Christ, who desires to live out His life through the believer.

The results of such abiding have been outlined by Chafer as "pruning (v. 2), prayer effectual (v. 7), joy celestial (v. 11), and fruit perpetual (v. 16)."[225] The last of these is particularly prominent in the development of the figure of the vine and the branches. Thus, the question arises, What is the fruit that the vine produces in the branches? From the immediate context it appears that the fruit produced is love. The abiding life expresses itself in abounding love. This is also the teaching of 1 John 2:10: "He that loveth his brother abideth in the light."

The nature of this fruit is more fully explained by the apostle Paul: "But the fruit of the Spirit is love, joy, peace, longsuffering, kindness, goodness, faithfulness, meekness, self-control" (Gal 5:22-23*b*, ASV). In this passage, the fruit [*karpos*, singular] of the Spirit is contrasted with the aforementioned works [*erga*, plural] of the flesh. *Erga* directs the attention to outward activity; *karpos* emphasizes inward ability. A machine can work, but only that which has life can produce fruit. Lenski draws out this contrast of works and fruit:

225. Chafer, 4:60-61.

> He [Paul] does not say, "the *works* of the spirit" (v. 20, "the works of the flesh") but uses the nobler word, "the *fruit* of the spirit." Compare the significant expression, "the unfruitful works of darkness" (Eph. 5:11). "Fruit" is also singular although it is a collective. The flesh spreads out in many directions with its evil works; all its many activities are bad. The spirit follows one direction, *produces unit fruit* [italics not in the original].[226]

Thus, the fruit of the Spirit is a unity—not to be separated—and is the product of a life—the life of Christ lived out in the Christian by the Spirit.|| || || || || The Holy Spirit reproduces the life of Christ. This is the essence of Paul's thoughts in Galatians 4:19: "My little children, of whom I travail in birth again until *Christ be formed in you*" [italics not in the original].

When the apostle Paul proceeds to name the individual elements of the fruit unit, he begins with love. Whether one believes that love is the fruit of the Spirit and all else is a development of love, or that love is simply one of a ninefold fruit that is the result of the Holy Spirit producing the life of Christ in the believer, the fact remains that love is an inseparable part of the fruit unity and will be present in the life of the one who is abiding in Christ.

When one returns, then, to the upper room discourse he finds a strong emphasis on the fruit of the Spirit, which is love (cf. John 13:34-35; 14:15, 21, 23-24; 15:9-10, 12, 17; 17:26). The final words of the Lord's prayer to the Father are: "I have declared unto them thy name, and will declare it: that the love wherewith thou hast loved me may be in them, and I in them" (17:26). And this is precisely the work of the Holy Spirit—to produce the life of Christ in the believer. The abiding life results in abounding love. Only by this kind of life, Christ says,

226. Lenski, p. 290.

|| || || || ||The genitive of source (*tou pneumatos*) indicates that the fruit is from the Holy Spirit and not from the believer's efforts. This coincides with the teaching of the vine and the branches.

"shall all men know that ye are my disciples, if ye have love one to another" (John 13:35).

Inherent in this figure, then, is a principle of inestimable worth to the contemporary ecumenical emphasis of the churches. Contrary to the current emphasis, the stress here is not on the outward unification of organizational and denominational machinery. Rather, the emphasis is on the inward production of the life of Christ in those who are "in Christ." As Paul expressed it: "Christ formed in you" (Gal 4:19*b*). And as Christ prayed: "I in them" (John 17:26*b*). This kind of fruit will bring about a church unity that is not halted by denominational barricades. Rather, it will transcend them and reveal the true unity of the church of Jesus Christ. Thus, there is a spiritual unity that already exists because of the union of the branches in the Vine, but the manifestation of that unity depends upon the branch's abiding in the Vine. Christian unity, then, is not primarily a matter of organization, but of the "communion of the saints."

In summary, then, the figure of the vine and the branches has its unique contribution to the doctrine of the nature of the church. In the first place, it reveals in a unique way the inseparable relationship of the members of the church to their Lord. Christ does not say that He is the stem, but the Vine, of which His disciples are the branches. The whole includes the parts. Second, this figure vividly describes the results of this identification of the members of the church with their Lord. Because they are branches in the Vine, the fruit that is produced is not their fruit. The branches simply bear the fruit, and the fruit is the life of Christ Himself, which the Holy Spirit will form in every member of the church who is abiding in the Vine. This life of Christ will be manifested in love for the brethren—the other branches of the Vine.

7

THE DOCTRINE OF THE LOCAL CHURCH

To stop with the doctrine of the universal church would be neither honest scholarship nor intelligent biblical interpretation, for the body of Christ is not the working entity of God in the world today. The working method of God in the world at any given time is to carry out His purpose through the members of the body of Christ who are living in the world at that time, and the New Testament always views these members of the body as banded together in groups known as local churches. Thus the church is in the world in the form of local churches, which are physical organizations with physical relationships and definite physical responsibilities. The local church is God's agency in the world, transacting God's business. Any relationship or responsibility encumbent upon the universal church must eventually find its outworking through the localized counterpart. That these local churches hold a place of prime importance in the mind of God and are the means through which God's program is to be accomplished can be clearly shown by a careful study of the New Testament revelation.

I. THE REVELATION OF THE LOCAL CHURCH

THE DEVELOPMENT OF MEANING

In the previous discussion of *ekklesia* in chapter 4, it has been demonstrated that in its common, historical, nontechnical usage the word *ekklesia* simply means "an assembly"—a physical unity. When the word came to be used by Christ, however, it took on a specific Christian content, so that the "Jesus *ekklesia*" was quite different from the "Jewish *ekklesia*" or the "secular *ekklesia*" down the street. Thus, in the development of the word, it took on this specific Christian content and came to be used in a technical sense to mean "a Christian assembly"—both physical and spiritual unity. Concerning this development it has been observed that the meanings do not shade off into one another in abrupt, sudden changes, but in gradual, almost imperceptible growth.[1] In the earliest Christian usages of *ekklesia,* therefore, before the word had taken on a very definite Christian content, there is an extensive use of descriptive modifiers, for example, "the church of the Thessalonians which is in God the Father and in the Lord Jesus Christ" (1 Thess 1:1). As time progressed, however, the descriptive modifiers were dropped and the technical usage—both physical and spiritual unity—became the predominent usage.

THE FREQUENCY OF USAGE

In theological statement the technical usage of *ekklesia* speaks of the local church. The great majority of the usages of *ekklesia* in the New Testament are technical usages. While the number of times a word is used in a specific way does not prove anything conclusively, it establishes a certain pattern, which may reveal a basic underlying trend of thought. Thus, an examination of the New Testament reveals that out of a total of one hundred and fourteen occurrences, *ekklesia* refers to the local church at least ninety times.* In the singular it is used to

1. E. C. Dargan, *Ecclesiology,* p. 29.

*Matt 18:17 (2); Acts 5:11; 8:1, 3; 11:22, 26; 12:1, 5; 13:1; 14:23, 27; 15:3, 4, 22, 41; 16:5; 18:22; 20:17, 28; Rom 16:1, 4, 5, 16, 23; 1 Cor 1:2; 4:17; 6:4; 7:17; 11:16, 18, 22; 14:4, 5, 12, 19, 23, 28, 33, 34, 35; 16:1, 19 (2); 2 Cor 1:1; 8:1, 18, 19, 23, 24; 11:8, 28; 12:13; Gal 1:2, 22; Phil 4:15; Col 4:15, 16; 1 Thess 1:1; 2:14; 2 Thess 1:1, 4; 1 Tim 3:5, 15; 5:16; Philem 2; James 5:14; 3 John 6, 9, 10; Rev 1:4, 11, 20 (2); 2:1, 7, 8, 11, 12, 17, 18, 23, 29; 3:1, 6, 7, 13, 14, 22; 22:16.

denote either a single assembly in a particular locality (cf. Acts 8:1) or all local churches generally, without reference to any specific locality (cf. Acts 12:1). In the plural it refers to the sum of individual local churches in a named region (cf. 1 Thess 2:14), an indefinite region (cf. 1 Cor 7:17), or neither of the foregoing (cf. 2 Cor 11:8).

While the fact of extensive usage does not in itself prove that the local church is God's means of working in the world today, it offers undeniable proof that there is such an organization or institution known as the local church, and that it holds a place of great importance in the mind of God.

II. THE RELATIONSHIP BETWEEN THE UNIVERSAL AND THE LOCAL CHURCHES

A recognition of both the universal and local aspects is essential to any proper understanding of what the Scripture teaches about the church.† In the final analysis, however, the basic issue is how these two aspects of the church relate to each other. Are there two churches, different in their constitution, quality, membership, and sphere? Or is there just one church in which is found these two aspects? And if there is just one, how can the universal and local ideas concur or correspond? The dilemma may be resolved by observing what the Scripture says about the beginning and the growth of the church.

THE RELATION OF THE CHURCHES IN THEIR INAUGURATION

Previous discussion has demonstrated that the church had its beginning on the day of Pentecost. No other date fits the data furnished by the New Testament. And this testimony has been so convincing that Dosker says without qualification: "The almost universal opinion among theologians and exegetes is this:

†Confusion in this area led B. H. Carroll to make the following statement: "The theory of the coexistence, side by side, on earth of two churches of Christ, one formal and visible, the other real, invisible and spiritual, with different terms of membership, is exceedingly mischievous and is so confusing that every believer of it becomes muddled in running the lines of separation." *Ecclesia—The Church*, p. 23.

that Pentecost marks *the founding of the Christian church as an institution*."[2] The crucial question that must be answered here, then, is, What church began on the day of Pentecost? Was it the body of Christ, or was it the local church? The futility of attempting to solve this on the basis of the use of *ekklesia* itself is evidenced by Schmidt's survey of certain lexicographers.

> Grimm-Thayer puts the local Church first: "those who anywhere, in city or village, constitute such a company and are united in one body"; and gives second place to "the whole body of Christians scattered throughout the earth." Preuschen-Bauer does the same, but the Catholic Zorell reverses the order: first "the whole body of Christ," and second, "any particular Church, i.e. believers in Christ in any region or city. . . ." It is sometimes hard to decide which of these meanings to give to *ekklesia* and the dictionaries do not always agree.[3]

An examination of the implications of the advent of the Holy Spirit at Pentecost as well as the content of Acts 2 sheds much light on this area of disagreement.

Luke calls this basic group of individuals who were baptized with the Holy Spirit, to which others were added that same day and on subsequent days, simply "the church" (Acts 2:47; cf. also 5:11). He does not specify whether this is the local church or the universal church. On the one hand, the statement of the Apostle Paul in 1 Corinthians 12:13 concerning the baptism by the Holy Spirit into the body of Christ, which is the church (cf. Col 1:24), makes it certain that the universal church began on that momentous day. On the other hand, however, Thiessen makes an interesting observation about the local church.

> The local Church was founded at the same time. We read that there were 120 waiting for the promise of the Spirit when the day of Pentecost came. These 120 were the first ones to be

2. Henry E. Dosker, "Pentecost," in *The International Standard Bible Encyclopaedia*, ed. James Orr, 4:2318.
3. Karl Ludwig Schmidt, "The Church," in *Bible Key Words from Gerhard Kittel's Theologisches Wörterbuch zum Neuen Testament*, ed. and trans. J. R. Coates and H. P. Kingdon, 1. 2:1.

> baptized with the Spirit, and they became the charter members of the Jerusalem church. In response to the preaching of Peter and the other Apostles, 3,000 "received the word gladly," were baptized, and added unto them "that day" (Acts 2:14, 41). A little later this local church had grown to 5,000 (Acts 4:4). It is clear that the believers acted as a corporate unit. They had a definite doctrinal standard (Acts 2:42); they had fellowship with one another as believers *(Ibid);* they observed the ordinances of baptism and the Lord's Supper (vss. 42, 47); they met for public worship (vs. 46); and they contributed to the support of the needy (vs. 44, 45). Surely, we have here the marks of an organized local church, even if the organization was only loose as yet.[4]

One is almost driven to the conclusion that the church in both its universal and local aspects began at the very same moment and that in the pages of Scripture it is called merely "the church." And once it is admitted that both began on the day of Pentecost, the conclusion follows logically that the universal church and the local church, on the day of their commencement, were actually one and the same. This first local church was in reality the universal church; and the universal church, the body of Christ, expressed itself in one visible local church, the church at Jerusalem. For a brief period of time, at least, every member of the body of Christ was living on earth and was a part of the one local church. That one assembly was the visible expression of the universal church, the body of Christ. "We must remember," says McClain, "that in the beginning the spiritual Body of Christ was in the local church at Jerusalem. There was for a brief season one Body and one local Church."[5] In all probability it was composed exclusively of believers, for the opposition and persecution of unbelievers, as well as the general reproach of the name of Christ would have kept it pure.

Cremer senses this closeness between the universal and local

4. Henry Clarence Thiessen, *Introductory Lectures in Systematic Theology,* p. 410.
5. Alva J. McClain, "The Church."

aspects. He points out that basically *ekklesia* is the "redeemed community," but sometimes it means the whole Christian body, and sometimes the same New Testament redeemed community localized. He further points out that it is not always possible to differentiate between two meanings.[6] Getting right at the heart of the present discussion, Zorell remarks that Acts 2:47 and 5:11 and other passages may be understood in either sense, in view of the fact that at the beginning the universal church and the local church were one and the same.[7]

It seems reasonable to conclude, then, that ideally, in the mind of God, the local church and the universal church are closely related, the one being simply the active, working, visible counterpart of the other, and certainly the first church in Jerusalem, in its institution, fulfilled this ideal. Ideally, in the mind of God, every member of a local church is to be a true believer, a member of the body of Christ. In this sense, the membership is identical. It seems that, from God's viewpoint, this is what every local church is to be.

Recently, numerous writers have given expression to this viewpoint. Having spoken of the nature of the universal church, Fleming goes on to point out the strategic importance of the local churches: "These local congregations were expressions in this world of the true Church, microcosms which bore the same relation to the 'Head' as the universal Church itself did."[8] McClain sees them as the external and visible form of manifestation of the universal body of Christ. He says: "To employ a Kantian expression: they are the external framework through which the ideal Church is schematized."[9] Again, Stibbs explains:

> It is very important to recognise, as the Scriptural use of the unqualified name *ecclesia* explicitly indicates, that what is thus

6. Hermann Cremer, *Biblico-Theological Lexicon of New Testament Greek,* trans. William Urwich, pp. 334-35.
7. In Schmidt, 1. 2:2.
8. Peter Fleming, *The Church,* pp. 8-9.
9. McClain.

> locally constituted, and made visible and functioning, is genuine "Church." One may find a suggestive illustration in our regular method of reference to the moon. When one sees a thin crescent moon in the sky, one says, not, "There is a part of the moon," but "There is the moon." For the part that is visible is genuine moon; and, what is more, it is actually, though to us invisibly, united with all the rest of the moon. Similarly, a local Christian congregation is genuine Church become visible.[10]

It is interesting and significant to note the words of Barth on this subject.

> The first congregation was a visible group, which caused a visible public uproar. If the Church has not this visibility, then it is not the Church. When I say congregation, I am thinking primarily of the concrete form of the congregation in a particular place. . . . The mystery of the Church is that for the Holy Spirit it is not too small a thing to have such forms. Consequently, there are in truth not many Churches but *one* Church in terms of this or that *concrete* one, which should recognize itself as the one Church and in all the others as well. . . . In faith I attest that the concrete congregation to which I belong and for the life of which I am responsible, is appointed to the task of making in this place, in this form, the one, holy, universal Church visible.[11]

Finally, Schmidt concludes with these significant words:

> As the Church of the N. T. cannot be explained by playing off idea against reality, so also it cannot be explained by playing off the Church as the whole body of believers against the individual congregation. . . . Every true congregation of the primitive Church represented the whole body as really as the congregation at Jerusalem.[12]

In the various descriptions given, these men are attempting to

10. Alan M. Stibbs, *The Church Universal and Local,* p. 69.
11. Karl Barth, *Dogmatics in Outline,* pp. 142-45.
12. Schmidt, 1. 2:68-69.

point up a very important principle: the local church in its function and character stands in the same relation to Christ as the universal church. It is the church in miniature, a replica of the whole, giving visible and temporal expression to the invisible and eternal church.

> There is then only one church but it may be viewed universally because viewed from union with its Head or it may be viewed locally because viewed from the membership in a particular place.[13]

If this be true, then it is the believer's responsibility in establishing a local congregation to see to it that it corresponds to and is patterned after the nature of the true church. Thus, it remains to be seen if the rest of the New Testament teaches this close relationship that seems to have been true of the first local church of Jerusalem.

THE RELATION OF THE CHURCHES IN THEIR CONTINUATION

The question arises, Does the subsequent history of the early church in the Scripture substantiate this idea of the relationship between the local and universal church? Several lines of evidence seem to demand an affirmative answer to this question.

The relationship in the book of Acts

Appeal could be made to numerous examples in Acts, but two passages are especially significant. The first is found in Acts 9. As Saul journeyed to the city of Damascus to purge that city of Christians, he saw a great light, and falling to the earth he heard a voice speaking unto him, "Saul, Saul why persecutest thou me?" (v. 4). From the previous chapter (8:3) it is learned that Paul was actually persecuting the church, yet Christ asks, "Why persecutest thou me?" This comparison has often been used to teach the oneness of Christ and His body, the

13. Bruce Shelley, *Introducing Laymen to Their Church: Studies in Ecclesiology,* p. 3.

universal church. "Saul's first lesson was the mystical union between Christ and His Church."‡

As has been noted previously, this is a valid interpretation; the universal church is intrinsic to the meaning here, but the factor to be noted is that Paul was actually persecuting the visible church, the local churches of that day without reference to locality. Even as both ideas were present in Luke's description of the commencement of the church, so throughout his account of the Acts of the Apostles his usage of the word *ekklesia* involves both the universal and local aspects of the church. In his mind they seem to be closely related. It is inconceivable that he should use the same word, in the same book, alternatively filling it with such vastly different meaning, without some kind of explanation. Concerning this rather loose usage of *ekklesia* Schmidt declares:

> It must be . . . emphasized that Singular and Plural are used promiscuously. This does not mean that the *ekklesia* is divided into *ekklesiai,* or that, *vice versa,* it is formed by the coming together of the latter. It means that the *ekklesia* is present in a certain place, and this is not affected by the mention of *ekklesiai* elsewhere.[14]

Thus, this coincidence of the local and universal aspects in the early church is indicated in the Acts 9 passage.

Another significant passage is Acts 20:28. While his ship remained in harbor at Miletus, Paul sent a message to Ephesus, which was about thirty miles away; in that message he asked the elders of the church in that city to come and see him. The charge he gives to them is quite distinctive in that it is the only recorded Pauline speech delivered to Christians. It has a sense of urgency in it, for Paul perceives that the opposition to his

‡R. J. Knowling, "The Acts of the Apostles," in *The Expositor's Greek Testament,* ed. W. Robertson Nicoll, 2:232. This mystical union between Christ and the believers had already been taught in such passages as John 10:16; 14:20; 15:5.

14. Schmidt, 1. 2:7.

teaching in the Ephesian church will increase and that heretical teachers may be expected to arise—"fierce wolves . . . not sparing the flock" (v. 29, RSV). Therefore, the elders have a solemn responsibility to act as true shepherds to the sheep that have been entrusted to their care by the Holy Spirit Himself. Thus, he charges them:

> Take heed therefore unto yourselves, and to all the flock, over which the Holy Ghost hath made you overseers, to feed [shepherd] the church of God, which he hath purchased with his own blood (Acts 20:28).

When Paul says that the elders must shepherd the church of God, the local element is undoubtedly present, for it was their particular local church of God that they were to nourish. But the universal element is not absent. Bruce observes:

> Their responsibility was all the greater in that the flock which they were called upon to tend was no other than the congregation of God which He had purchased for Himself . . . and the ransom-price was nothing less than the life blood of His beloved Son.[15]

Ephesians 1 places the idea of redemption through Christ's blood, a blessing the believer had in Christ, as a member of the body of Christ, in the realm of "body truth." But in the present passage it is related to the flock among them in Ephesus.

Speaking of Paul's last words to the Ephesian elders, Hort states:

> They are part of St. Paul's solemn farewell to the cherished Ecclesia of his own founding. He begins with the actual circumstances of the moment, the local Ephesian community, which was the flock committed to the Ephesian Elders, and then goes on to say that that little flock had a right to believe itself to be the Ecclesia of God which He had purchased to be His own possession at so unspeakable a price. Of course in strictness

15. F. F. Bruce, *Commentary on the Book of the Acts,* p. 416.

> the words belong only to the one universal Christian Ecclesia: but here they are transferred to the individual Ecclesia of Ephesus, which alone these Elders were charged to shepherd.[16]

Thus, although today one sometimes finds those who perceive a clear-cut dichotomy between the two aspects of the church, in the minds of the human authors of Scripture there was not that dichotomy. Rather, the particular local *ekklesia* represents the universal *ekklesia,* and, through participation in the redemption of Christ, mystically comprehends the whole of which it is the local manifestation.

The relationship in the epistles

The close relationship of the universal and local aspects of the church is amply attested in the epistles. Of special significance in this regard are the salutations of certain epistles and the figures of the local church. Some have expressed the belief that the local church is a man-made affair and of little consequence compared with the spiritual body. The evidence presented in the salutations to the local churches seems to militate against this idea. Paul writes to "the church of the Thessalonians which is in God the Father and in the Lord Jesus Christ" (1 Thess 1:1). Using the plural, he writes: "For ye, brethren, became followers of the churches of God which in Judaea are in Christ Jesus" (1 Thess 2:14). In both 1 Corinthians 1:2 and 2 Corinthians 1:1 Paul calls the believers he is addressing "the church of God which is at Corinth." The phrase "church of God" has definite universal connotations; it is vast and all-embracing. But Paul writes to the church of God at Corinth. This universal church of God has distinct visible expression in the local church at Corinth. Paul "associates them with a larger whole, of which they are only one of the members."[17] "Of this

16. Fenton John Anthony Hort, *The Christian Ecclesia,* pp. 102-3.
17. Frederick Louis Godet, *Commentary on the First Epistle of St. Paul to the Corinthians,* 1:45.

universal Church, each local church is a miniature pattern."[18] In Romans 16:16 Paul says, "The churches of Christ salute you." These salutations and others confirm the fact that, rather than being only man-made, the local churches are directly related to Christ and are owned by Him. The close identity of the two aspects (human and divine), as well as the expression of the universal in the local, is clearly seen in these salutations.

The relation of the local assembly to the universal church is also seen in the divinely intended characteristics that are clearly expressed in the figures of the local church. From these figures the local churches can learn from the Scripture itself more of the ways in which God himself intended them to function. Out of the many meaningful metaphors come at least four that are used on different occasions to describe both the church universal and the local church, namely temple, body, bride, and flock. The very fact that these are used of both the universal and local aspects of the church is very significant to the present argument.§ As Fleming says:

> A very important principle may be seen: the local church in its function and character stands in the same relation to Christ as the universal Church. It is the Church in miniature, a replica of the whole, giving visible and temporal expression to the invisible and eternal Church.[19]

The first of these figures, the temple metaphor, finds its major application to the local church in 1 Corinthians 3:16-17. Paul writes:

> Know ye not that ye are the temple of God, and that the Spirit of God dwelleth in you? If any man defile the temple of God, him shall God destroy; for the temple of God is holy, which temple ye are.

18. Joseph A. Beet, *A Commentary on St. Paul's Epistles to the Corinthians,* p. 223.

§Because this close relationship exists, much of what was said under the development of this subject in chapter 5 may be applied at this point.

19. Fleming, p. 10.

In the previous verses Paul speaks of the local church at Corinth under the metaphor of a building ("ye are God's building" [v. 9]). Paul was the expert master-builder who laid the foundation in Christ, and others built upon the foundation. After issuing a warning as to the kind of materials men use in the construction, Paul reminds them of the seriousness of their labors, for this is not just any kind of a building. It is the temple of God. Findlay explains:

> The expression *naos Theou* . . . accentuates the *Theou oikodome,* expounded since ver. 9: "Do you not know that you are (a building no less sacred than) *God's temple?"*[20]

The word *naos is* anarthrous and should not be translated *"the* temple"; but neither should it be translated *"a* temple," which seems to take away from the qualitative force of the anarthrous construction.[21] Plummer's explanation seems more to the point:

> Not "a temple of God" but "God's Temple." There is but one Temple, embodied equally truly in the whole Church, in the local Church, and in the individual Christian; the local Church is meant here.[22]

The meaning of *naos* as contrasted to *hieron* has been examined previously; however, it should be remembered that in the Temple structure the *naos* is the Temple in the restricted sense—the Holy of Holies and the Most Holy Place—whereas, the *hieron* included the entire compass of the sacred enclosure. The *naos* was the habitation of God. Under such sacred terminology, Paul describes the local church (even the church at Corinth). The local church is the holy sanctuary of God. It is the dwelling place of God.

It is not surprising then that such strong words of condem-

20. G. G. Findlay, "The First Epistle of Paul to the Corinthians," in *The Expositor's Greek Testament,* ed. W. Robertson Nicoll, 2:793.
21. William Douglas Chamberlain, *An Exegetical Grammar of the Greek New Testament,* p. 57.
22. Archibald Robertson and Alfred Plummer, *A Critical and Exegetical Commentary on the First Epistle of St. Paul to the Corinthians,* p. 66.

nation fall upon those who would attempt to destroy the character and testimony of the local church. The King James Version mars the effect by translating the verb first "defile" and then "destroy." There is a solemn repetition of the same verb in the future active indicative (cf. *phtheirei* with *phtherei*). "One destruction is requited by another destruction."[23] Robertson's comments on these words are striking:

> This old verb *phtheiro* means to corrupt, to deprave, to destroy. It is a gross sin to be a church-wrecker. There are actually a few preachers who leave behind them a ruin like a tornado in their path. Him shall God destroy (*phtherei touton ho theos*). . . . The condition is the first class and is assumed to be true. Then the punishment is certain and equally effective. *The church-wrecker God will wreck* [italics not in the original].[24]

God's local assembly is a "holy" institution and it is not to be tampered with without grave danger. A temple is a meeting place of God and man—a place of worship. Woe be to that man who would destroy the sanctity of the local assembly of believers. Speaking of these who seek to destroy, Ironside says:

> I tremble when I think of what it will mean for men who today profess to be servants of Christ and ministers of God but despise this Book and deny every fundamental truth of Holy Scripture, and yet for filthy lucre's sake get into pulpits of orthodox churches, and instead of building gold, silver or precious stones are only building wood, hay, and stubble, and they are destroying, as much as in them is, the temple of God. God says, "I will destroy them; they will have to account to Me by-and-by."[25]

This figure, then, serves as a major contribution to the discussion of the character of the local church. When the local assem-

23. Robertson and Plummer, p. 67.
24. A. T. Robertson, *Word Pictures in the New Testament,* 4:99.
25. H. A. Ironside, *Addresses on the First Epistle to the Corinthians,* p. 135.

bly of believers meets together, it should recognize itself as a dwelling place of God, the Holy Spirit. As Stibbs says: "This should be the first inescapable reality in a Christian congregation; God is here. This is 'the church of the living God.' "[26]

A second metaphor used to describe both the church universal and the local church is that of the body. Paul says to the Christians at Corinth: "Now ye are the body of Christ and members in particular" (1 Cor 12:27). In verses 14-26 Paul had developed with deliberateness and completeness the figure of the *body*. Although the spiritual gifts he mentioned in the previous context may be many and various, yet those who are endowed with them constitute one organic whole. Thus, the purpose of the body metaphor was to stress the unity of a living organism. No two parts are exactly alike, but all discharge different functions for the good of the whole. After developing the figure, Paul applies it to the Christians at Corinth: "Now ye are body of Christ." The article before "body of Christ" is noticeably absent. Lenski analyzes the problem:

> Paul is writing to the Corinthians and therefore cannot use the article: you are *"the"* body of Christ, for this might make the impression that they are Christ's entire body. Yet the absence of the article does not mean that the Corinthians are "a body" of Christ, for no plurality of bodies of Christ exists.[27]

A similar situation was faced in the previous discussion of the local church as a temple. It was observed that the absence of the article brought emphasis to the qualitative aspect. As Dana and Mantey state: "Sometimes with a noun which the context proves to be definite the article is not used. This places stress upon the qualitative aspect of the noun rather than its mere identity."[28] If this be true, then Paul is saying that the local

26. Stibbs, p. 71.
27. R. C. H. Lenski, *The Interpretation of St. Paul's First and Second Epistle to the Corinthians*, p. 535.
28. H. E. Dana and Julius R. Mantey, *A Manual Grammar of the Greek New Testament*, p. 149.

church at Corinth is of the same quality as the universal church, the body of Christ. As Lenski explains, the Corinthian church is not one of many bodies of Christ, but rather, "just what Christ's body is as to nature and quality, that you Corinthians are."[29] The members of which he speaks are the Corinthian believers.

A very helpful, expanded explanation of this concept of 1 Corinthians 12:27 is given by Robertson and Plummer:

> "Body of Christ" is the quality of the whole which each of them individually helps to constitute. . . . It does not mean, "Ye are *the* Body of Christ," although that translation is admissible, and indicates the truth that each Christian community is the Universal Church in miniature; nor, "Ye are Christ's Body," which makes "Christ's" emphatic, whereas the emphasis is on *soma* as the antithesis of *mele*. Least of all does it mean, "Ye are a Body of Christ," as if St. Paul were insisting that the Corinthians were only *a* Church and not *the* Church, a meaning which is quite remote from the passage. Nowhere in the Pauline Epistles is there the idea that the one Ecclesia is made up of many Ecclesiae. . . . He means here that the nature of the whole of which the Corinthians are parts is that it is Body of Christ, not any other kind of whole. Consequently, whatever gift each one of them receives is not to be hidden away, or selfishly enjoyed, or exhibited for show, but to be used for the good of the whole community.[30]

Here, then, is strong biblical evidence for the contention that each local church is in itself an expression, or miniature pattern, of the universal church, the body of Christ.

Again, the bride metaphor is used of the local church as well as of the universal church. Being anxious over the church at Corinth lest it fall victim to the subtleties of Satan, Paul writes this reminder: "For I am jealous over you with godly jealousy: for I have espoused you to one husband, that I may present you

29. Lenski, p. 535.
30. Robertson and Plummer, pp. 277-78.

as a chaste virgin to Christ" (2 Cor 11:3). This local assembly was like an engaged maiden. It had been espoused by the apostle to one husband, even Christ. Lenski explains: "The bride did not betroth herself. Her parents, her father, or whoever was the head of the house did that. Paul acts this part. He had founded the Corinthian congregation, he was its father."[31] Thus, Paul pledged the Corinthian church in betrothal to her husband—to Christ. Tasker notes:

> Paul looks forward to the Lord's return, not least because then the time for the marriage of the bride will have come (see Rev. xix. 7), and he will have the inestimable privilege of presenting his converts, the church of God at Corinth among them, as *a chaste virgin to Christ*, the heavenly Bridegroom.[32]

Although this bride metaphor may, by extension, be applied to the universal church (cf. Eph 5:27), in this context the primary interpretation is of the local church at Corinth. "Paul's relation was so intimate with the Corinthians as author of their espousals to Christ, that he could not fail to feel the deepest interest in their fidelity."[33] This stands as further evidence, then, of the close relation in which the apostle Paul holds the church universal and the local church.

The final figure used of both aspects of the church is that of the flock. The usage of this flock metaphor in 1 Peter 5:2-4 is especially significant in this discussion of the relation of the universal and local aspects of the church. Although this has been discussed previously, it is necessary to summarize the teaching at this point. Peter commands the elders among the saints scattered throughout Pontus, Galatia, Cappadocia, Asia, and Bithynia to "feed the flock of God which is among you" (v. 3). God has only one flock—the universal church—but it has been distributed in the different localities where the elders

31. Lenski, p. 1236.
32. R. V. G. Tasker, *The Second Epistle of Paul to the Corinthians*, p. 145.
33. Charles Hodge, *An Exposition of the Second Epistle to the Corinthians*, pp. 251-52.

live and work. As is stated in verse 3, portions of the flock have been entrusted to the elders in the various geographical areas. It has been portioned out among the shepherds. They are charged with shepherding, not "lording it over," those portions of God's flock assigned to them. In so doing, they will become an example, or pattern, for the entire flock. Thus, the close relation of the universal and local aspects is clearly exhibited here.

Now, when one turns to Acts 20:28 he finds that the Ephesian "portion" (cf. 1 Pet 5:3) of the flock is itself called "the flock" (*toi poimnioi*). In fact, it is referred to as "all [*panti*] the flock." This local group is in turn related to "the church of God, which he hath purchased with his own blood." Thus, when the elders shepherd their local flock, they are in actuality shepherding "the church of God"—the universal church.

Without laboring this point any further, it seems that Scripture gives ample evidence of the intimate relationship that exists between the universal and local aspects of the church. The New Testament is clear as to what the local churches ought to be, what God has intended for them to be. It seems significant that three of these four figures are spoken of the church at Corinth, a most unlikely prospect for such designations. Surely, it is a sobering thought, for example, for the local church to realize that it is "the temple of God," the sanctuary and habitation of God.

The relationship in the Apocalypse

Even as the church universal is to look to Christ, the Head of the church, for its direction and guidance, so each individual local church is directly responsible to Christ. It is doubtful that any passage in the New Testament contains more clear, concise, and comprehensive instruction on the life and work of the local church than the second and third chapters of the book of Revelation. In a very vivid portrayal, John presents Christ as walking about in the midst of the churches. Not only does He walk among them, however, but also He is intimately acquainted with them. In each of the seven letters to the churches Christ begins with the phrase "I know." He is the divine overseer of the churches. He dwells with them. He walks among them. He inspects them. He knows them. Stott says:

> He is walking among the lampstands, patrolling and supervising His churches. He is the chief pastor, the chief bishop. Then what is His view of His Church? In each of the seven letters which follow, the risen Christ lays emphasis, either in rebuke or in commendation, on one particular characteristic of an ideal church. Put together, these characteristics constitute the seven marks of a true and living church. They tell us what Christ thinks of His Church, both as it is and as it should be.[34]

Thus, in these seven epistles to the churches as in the other epistles, there is no lack of clarity as to God's revealed will concerning the pattern of the local church. Unfortunately, however, there is evidence of a lack of apprehension of this truth on the part of the members of the local churches. For this reason, oftentimes a local church loses its opportunity as a "candlestick," or testimony, for Jesus Christ.

This tendency to drift from the New Testament pattern cannot be denied, and perhaps no Scripture more vividly portrays this departure than the address to the church of Laodicea in Revelation 3:14-19.|| Here in Laodicea was a local assembly that had lost the New Testament concept of the church. So far had it departed from the pattern that it could no longer be considered a visible manifestation or representation of the church universal. No longer could it be considered God's working agent here on earth, for Christ was forced to say of them, "I will spue thee out of my mouth" (v. 16). Thus, McClain says, "A

34. John R. W. Stott, *What Christ Thinks of the Church,* p. 20.

||Cf. also 1 Tim 1:3-7; 6:3-5; 2 Tim 2:20-21; 4:3-4; Titus 1:10-16; 2 Pet 2:1-22; 3:3; 1 John 2:19; 2 John 7; Jude 4; 18-19.

local church may depart so far from the New Testament ideal that Christ may disown it."[35] Yet even for this tepid church the day of grace was not ended, for if such were the case there would have been no reason for the epistle. The King James Version translates the phrase "I will spue thee out of my mouth" as if the verb were *thelo;* however, it is *mello,* "I am about to." The act is impending; the Lord is still waiting.[36] Trench explains:

> The threat does not present itself as one about to be put into *immediate* execution. The long-suffering of Christ has not been all exhausted; *mello se emesai,* "I am about," or "I have it in my mind to spue thee out of my mouth. . . ." But if executed, it implies nothing less than absolute rejection, being equivalent to that *"I will remove* thy candlestick out of his place" (ii. 5), uttered against the Ephesian Angel."[37]

It must be admitted, then, that although it ought not to be, it is possible that a person may be in a local church, but outside of the body of Christ. Consequently, it becomes necessary to emphasize the distinction between the two so that the basic issue of salvation be not clouded. And while Scripture does not emphasize it, it certainly does allow for it, by teaching the existence of a universal church, by revealing the existence of local churches, and by indicating the presence of unbelievers in local churches.

This constant possibility of permeation of the local church by unbelief emphasizes the fact that no church has a secure and permanent place in the world. The local church is continuously on trial. A solemn reminder of this is seen in the warning given to the church of Ephesus, which had been well taught by the apostle Paul:

> Remember therefore from whence thou art fallen, and re-

35. McClain.
36. William F. Arndt and F. Wilbur Gingrich, *A Greek-English Lexicon of the New Testament and Other Early Christian Literature,* pp. 501-2.
37. Richard Chenevix Trench, *Commentary on the Epistles to the Seven Churches in Asia,* p. 198.

> pent, and do the first works; or else I will come unto thee quickly, and will remove thy candlestick out of his place, except thou repent (Rev 2:6).

Apparently the church rallied to the appeal, since in the next generation Ignatius could address them thus:

> Ignatius, who is [also called] Theophorus, to the Church which is blessed in the greatness of God the Father, and perfected; to her who was selected from eternity, that she might be at all times for glory, which abideth, and is unchangeable, and is perfected and chosen in the purpose of truth by the will of the Father of Jesus Christ our God; to her who is worthy of happiness; to her who is at Ephesus, in Jesus Christ, in joy which is unblameable: [wishes] abundance of happiness.
>
> Inasmuch as your name, which is greatly beloved, is acceptable to me in God, [your name] which ye have acquired by nature, through a right and just will, and also by the faith and love of Jesus Christ our Saviour, and ye are imitators of God, and are fervent in the blood of God, and have speedily completed a work congenial to you.[38]

But later it lapsed again, and the church of Ephesus was removed out of its place of testimony. The results of this solemn divine visitation are related by Swete:

> The little railway station and hotel and a few poor dwelling-houses of Ayasaluk (*Hágiois Theológos*), which now command the ruins of the city, are eloquent of the doom which has overtaken both Ephesus and its church.[39]

A traveler visiting the village "found only three Christians there," writes Trench, "and these sunken in such ignorance and apathy as scarcely to have heard the names of St. Paul or St. John."[40] Such an example should prove to be sufficient warning for those who would contemplate a departure from the New

38. Ignatius *The Second Epistle of Ignatius to the Ephesians* Salutation-1.
39. Henry Barclay Swete, *The Apocalypse of St. John*, p. 28.
40. Trench, p. 81.

Testament pattern of the church. The warning to Ephesus is just as appropriate to local churches today.

III. THE RESULTANT IMPLICATIONS OF THIS RELATIONSHIP

While the New Testament does allow for a distinction that must be clearly understood, especially as it pertains to matters of salvation, the close relationship that God intends is what ought to concern believers today in the organization and administration of the local churches and in their service for the Lord through this God-intended agency, the local church. The fact that each local assembly is in itself (or ought to be) an expression of the body of Christ has pertinent and practical implications affecting the overall approach of each local church. Local Christian congregations are only likely to walk more worthily of their high calling if they first learn from Scripture itself more of the ways in which God Himself intends for them to function.

IT DEMANDS A REGENERATE MEMBERSHIP

The force of this statement operates in two directions. The local church may include *only* the regenerate as members, but it also includes *all* the regenerate as members.

It includes only the regenerate

The Word of God represents regeneration not as a process of gradual growth unto godliness, but as a radical and thorough change in man's spiritual condition, which change is totally the work of God. It is pictured as a new birth (John 3:3-7), a new creation (2 Cor 5:17), and a quickening (Eph 2:5). Thus, the subjects "have passed from death unto life." Concerning these figures of regeneration, Marsh says:

> They show that it is not a development, but a creation; that it is to the soul what natural birth is to the man, or what resur-

> rection is to the body. The idea of its necessity did not originate with man.[41]

This fact of regeneration is the portion of every member of the body of Christ. Each member of the church universal has been called "out of darkness into his marvellous light" (1 Pet 2:9). So, then, if each local church is a miniature pattern of the universal church, only the truly regenerate make up its membership. Kuiper writes:

> Very strictly speaking, the membership of the visible church coincides with that of the invisible church. And since the invisible church consists of the regenerate, only they rate as members of the visible church. To use a Biblical expression, only the regenerate are *of* the visible church (1 John 2:19).[42]

This was surely the viewpoint of the New Testament writers. The church at Rome "are the called of Christ Jesus" (Rom 1:6-7). The church at Corinth "are sanctified in Christ Jesus, called to be saints" (1 Cor 1:2). The Colossians are "saints and faithful brethren in Christ" (Col 1:2). The church of the Thessalonians was "in God the Father and in the Lord Jesus Christ" (1 Thess 1:1). Similar statements could be cited for each of the local churches addressed. Although the appellations "pure witness," "pure church," and "true church" are used satirically by some modern writers,[43] the goal is, nevertheless, an entirely biblical one.

This kind of demand, however, cuts directly across the grain of many contemporary expressions of the nature of the local church. Some would plead scriptural precedent for a mixture of good and evil men within the church on the basis of the wheat and tares of Matthew 13. A representative of this position says:

> After all, it is not our duty to draw the circle of fellowship; our duty is to live in it. We are not to pull out the tares; Christ

41. W. H. H. Marsh, *The New Testament Church*, p. 140.
42. R. B. Kuiper, *The Glorious Body of Christ*, p. 26.
43. See Edward John Carnell, "Orthodoxy: Cultic vs. Classical," *Christian Century* 77:378.

> has assigned that job to the angels at the end of the age, and He tells us why: *"Lest in gathering the tares you root up the wheat along with them."*[44]

Even a cursory reading of this passage, however, reveals that the Lord is not speaking of membership in a local church. In the first place, the church was not even a matter of revelation at the time of Matthew 13. Not until Matthew 16:18 does the Lord announce the *future* building of His church. Nowhere in this passage is the church even mentioned. Secondly, the chapter simply presents the course of Christendom between the first and second advents of Christ.#

An even more extreme view among some contemporary neo-evangelicals is that the presence or absence of heretics in the church has nothing to do with the nature of the church.[45] Setting Machen aside as one having a "cultic" mentality, Carnell asks:

> Does the church become apostate when it has modernists in its agencies and among its officially supported missionaries? The older Presbyterians knew enough about Reformed ecclesiology to answer this in the negative. Unfaithful ministers do *not* render the church apostate.[46]

Thus, it is his belief that so long as the creed of the churches has not been changed, conservatives are free to remain in them no matter how large the liberal majority may be. One should "judge the claims of a church by its official creed or confession, not by the lives of its members."[47] As support for this view, appeal is repeatedly made to the extreme corruption of Israel and the Temple, from which the prophets and priests of God

44. Donald Grey Barnhouse, "We Are One Body in Christ," *Eternity* 8:42.
#Cf. E. W. Palmer, *The Key to the Bible: The Parables of Matthew Thirteen*, p. 6: "There is in Matthew 13 a sevenfold picture of the rule, or government, of Heaven in the present-day world, largely through Christendom. This is *not the church* which is made up of only saved, born-again individuals, but is a mixture of saved and lost members, possessing and professing followers of Jesus Christ."
45. Edward John Carnell, *The Case for Orthodox Theology*, p. 136.
46. Ibid., p. 115.
47. Ibid., pp. 133-34.

did not separate themselves.[48] It seems strange, indeed, to appeal to the nation Israel as a pattern for developing a doctrine of the nature of the church, which began as an entirely new entity at Pentecost. Surely, the New Testament gives sufficient information as to the nature of the local church, which is the temple of the Holy Spirit, the body of Christ, the bride of Christ, the flock of God.

The end result of this inclusivist policy is disastrous. In its series on "Great Churches of America," *The Christian Century* reported on one large institution that takes in eight to ten persons a Sunday, most of whom have never been seen before. When the leaders are warned of the dangers inherent in such a mass approach, they say:

> Maybe. But what is a church? It certainly isn't a club of saints. We believe it is a fellowship of those who are seeking after righteousness, and we believe that when they knock at the doors of the Church, then is the time to swing them open and take them in. Our major responsibility starts once they cross that threshold. Our principle, in other words, isn't exclusion; it's inclusion, and then using every bit of resources we have here, both personal and material, to do the best job of Christian nurture of which we are capable.[49]

It was against just such a careless attitude toward the visible church that Machen spoke when he asked:

> But what is the trouble with the visible Church? What is the reason for its obvious weakness? . . . One cause is perfectly plain—the Church of today has been unfaithful to her Lord by admitting great companies of non-Christian persons, not only into her membership, but into her teaching agencies. . . . The greatest menace to the Christian Church today comes not from the enemies outside, but from the enemies within.[50]

48. Ibid., pp. 115-16, 134.
49. "Deep in the Heart of Texas: Highland Park Methodist, Dallas—A Mighty Church in the Booming Southwest," *Christian Century* 69:1315.
50. J. Gresham Machen, *Christianity and Liberalism*, pp. 159-60.

Such policies of compromise as are advocated by some contemporary writers can never produce the church unity they desire. Rather, it can only serve to destroy the local churches and their testimony. Herman Sasse, former professor of church history at the University of Erlangen and for ten years active in the World Conference on Faith and Order, has stated:

> Will the Commission on Faith and Order understand that no true unity can ever be attained through its present methods of compromise? . . .
>
> . . . *The reason for our inability to express doctrinal consensus* is to be found in the *tragic fact that modern Protestantism has lost, along with the understanding of the dogma of the Church,* in her nature, her function, and her content, *the ability to think dogmatically,* that is, to think *in terms of a trans-subjective truth which is given to us in the revelation of God. This is also the reason we are no longer able to reject error and heresy.*[51]

There is no real paradox** between the purity and the unity of the church. There is a harmony between the two. This harmony cannot be achieved, however, by compromising the purity of the church. True spiritual unity can only be achieved among those who share a common life with the Lord Jesus Christ. In this light, Sanderson says:

> A greater appreciation then of the doctrine of the Church can serve to correct false tendencies and perhaps to hold errant emotions in check as wild charges are brought to the full-orbed Scripture doctrine. When this is done, purity and unity will be seen in their true light, and neither will be sacrificed for the other.[52]

Thus, having seen in the previous study the exclusive estate

51. Hermann Sasse, "Facing New Delhi: Crisis of the Ecumenical Movement," *Christianity Today* 5:582.

**See J. I. Packer, *Evangelism and the Sovereignty of God,* pp. 19-20: "The point of a paradox . . . is that what creates the appearance of contradiction is not the facts, but the words. The contradiction is verbal, but not real."

52. John W. Sanderson, *Fundamentalism and Its Critics,* p. 39.

of the local church and its responsibility to be a miniature pattern of the church universal, it behooves the membership of these churches to maintain an eternal vigilance to see that only those who are truly born again share in and create the intimacy of the local fellowship. Membership procedures ought to be sufficiently thorough to exclude any whose salvation is in doubt. The body of Christ consists of persons who have been joined to Christ by faith in His shed blood. The local body needs to demand the same.

It includes all the regenerate

Even as the New Testament knows of no church member who is unregenerate, so also it knows of no regenerate person who is not a member of a local church. As has been seen previously, the local churches are owned by Christ (cf. Rom 16:16). They were established throughout the Roman Empire by God's order to unite all believers in Christ in any convenient geographical area into autonomous, Spirit-directed congregations. The local church is a body in which every member is obligated to assume his part. McClain states:

> *The necessity of membership in the local church is never questioned in the New Testament.* It is taken for granted. Had we asked the believers of the Apostolic period whether it was essential to join a church, they would not have known what we were talking about. Every believer became a member of a church. It was involved in the very profession he made in Christ. . . . Furthermore, when the history of the church upon earth is prophetically written, the Holy Spirit speaks of it as consisting of local churches. Rev. 1-3. . . . There is no authority for abandoning the local church altogether for a purely individualistic Christian existence.[53]

Two passages of Scripture seem especially significant in this regard. The first of these is Acts 2:47: "And the Lord added

53. McClain.

to the church daily such as should be saved." The present passive participle *sozomenous* is more correctly rendered in the American Standard Version: "those that were being saved" (cf. 1 Cor 1:18; 2 Cor 2:15). Thus, the Lord Himself was adding to the local as well as the universal church, day by day, those who were being saved. Kuiper states:

> Not only does the Lord Christ require of those who are saved that they unite with the church; He Himself joins them to the church. And the reference is unmistakably to the *visible* church.[54]

It is the Lord whose prerogative it is to add new members to His own community. Thus, the true local church is not built by man, but by God.

A second significant passage is Hebrews 10:24-25:

> And let us consider one another to provoke unto love and to good works: Not forsaking the assembling of ourselves together, as the manner of some is; but exhorting one another: And so much the more as ye see the day approaching.

This is the third in a series of three exhortations given to believer-priests on the basis of their superior privileges of access to God as the result of the removal of barriers by their great High Priest (vv. 19-21). Despite these high privileges, these believers are in need of exhortation. They are not worshiping, for they have lost their confidence; because they have lost their confidence, they are renouncing and abandoning the assembly—the local church—itself. The writer reminds them, however, that it is their duty to keep on considering how to provoke one another unto love and good works. And there was one particular way in which they could do this, "by not forsaking the assembling of ourselves together, as the manner of some is; but exhorting one another." The word "forsaking" (*egkataleipontes*)

54. Kuiper, p. 112.

has the idea of "not leaving behind, not leaving in the lurch."[55] And *episunagoge* is more than the act of assembling; it is the assembly itself.[56] Thus, they were not to leave the assembly in the lurch. Rather, the Christian duty of stimulating others to love and good works was to be achieved through the fellowship of the local assembly. Griffith Thomas writes:

> Isolation is a certain danger and involves inevitable weakness. While we are justified in relation to Christ solitarily and alone, we are sanctified in connection with other Christians, and we shall never know what it is to be a "saint" unless we make much of "the communion of saints."[57]

Mackintosh has very aptly pointed out that the word *saint* never occurs in the singular, and that "invariably it is plural."[58]

Thus, God demands that Christians not neglect the fellowship with His people in the local church. Failure on the part of Christians to unite with the local church is an evidence of spiritual coldness and declension. On the other hand, there is strength in legitimate union.

IT DEMANDS AN AUTONOMOUS MEMBERSHIP

Whatever term one may use to describe this factor seems to require explanation. The local church of the New Testament was autonomous; that is, in its government it was independent of outside earthly rulership, whether religious or secular. The relationship to the church universal, however, emphasizes the fact that this was much more than the exercise of the right of self-government. For example, as a representative of the body of Christ, this self-government was exercised in loyalty to the headship of Jesus Christ. As Fleming has said:

55. Robertson, 5:412.
56. Brooke Foss Westcott, *The Epistle to the Hebrews: The Greek Text with Notes and Essays*, p. 325.
57. W. H. Griffith Thomas, *Let Us Go On: The Secret of Christian Progress in the Epistle to the Hebrews*, p. 134.
58. H. R. Mackintosh, *The Divine Initiative*, p. 100.

> We will . . . never look for the Head of the Church to be found on earth. For as Christ in the heavens is Head of the whole Church, so He is also Head of every local assembly of believers. Thus, the churches should recognize no supreme earthly ruler of the faithful, no human vicar, no special representative of God on earth; their "Head" is in heaven.[59]

One might add, however, that the Head of the local church is pictured in Scripture as actively supervising "in the midst" (Rev 2:1) of the churches. Each local church is directly responsible to Christ and dependent on Him for leadership and sustenance, even as is the body of Christ in its entirety.

The independence of the local church from external, earthly rulership is also evidenced in the fact that it is the temple of the Holy Spirit. Even as the New Testament church is a creation of the Holy Spirit, so it is His temple—His sanctuary. Thus, it is to be administered under the guidance of the Holy Spirit. The presence and guidance of the Holy Spirit in the early church is amply attested in the book of Acts.†† One clear and specific instance is His charge to the church at Antioch: "Separate me Paul and Barnabas for the work whereunto I have called them" (Acts 13:2). Here the Holy Spirit not only supervises the affairs of a local church, but asserts the prerogative of directing the carrying out of the final commission. Gordon writes:

> The Holy Spirit, the sovereign administrator of the church, commissions those whom he sovereignly chooses, instead of recruiting those who may judge themselves fit for his service.[60]

This is to be the pattern of government in the local church. To this sovereign leadership of the Holy Spirit the local church is to be responsive and submissive. Its corporate action is either declarative of this, or else it is an act of rebelliousness. A solemn fact is that it is possible for a local church to quench the minis-

59. Fleming, p. 10.
††Cf. Acts 5:3, 9; 13:2, 4; 15:28; 20:28.
60. A. J. Gordon, *The Holy Spirit in Missions*, p. 81.

try of the Holy Spirit in its assembly (cf. 1 Thess 5:19).‡‡ It remains, then, to seek out the results of the application of this principle in relation to other churches and in relation to civil government.

In relation to other churches

Recognizing the Holy Spirit, who dwells in the churches, as an all-sufficient guide, Cody states:

> If a local church has the Holy Spirit indwelling in it there exists no need to subject it to any other body because no other body can possibly have anything greater or wiser than the Holy Spirit. Equality and independence follows as inevitably from the gift of the Holy Spirit as does individual equality and independence.[61]

Because of this headship of Christ and indwelling of the Holy Spirit, no church or council of churches had the right to dictate to a local church. There was no super-organization seeking to impose its will on the individual churches. Actions of local New Testament churches and specific statements in the New Testament repeatedly affirm the truth of this autonomy of the local church. Evidence supporting the supreme authority of the local church in its own affairs is summarized in outline form by McClain:

> (1) *The local church has authority to judge its own membership* (1 Cor. 5:13). Even an apostle does not assume to excommunicate a member, but calls upon the local church to do it.
>
> (2) *The local church has authority to elect its own officers* (Acts 6:1-6). Not even the apostles assume to choose the officers of a local church, but call upon the church to do it.
>
> (3) *The local church has authority to guard and observe the*

‡‡In 1 Thessalonians 5:19 ff, Paul is warning the churches of a mechanical order that would discourage the manifestation of the Spirit and His free operation. Cf. C. F. Hogg and W. E. Vine, *The Epistles to the Thessalonians*, pp. 194-96.

61. In J. Clyde Turner, *The New Testament Doctrine of the Church*, pp. 47-48.

ordinances (1 Cor. 11:23 "I delivered unto you"). Not to the *clergy,* the elders or bishops. This means that no church can be deprived of these sacred rites, as the hierarchy of Rome assumes. Even if all ministers should be withdrawn, the local church could elect others to lead its services.

(4) *The local church has authority to settle its own internal difficulties* (1 Cor. 6:1-5). Paul doesn't appoint a committee, but directs the *Church* to look after the matter. . . .

(5) *The local church has authority in matters involving the relations of different local churches* (Acts 15:1-2, 22, 23, 25, 30). This was not a conference of ecclesiastical overlords, but of two local churches, each sovereign in its own affairs. One protests through chosen delegates (2). The other answers through chosen delegates (22). Even the apostles do not assume exclusive authority in the matter.

(6) *All "Church Government in the New Testament applies only to local bodies."* (See Forrester in I.S.B.E.).

(7) *The authority of the local church is final as far as its own affairs are concerned.* (See Matt. 18:17). There is no higher court.§§

Thus, no denominational affiliations are indicated anywhere in Scripture. Local churches are not organizationally related to other local churches. Such organizational alignments only serve to obscure the true nature of the church.

This fact of the independence and autonomy of the local church gives rise to the question of how matters of common interest to all the churches may be attended to. Although there is not a great deal of scriptural evidence on the matter of cooperation between churches, there are two New Testament precedents that throw very instructive light on the subject. The first of these is the Jerusalem conference recorded in Acts 15. Certain individuals in the church at Jerusalem did try to control the policies of the church at Antioch by trying to make them submit to the rite of circumcision (v. 1). Messengers from the

§§McClain. For an extended discussion of the several points see Augustus Hopkins Strong, *Systematic Theology,* pp. 904-8.

church at Antioch were appointed and sent to Jerusalem to discuss their common problem. The result was a repudiation of the troublemakers and a friendly letter of recommendations to the church at Antioch: "Then pleased it the apostles and elders with the whole church, to send chosen men of their own company to Antioch with Paul and Barnabas" (v. 22). The latter meeting, which is recorded in Acts 15:22-29, contains no note of authority, but exhorts Gentile Christians to abstain from certain practices that would give offense to their Jewish brethren. If any church could have laid claim to the right to dictate to another church, it would have been the church at Jerusalem, for it was the first church and for some time the only church. But it made no effort to dictate. Rather, a plan of cooperation was achieved under the direction of the Holy Spirit.

A second New Testament precedent bearing upon the matter of cooperation between churches is Paul's collection for the destitute saints in Jerusalem (cf. Acts 24:17; Rom 15:25-26, Gal 2:10). Paul called on all the churches to participate in this work of charity, and they made a willing and ready response. When the money was raised it was delivered to a committee selected from various local churches; that committee was to carry the money to Jerusalem and disburse it in accord with the best judgment of the committee, under the guidance of the Holy Spirit (cf. Acts 20:4; 2 Cor 8:19).

Thus, there seems to be good ground in the New Testament for interchurch cooperation, but care should be exercised not to infringe upon the rights of the local church.

In relation to civil government

As the churches are not to be dominated by any external ecclesiastical authority, so they are not to be interfered with, in their church life, by civil government. The focal point of this teaching is prominently identified in contemporary discussion as the separation of church and state. This teaching of religious liberty, which teaching has had such a vital and welcome influence on the history of the church in America, stems largely from the biblical emphasis of the "left-wing" reformers.|| || While it is not the purpose of this writer to expound on the issues of separation of church and state, the basic principles should be noted.

According to the principles of Christ, the areas of church and state present two distinct and separate responsibilities to the Christian. The guiding principle is given in Matthew 22:21. "Render therefore unto Caesar the things which are Caesar's; and unto God the things that are God's." Here are two distinct spheres of obligation, which spheres are to be kept separate. On the one hand, there are certain duties the Christian owes to his government. These are spoken of at some length by both Paul (Rom 13:1-7) and Peter (1 Pet 2:13-17). On the other hand, there are duties a Christian owes to God, and these are supreme. When there is a conflict between the laws of man and the laws of God, the Christian must obey God. Thus, Peter and the other apostles were bold to affirm, "We ought to obey God rather than men" (Acts 5:29). Thus, Forrester states: "It follows that only where the life of a church touches the civic life of a community has the civil authority any right to interfere."[62] The grave dangers arising today from failure to maintain the biblical distinction are summarized by Turner.

> The danger is twofold. There is a growing tendency on the part of the government to invade the realm of religion and impose restrictions on the churches. On the other hand, there is a persistent effort on the part of certain religious organizaitons to bring the church and state into partnership. This is true especially in education.[63]

|| ||Several contemporary writers have given themselves to a defense of "free church" principles. Cf. Gunnar Westin, *The Free Church Through the Ages;* Franklin Hamlin Littell, *The Free Church;* also by Littell, *The Anabaptist View of the Church: A Study in the Origins of Sectarian Protestantism.*

62. E. J. Forrester, "Church Government," in *The International Standard Bible Encyclopaedia,* ed. James Orr, 1:655.
63. Turner, p. 51.

An assured result of the union of church and state is the destruction of local church autonomy.

By way of summary, then, the local congregation is a "church of Christ," related directly to Christ as its Head, and a temple of the Holy Spirit, who indwells and guides the assembly. Such a group must not be subjected to any external authority, whether ecclesiastical or civil. Such churches are wholly competent to govern their own affairs.

IT DEMANDS AN ORDERED AND PURPOSEFUL MEMBERSHIP

If any general impression is gained from a reading of 1 Corinthians 12, it is certainly the orderliness and purpose of the body of Christ. There are differences of gifts, there are diversities of administration, but there is order and purpose. Each member is in the proper place and doing the proper thing at the proper time. Thus, when Paul said, "Ye are the body of Christ," emphasizing the qualitative relation to the universal body of Christ, there were significant implications as to the order that should characterize their assembly. The word "order" occurs four times in connection with the proper direction and control of church affairs. Twice it is used in relation to the regulation of the service of worship by the church (cf. 1 Cor 11:34; 14:40) and twice it is used in connection with the organization of the church (cf. Col 2:5; Titus 1:5).[64] The Greek term for *order* is *taxis,* from the verb *tasso.* It was primarily a military term that was in common use to express the most precise and exact order. It was commonly used of "drawing up in rank and file, order or disposition of an army." Again, it was the "battle array, order of battle."[65] This order is to be evidenced in the use of spiritual gifts and in the application of the principles of church government.

64. Marsh, pp. 235-37.
65. Henry George Liddell and Robert Scott, *A Greek-English Lexicon,* p. 1756.

As evidenced in the gifts

God's Word explicitly states that every member of the body of Christ is gifted for service (cf. 1 Cor 12:7; Eph 4:7; 1 Pet 4:10) and that every member is to be using the gift or gifts God has bestowed. "As every man hath received the gift, even so minister the same one to another, as good stewards of the manifold grace of God" (1 Pet 4:10). The implication for the local church is quite apparent. There ought to be no idle members, but rather opportunities for service for every person. These responsibilities ought to be accepted joyfully and carried out diligently and in orderliness for God's glory.

This principle of order in the use of the gifts was applied by Paul to the Corinthian church because of its disorderly use of one of the gifts. He rebuked the Corinthians for their self-elation because of the possession of special gifts and for the confusion occasioned thereby in the services of the church. He reminds them that "God is not the author of confusion, but of peace, as in all churches of the saints" (1 Cor 14:33). Thus, Robertson remarks, "Orderly reverence is a mark of the churches."[66] The character of God Himself and the practice of all the churches of the saints stand behind Paul's final exhortation to the local church at Corinth: "Let all things be done decently and in order" (1 Cor 14:40). The adverb decently (*euschemonos*) is from an adjective meaning well formed, hence, symmetrical, adapted to attract and make a favorable impression upon the spectator.[67] Robertson and Plummer explain:

> Ecclesiastical decorum is meant; beauty and harmony prevail in God's universe, where each part discharges its proper function without slackness or encroachment; and beauty and harmony ought to prevail in the worship of God.[68]

The phrase "in order" translates *kata taxin,* a phrase that occurs

66. Robertson, 4:185.
67. Liddell and Scott, p. 734.
68. Robertson and Plummer, p. 328.

nowhere else in either the New Testament or the Septuagint, but is used of the Greeks' manner of fighting at Salamis as opposed to the disorderly efforts of the barbarians.[69] Taking the two expressions together (*euschemonos kai kata taxin*) Milligan says that they are used "to express the beauty and harmony that result in the Church from every member's keeping his own place."[70] "Not tumultuously as in a mob," says Hodge, "but as a well-ordered army, where every one keeps his place, and acts at the proper time and in the proper way."[71]

Behind all these statements one can see the symmetry, beauty, decorum, and orderliness of the body of Christ, which is to have its manifestation in the local churches, especially with regard to the use of the gifts. Where gifts need to be developed and training is lacking, it is the responsibility of the local church to develop the gifts and provide the training so that the local assembly may increase unto the edifying of itself, even as the body (cf. Eph 4:7-16). Thus, there is a goal toward which the use of the gifts is to contribute. And that goal should be attained through the most orderly, efficient, capable means possible. That is the way God has constructed the body of Christ. Now He has left to believers the responsibility of conducting the local churches after the same pattern.

As evidenced in the government

Sending Titus to Crete, Paul instructs him to "set in order the things that are wanting" (Titus 1:5). This implies that some sort of government had been established previously in the churches to which Titus was sent, but that it was not yet perfectly organized. Reconstructing the situation, White says:

> As I left you in Crete to carry out completely the arrangements for the organization of the Church there, which I set

69. Ibid.
70. George Milligan, *St. Paul's Epistles to the Thessalonians*, p. 54.
71. Charles Hodge, *An Exposition of the First Epistle to the Corinthians*, pp. 307-8.

> before you in detail, let me remind you of the necessary qualifications of presbyters.[72]

Thus, Paul is concerned that the local churches be organized not partially, but completely after the pattern he had given them under inspiration of the Holy Spirit. Incomplete organization is often the occasion of the most serious disorder.

Again, to the Colossians, Paul says: "I am with you in spirit, joying and beholding your order, and the steadfastness of your faith in Christ." Here again he uses the Greek term *taxin,* which implies the most precise and exact order. Contrary to Paul's concern over the Cretan churches because of their incomplete organization, here he is joyful upon beholding their order and their faith. Nicholson says:

> Notice the words *"orderly array,"* which means each one in his place, submissive to discipline, submissive to them that are over them in the Lord, no self-will, no isolated action. . . . Order and faith are thus united, and the provision of either without the other marks an unprosperous church, for in that case the one becomes formalism and the other fanaticism.[73]

Thus, not only is the local church a temple of the Holy Spirit in which each member exercises the privileges of a believer-priest, but it is also a flock in which the members submit to the rulership of the undershepherds, who are responsible to the Chief Shepherd for their souls.

> Obey them that have the rule over you, and submit yourselves: for they watch for your souls, as they that must give an account, that they may do it with joy, and not with grief: for that is unprofitable for you (Heb 13:17).

That things were to be done orderly and systematically, even as Paul commanded the Corinthians (1 Cor 14:40) and for

72. Newport J. D. White, "The Epistle to Titus," in *The Expositor's Greek Testament,* ed. W. Robertson Nicoll, 4:186.
73. W. R. Nicholson, *Oneness with Christ: Popular Studies in the Epistle to the Colossians,* ed. James M. Gray, p. 183.

which he commended the Colossians (Col 2:5), was carried out throughout the organizational structure of the local church. Because it is not within the scope of this book to treat these factors, they can only be noted in passing as supporting evidence of the orderliness of the local church. There were local church officers (Acts 6:1-6; 1 Tim 3:1-16; Titus 1:5-9), and proper submission to them is scriptural (Heb 13:17; 1 Pet 5:1-5). There was what closely approximates an orderly local church election in Acts 6:1-6.## There were local church rolls, at least for the widows who were to receive help (1 Tim 5:9, ASV), and evidence seems to support the fact that there were carefully kept membership records, for all were associated with a particular local church. The numbers were known (Acts 1:15; 2:41; 4:4); election of officers assumes a roll (Acts 6:2-5); and church discipline assumes a roll (1 Cor 5: 13).*** There were rules for orderly procedures and practices in the local churches (1 Cor 11:1-34; 14:1-40). There was an orderly system of local church finances (1 Cor 16:2). The example of these early New Testament churches becomes the pattern for local churches today. As a representation of the church universal, the body of Christ, each local church should have the symmetry, the beauty, the decorum, the orderliness characteristic of the archetype.

IT DEMANDS A UNIFIED MEMBERSHIP

The subject of the unity of the church is one of the most

##Cf. Marsh, pp. 243-44: "The Hellenistic Jews in the body of believers complained to the apostles that 'their widows were neglected in the daily ministration.' Then the multitude of the disciples were called together by the apostles. The word rendered multitude is *plēthos*. It never denotes a small number. By no sort of linguistic jugglery can it be made to mean a few individuals, or a committee sent by the church to confer with the apostles about the matter. It here denotes the whole body of believers who by this time were termed the church. . . . This is the first corporate act of a New Testament church of which we have a record."

***Cf. McClain. Speaking of 1 Corinthians 5:19, he says: "Surely this did not mean exclusion from the ordinary meetings of the church. How could the sinner be helped if thus excluded? Obviously, it meant formal severance of his membership in the local church. This would require a vote, and hence the determination of the voters."

prominent, if not *the most* prominent, subjects of contemporary theological discussion. So commonplace has it become that the Greek word *oikoumene,* the slogan of the ecumenicists, comes across the lips of layman and theologian alike. The goal of these advocates of ecumenicity is one universal church, a superchurch. In his chapter "The Future Goal of the Ecumenical Movement," David Hedegard thoroughly documents this ecumenical intention. Summarizing the position, he says:

> Thus the merging of all churches into one united but very differentiated church is regarded as being the real solution. It is also pointed out that this church should have some sort of supreme government.[74]

This, then, leads to the major question, What is the organizational unity described in the New Testament?

Ecumenical unity denied

In the past it has been common, especially among liberal scholars, to assume the organizational unity of the apostolic church.[75] More recently, however, liberal scholars have admitted that such was plainly not the case.

> We have seen that there was no single comprehensive organization of the churches; nor can a universal pattern of organization be traced among all the churches severally. . . . Not only was there no such thing as "organic union"; there was a great amount of regional, even local, independence.[76]

Most significant at this point are the results of J. Theodore Meuller's study of Revelation 2-3:

> There is in these two dynamic chapters no stress whatever on outward church organization as it is being urged in many areas of Christendom today. The seven representative churches

74. David Hedegard, *Ecumenism and the Bible,* p. 215.
75. F. W. Dillistone, *The Structure of the Divine Society,* p. 87.
76. John Knox, *The Early Church and the Coming Great Church,* p. 83.

> of Asia, humanly speaking, were greatly in need of such organization, for they were troubled by spiritual foes in many ways. But nowhere does the Holy Spirit suggest any group organization of these churches as a means of offense or defense. Every congregation is addressed as an independent unit and is exhorted both to preserve the doctrine delivered to it by the apostolic proclamation and to reject all errors opposing that doctrine. That, too, is the method of St. Paul, who consistently admonishes the local churches to preserve the apostolic doctrine and practice together with their sister churches. "We have no such custom, neither the churches of God" (1 Cor. 11:16). "As in all churches of the saints, let your women keep silence in the churches" (1 Cor. 14:34). The apostolic emphasis is always on unity of doctrine and practice, but never on external church organization.[77]

The lack of such organizational unity among the New Testament churches, however, does not deter the present-day ecumenicists in their drive for the superchurch. In his study of contemporary ecclesiological thought, J. Robert Nelson reminds his readers that few of today's church leaders look to the New Testament for the model of church form and order. He explains:

> In view of the profound difference between first-century and twentieth-century society, primitive forms can hardly be considered binding upon the Church today, particularly when the Church is known as a religious, rather than a sociological, entity. That the continuing Church is dynamic and changing, rather than static and changeless, in form hardly needs to be argued, even with those who hold most rigidly to the ancient traditions.[78]

But is all one finds in the New Testament simply a product of the first century? Or does inspiration of the Scriptures consti-

77. "Symposium: The Body Christ Heads," *Christianity Today* 1:9.
78. J. Robert Nelson, *The Realm of Redemption*, p. 2.

tute it in principle an enduring authority, even in matters of church form and order, for the contemporary world?

Local church unity demanded

While the New Testament does not give even the slightest hint of organizational unity beyond the local church, it specifically commands both organizational and spiritual unity within the bounds of the local church. This is achieved by a series of "submissions" in the local church. In the first place, the entire assembly is to be submissive to the Holy Spirit and His guidance in the choosing of officers and representatives (cf. Acts 6:3; 13:2-4) so that the resultant elected leadership may be said to have been set apart by the Holy Spirit (cf. Acts 13:2-4; 20:28). Having selected these men as leaders of the local organized assembly, the members of that assembly are commanded to submit to them (Heb 13:17). In turn, the officers of each local church, as undershepherds, are directly responsible to the Chief Shepherd (1 Pet 5:4; Heb 13:17). Such a pattern of submission is certainly in keeping with the thesis that the local church is a miniature manifestation of the universal body of Christ. Because of proper submission, there is in the human body diversity of function within a perfect unity. Failure of any member of the human body in this submission is classified as a freak or monstrosity. Such is also the case with the body of Christ and its local manifestation. In summarizing the teaching of Hebrews 13:15-17, Pink states:

> Most comprehensive and all-inclusive are the exhortations found in vv. 15-17. The first respects our *spiritual* obligation, Godwards, rendering unto Him that which is His due (v. 15). The second respects our *social* obligation, rendering unto our needy fellows that which the requirements of charity dictates, according to our ability. The third has respect to our *ecclesiastical* obligation, rendering unto these officers in the church that

> submission and respect to which they are entitled by virtue of position and authority which Christ has accorded them. This is a Gospel institution, which can only be disregarded to the manifest dishonour of the Lord and to our own great loss.[79]

Finally, and very important, it must be recognized that central to the maintenance of this unity is a strict adherence to the doctrine that has been delivered in the infallible, inerrant Word of God. Speaking to the churches Paul says, "mark them which cause divisions and offences contrary to the doctrine which ye have learned; and avoid them" (Rom 16:17). Again, "If any man preach any other gospel unto you than that ye have received, let him be accursed" (Gal 1:9). It should be carefully noted that where doctrinal dissipation occurs, ecclesiastical submission disappears. Thus, the basic principle of Christian unity is Christ Himself and the doctrine concerning Him, which doctrine the apostles faithfully transmitted to the churches. This was the repeatedly resounding appeal to the seven churches in Asia: "He that hath an ear, let him hear what the Spirit saith to the churches." The issue was repeatedly doctrinal. And this is precisely the point that seems to escape the thinking of the modern ecumenical movement, which is willing to have unity on the basis of the least common denominator of doctrinal agreement.[80] As Berkouwer warns, the church dare not neglect its "uniqueness" in its drive for "unity."[81] This uniqueness is found in its Christ-centered doctrinal content.

Two factors, then, are particularly pertinent to the idea of unity. First, although the New Testament teaches the spiritual unity of the universal church, organizational unity never goes beyond the local church. Second, this organizational unity will falter and fail unless it is accompanied by a steady and strict adherence to the unique doctrinal truth centered in Jesus Christ.

79. Arthur W. Pink, *An Exposition of Hebrews*, 3:325.
80. Sasse, 5:580-82.
81. "Symposium: The Body Christ Heads," 1:4-5.

IT DEMANDS A GROWING MEMBERSHIP

Without this factor all that has been advocated to this point becomes cold and sterile. This is the goal of the decorum and order, the gifts and government, the unity and uniqueness. God never intended that the local church should be a static organization. It is built out of living stones, regenerate persons, who are provided with all the spiritual gifts and resources necessary in order that there might be increase, both qualitatively and quantitatively. Kuiper writes:

> When the question arises whether the task of the church is to build up its members in the faith or to bring the gospel to those who are outside the church, some choose for one of these to the practical exclusion of the other. But that betrays a serious lack of balance. The church must do both.[82]

Qualitative growth

He who would evangelize those outside the church while neglecting the building up of those within the church is much like a general who leads his army forth to conquer other lands but fails to keep strong the base of operations in his own land. The ultimate purpose of Christ in giving gifted men to the church was "for the perfecting of the saints, unto the work of ministering, with the building up of the body of Christ" (Eph 4:12, ASV). If this is the case then they would

> be no longer children, tossed to and fro and carried about with every wind of doctrine by the sleight of men, in craftiness, after the wiles of error; but speaking the truth in love, may grow up in all things into him, who is head, even Christ (Eph 4:14-15, ASV).

Now this purpose of God for the entire body of Christ finds its outworking and visible manifestation in the local body, which is the working agency of God on earth. It is God's front line. The problem with many local assemblies, however, is that

82. Kuiper, p. 158.

they never experience this growth and thus make poor front line material. As Robertson says, "Some Christians are quite content to remain 'babes' in Christ and never cut their eyeteeth (Heb 5:11-14), the victims of every charlatan who comes along."[83] Many are the local churches that for years have simply existed. Their leadership remains as unqualified as in its inception. The spiritual gifts and gifted men God has provided continue to be resources largely untapped. The local church is not an end in itself, but a means to the end. As is pointed out in Hebrews 10:24-25, faithfulness to the local assembly provides the key opportunity for considering one another and provoking the brethren unto love and good works. Lang states:

> This is no easy-going friendliness. "To consider" means to consider diligently and earnestly (katanoomen). "To provoke" is the English word paroxysm, an intense word. This demands an intensity of love which can set others on fire with love.[84]

Delitzsch interprets this provocation as "a stirring up the brethren to a rivalry in good works."[85] As one directs his attention to his Christian brother's circumstances and situation, his purpose is to spur that brother on to realize the mighty potentialities of God's gifts within him and to allow the Holy Spirit to live out Christ's life through him.

The apostle Paul reminds the local church at Corinth that this growth is to be a continual process among them. Using the figure of the local church as God's husbandry (*georgion*†††), he says, "I have planted, Apollos watered; but God gave the increase" (1 Cor 3:6). Paul had started the church and Apollos had succeeded him as the minister, but God caused the growing.

83. Robertson, 4:538.
84. George Henry Lang, *Epistle to the Hebrews: A Practical Treatise for Plain and Serious Readers*, p. 169.
85. Franz Delitzsch, *Commentary on the Epistle to the Hebrews*, trans. Thomas L. Kingsbury, 2:181.
†††Arndt and Gingrich (p. 156) translate this as "cultivated land."

There is a very significant change in tenses from aorists to imperfect to be noted here:

> The aorists sum up, as wholes, the initial work of Paul (Acts xviii. 1-18) and the fostering ministry of Apollos (Acts xviii. 24-xix. 1): the imperfect indicates what was going on *throughout;* God was all along causing the increase (Acts xiv. 27, xvi. 14).[86]

Perhaps, a failure to understand that the church must always look to God for its increase and growth and not to man explains why the Corinthian church ceased in its growth, thus forcing Paul to address them as babes.

The local church is to grow qualitatively, but this may be abruptly halted by a myopic vision that fails to see beyond church leaders to God, who alone causes increase. The danger here is far from imaginary, for the church that fails to build up its constituency qualitatively will soon have no quantitative outreach.

Quantitative growth

When the membership of a local church is growing qualitatively, it will have the burden of quantitative growth. The stagnant character of many local churches is simply evidence of their spiritual immaturity. When the local church begins to share the heart of Christ and to see the multitudes as He saw them, they get a burden for outreach—for missions, both at home and abroad. A contemporary authority in the field of local church extension, Luther L. Grubb, has stated: "The reason for the existence of the church is missions."[87] Certainly this was central to the thinking of the early church, whose members propagated the name of Jesus regardless of the warnings of torture and even death. Luke writes: "And daily in the temple, and in every house, they ceased not to teach and preach Jesus Christ" (Acts 5:42). Surely this is the appropriate response to

86. Robertson and Plummer, p. 57.
87. Luther L. Grubb, "The Genius of Church Extension."

the divinely appointed commission to the church: "Go ye therefore and make disciples of all the nations, baptizing them in the name of the Father and of the Son and of the Holy Ghost: teaching them to observe whatsoever things I have commanded you" (Matt 28:19, ASV). Thus, the scope of the commission to the church at any particular time is the entire earth. Such a task demands a vigorous evangelical testimony that results in a continually expanding outreach. The Thessalonian assembly forms a splendid pattern: "For not only has the word of the Lord sounded forth from you . . . but your faith in God has gone forth everywhere" (1 Thess 1:8, RSV).

It is not enough to say that "missions" is the reason for the existence of the local church. Looking at this task from a slightly different perspective, it must be stressed that the local church is the key to missions. No one would want to deny the good being done by the various agencies of Christian service outside the local church, but "the basic and central institution for witnessing and general outreach is the *local church.*"[88] Missions are dependent on a vital local church program. This is true whether the particular endeavor of missionary outreach is, for example, Unevangelized Fields Mission, United Indian Missions, Campus Crusade for Christ, Young Life Campaign, Navigators, or Youth For Christ. The preparation, inspiration, and resources for all these stem from the local church. Any Christian enterprise has its inception in the local church. Because of this strategic position of the local church, one can begin to understand the significance of Grubb's statement that "The pastor of the local church is God's key man on earth."[89]

This does not by any means deprecate the work of the various "arms of the church," but it does stress that these organizations should work hand in hand with the central working agency of God on earth—the local church. Stibbs points up this New Testament pattern:

88. Ibid.
89. Ibid.

> Evangelism can only worthily be done when whole congregations give themselves to its support. So, when God called Barnabas and Paul to go forth to preach to the Gentiles, He also called the local Church at Antioch, *of which Paul and Barnabas were at that time members*, to share in the responsibility for sending them forth. Again, much later in his life, when Paul was hoping to go to Spain, he wrote to the Christians at Rome to tell them of his plans, and to express the hope that they would help him forward on his journey. This means, therefore, that when individual missionaries go forth to preach the Gospel, whether in distant lands or to the godless nearer home, they ought to go not only as sent by God, but also as workers publicly separated to this service by a local church.[90]

In recent years there has been a tendency among some Christian enterprises, which received their material and resources from the local church, to fail to maintain a reciprocal relationship with the local church. Failing to recognize the centrality of the local church in the carrying out of God's program, some have failed to inculcate a healthy respect for the local church in the minds of their converts. Some have placed a strong emphasis on the "invisible church," which is the "true church" almost to the exclusion of the local church. This is not a healthy situation, and the lack of a close working relationship has caused difficulties for both sides in certain quarters. Fortunately, among some of these "arms of the church" there has been a wholesome emphasis on the centrality of the local church. A case in point is the statement of purpose of the Word of Life Bible Clubs, an organization attempting to help meet the needs of teenagers. It states its aim as follows:

> The club program has adopted a system of 3 progressive levels that have been designed to give incentive and put the teenager to work *within the structure of the local church.* The teen will receive a certificate upon completion of the necessary requirements in each level. The outstanding assignment is the

90. Stibbs, p. 74.

> Christian service assignment. This must be maintained for a definite number of weeks. *The assignments are afforded by the local church, thus giving a direct tie-in to that ministry* [italics not in the original].

This seems to be in harmony with the New Testament pattern of evangelical outreach.

In summary, then, the local church is to be a growing organization, both qualitatively and quantitatively. Thus, a double responsibility falls upon the shoulders of the local assembly. The decline of either will result in the stagnation or decease of the other. Because the local church is God's working agency on earth, it behooves all Christian organizations to maintain a close working relationship with "the churches of Christ" (Rom 16:16).

8

SUMMARY AND CONCLUSION

The ecumenical dialogue concerning the nature of the church has really only just begun. As the last pages of this book are written (1962), the ecumenical movement reaches a significant milestone with the convening of the third assembly of the World Council of Churches in New Delhi, India. This will undoubtedly prove to be another move in the direction and eventual emergence of the long-feared superchurch. Of significance is the fact that for the first time, the Vatican has authorized observers (five) to attend a World Council of Churches meeting.[1] Perhaps this is a feeler in preparation for the coming ecumenical council of the Roman Catholic Church, which is making renewed and intensive efforts to realize her concept of the church, a universal visible institution under the autocratic headship of one man who is supposed to be the vicar of Christ. But, whether liberal Protestant or Roman Catholic, the goal is much the same—visible, corporate unity.

It has not been the purpose of this study, however, simply to discover and descry the inherent defects of the ecumenical emphasis. This purpose in itself would hardly be worth the time expended. To the contrary, it has been seen that some very serious problems face the theologian of orthodox persuasion concerning the nature of the church, especially as he relates the local assembly to the body of Christ. The apparent unbal-

1. "New Delhi Marks Ecumenical Milestone," *Christianity Today* 6:146.

ance that presently exists in much contemporary orthodox discussion concerning the "relationship" of these aspects of the church has formed the core of the desire for this present investigation. All too frequently even among evangelical Christians there is a lack of appreciation for the church.

Realizing that it is much easier to understand the present if one has some knowledge of its roots in the past, this writer has assayed to evaluate the evidence of history and its explanation of the church (chap. 2). The study of the early church Fathers failed to produce any exact definitions of the church, but it did uncover some trends, or budding emphases that became most significant when they reached their full bloom. It is very clear that the earliest of the Fathers placed a strong emphasis on the local church, especially on the unity of that group as a fellowship of believers. But there is sufficient evidence to indicate that these writers were not unaware that these local churches were visible representations of the church, the body of Christ, to which all believers in Christ belong. Before long, however, the rise of persecution without and heresies within brought about the desire for organizational unity of all the churches and centralization of power. This opened the way for a hierarchal development that reached its climax doctrinally in the ecclesiology of Cyprian and Augustine. The historical outworking of this development was seen in the rise of the papacy and in the universal church on earth. Contrary to the early church emphasis, which limited organizational unity to the local assembly, the medieval writers extended the organizational aspect to all Christendom. The church was equated with the kingdom of God on earth headed by the pope, Christ's vicar on earth. A natural conclusion of such a teaching was that outside of this earthly hierarchal organization there was no salvation or forgiveness of sin.

The Reformers recovered part of the early church teaching, but most of them were still interested in maintaining the medieval pattern of the universal church on earth. Although they were interested in purifying its doctrine, the Lutheran, Reformed, and Anglican churches all saddled their members with a state-controlled church. It is true that they made a decisive break with the organizational unity of Rome, but they put a sacramental unity in its place. While they attempted to separate ecclesiology and soteriology, they never quite succeeded, for they felt that there was no salvation outside the universal church on earth. A strong distinction between the "invisible church" and the "visible church" seems to have been used by them as an escape from the charge of unregenerate persons in the church. The parable of the wheat and the tares was commonly used as a defense of this position.

A more thorough reform was made by the "radical," or "left-wing," Reformers, who demanded a complete separation of the church from the state. They emphasized that the church was a voluntarily gathered assembly of baptized believers exercising discipline apart from control by the state. This teaching had its beginnings long before the Reformation in the various groups that persistently opposed the hierarchal organization. But it reached its most forceful and consistent defense among the radical Reformers, namely, the Anabaptists of the continental reformation and the Separatists of the English reformation. The ecclesiology of these groups has had a most notable influence on the growth and development of the church in America.

The history of the church in America has not developed the doctrine of the church beyond that which was evident in the four streams of Reformation thought. Rather, it has adopted and maintained one or the other of the various presentations of the ecclesiological doctrine that came out of the Reformation. It has been seen, however, that the free atmosphere of the American scene provided a choice of opportunity for the propagation of the free church principles. Thus, while there was no development of new doctrine, there was a place to practice that which had previously been restricted by established church systems.

Not until the twentieth century and, more particularly, the initial meeting of the World Council of Churches, in Amsterdam, was a new burst of energy expended in the examination of the nature of the church. This inaugurated a new age of interest in the church, which age presents a pattern of viewpoints equally as variegated as that of the Reformation. Common to all the viewpoints is an attempt to deal with the matter of the unity of the church. A survey of these contemporary viewpoints has been set forth in chapter three. It has been seen that the Roman Catholic doctrine of the church falls into two divisions, namely, the mystical body of Christ and the church on earth. These do not refer to two different churches, for the constituency of each is the same, but they refer to two aspects of the church. Because of the identification of the mystical body with the visible church, the Roman Catholic conclusion is that there is no salvation outside the visible church. Although there are numerous books on the Roman Catholic-Protestant dialogue and ecumenical interests, it has been noted that any "return" of Protestants to Rome must involve the recognition of the pope as the viceregent of Christ.

The examination of contemporary Protestantism evidences great diversity of opinion about the church as compared to the unanimity that characterizes (as one might expect) the Roman Catholic dogmatism. Liberalism, being strongly influenced by the social gospel, saw little need for the local churches, which simply impeded the progress of the transformation of society by feverishly clinging to their ecclesiastical dogmas and traditions. The church was regarded as being a strictly human, mundane organization that was extraneous to the Christian faith.

Neoliberalism, reacting against the worldly, human organization of the liberals, brought in a new sense of the importance of the church. Neoliberals have come to believe that there is a church over and beyond the split denominations. It is a living society, begun in the work of Jesus and continuing that work through the ages. Thus, it is not simply a social organization; it is a divine institution, founded by God. This institution is often referred to by neoliberals as the *koinonia,* the spiritual fellowship of all those who have committed themselves to the reign of God. One must not be deceived by the seeming orthodoxy, for in reality it is a subtle form of existentialism: the church is simply a subjective state of being as regards the I-Thou encounter. Neoliberalism denies that the organized church was in the plan of Christ.

Neoorthodoxy has some striking similarities to neoliberalism as regards the doctrine of the church, especially concerning the fluid nature of it. The church is an "event"; that is, the church is not constituted once for all; rather, it is continually being recreated by renewed divine activity. There are striking differences, however. Not only does Barth give much greater place to the Holy Spirit as the Creator of the church, but, whereas neoliberalism tends to think of the organized church as a necessary evil, Barth feels that it is *the church.* Finally, he believes that the one, holy, universal church exists in each of the local congregations.

Neoevangelicalism finds one of its most serious differences with fundamentalism in its doctrine of the church. Neoevangelicalism tends to sacrifice the purity of the church for the peace and unity of the church. It is the neoevangelicals' opinion that heretics and unbelievers within the church do not affect the nature of the church. Thus, they are willing to sacrifice purity for unity and opportunity. The job of separating the wheat from the tares, they say, will be Christ's at the second advent. Little attention is given to the New Testament passages demanding definite discipline and purgation in the church. Because the neoevangelical believes that rapproachment can be effected with liberalism and neoorthodoxy, he is willing to subordinate doctrinal particularity.

Fundamentalism is most concerned with the purity of the church; thus the fundamentalist cries out for a separation from modernism and unbelief. No true unity can be achieved, he says, when you have an amalgamation of believers and unbelievers. "Uniqueness" as well as "unity" is demanded by the Scriptures. In an attempt to maintain this separation, the fundamentalist was inclined to make a sharp distinction between the nature of the visible church and the nature of the invisible church. At times fundamentalists overstated the case and gave the impression that there are two distinct and separate churches, the invisible and the visible. Among other fundamentalists, however, there has been a denial of anything beyond the local church. This tension point between the universal-local church theory and the local church theory, together with the various other concepts of the nature of the church, made necessary an extensive examination of the usage of *ekklesia.*

This examination of the usage of *ekklesia* has been set forth in chapter four. It has been seen that *ekklesia* brought with it many historical and linguistic associations. It is a word with a double history—both Jewish and Greek; thus, it was necessary to examine its usage in the classical Greek and in the Septuagint before approaching the New Testament. In classical Greek, *ekklesia* (derived from *ekkaleo,* "to call out") signified primarily the assembly of citizens in a self-governed state. Thus, the major idea in the word is that of summoning, and not segregation, as has been popularly supposed. Furthermore, in ordinary usage *ekklesia* meant only an assembly, a meeting, and not the body of people assembled or met together. It is generally agreed that the contribution of the classical usage of this word to New Testament writings must be limited to external organization. The classical *ekklesia* was always local and autonomous, but it had no religious associations.

A second area of investigation was the Septuagint usage of *ekklesia.* A comparison of the seventy-seven passages in which *ekklesia* is used has revealed that an *ekklesia* may meet for any purpose (religious, political, military, judicial, national, or racial), but there always seems to be some deliberative purpose for the meeting. The word itself does not signify the nature or the purpose of its constituency: it only points to the group identity and autonomous prerogatives. Second, the qualifications for the constituency may vary to a great extent, yet one qualification is constant: to be a member of an *ekklesia* a person must be physically present at the assembly. The *ekklesia* is never contemplated as a spiritual fact, independent of spatial and temporal limitations. It always describes a corporeal, physical unity of people. Finally, as was the case in the classical writings, there is no evidence whatever that the word acquired a specifically religious connotation in the Septuagint. All uses of the word never go beyond the simple meaning of *an assembly.* Thus, there is no basis for reading the church of the New Testament back into the Old Testament on the basis of the prevalent usage of *ekklesia.*

It has been seen then that all the usages of *ekklesia* prior to the New Testament never go beyond the simple, nontechnical meaning of "an assembly." When the writers of the New Testament, whose Bible was the Septuagint, used *ekklesia,* they were not inventing a new term. They found the term in common use and simply employed what was at hand. But a question arose, however, as to whether they used *ekklesia* in its established nontechnical and general sense, or in a specific and technical sense. In other words, the final authority on any word does not lie in its etymological or historical connotation, but in its actual use. Examination of its usage has revealed that there is a progressive development in the New Testament from a nontechnical through a technical and to a metaphorical usage. The nontechnical usage is found five times, and in these cases *ekklesia* simply refers to an autonomous group of people physically united. In the literary development of the word, however, there was an unconscious process whereby it assumed a technical character because of its restricted application. It became so completely identified with a new kind of assembly—an assembly of unified Christians—that it was applied to that type of assembly. The Christian, or spiritual, characteristic became accepted as a part of the word itself. The transition between the nontechnical and technical usages can be easily noticed, for in the earlier usages there seemed to be a necessity for using extensive descriptive modifiers in order to differentiate the Christian *ekklesia* from the secular *ekklesia.* In the later writings of the New Testament these modifiers gradually disappear as *ekklesia* takes on its definite technical meaning. Thus, in the development of the word *ekklesia,* the technical use of the word came to mean not only a physical assembly, but a physical assembly characterized by a distinctly Christian unity. This is the usage, then, that became overwhelmingly predominant in the New Testament. Here was a new kind of *ekklesia*—a Christian *ekklesia*—and it was distinct from every other *ekklesia* because it had the content Jesus Christ gave it. This Christian *ekklesia* has been defined, then, as a local, autonomous assembly spiritually united in Christ.

The growth of the word *ekklesia* did not stop with the technical usage. It acquired what has been termed in this book a metaphorical usage. While in the great majority of places where the word *ekklesia* occurs the meaning is unmistakably that of the local church (physical and spiritual unity), there are those usages that go beyond this and have a spiritual unity without physical unity. This metaphorical usage has been variously described as "spiritual," or "ideal," or "universal," or "invisible." Investigation has revealed nineteen instances of this usage in the New Testament. The peak of this development in Paul's usage of *ekklesia* is seen in Ephesians and Colossians.

Finally, in the setting forth of this usage, it has been strongly emphasized that the metaphorical usage of *ekklesia* is in the realm of conception, not ecclesiastical practice; and individual *ekklesiai,* banded together by any sort of tie, whether name or organization, do not constitute this *ekklesia.* It is an *ekklesia* growing out of the immediate relationship of an individual believer to God in Christ. It implies spiritual unity alone, without reference to physical or organizational unity. This eliminates the ecumenical organizational effort.

After the usages of *ekklesia* in the New Testament had been examined, the next item of concern was the commonly referred-to usages not found in the New Testament. Thus, it has been seen that it is improper to speak of the *ekklesia* as a building, a denomination, or a state or a national church. Also, it is imperative that it be recognized that the *ekklesia* is not to be confused with Israel or the kingdom of God. The *ekklesia* is a unique dispensational work of God in this age. This conclusion cuts directly across the grain of many contemporary writings that describe the church as the continuation of Israel.

Having arrived at these meanings of *ekklesia,* it became the purpose of chapters five through seven to develop them theologically. The doctrine of the universal church (chap. 6) arises out of an inductive systematization of the metaphorical usages of *ekklesia* as well as certain biblical figures in the New Testament. In this usage, which is found predominantly in Ephesians and Colossians, Paul conceives of an entire world of individual Christians related to Christ apart from local *ekklesiai,* and he terms them simply the (only) *ekklesia.* Thus, the concept of the physical assembly gives way to the spiritual assembly.

Before entering upon a detailed study of the universal church, however, it was necessary to investigate certain introductory matters (chap. 5). One of these areas of concern was the unfavorable extremes that have been a menace to the doctrine of the universal church. Careless applications of the doctrine have led some to reject it entirely. Others have put such stress on the universal body of Christ that they have neglected the local church, considering it of little importance. Some Christian enterprises, which started as a so-called "arm of the church" and received their material and resources from the local church, have become quite nonreciprocal and thus have caused bitter feelings. Finally, there is the problem of the modern ecumenical movement, which sees in the doctrine of the universal church the latent potential of worldwide organizational unity of all local churches. It has been the purpose of this book to avoid these nonbiblical extremes and to preserve the biblical balance.

As is so often the case, much of the misunderstanding about this doctrine is a problem of semantics. The choice of the wrong literary vehicle results in a lack of communication. Without attempting to be exhaustive, this writer has discussed the more popular nomenclature, namely, "invisible," "ideal," "spiritual," and "universal." It has been shown that each of these terms has had a wrong interpretation, yet each of them also has a certain legitimacy. In a very real sense, the church may be designated an invisible, ideal, spiritual, universal organism, which organism, to aid in the facility of expression for the purposes of this book, has been termed the universal church.

One of the most significant problems relative to the universal church is its historical beginning. Although some theologians, such as Bultmann, deny the divine origin of the church in the plan of God, conservative theologians agree that it is a divine institution. Concerning its historical beginning, however, there is no such unanimity of opinion. The times of Adam, Abraham, Christ, and Paul have all been suggested as dates of origination. This book has defended the thesis, however, that the church could not have had its historical beginning before the day of Pentecost. Several lines of argument support this date. First, the mystery concept of Ephesians 3 demands a beginning in this present dispensation. The church is not a continuation of Judaism, nor is it to be identified with Israel, for Paul claims that the church, the body of Christ and a mystery hid from eternity past in the mind of God, is only now, in this dispensation, revealed to His holy apostles and prophets. Second, not only was the church unknown in the Old Testament, but also it had not yet come into being when Jesus Christ was living on the earth. Christ stated that in the future He was going to establish an *ekklesia* that would be a completely new and distinct *ekklesia* from anything the Jews knew about. Third, the possibilities of its beginning are further narrowed down by the fact of the necessity of the death, resurrection, and ascension of Christ. The foundation of it was His death, and He could not become Head over the church until after His resurrection and ascension. Finally, the precise event that inaugurated the church was the advent of the Holy Spirit on the day of Pentecost, at which time those persons who were tarrying in the upper chamber at Jerusalem, waiting for the promise of the Father, were baptized by the Holy Spirit into one body and thus became the first members of the church.

The nature of the universal church has been discussed in chapter six by using the biblical figures for the source material. No richer or more complete statement of the nature of the church could be found than those biblical figures the apostles paint. A number of figures are used by these writers, for no one figure could portray adequately all the truth. This study has made examination of the six major figures of the church: the body of Christ, the bride of Christ, the building, the royal priesthood, the flock, and the branches of the vine. The greatest of these pictures seems to be that which was studied first—the body of Christ. Discussions concerning the body of Christ divide into two major interpretations—literal and metaphorical. The literal interpretation views the church as "the extension of the incarnation." In the main this is the view of most Roman Catholic writers; however, it is gaining a definite popularity among liberal Protestantism and even neoevangelicalism. This view is at the very heart of Roman Catholicism, because if the church is literally the incarnation extended, it has the same mission and same authority as Christ had. The fact that liberalism is espousing this view is simply one further step as the liberals lead and pave the road to Rome and the recovery of the "Great Church." Among most evangelical writers the figure of the body is interpreted metaphorically, or analogically. Several implications are derived from this interpretation. As the governmental Head of the body, Christ is preeminent. As the vital Head, He is the originating cause of the body's life. Furthermore, He is the continually active source of both sustenance and unity, the channels of communication of which are the members of the body.

The study of the bride metaphor has also revealed significant truths. Both the body metaphor and the bride metaphor speak of the inseparable and vital union that exists between Christ and His church, but each has its own facet of this to express. The former is a relationship of life and the latter a relationship of love. No more vivid expression of this love could be demonstrated than that pictured in the figure of the bride. A study of this relationship in the light of the Oriental marriage customs has helped to organize the eschatological truth relative to the future presentation of the bride by Christ to Himself and relative to the subsequent marriage supper. Thus, while this figure is basically a manifestation of the knowledge-surpassing love of Christ for the church, it is also a marvelous, panoramic view of the exalted position of the church, both now and for all eternity.

In the figure of the building the whole church is regarded as a great structure in which Gentile and Jew share equal family privileges in the household of God. Each member, being a living stone, is part of this great spiritual house built upon the foundation of the apostles and prophets of the New Testament. These living stones are secured by the Cornerstone, the Stone that gives unity to all the superstructure rising from it. The result is that all the building, being welded into one, is growing into a holy temple that is even now the permanent spiritual dwelling place of God. Thus, at the end of the vista, seen in the interim through the perspective glass of prophecy, a majestic edifice, absolutely faultless, looms into view.

The figure of the royal priesthood presents a significant contrast to the former dispensations. Whereas Israel *had* a priesthood, the church *is* a priesthood. A study of the central passages has revealed that every believer in this age, be he ever so humble, is a priest before God and has free access to the throne of grace. His exalted privilege begets to him certain responsibilities, for the privilege has a purpose. Thus, the believer is to offer spiritual sacrifices, the first of which is a presentation of himself, which presentation inaugurates him into his priestly ministry. Having taken this step, the believer-priest has many opportunities for sacrificial service open to him, chief among them being the sacrifice of praise to God. This thank offering, which is his continual responsibility, eventuates in the service of sacrifice to others and includes the sharing of substance as well as the proclamation of the excellencies of the Saviour. With this twofold offering of spoken witness and practical loving-kindness, God is well pleased.

The study of the figure of the flock has reemphasized certain of the truths found repeatedly in the other figures—truths such as the unity and oneness of the church. As each figure has had special contributions of its own to make, however, so the flock metaphor has contributions unique to itself. This figure seems to come closer to showing the relationship of the universal and local churches than does any other. The charge of portions of the flock in various local situations is allotted to undershepherds who in turn are responsible to the Chief Shepherd. This "oversight" on the part of the undershepherd is limited to the specific portion of the flock allotted to him in his local area.

As a shepherd he is responsible to provide for the sheep in various areas, such as government, guidance, and protection, but most especially is he to provide a well-balanced diet of spiritual food. On the other hand, the sheep are to be in subjection to the shepherd. This figure, then, guards against the possible misuse of the believer-priest teaching, which, if it were taken to an extreme, could eliminate subjection to any local church organization. Here again is evidence, then, of the need of all these biblical figures in order to understand the true nature of the church.

The final figure, the figure of the branches and the vine, has been seen to have its unique contribution to the doctrine of the nature of the church. First, it reveals in a way not paralleled by any of the other figures the inseparable relationship of the members of the church to their Lord. Christ does not say that He is the stem; He says that He is the Vine, of which His disciples are the branches. The whole includes the parts. Secondly, this figure vividly describes the results of this identification of the members of the church with their Lord. Because they are branches in the Vine, the fruit produced is not their responsibility or the result of their efforts. The branches simply bear the fruit, and the fruit is the life of Christ Himself, which life the Holy Spirit will form in every member of the church who is abiding in the Vine. This life of Christ formed in them by the Holy Spirit will be manifested in love for the brethren—the other branches of the Vine.

Perhaps the most relevant chapter to contemporary discussion is chapter seven, for the visible, local church is God's working entity in the world today. It is God's agency in the world, transacting God's business. Any relationship or responsibility incumbent upon the universal church must eventually find its outworking through the localized counterpart. The importance of this institution is certainly indicated by the fact that the great majority of the usages of *ekklesia* in the New Testament (at least ninety-two of them) are technical usages; that is, they refer to the local church (physical and spiritual unity).

The only way truly to understand the nature of the local church is to see it in its relation to the universal church. These are not two separate and distinct churches; rather, they are two aspects of the same church. Thus, extensive attention has been devoted to a development of the relationship set forth in Scripture. The first evidence of their close relationship has been seen in the fact that both have their beginning at Pentecost without any distinction between them, for on the day of their commencement they were actually one and the same. This first local church was in reality the universal church; and the universal church, the body of Christ, expressed itself in one visible local church, the church at Jerusalem. The latter was simply the active, working, visible counterpart of the other. The membership of both was identical. It seems that, from God's viewpoint, this is what every local church is to be. Every member of a local church is to be a true believer, a member of the body of Christ. If this is true, it is the believers' responsibility in establishing a local congregation to see to it that it corresponds to and is patterned after the nature of the universal church.

Further research was made to determine whether or not the subsequent history of the early church substantiates this idea of the relationship between the local and universal church. Several lines of evidence supported an affirmative answer. First, even as both ideas were present in Luke's description of the commencement of the church, so throughout his account of the Acts of the Apostles his usage of the word *ekklesia* involves both the universal and local aspects of the church. The particular local *ekklesia* represents the universal *ekklesia* and, through participation in the redemption of Christ, mystically comprehends the whole of which it is the local manifestation.

This same truth was seen to be amply attested in the epistles. Of special significance in this regard are the salutations of certain epistles and the figures of the local church. The former assert that the local churches belong to Christ and are "in God the Father and in the Lord Jesus Christ." More of the divinely-intended characteristics are clearly expressed in the figures of the local church: the temple, the body, the bride, and the flock. The very fact that these are all used of both the local and universal aspects of the church is strong supporting evidence of the close relationship. The figure of the temple presents a solemn reality. When the local assembly of believers meets together, it should recognize itself as the dwelling place of God, the Holy Spirit. Woe be to that man who would destroy the sanctity of the local assembly of believers. The body metaphor stresses the unity of the living organism. No two parts are exactly alike, but all discharge different functions for the good of the whole. The bride metaphor stresses the intimate relationship of the local assembly to Christ. The flock metaphor brings the two aspects especially close together. God has only one flock—the universal church—but it has been distributed in different localities where the elders live and work. These "portions" are also called the flock. Thus, Scripture gives ample evidence of the intimate relationship between the universal and local aspects of the church. The evidence is clear as to what the local churches ought to be, what God intended for them to be.

The evidence from the Apocalypse especially points up the direct relationship between the local church and Christ, even as is true of the universal church. There is evidence here, however, of a lack of apprehension of this relationship on the part of members of some local churches. Thus, a local church may depart so far from the pattern that Christ will actually disown it. That church's testimony in the world is removed and given to another. It must be admitted, then, that although it ought not to be, it is possible that a person may be in a local church, but outside the body of Christ. Thus, it is necessary to make a distinction between the two so that the basic issue of salvation be not clouded. This fact should be a solemn warning to the local church, which is continuously on trial. It has no secure and permanent place in the world.

Finally, the resultant implications of this close relationship between the universal and local aspects of the church have been set forth. The fact that each local assembly is in itself (or ought to be) a visible expression of the body of Christ has pertinent and practical implications affecting the overall approach of each local church. First, this relationship demands that only the regenerate compose its membership. The local church is not to comprise "wheat and tares" indifferently, nor is it to be an institution for nurturing unbelievers. It is the sanctuary of the living God, who has no fellowship with the unsaved. Not only is the local church to include *only* the regenerate, but also it is to include *all* the regenerate. Scripture knows of no Christian who belongs to the universal church but has not united with the local church. Every believer is obligated to assume his part and exercise his gift in a local church. Not only does Christ require this, but also Scripture represents Christ as adding the members to the local church.

Second, as a representative of the body of Christ, the local church is independent of outside earthly rulership, whether religious or secular. Because the Holy Spirit indwells the local church and Christ personally directs it, there exists no need to subject it to any other body, since it could not possibly have any greater or wiser source of authority. This does not eliminate cooperation between churches. In fact, cooperation is encouraged. But the local church under the direction of Christ is wholly competent to govern its own affairs.

A third demand that has been seen is an ordered and purposeful membership. Everything is to be done decently and in order. This is evidenced in the provision of spiritual gifts for every member. Thus, there ought to be no idle members; rather there should be opportunities of service for everyone. Even as the body of Christ pictures great diversity in perfect unity, so the local church is to conduct itself not tumultuously, like a mob, but like a well-ordered army, where everyone keeps his place and acts at the proper time and in the proper way. This is evidenced not only in the use of the gifts but also in the exercise of government. Each one is to be in his place, submissive to discipline, submissive to those who are over him in the Lord—no self-will, no isolated action. Thus, not only is the local church a temple of the Holy Spirit in which each member exercises the privileges of a believer-priest, but it is also a flock in which the members submit to the rule of the undershepherds, who are responsible to the Chief Shepherd.

Fourth, this relationship demands a unified membership. Contrary to the modern emphasis, the Scriptures never teach any organizational unity beyond the local church. Even recent liberal scholarship has admitted this, but the liberals care not for a first century pattern in the twentieth century. Those who defend the infallibility of Scripture, however, find therein an enduring authority, even in the matters of church form and order, for the contemporary world. It has been seen that while the New Testament does not give even the slightest hint of organizational unity beyond the local church, it specifically commands both organizational and spiritual unity within the bounds of the local church. This is accomplished by the Spirit-directed selection of church officers. Central to the maintenance of this unity, however, is a strict adherence to the doctrine that has been delivered in the infallible, inerrant Word of God. The church dare not seek to have "unity" apart from this doctrinal "uniqueness" centered in Jesus Christ.

Finally, this relationship of the local assembly to the universal body of Christ demands a growing membership in the local church. Without this factor all that has been advocated to this point becomes cold and sterile. The church is not a static organization; it is a house of God, built out of living stones, regenerate persons, who are provided with all the spiritual gifts and resources necessary in order that there might be increase, both qualitatively and quantitatively. The church should be continually experiencing an inward spiritual maturity. Leadership should become more competent. Teachers should acquire greater skill and proficiency. Failure to build a strong home base is certain to destroy the plans for evangelistic outreach, which provides for the necessary quantitative growth. This is *the reason* for the existence of the local church. Unless it experiences this growth it is failing. Because the local church is the central agency of God for outreach on earth, it is imperative that other Christian agencies work closely with this divine institution and channel their work through it.

This, then, is the doctrine of the nature of the church, both in its universal and in its local aspects, as patterned in the New Testament. Deviation from the pattern can bring nothing but failure. Adherence to it will make known the manifold wisdom of God unto the principalities and powers in the heavenlies (Eph 3:10). "Unto him be glory in the church by Christ Jesus throughout all ages, world without end. Amen" (Eph 3:21).

APPENDIX 1

THE USAGE OF *EKKLESIA* IN THE SEPTUAGINT*

Deut 9:10	"Jehovah spake with you in the mount out of the midst of the fire in the day of the assembly."
Deut 18:16	"in Horeb in the day of the assembly"
Deut 23:1	"shall not enter into the assembly of Jehovah"
Deut 23:2	"shall none of his enter into the assembly of Jehovah"
Deut 23:3	"shall none belonging to them enter into the assembly of Jehovah"
Deut 23:8	"shall enter into the assembly of Jehovah"
Deut 31:30	"And Moses spake in the ears of all the assembly of Israel the words of this song"
Josh 8:35	"Joshua read . . . before all the assembly of Israel"
Judg 20:2	"And the chiefs of all the people . . . presented themselves in the assembly of the people of God"
Judg 21:5	"And the children of Israel said, Who is there among all the tribes of Israel that came not up in the assembly unto Jehovah?"
Judg 21:8	"There came none to the camp from Jabesh-gilead to the assembly"
1 Sam 17:47	"That all this assembly may know that Jehovah saveth not with sword and spear"
1 Sam 19:20	"when they saw the company of the prophets prophesying"
1 Kings 8:14	"the king . . . blessed all the assembly of Israel"

*The only instances cited are those in which *ekklesia* translates *qahal* in the canonical books of the Old Testament. Chapters and verses are given according to the American Standard Version.

1 Kings 8:22	"Solomon stood before the altar of Jehovah in the presence of all the assembly of Israel"
1 Kings 8:55	"and he stood, and blessed all the asesmbly of Israel with a loud voice"
1 Kings 8:65	"and all Israel with him, a great assembly"
1 Chron 13:2	"And David said unto all the assembly of Israel"
1 Chron 13:4	"And all the assembly said that they would do so"
1 Chron 28:2	"Then David the king stood up upon his feet [in the midst of the assembly]." Nothing in the Hebrew text for the words in brackets, and hence nothing in the English version.
1 Chron 28:8	"in the sight of all Israel, the assembly of Jehovah"
1 Chron 29:1	"David the king said unto all the assembly"
1 Chron 29:10	"David blessed Jehovah before all the assembly"
1 Chron 29:20	"David said to all the assembly"
1 Chron 29:20	"And all the assembly blessed Jehovah"
2 Chron 1:3	"So Solomon, and all the assembly with him, went to the high place"
2 Chron 1:5	"and Solomon and the assembly sought unto it"
2 Chron 6:3	"the king turned his face, and blessed all the assembly of Israel"
2 Chron 6:3	"and all the assembly of Israel stood"
2 Chron 6:12	"And he stood before the altar of Jehovah in the presence of all the assembly of Israel"
2 Chron 6:13	"kneeled down upon his knees before all the assembly of Israel"
2 Chron 7:8	"Solomon held the feast . . . and all Israel with him, a very great assembly"
2 Chron 20:5	"And Jehoshaphat stood in the assembly of Judah and Jerusalem, in the house of Jehovah, before the new court"
2 Chron 20:14	"Then upon Jahaziel . . . came the Spirit of Jehovah in the midst of the assembly"
2 Chron 23:3	"And all the assembly made a covenant with the king in the house of God"

2 Chron 28:14	"So the armed men left the captives and the spoil before the princes and all the assembly"
2 Chron 29:23	"And they brought . . . the sin-offering before the king and the assembly"
2 Chron 29:32	"And the number of the burnt-offerings which the assembly brought"
2 Chron 30:2	"For the king had taken counsel, and his princes, and all the assembly in Jerusalem, to keep the pass-over in the second month"
2 Chron 30:4	"And the thing was right in the eyes of the king and of all the assembly"
2 Chron 30:13	"And there assembled at Jerusalem . . . a very great assembly"
2 Chron 30:17	"For there were many in the assembly that had not sanctified themselves"
2 Chron 30:23	"And the whole assembly took counsel to keep other seven days"
2 Chron 30:24	"For Hezekiah . . . did give to the assembly for offerings a thousand bullocks and seven thousand sheep; and the princes gave to the assembly a thou-sand bullocks and ten thousand sheep"
2 Chron 30:25	"And all the asesmbly of Judah . . . rejoiced"
2 Chron 30:25	"and all the assembly that came out of Israel . . . rejoiced"
Ezra 2:64	"The whole assembly together was forty and two thousand three hundred and threescore"
Ezra 10:1	"there was gathered together unto him out of Israel a very great assembly"
Ezra 10:8	"and himself separated from the assembly of the captivity"
Ezra 10:12	"Then all the assembly answered"
Ezra 10:14	"Let now our princes be appointed for all the as-sembly"
Neh 5:7	"And I held a great assembly against them"
Neh 5:13	"And all the assembly said, Amen"

Neh 7:66	"The whole assembly together was forty and two thousand three hundred and threescore"
Neh 8:2	"Ezra the priest brought the law before the assembly, both men and women, and all that could hear with understanding"
Neh 8:17	"And all the assembly of them that were come again out of the captivity made booths"
Neh 13:1	"an Ammonite and a Moabite should not enter into the assembly of God for ever"
Job 30:28	"I stand up in the assembly, and cry for help"
Psalm 22:22	"In the midst of the assembly will I praise thee"
Psalm 22:25	"Of thee cometh my praise in the great assembly"
Psalm 26:5	"I hate the assembly of evil-doers"
Psalm 26:12	"In the congregations will I bless Jehovah"
Psalm 35:18	"I will give thee thanks in the great assembly"
Psalm 40:9	"I have proclaimed glad tidings of righteousness in the great assembly"
Psalm 68:26	"Bless ye God in the congregations"
Psalm 89:5	"Thy faithfulness also in the assembly of the holy ones"
Psalm 107:32	"Let them exalt him also in the assembly of the people"
Psalm 149:1	"Sing . . . his praise in the assembly of the saints"
Prov 5:14	"I was well-nigh in all evil in the midst of the assembly and congregation"
Lam 1:10	"that they should not enter into thine assembly"
Ezek 32:3	"I will spread out my net upon thee with a company of many peoples"
Ezek 32:23	"and her company is round about her grave"
Joel 2:16	"gather the people, sanctify the assembly"
Mic 2:5	"thou shalt have none that shall cast the line by lot in the assembly of Jehovah"

APPENDIX 2

THE USAGES OF *EKKLESIA* IN THE NEW TESTAMENT*

1. Nontechnical Usage

Acts 7:38	"This is he, that was in the church in the wilderness"
Acts 19:32	"for the assembly was confused"
Acts 19:39	"determined in a lawful assembly"
Acts 19:41	"thus spoken, he dismissed the assembly"
Heb 2:12	"in the midst of the church will I sing praise unto thee"

2. Subtechnical Usage

1 Thess 1:1	"the church of the Thessalonians which is in God the Father and in the Lord Jesus Christ"
1 Thess 2:14	"the churches of God which in Judaea are in Christ Jesus"
2 Thess 1:1	"the church of the Thessalonians in God our Father and the Lord Jesus Christ"
2 Thess 1:4	"in the churches of God"

3. Technical Usage

Matt 18:17	"tell it unto the church"
Matt 18:17	"but if he neglect to hear the church"
Acts 2:47	"the Lord added to the church daily"
Acts 5:11	"fear came upon all the church"
Acts 8:1	"the church which was at Jerusalem"
Acts 8:3	"He made havock of the church"

*Scripture citations are from the King James Version.

Acts 11:22	"the church which was in Jerusalem"
Acts 11:26	"assembled themselves with the church"
Acts 12:1	"to vex certain of the church"
Acts 12:5	"prayer was made without ceasing of the church unto God for him"
Acts 13:1	"Now there were in the church that was at Antioch"
Acts 14:23	"ordained them elders in every church"
Acts 14:27	"had gathered the church together"
Acts 15:3	"And being brought on their way by the church"
Acts 15:4	"they were received of the church"
Acts 15:22	"Then pleased it the apostles and elders with the whole church, to send chosen men of their own company"
Acts 15:41	"went through Syria and Cilicia, confirming the churches"
Acts 16:5	"so were the churches established in the faith"
Acts 18:22	"And when he had . . . saluted the church"
Acts 20:17	"he sent to Ephesus, and called the elders of the church"
Rom 16:1	"a servant of the church which is at Cenchrea"
Rom 16:4	"all the churches of the Gentiles"
Rom 16:5	"the church that is in their house"
Rom 16:16	"The churches of Christ salute you"
Rom 16:23	"the whole church, saluteth you"
1 Cor 1:2	"the church of God which is at Corinth"
1 Cor 4:17	"as I teach every where in every church"
1 Cor 6:4	"who are least esteemed in the church"
1 Cor 7:17	"And so ordain I in all churches"
1 Cor 10:32	"Give none offence, neither to the Jews, nor to the Gentiles, nor to the church of God"
1 Cor 11:16	"we have no such custom, neither the churches of God"
1 Cor 11:18	"when ye come together in the church"

1 Cor 11:22	"or despise ye the church of God"
1 Cor 14:4	"he that prophesieth edifieth the church"
1 Cor 14:5	"that the church may receive edifying"
1 Cor 14:12	"seek that ye may excel to the edifying of the church"
1 Cor 14:19	"in the church I had rather speak five words"
1 Cor 14:23	"the whole church be come together into one place"
1 Cor 14:28	"let him keep silence in the church"
1 Cor 14:33	"as in all churches of the saints"
1 Cor 14:34	"Let your women keep silence in the churches"
1 Cor 14:35	"it is a shame for women to speak in the church"
1 Cor 16:1	"as I have given order to the churches of Galatia"
1 Cor 16:19	"The churches of Asia salute you"
1 Cor 16:19	"with the church that is in their house"
2 Cor 1:1	"the church of God which is at Corinth"
2 Cor 8:1	"the churches of Macedonia"
2 Cor 8:18	"the gospel throughout all the churches"
2 Cor 8:19	"was also chosen of the churches to travel with us"
2 Cor 8:23	"they are the messengers of the churches"
2 Cor 8:24	"to them, and before the churches"
2 Cor 11:8	"I robbed other churches, taking wages of them"
2 Cor 11:28	"the care of all the churches"
2 Cor 12:13	"were inferior to other churches"
Gal 1:2	"unto the churches of Galatia"
Gal 1:22	"unto the churches of Judaea"
Phil 4:15	"no church communicated with me"
Col 4:15	"the church which is in his house"
Col 4:16	"in the church of the Laodiceans"
1 Tim 3:5	"how shall he take care of the church of God?"
1 Tim 3:15	"in the house of God, which is the church of the living God, the pillar and ground of the truth"

1 Tim 5:16	"let not the church be charged"
Philem 2	"to the church in thy house"
James 5:14	"let him call for the elders of the church"
3 John 6	"thy charity before the church"
3 John 9	"I wrote unto the church"
3 John 10	"and casteth them out of the church"
Rev 1:4	"John to the seven churches which are in Asia"
Rev 1:11	"send it unto the seven churches which are in Asia"
Rev 1:20	"The seven stars are the angels of the seven churches"
Rev 1:20	"and the seven candlesticks which thou sawest are the seven churches"
Rev 2:1	"Unto the angel of the church of Ephesus"
Rev 2:7	"hear what the Spirit saith unto the churches"
Rev 2:8	"unto the angel of the church in Smyrna"
Rev 2:11	"hear what the Spirit saith unto the churches"
Rev 2:12	"to the angel of the church in Pergamos"
Rev 2:17	"hear what the Spirit saith unto the churches"
Rev 2:18	"unto the angel of the church in Thyatira"
Rev 2:23	"all the churches shall know that I am he which searcheth the reins and hearts"
Rev 2:29	"hear what the Spirit saith unto the churches"
Rev 3:1	"unto the angel of the church in Sardis"
Rev 3:6	"hear what the Spirit saith unto the churches"
Rev 3:7	"to the angel of the church in Philadelphia"
Rev 3:13	"hear what the Spirit saith unto the churches"
Rev 3:14	"unto the angel of the church of the Laodiceans"
Rev 3:22	"hear what the Spirit saith unto the churches"
Rev 22:16	"to testify unto you these things in the churches"

4. Submetaphorical Usage

Acts 9:31	"So the church throughout all Judaea and Galilee and Samaria had peace" (ASV)

Acts 20:28	"to feed the church of God"
1 Cor 15:9	"I persecuted the church of God"
Gal 1:13	"I persecuted the church of God"
Phil 3:6	"Concerning zeal, persecuting the church"

5. Metaphorical Usage

Matt 16:18	"I will build my church"
1 Cor 12:28	"And God hath set some in the church"
Eph 1:22	"and gave him to be the head over all things to the church"
Eph 3:10	"might be known by [through] the church the manifold wisdom of God"
Eph 3:21	"Unto him be glory in the church by Christ Jesus throughout all ages"
Eph 5:23	"Christ is the head of the church"
Eph 5:24	"as the church is subject unto Christ"
Eph 5:25	"as Christ also loved the church"
Eph 5:27	"That he might present it to himself a glorious church"
Eph 5:29	"nourisheth and cherisheth it, even as the Lord the church"
Eph 5:32	"I speak concerning Christ and the church"
Col 1:18	"And he is the head of the body, the church"
Col 1:24	"for his body's sake, which is the church"
Heb 12:23	"To the general assembly and church of the first-born"

BIBLIOGRAPHY

I. Books

Adam, Karl. *One and Holy.* Translated by Cecily Hastings. New York: Sheed & Ward, 1951.

Allis, Oswald T. *Prophecy and the Church.* Philadelphia: Presby. & Ref., 1945.

Anderson, Robert. *The Coming Prince: The Marvelous Prophecy of Daniel's Seventy Weeks Concerning the Antichrist.* 13th ed. London: Pickering & Inglis, n.d.

Aquinas, Thomas. *The Summa Theologica of Saint Thomas Aquinas.* Translated by Fathers of the English Dominican Province. Revised by Daniel J. Sullivan. Great Books of the Western World, edited by Robert Maynard Hutchins, vols. 19-20. Chicago: Benton, 1952.

Augustine. "Of Holy Virginity." Translated by C. L. Cornish. In *St. Augustin: On the Holy Trinity, Doctrinal Treatises, Moral Treatises.* A Select Library of the Nicene and Post-Nicene Fathers of the Christian Church, 1st series, edited by Philip Schaff, vol. 3, pp. 415-38. Grand Rapids: Eerdmans, 1956.

———. "On Baptism, Against the Donatists." In *The Works of Aurelius Augustine, Bishop of Hippo,* edited by Marcus Dods. Edinburgh: T. & T. Clark, 1886-89. Vol. 3, *Writings in Connection with the Donatist Controversy,* translated by J. R. King, 1872. Pp. 3-228.

———. "On Rebuke and Grace." In *Saint Augustin: Anti-Pelagian Writings,* revised translation by Benjamin B. Warfield. A Select Library of the Nicene and Post-Nicene Fathers of the Christian Church, 1st series, edited by Philip Schaff, vol. 5, pp. 467-91. Grand Rapids: Eerdmans, n.d.

———. "On the Creed: A Sermon to the Catechumens." Translated by H. Browne. In *St. Augustin: On the Holy Trinity, Doctrinal Treatises, Moral Treatises.* A Select Library of the Nicene and Post-Nicene Fathers of the Christian Church, 1st series, edited by Philip Schaff, vol. 3, pp. 367-75. Grand Rapids: Eerdmans, 1956.

———. "Sermons on Selected Lessons of the New Testament." Edited by Philip Schaff. Translated by R. G. MacMullen. In *Saint Augustin: Sermon on the Mount, Harmony of the Gospels, Homilies on the Gospels.* A Select Library of the Nicene and Post-Nicene Fathers of the Christian Church, 1st series, edited by Philip Schaff, vol. 6, pp. 237-545. Grand Rapids: Eerdmans, n.d.

Baker, Charles F. *Bible Truth—What We Believe and Why We Believe It.* Milwaukee: Milwaukee Bible College, Grace Gospel Fellowship, Worldwide Grace Testimony, 1956.

Bannerman, D. Douglas. *The Scripture Doctrine of the Church.* Grand Rapids: Eerdmans, 1955.

Barclay, William. *The Mind of St. Paul.* New York: Harper, 1958.

———. *More New Testament Words.* New York: Harper, 1958.

———. *A New Testament Wordbook.* New York: Harper, n.d.

———. *The Promise of the Spirit.* Philadelphia: Westminster, 1960.

Barrows, E. P. *Companion to the Bible.* New York: Am. Tract Soc., 1867.

Barth, Karl. *The Church and the Churches.* Grand Rapids: Eerdmans, 1936.

———. *Die Kirchliche Dogmatik.* Zollikon-Zurich, Switz.: Evangelischer Verlag, 1948.

———. *The Doctrine of the Word of God.* Translated by G. T. Thomson. Edinburgh: T. & T. Clark, 1936.

———. *Dogmatics in Outline.* New York: Harper, 1959.

Bass, Clarence B. *Backgrounds to Dispensationalism.* Grand Rapids: Eerdmans, 1960.

Baxter, Richard. *A Holy Commonwealth; or, Political Aphorisms Opening the True Principles of Government.* London: Underhill & Tyton, 1659.

Berkhof, Louis. *The History of Christian Doctrines.* Grand Rapids: Eerdmans, 1953.

———. *Systematic Theology.* Grand Rapids: Eerdmans, 1953.

Berkouwer, Gerrit Cornelius. *The Conflict With Rome.* Translated by H. De Jongste under the supervision of David H. Freeman. Philadelphia: Presby. & Ref., 1958.

Best, Ernest. *One Body in Christ.* London: S.P.C.K., 1955.

Bettenson, Henry. *Documents of the Christian Church.* New York: Oxford U., 1947.

Blackman, Edwin Cyril. *Marcion and His Influence.* London: S.P.C.K., 1948.

Bogard, Ben. M. *The Baptist Way Book.* Texarkana, Ark.-Tex.: Bapt. S. S. Committee, 1945.

Bradshaw, William. *A Protestation of the Kings Supreamacie, Made by the Nonconforming Ministers, Which Were Suspended or Deprived.* London: Royston, 1647.

Bright, John. *The Kingdom of God: The Biblical Concept and Its Meaning for the Church.* Nashville: Abingdon-Cokesbury, 1953.

Bromiley, G. W. *The Unity and Disunity of the Church.* Grand Rapids: Eerdmans, 1958.

Brown, Robert McAfee. *The Significance of the Church.* Philadelphia: Westminster, 1956.

———, and Weigel, Gustave, S. J. *An American Dialogue: A Protestant Looks at Catholicism and a Catholic Looks at Protestantism.* New York: Doubleday, 1961.

Brown, William Adams. *Christian Theology in Outline.* New York: Scribner's, 1907.

———. *The Church: Catholic and Protestant.* New York: Scribner's, 1935.

Browne, Robert. *A Treatise of reformation without tarying for anie, and of the wickednesse of those Preachers, which will not reforme till the Magistrate commaunde or compell them.* Middleburgh: 1582.

Brunner, Emil. *The Misunderstanding of the Church.* Philadelphia: Westminster, 1953.

Bullinger, Ethelbert W. *The Foundations of Dispensational Truth.* London: Eyre & Spottiswoode, 1930.

———. *How to Enjoy the Bible.* London: Eyre & Spottiswoode, 1907.

———. *The Mystery.* London: Eyre & Spottiswoode, n.d.

Burrage, Champlin. *Early English Dissenters in the Light of Recent Research.* 2 vols. New York: Putnam, 1912.

Burrows, Millar. *The Basis of Israelite Marriage.* New Haven, Conn.: Am. Oriental Soc., 1938.

Cairns, Earle E. *Christianity Through the Centuries.* Rev. ed. Grand Rapids: Zondervan, 1967.

Calvin, John. *Institutes of the Christian Religion.* Edited by John T. McNeill. Translated by Ford Lewis Battles. The Library of Christian Classics, edited by John Baillie, John T. McNeill, and Henry P. Van Dusen, vols. 20-21. Philadelphia: Westminster, 1960.

Cameron, James R. *God the Christlike.* Nashville: Cokesbury, n.d.

Carnell, Edward John. *The Case for Orthodox Theology.* Philadelphia: Westminster, 1959.

Carroll, B. H. *Baptists and Their Doctrines.* New York: Revell, 1913.

———. *Ecclesia—The Church.* Louisville: Bapt. Book Concern, 1903.

Carver, William Owen. *The Glory of God in the Christian Calling: A Study in the Ephesian Epistle.* Nashville: Broadman, 1949.

Cedarholm, B. Myron. *The Witness of the Local Church.* Minneapolis: Central Conserv. Bapt. Press, n.d.

Cerfaux, Lucien. *The Church in the Theology of St. Paul.* New York: Herder & Herder, 1959.

Chafer, Lewis Sperry. *Systematic Theology.* 8 vols. Dallas: Dallas Seminary, 1948.

Clearwaters, Richard V. *The Local Church of the New Testament.* Chicago: Conserv. Bapt. Assoc. of Am., 1954.

Clement. "An Anonymous Sermon, Commonly Called Clement's Second Letter to the Corinthians. In *Early Christian Fathers,* edited and translated by Cyril C. Richardson. The Library of Christian Classics, edited by John Baillie, John T. McNeill, and Henry P. Van Dusen, vol. 1, pp. 183-202. Philadelphia: Westminster, 1953.

———. "The Letter of the Church of Rome to the Church of Corinth, Commonly Called Clement's First Letter." In *Early Christian Fathers,* edited and translated by Cyril C. Richardson. The

Library of Christian Classics, edited by John Baillie, John T. McNeill, and Henry P. Van Dusen, vol. 1, pp. 33-73. Philadelphia: Westminster, 1953.

Clifford, Paul Rowntree. *The Mission of the Local Church.* London: SCM, 1953.

Craig, Clarence Tucker. *The One Church.* New York: Abingdon-Cokesbury, 1951.

Cross, I. K. *Cross Reviews Van Gilder.* Somerset, Ky.: Eastern Bapt. Inst., n.d.

Cullmann, Oscar. *The Early Church.* Philadelphia: Westminster, 1956.

———. *Peter: Disciple, Apostle, Martyr.* Philadelphia: Westminster, 1953.

Cyprian. *The Epistles of S. Cyprian, Bishop of Carthage and Martyr, with the Council of Carthage on the Baptism of Heretics.* Edited by E. B. Pusey. A Library of Fathers of the Holy Catholic Church, Anterior to the Division of the East and West, edited by E. B. Pusey, John Keble, J. H. Newman, and C. Marriott. Oxford: Parker, 1844.

———. "The Unity of the Catholic Church." In *Early Latin Theology,* edited and translated by S. L. Greenslade. The Library of Christian Classics, edited by John Baillie, John T. McNeill, and Henry P. Van Dusen, vol. 5, pp. 119-42. Philadelphia: Westminster, 1956.

Dana, H. E. *Christ's Ecclesia.* Nashville: Broadman, 1926.

———. *A Manual of Ecclesiology.* Kansas City, Kansas: Central Seminary, 1944.

———. *Searching the Scriptures.* New Orleans: Bible Inst. Memorial Press, 1936.

Darby, John Nelson. *The Collected Writings of J. N. Darby.* Edited by William Kelly. 35 vols. London: Morrish, 1857-67.

———. *Synopsis of the Books of the Bible.* Rev. ed. 5 vols. New York: Loizeaux, n.d.

Dargan, E. C. *Ecclesiology.* Louisville: Dearing, 1897.

Deissmann, G. A. *Light from the Ancient East.* Translated by Lionel R. M. Strachan. London: Hodder & Stoughton, 1910.

———. *The Philology of the Greek Bible.* Translated by Lionel R. M. Strachan. London: Hodder & Stoughton, 1908.

DeWolf, L. Harold. *The Case for Theology in Liberal Perspective.* Philadelphia: Westminster, 1959.

———. *A Theology of the Living Church.* New York: Harper, 1953.

Dillistone, F. W. *The Structure of the Divine Society.* Philadelphia: Westminster, 1951.

Dod, C. H. *History and the Gospel.* London: Nisbet, 1938.

Edersheim, Alfred. *The Life and Times of Jesus the Messiah.* New Amer. ed. 2 vols. Grand Rapids: Eerdmans, 1956.

———. *Sketches of Jewish Social Life in the Days of Christ.* Grand Rapids: Eerdmans, 1957.

———. *The Temple: Its Ministry and Services as They Were at the Time of Jesus.* Grand Rapids: Eerdmans, 1954.

Evans, Austin P. *An Episode in the Struggle for Religious Freedom: The Sectaries of Nuremburg, 1524-1528.* New York: Columbia U., 1924.

Fairbairn, A. M. *Studies in the Life of Christ.* New York: Doran, 1880.

Farrar, Frederic W. *The History of Interpretation.* London: Macmillan, 1886.

Feinberg, Charles L. ed. *The Fundamentals for Today.* 2 vols. Grand Rapids: Kregel, 1958.

Findlay, J. Alexander. *A Portrait of Peter.* New York: Abingdon, 1935.

Fish, E. J. *Ecclesiology: A Fresh Inquiry as to the Fundamental Idea and Constitution of the New Testament Church.* New York: Author's Pub. Co., 1895.

Fleming, Peter. *The Church.* Oak Park, Ill. Midwest Christian Publishers, n.d.

Flew, R. Newton. *Jesus and His Church.* London: Epworth, 1938.

———, ed. *The Nature of the Church.* New York: Harper, 1952.

Foster, John. *Why the Church?* London: SCM, 1954.

Garrett, James Leo. *The Nature of the Church According to the Radical Continental Reformation.* Fort Worth: Southwestern Bapt. Theol. Sem., 1957.

Getz, Gene A. *Sharpening the Focus of the Church.* Chicago: Moody, 1974.

Gill, John. *Body of Divinity.* Grand Rapids: Baker, 1951.

Girdlestone, Robert Baker. *Synonyms of the Old Testament.* Grand Rapids: Eerdmans, 1956.

Gordon, A. J. *The Holy Spirit in Missions.* New York: Revell, 1893.

Gore, Charles. *The Holy Spirit and the Church.* New York: Scribner's, 1924.

Graves, J. R. *Old Landmarkism: What Is It?* Texarkana, Ark.-Tex.: Bapt. S. S. Committee, 1928.

Griffiths, Michael. *God's Forgetful Pilgrims.* Grand Rapids: Eerdmans, 1976.

Gwatkin, Henry Melvill. *Early Church History to A.D. 313.* 2 vols. London: Macmillan, 1909.

Hanbury, Benjamin. *Historical Memorials Relating to the Independents and Congregationalists from Their Rise to the Restoration of the Monarchy.* 2 vols. London: Congregational Union of England and Wales, 1839.

Hanke, Howard A. *Christ and the Church in the Old Testament: A Survey of Redemptive Unity in the Testaments.* Grand Rapids: Zondervan, 1957.

———. *From Eden to Eternity.* Grand Rapids: Eerdmans, 1960.

Hanson, Stig. *The Unity of the Church in the New Testament: Colossians and Ephesians.* Uppsala, Sweden: Almqvist & Wiksells Boktryckeri AB, 1946.

Hedegard, David. *Ecumenism and the Bible.* Amsterdam: International Council of Christian Churches, 1954.

Henry, Carl F. H. *Evangelical Responsibility in Contemporary Theology.* Grand Rapids: Eerdmans, 1957.

Hodge, Archibald Alexander. *Outlines of Theology.* Rewritten and enlarged edition of 1878. Grand Rapids: Eerdmans, 1957.

Hodge, Charles. *Systematic Theology.* 3 vols. New York: Scribner's, 1883.

Hodges, Jesse Wilson. *Christ's Kingdom and Coming.* Grand Rapids: Eerdmans, 1957.

Hogg, C. F. and Vine, W. E. *The Epistle to the Galatians.* Fincastle, Va.: Bible Study Classics, 1959.

Hordern, William. *A Layman's Guide to Protestant Theology.* New York: Macmillan, 1960.

Hort, Fenton John Anthony. *The Christian Ecclesia.* London: MacMillan, 1914.

Horton, Walter Marshall. *Christian Theology: An Ecumenical Approach.* New York: Harper, 1955.

———. *Realistic Theology.* New York: Harper, 1943.

———. *Theology in Transition.* New York: Harper, 1943.

Hoskyns, Edwyn, and Davey, Noel. *The Riddle of the New Testament.* London: Faber & Faber, 1947.

Huegel, F. J. *Bone of His Bone.* 6th Am. Ed. Grand Rapids: Zondervan, n.d.

Hunt, George L. *Rediscovering the Church.* New York: Association Press, 1956.

———, ed. *Ten Makers of Modern Protestant Thought.* New York: Association Press, 1958.

Hunter, A. M. *The Message of the New Testament.* Philadelphia: Westminster, 1944.

Hutchinson, Thomas. *The History of the Colony of Massachusetts Bay.* 2 vols. Boston: Prince Soc., 1865.

Ignatius. "The Second Epistle of Ignatius to the Ephesians." In *The Apostolic Fathers—Justin Martyr—Irenaeus.* The Ante-Nicene Fathers: Translations of the Writings of the Fathers down to A.D. 325, edited by Alexander Roberts and James Donaldson, revised by A. Cleveland Coxe, vol. 1, pp. 101-2. Grand Rapids: Eerdmans, n.d.

———. "The Epistle of Ignatius to the Philadelphians: shorter and longer versions." In *The Apostolic Fathers—Justin Martyr—Irenaeus.* The Ante-Nicene Fathers: Translations of the Writings of the Fathers down to A.D. 325, edited by Alexander Roberts and James Donaldson, revised by A. Cleveland Coxe, vol. 1, pp. 79-85. Grand Rapids: Eerdmans, n.d.

———. "The Epistle of Ignatius to the Smyrnaeans: shorter and longer versions." In *The Apostolic Fathers—Justin Martyr—Irenaeus.* The Ante-Nicene Fathers: Translations of the Writings of the Fathers down to A.D. 325, edited by Alexander Roberts and James Donaldson, revised by A. Cleveland Coxe, vol. 1, pp. 86-92. Grand Rapids: Eerdmans, n.d.

Irenaeus. "Against Heresies." In *The Apostolic Fathers—Justin*

Martyr—Irenaeus. The Ante-Nicene Fathers: Translations of the Writings of the Fathers down to A.D. 325, edited by Alexander Roberts and James Donaldson, revised by A. Cleveland Coxe, vol. 1, pp. 309-567. Grand Rapids: Eerdmans, n.d.

Johnson, Edward. *The Wonder Working Providences of Zion's Saviour in New England*. Original Narratives of Early American History, edited by J. Franklin Jameson, vol. 15, New York: Barnes and Noble, 1959.

Johnston, George. *The Doctrine of the Church in the New Testament*. Cambridge: Cambridge U., 1943.

Jones, Rufus. *Mysticism and Democracy in the English Commonwealth*. Cambridge: Harvard U., 1932.

Justin Martyr. "The First Apology of Justin Martyr." In *The Apostolic Fathers—Justin Martyr—Irenaeus*. The Ante-Nicene Fathers: Translations of the Writings of the Fathers down to A.D. 325, edited by Alexander Roberts and James Donaldson, revised by A. Cleveland Coxe, vol. 1, pp. 159-87. Grand Rapids: Eerdmans, n.d.

Kelly, William. *Lectures on the Church of God*. London: Morrish, 1918.

Kerr, Hugh Thomson, ed. *A Compend of Luther's Theology*. Philadelphia: Westminster, 1943.

Kik, Marcellus J. *Ecumenism and the Evangelical*. Philadelphia: Presby. & Ref., 1958.

Kittel, Rudolf. *Biblia Hebraica*. 7th ed. Stuttgart: Privileg. Wurtt. Bibelanstalt, 1954.

Knox, John. *The Early Church and the Coming Great Church*. New York: Abingdon, 1955.

———. *Marcion and the New Testament*. Chicago: U. of Chicago, 1942.

Kraus, C. Norman. *The Community of the Spirit*. Grand Rapids: Eerdmans, 1974.

———. *Dispensationalism in America*. Richmond, Va.: John Knox, 1958.

Kuen, Alfred. *I Will Build My Church*. Chicago: Moody, 1971.

Kuiper, R. B. *The Glorious Body of Christ*. Grand Rapids: Eerdmans, n.d.

Ladd, George Eldon. *The Gospel of the Kingdom.* Grand Rapids: Eerdmans, 1959.

Lambie, Thomas. *The Church, the Body of Christ.* New York: Revell, 1946.

Latourette, Kenneth Scott, ed. *The Gospel, the Church, and the World.* New York: Harper, 1946.

Lightner, Robert P. *Neo-Evangelicalism.* Findlay, Ohio: Dunham, n.d.

———. *Neo-Liberalism.* Chicago: Regular Bapt. Press, 1959.

Littell, Franklin Hamlin. *The Anabaptist View of the Church: A Study in the Origins of Sectarian Protestantism.* 2nd ed. Boston: Starr King, 1958.

———. *The Free Church.* Boston: Starr King, 1957.

McCall, Duke, ed. *What Is the Church?* Nashville: Broadman, 1958.

McClain, Alva J. *The Greatness of the Kingdom.* Grand Rapids: Zondervan, 1959.

McDaniel, George W. *The Churches of the New Testament.* Nashville: S. S. Board of the Southern Bapt. Convention, 1921.

McElhinney, John J. *The Doctrine of the Church: A Historical Monograph.* Philadelphia: Claxton, Remsen, & Haffelfinger, 1871.

McGee, J. Vernon. *Christ, His Cross, His Church.* 2nd ed. Los Angeles: Church of the Open Door, n.d.

MacGregor, Geddes. *Corpus Christi: The Nature of the Church According to the Reformed Tradition.* Philadelphia: Westminster, 1958.

Machen, J. Gresham. *Christianity and Liberalism.* Grand Rapids: Eerdmans, 1923.

Mackintosh, H. R. *The Divine Initiative.* London: SCM, 1921.

Manley, G. T. *Christian Unity.* London: Intervarsity Fellowship, 1945.

Marsh, W. H. H. *The New Testament Church.* Philadelphia: Am. Bapt. Publishing Soc., 1898.

"The Martyrdom of Polycarp, Bishop of Smyrna, as Told in the Letter of the Church of Smyrna to the Church of Philomelium," edited and translated by Massey Hamilton Shepherd, Jr. In *Early*

Christian Fathers, edited and translated by Cyril C. Richardson. The Library of Christian Classics, edited by John Baillie, John T. McNeill, and Henry P. Van Dusen, vol. 1, pp. 141-58. Philadelphia: Westminster, 1953.

Mason, Roy. *The Church That Jesus Built.* 10th ed. n.c.: n.p., n.d.

Mather, Cotton. *Magnalia Christi Americana; or, The Ecclesiastical History of New-England, from Its First Planting in the Year 1620 unto the Year of Our Lord, 1698.* 2 vols. 1st Am. ed. from the London ed. of 1702. Hartford: Andrus, 1820.

Mielziner, M. *The Jewish Law of Marriage and Divorce in Ancient and Modern Times, and Its Relation to the Law of the State.* Cincinnati: Block, 1884.

Miller, Donald G. *Nature and Mission of the Church.* Richmond, Va.: John Knox, 1957.

Miller, Perry. *Orthodoxy in Massachusetts, 1630-1650.* Cambridge: Harvard U., 1933.

Morrison, Charles Clayton. *The Unfinished Reformation.* New York: Harper, 1953.

Nelson, J. Robert. *The Realm of Redemption.* London: Epworth, 1953.

Nestle, D. Eberhard. *Novum Testamentum Graece.* New York: A. B. S., 1952.

Neufeld, E. *Ancient Hebrew Marriage Laws.* New York: Longmans, Green, 1944.

Neve, J. L. *Churches and Sects of Christendom.* Blair, Nebr.: Luth. Pub. House, 1952.

———. *A History of Christian Thought.* With contributions by O. W. Heick on the Middle Ages and Catholicism. 2 vols. Philadelphia: Muhlenberg, 1946.

Nygren, Anders. *Christ and His Church.* Philadelphia: Westminster, 1956.

———. *This Is the Church.* Philadelphia: Muhlenberg, 1943.

Oehler, Gustave Friedrich. *Theology of the Old Testament.* Revised by George E. Day. Reprint. Grand Rapids: Zondervan, n.d.

O'Hair, J. C. *A Dispensational Study of the Bible.* Chicago: O'Hair, n.d.

Origen. "Origen Against Celsus." In *Tertullian, Part Fourth; Minucius Felix; Commodian; Origen, Parts First and Second.* The Ante-Nicene Fathers: Translations of the Writings of the Fathers down to A.D. 325, edited by Alexander Roberts and James Donaldson, revised by A. Cleveland Coxe, vol. 4, pp. 395-669. Grand Rapids: Eerdmans, n.d.

Orr, James. *The Progress of Dogma.* Grand Rapids: Eerdmans, 1952.

Otten, Bernard John. *Manual of the History of Dogmas.* 2 vols. St. Louis: Herder, 1918.

Overby, Edward H. *The Meaning of Ecclesia in the New Testament.* Alderson, W. Va.: Overby, n.d.

Pache, Rene. *The Ecumenical Movement.* Dallas: Dallas Theol. Sem., 1950.

Packer, J. I. *Evangelism and the Sovereignty of God.* Chicago: InterVarsity, 1961.

Paget, John. *A Defence of Church Government Exercised in Presbyteriall, Classical, and Synodall Assemblies; According to the Reformed Churches.* London: Underhill, 1641.

Palmer, E. W. *The Key to the Bible: The Parables of Matthew Thirteen.* Chicago: Moody, 1957.

Palmer, William. *A Treatise on the Church of Christ.* 2 vols. New York: Appleton, 1841.

Pelikan, Jaroslav. *The Riddle of Roman Catholicism.* New York: Abingdon, 1959.

Pentecost, J. Dwight. *Prophecy for Today.* Grand Rapids: Eerdmans, 1961.

———. *Things to Come: A Study in Biblical Eschatology.* Findlay, Ohio: Dunham, 1958.

Peters, George N. H. *The Theocratic Kingdom of Our Lord Jesus, the Christ, as Covenanted in the Old Testament and Presented in the New Testament.* 3 vols. Grand Rapids: Kregel, 1957.

Pfleiderer, Otto. *Paulinism: A Contribution to the History of Primitive Christian Theology.* Translated by Edward Peters. 2 vols. London: Williams & Norgate, 1877.

Pink, Arthur W. *Why First Corinthians Twelve Does Not Refer to the Church Universal.* Willowdale, Ont.: Gospel Tract Depot, n.d.

Preus, Aerman Amberg. *The Communion of Saints, A Study of the Origin and Development of Luther's Doctrine of the Church.* Minneapolis: Augsburg, 1948.

Price, Oliver W. *The Bible and the Church, Which Came First?* Findlay, Ohio: Dunham, 1958.

Rahlfs, Alfred, ed. *Septuaginta.* 2 vols. New York: A. B. S., 1949.

Ramm, Bernard. *Protestant Biblical Interpretation: A Textbook of Hermeneutics for Conservative Protestants.* Rev. Ed. Boston: Wilde, 1956.

Ramsay, W. M. *St. Paul: The Traveller and Roman Citizen.* 4th ed. London: Hodder & Stoughton, 1898.

Rea, James Edward. *The Common Priesthood of the Members of the Mystical Body.* Westminster, Md.: Newman Bookshop, 1947.

Riley, William B. *Rethinking the Church.* New York: Revell, 1940.

Robertson, A. T. *Word Pictures in the New Testament.* 4 vols. Nashville: Broadman, 1930.

Robinson, John. *Works.* Edited by Robert Ashton. 3 vols. Boston: Doctrinal Tract and Book Soc., 1851.

Robinson, William. *The Biblical Doctrine of the Church.* St. Louis: Bethany, 1948.

Rutenbar, Culbert Gerow. *The Dagger and the Cross.* New York: Fellowship Publications, 1950.

Ryrie, Charles Caldwell. *The Basis of the Premillennial Faith.* New York: Loizeaux, 1953.

———. *Biblical Theology of the New Testament.* Chicago: Moody, 1959.

Sanderson, John W. *Fundamentalism and Its Critics.* Philadelphia: S. S. Times, 1961.

Saucy, Robert. *The Church in God's Program.* Chicago: Moody, 1972.

Sauer, Erich. *From Eternity to Eternity.* Translated by G. H. Lange. Grand Rapids: Eerdmans, 1954.

———. *In the Arena of Faith: A Call to a Consecrated Life.* London: Paternoster, 1955.

Schaeffer, Francis A. *The Church at the End of the Twentieth Century.* Downers Grove, Ill.: Inter-Varsity, 1970.

Schaff, Philip. *The Creeds of Christendom, With a History and Critical Notes.* 3 vols. New York: Harper, 1919.

Schneider, Herbert Wallace. *The Puritan Mind.* Ann Arbor, Mich.: U. of Mich., 1958.

Scofield, C. I. *The Scofield Bible Correspondence School.* 3 vols. London: Morgan & Scott, 1907.

———, ed. *The Scofield Reference Bible.* New York: Oxford U., 1909.

Shank, Robert. *Life in the Son.* Springfield, Mo.: Westcott, 1960.

Shedd, Russell Philip. *Man in Community.* London: Epworth, 1958.

Shelley, Bruce. *Introducing Laymen to Their Church: Studies in Ecclesiology.* Seminary Study Series. Denver, Colo.: Conserv. Bapt. Theol. Sem., n.d.

Smith, George D., ed. *The Teaching of the Catholic Church.* 2 vols. New York: Macmillan, 1949.

Smyth, F. H. *Manhood into God.* New York: Round Table, n.d.

Spilman, T. E. *Scripture Emblems of God's People.* Butler, Ill.: Messenger Print, 1879.

Spinka, Matthew, ed. *Advocates of Reform: From Wyclif to Erasmus.* The Library of Christian Classics, edited by John Baillie, John T. McNeill, and Henry P. Van Dusen, vol. 14. Philadelphia: Westminster, 1953.

Stibbs, Alan M. *The Church Universal and Local.* London: Church Book Room, 1948.

Strong, Augustus Hopkins. *Systematic Theology.* Philadelphia: Judson, 1907.

Stuart, C. E. *Simple Papers on the Church of God.* New York: Loizeaux, n.d.

Taylor, Vincent. *The Names of Jesus.* New York: St. Martin's, 1953.

Thiessen, Henry Clarence. *Introductory Lectures in Systematic Theology.* Grand Rapids: Eerdmans, 1951.

Thomas, Jesse B. *The Church and the Kingdom.* Louisville: Bapt. Book Concern, 1914.

Thornton, Lionel S. *The Common Life in the Body of Christ.* London: Dacre, 1950.

Todd, John Murray. *Catholicism and the Ecumenical Movement.* London: Longmans, Green, 1956.

Torrance, T. F. *Kingdom and Church: A Study in the Theology of the Reformation.* Fair Lawn, N. J.: Essential Books, 1956.

———. *Royal Priesthood.* Edinburgh: Oliver & Boyd, 1955.

Trench, Richard Chenevix. *Synonyms of the New Testament.* 9th ed. Grand Rapids: Eerdmans, 1953.

Troeltsch, Ernst. *The Social Teaching of the Christian Churches.* 2 vols. Translated by Olive Wyon. New York: Harper, 1960.

Tulga, Chester E. *The Doctrine of the Church in These Times.* Chicago: Conserv. Bapt. Assoc. of Am., 1953.

———. *New Testament Baptists and the Nature of the Church.* Chicago: Conserv. Bapt. Assoc. of Am., n.d.

Turner, J. Clyde. *The New Testament Doctrine of the Church.* Nashville: Convention Press, 1951.

Unger, Merrill F. *The Baptizing Work of the Holy Spirit.* Chicago: Scripture Press, 1953.

———. *Principles of Expository Preaching.* Grand Rapids: Zondervan, 1955.

Van Gilder, H. O. *The Church Which Is His Body.* El Cerrito, Calif., College Press, n.d.

Van Noort, G. *Dogmatic Theology.* Edited by J. P. Verhaar. Translated and revised by John J. Castelot and William R. Murphy. 5th ed. 3 vols. Westminster, Md.: Newman, 1959.

Van Oosterzee, J. J. *Christian Dogmatics.* Translated by John Watson and Maurice J. Evans. 2 vols. New York: Scribner's, 1873.

Vincent, Marvin R. *Word Studies in the New Testament.* 4 vols. Grand Rapids: Eerdmans, 1924.

Vos, Geerhardus. *The Kingdom and the Church.* Grand Rapids: Eerdmans, 1951.

Walker, Williston. *The Creeds and Platforms of Congregationalism.* Boston: Pilgrim, 1960.

———. *A History of the Congregational Churches in the United States.* The American Church History Series, vol. 3. New York: Christian Lit., 1894.

Walvoord, John F. *The Millennial Kingdom.* Findlay, Ohio: Dunham, 1959.

Watson, J. B. *The Church: A Symposium.* London: Pickering & Inglis, 1949.

Weigel, Gustave. *Catholic Theology in Dialogue.* New York: Harper, 1961.

Weiss, Johannes. *Earliest Christianity—A History of the Period A.D. 30-150.* New York: Harper, 1959.

Westin, Gunnar. *The Free Church Through the Ages.* Nashville: Broadman, 1954.

Whale, John Seldon. *Christian Doctrine.* Cambridge: Cambridge U., 1941.

Whitney, W. D. *The Life and Growth of Language.* New York: Appleton, 1897.

Williams, George Huntston, ed. *Spiritual and Anabaptist Writers.* The Library of Christian Classics, edited by John Baillie, John T. McNeill, and Henry P. Van Dusen, vol. 25. Philadelphia: Westminster, 1960.

Williams, Robert R. *A Guide to the Teachings of the Early Church Fathers.* Grand Rapids: Eerdmans, 1960.

Wilson, L. R. *The New Testament Church: A Divine Institution.* Austin, Tex.: Firm Foundation, 1953.

The World Council of Churches. *Man's Disorder and God's Design.* 5 vols. New York: Harper, 1949.

Wyngaarden, Martin J. *The Future of the Kingdom in Prophecy and Fulfillment: A Study of the Scope of "Spiritualization" in Scripture.* Grand Rapids: Baker, 1955.

Young, Alexander, ed. *Chronicles of the First Planters of the Colony of Massachusetts Bay, 1623-1636.* Law, Politics and History Series. Reprint. New York: Da Capo, n.d.

Young, G. Douglas. *The Bride and the Wife.* Minneapolis: Free Church Publications, 1959.

II. Commentaries

Abbot, T. K. *A Critical and Exegetical Commentary on the Epistles to the Ephesians and Colossians.* The International Critical Commentary on the Holy Scriptures of the Old and New Testaments, edited by Charles Augustus Briggs, Samuel Rolles Driver, and Alfred Plummer. New York: Scribner's, 1903.

Alford, Henry. *The Greek Testament.* Revised by Everett F. Harrison. 2 vols. Chicago: Moody, 1958.

Archer, Gleason L. *The Epistle to the Hebrews: A Study Manual.* Grand Rapids: Baker, 1957.

Barrett, C. K. *The Gospel According to St. John.* London: S. P. C. K., 1960.

Beet, Joseph A. *A Commentary on St. Paul's Epistles to the Corinthians.* 6th ed. London: Hodder & Stoughton, 1895.

Bigg, Charles. *A Critical and Exegetical Commentary on the Epistles of St. Peter and St. Jude.* 2nd ed. The International Critical Commentary. Edinburgh: T. & T. Clark, 1956.

Bruce, Alexander Balmain. "The Synoptic Gospels." In *The Expositor's Greek Testament,* edited by W. Robertson Nicoll, 1:3-651. Reprint. Grand Rapids: Eerdmans, 1956.

Bruce, F. F. *Commentary on the Book of the Acts.* Grand Rapids: Eerdmans, 1954.

Carroll, Benejah Harvey. *An Interpretation of the English Bible.* Edited by J. B. Cranfill and J. W. Crowder. 17 vols. New and complete ed. Nashville: Broadman, 1948.

Chafer, Lewis Sperry. *The Ephesian Letter Doctrinally Considered.* New York: Loizeaux, Bible Truth Depot, 1935.

Delitzsch, Franz. *Commentary on the Epistle to the Hebrews.* Translated by Thomas L. Kingsbury. 2 vols. Edinburgh: T. & T. Clark, 1870.

Eadie, John. *Commentary on the Epistle to the Ephesians.* Edited by W. Young. Reprint. Grand Rapids: Zondervan, n.d.

Ellicott, Charles J. *A Critical and Grammatical Commentary on St. Paul's Epistle to the Ephesians.* 2nd ed. Andover, Mass.: Draper, 1864.

———. *A Critical and Grammatical Commentary on St. Paul's Epistle to the Galatians.* Andover, Mass.: Draper, 1896.

Findlay, G. G. "The First Epistle of Paul to the Corinthians." In *The Expositor's Greek Testament,* edited by W. Robertson Nicoll, 2:727-953. Reprint. Grand Rapids: Eerdmans, 1970.

Gaebelein, Arno C. *The Acts of the Apostles.* New York: Our Hope, 1912.

———. *The Gospel of Matthew.* New York: Loizeaux, 1961.

Gerstner, John H. *The Epistle to the Ephesians: A Study Manual.* Grand Rapids: Baker, 1958.

Godet, Frederick Louis. *Commentary on the First Epistle of St. Paul to the Corinthians.* 2 vols. Grand Rapids: Zondervan, 1957.

———. *Commentary on the Gospel of John.* Revised and translated from the 3rd French ed. by Timothy Dwight. 2 vols. Grand Rapids: Zondervan, n.d.

———. *Commentary on St. Paul's Epistle to the Romans.* 2 vols. Edinburgh: T. & T. Clark, n.d.

Hackett, Horatio B. *A Commentary on the Acts of the Apostles.* Philadelphia: Am. Bapt. Publication Soc., 1882.

Hart, J. H. A. "The First Epistle General of Peter." In *The Expositor's Greek Testament,* edited by W. Robertson Nicoll, 5:1-80. Reprint. Grand Rapids: Eerdmans, 1956.

Henry, Carl F. H. "John." In *The Biblical Expositor,* edited by Carl F. H. Henry, 3:155-82. Philadelphia: Holman, 1960.

Hodge, Charles. *A Commentary on the Epistle to the Ephesians.* New York: Carter, 1856.

———. *An Exposition of the First Epistle to the Corinthians.* Grand Rapids: Eerdmans, 1950.

———. *An Exposition of the Second Epistle to the Corinthians.* Grand Rapids: Eerdmans, n.d.

Hogg, C. F. and Vine, W. E. *The Epistle of Paul the Apostle to the Galatians.* London: Pickering & Inglis, n.d.

———. *The Epistles to the Thessalonians.* Rev. ed. Fincastle, Va.: Bible Study Classics, 1959.

Hovey, Alvah, ed. *An American Commentary on the New Testament.* Philadelphia: Am. Bapt. Publication Soc., 1881-1890. *Commentary on the Gospel of Matthew,* by John A. Broadus, 1886.

Ironside, H. A. *Addresses on the First Epistle to the Corinthians.* New York: Loizeaux, 1952.

Knowling, R. J. "The Acts of the Apostles." In *The Expositor's Greek Testament,* edited by W. Robertson Nicoll, 2:1-554. Reprint. Grand Rapids: Eerdmans, 1956.

Lang, George Henry. *Epistle to the Hebrews: A Practical Treatise for Plain and Serious Readers.* London: Paternoster, 1951.

Lange, John Peter, et al. *A Commentary on the Holy Scriptures: Critical, Doctrinal and Homiletical.* Edited and translated by

Philip Schaff. Grand Rapids: Zondervan, n.d. *Revelation,* by John Peter Lange, n.d.

Leighton, Robert. *A Practical Commentary upon the First Epistle General of Peter.* 2 vols. Philadelphia: Presby. Board of Publication, 1864.

Lenski, R. C. H. *The Interpretation of St. Paul's Epistles to the Galatians, to the Ephesians, and to the Philippians.* Columbus, Ohio: Wartburg, 1946.

———. *The Interpretation of St. Paul's First and Second Epistle to the Corinthians.* Columbus Ohio: Wartburg, 1946.

Lightfoot, J. B. *The Epistle of St. Paul to the Galatians.* Reprint. Grand Rapids: Zondervan, n.d.

———. *Saint Paul's Epistles to the Colossians and to Philemon.* Reprint. Grand Rapids: Zondervan, n.d.

M'Neile, Alan Hugh. *The Gospel According to St. Matthew.* London: MacMillan, 1955.

Milligan, George. *St. Paul's Epistles to the Thessalonians.* Grand Rapids: Eerdmans, 1953.

Moffatt, James. "The First and Second Epistles to the Thessalonians." In *The Expositor's Greek Testament,* edited by W. Robertson Nicoll, 4:1-54. Reprint. Grand Rapids: Eerdmans, 1956.

Moule, H. C. G. *The Epistle to the Ephesians, with Introduction and Notes,* The Cambridge Bible for Schools and Colleges, edited by J. J. S. Perowne. Cambridge: Cambridge U., 1895.

Nicholson, W. R. *Oneness with Christ: Popular Studies in the Epistle to the Colossians.* Edited by James M. Gray. Grand Rapids: Kregel, 1951.

Peake, A. S. "The Epistle to the Colossians." In *The Expositor's Greek Testament,* edited by W. Robertson Nicoll, 3:475-547. Reprint. Grand Rapids: Eerdmans, 1956.

Pink, Arthur W. *An Exposition of Hebrews.* 3 vols. Grand Rapids: Baker, 1954.

Plummer, Alfred. *A Commentary on St. Paul's First Epistle to the Thessalonians.* London: Scott, 1918.

———. *An Exegetical Commentary on the Gospel According to St. Matthew.* Grand Rapids: Eerdmans, 1956.

Robertson, A. T. *Paul and the Intellectuals: The Epistle to the Colossians.* Edited and revised by W. C. Strickland. Nashville: Broadman, 1959.

Robertson, Archibald and Plummer, Alfred. *A Critical and Exegetical Commentary on the First Epistle of St. Paul to the Corinthians.* 2nd ed. The International Critical Commentary on the Holy Scriptures of the Old and New Testaments, edited by Samuel Rolles Driver, Alfred Plummer, Charles Augustus Briggs. Edinburgh: T. & T. Clark, 1955.

Robinson, J. Armitage. *St. Paul's Epistle to the Ephesians.* 2nd ed. London: Macmillan, 1904.

Salmond, S. D. F. "The Epistle to the Ephesians." In *The Expositor's Greek Testament,* edited by W. Robertson Nicoll, 3:201-395. Reprint. Grand Rapids: Eerdmans, 1956.

Sanday, William and Headlam, Arthur C. *A Critical and Exegetical Commentary on the Epistle to the Romans.* The International Critical Commentary on the Holy Scriptures of the Old and New Testaments, edited by Samuel Rolles Driver, Alfred Plummer, and Charles Augustus Briggs. Edinburgh: T. & T. Clark, 1898.

Scott, Walter. *Exposition of the Revelation of Jesus Christ.* 4th ed. London: Pickering & Inglis, n.d.

Selwyn, Edward Gordon. *The First Epistle of St. Peter.* 2nd ed. London: Macmillan, 1958.

Simpson, A. B. *The Highest Christian Life: Exposition of the Epistle to the Ephesians.* South Nyack, N. Y.: Christian Alliance, 1898.

Simpson, E. K. and Bruce, F. F. *Commentary on the Epistles to the Ephesians and the Colossians.* The New International Commentary on the New Testament, ed. Ned B. Stonehouse and F. F. Bruce. Grand Rapids: Eerdmans, 1957.

Stibbs, Alan M. *The First Epistle General of Peter.* Intro. by Andrew F. Walls. The Tyndale New Testament Commentaries, edited by R. V. G. Tasker. Grand Rapids: Eerdmans, 1959.

Stifler, James M. *The Epistle to the Romans—A Commentary Logical and Historical.* Chicago: Moody, 1960.

Stott, John R. W. *What Christ Thinks of the Church.* Grand Rapids: Eerdmans, 1958.

Summers, Ray. *Ephesians: Pattern for Christian Living.* Nashville: Broadman, 1960.

Swete, Henry Barclay. *The Apocalypse of St. John.* Grand Rapids: Eerdmans, 1954.

———. *The Gospel According to St. Mark.* 3rd ed. Reprint. Grand Rapids: Eerdmans, 1956.

Tasker, R. V. G. *The Second Epistle of Paul to the Corinthians.* The Tyndale New Testament Commentaries, edited by R. V. G. Tasker. Grand Rapids: Eerdmans, 1958.

Tenney, Merrill C. *John: The Gospel of Belief: An Analytic Study of the Text.* Grand Rapids: Eerdmans, 1953.

Thomas, W. H. Griffith. *Let Us Go On: The Secret of Christian Progress in the Epistle to the Hebrews.* 3rd ed. Grand Rapids: Zondervan, 1944.

Trench, Richard Chenevix. *Commentary on the Epistles to the Seven Churches in Asia.* 2nd ed. London: Parker, Son, & Bourn, 1861.

Westcott, Brooke Foss. *Saint Paul's Epistle to the Ephesians: The Greek Text with Notes and Addenda.* London: Macmillan, 1906.

———. *The Epistle to the Hebrews: The Greek Text with Notes and Essays.* Grand Rapids: Eerdmans, 1955.

———. *The Gospel According to St. John: The Authorized Version with Introduction and Notes.* Grand Rapids: Eerdmans, 1954.

White, Newport J. D. "The Epistle to Titus." In *The Expositor's Greek Testament,* edited by W. Robertson Nicoll, 4:185-202. Reprint. Grand Rapids: Eerdmans, 1956.

Wuest, Kenneth S. *First Peter in the Greek New Testament for the English Reader.* Grand Rapids: Eerdmans, 1956.

III. ESSAYS

Barker, Glenn W. "The Church of God." In *The Word for This Century,* edited by Merrill C. Tenney, pp. 108-30. New York: Oxford, 1960.

Barth, Karl. "The Church—The Living Congregation of the Living Lord Jesus Christ." In *Man's Disorder and God's Design,* by the World Council of Churches, 1:67-76. New York: Harper, 1949.

Carver, W. O. "Introduction." In *What Is the Church?,* edited by Duke McCall, pp. 1-14. Nashville: Broadman, 1958.

Craig, Clarence T. "The Church of the New Testament." In *Man's Disorder and God's Design,* by the World Council of Churches, 1:31-42. New York: Harper, 1949.

Craven, E. R. "Excursus on the Basileia." In *A Commentary on the Holy Scriptures: Critical, Doctrinal, and Homiletical,* by John Peter Lange et al., edited and translated by Philip Schaff. Grand Rapids: Zondervan, n.d. *Revelation,* edited by E. R. Craven, n.d. Pp. 93-100.

Graham, Aelred. "The Church on Earth." In *The Teaching of the Catholic Church,* edited by George D. Smith, 2:691-732. New York: Macmillan, 1949.

Gregg, John A. F. "One, Holy, Catholic, Apostolic Church." In *Man's Disorder and God's Design,* by the World Council of Churches, 1:59-66. New York: Harper, 1949.

Hodgson, Leonard. "The Doctrine of the Church as Held and Taught in the Church of England." In *The Nature of the Church,* edited by R. Newton Flew, pp. 121-46. New York: Harper, 1952.

Jeremias, Joachim. *"Gonia, Akrogoniaios, Kephale Gonias."* In *Theologisches Wörterbuch zum Neuen Testament,* herausgegeben von Gerhard Kittel, 1: 792-93. Stuttgart: Verlag von W. Kahlhammer, 1933.

———. *"Numphe, Numphios."* In *Theologisches Wörterbuch zum Neuen Testament,* herausgegeben von Gerhard Kittel, 4: 1092-99. Stuttgart: Verlag von W. Kahlhammer, 1942.

Kicklightner, R. W. "The Origin of the Church." In *What Is the Church?,* edited by Duke McCall, pp. 28-45. Nashville: Broadman, 1958.

Lewis, Leicester C. "The Anglican Church." In *The Nature of the Church,* edited by R. Newton Flew, pp. 309-18. New York: Harper, 1952.

Lindeskog, Gosta. "The Kingdom of God and the Church in the New Testament." In *This Is the Church,* edited by Anders Nygren with Gustaf Aulen, translated by Carl C. Rassmussen, pp. 136-47. Philadelphia: Muhlenberg, 1952.

Luther, Martin. "The Papacy at Rome." In *Works of Martin Luther,* 1:327-95. Philadelphia: Holman, n.d.

Myers, E. "The Mystical Body of Christ." In *The Teaching of the Catholic Church,* edited by George D. Smith, 2:659-90. New York: Macmillan, 1949.

Nelson, J. Robert. "Church." In *A Handbook of Christian Theology,* edited by Marvin Halverson and Arthur A. Cohen, pp. 53-58. New York: New Am. Lib., 1974.

Paget, John. "A Declaration and Plainer Opening." In *Historical Memorials Relating to the Independents and Congregationalists from Their Rise to the Restoration of the Monarchy,* by Benjamin Hanbury. 2 vols. London: Congregational Union of England and Wales, 1839.

Price, Theron D. "The Anabaptist View of the Church." In *What Is the Church?,* edited by Duke McCall, pp. 97-117. Nashville: Broadman, 1958.

Ryle, John C. "The True Church." In *The Fundamentals for Today,* edited by Charles L. Feinberg, 2:505-8. Grand Rapids: Kregel, 1958.

Schmidt, Karl Ludwig. "The Church." In *Bible Key Words from Gerhard Kittel's Theologisches Wörterbuch zum Neuen Testament,* edited and translated by J. R. Coates and H. P. Kingdon. Vol. 1. New York: Harper, 1951.

Steely, John E. "The Landmark Movement in the Southern Baptist Convention." In *What Is the Church?,* edited by Duke McCall, pp. 134-47. Nashville: Broadman, 1958.

Thornton, L. S. "The Body of Christ in the New Testament." In *The Apostolic Ministry,* edited by Kenneth E. Kirk, pp. 53-111. New York: Morehouse-Gorham, 1946.

Torbet, Robert G. "Landmarkism." In *Baptist Concepts of the Church,* edited by Winthrop Still Hudson, pp. 170-95. Philadelphia: Judson, 1959.

Yoder, John T. "The Prophetic Dissent of the Anabaptists." In *The Recovery of the Anabaptist Vision,* edited by Guy Franklin Hershberger, pp. 93-104. Scottdale, Pa.: Herald, 1957.

IV. PERIODICALS

Allen, E. L. "The Jewish Christian Church in the Fourth Gospel." *Journal of Biblical Literature* 74 (1955):175-87.

Arndt, W. "A Royal Priesthood, 1 Pet 2:9," *Concordia Theological Monthly* 19 (April 1948):241-49.

Barnhouse, Donald Grey. "Chain of Glory." *Eternity* 9 (March 1958):16-18.

———. "We Are One Body in Christ." *Eternity* 8 (March 1957):4-5, 39-43.

Barth, Markus. "A Chapter on the Church—The Body of Christ." *Interpretation* 12 (1958):129-56.

Berkouwer, G. C. "Election and Doctrinal Reaction." *Christianity Today* 5 (April 10, 1961):586-89.

Bernardin, Joseph Buchanan. "The Church in the New Testament." *Anglican Theological Review* 21 (July 1939):153-70.

Blake, Eugene Carson. "A Proposal Toward the Reunion of Christ's Church." *Christian Century* 77 (December 1960): 1508-11.

"Blueprint for Unity." *Time* 65 (January 24, 1955):42-44.

Brunner, Emil. "One Holy Catholic Church." *Theology Today* 4 (October 1947):319-31.

Bultmann, Rudolf. "The Idea of the Church." *Andover Newton Quarterly* 1 (September 1960):6-16.

———. "The Transformation of the Idea of the Church in the History of Early Christianity." *Canadian Journal of Theology* 1 (1955):73-81.

Campbell, J. Y. "The Origin and Meaning of the Christian Use of the Word *Ekklesia*," *Journal of Theological Studies* 49 (April 1948):130-42.

Carnell, Edward John. "Orthodoxy: Cultic vs. Classical." *Christian Century* 77 (March 30, 1960):377-79.

Davidson, Richard. "The Old Testament Preparation for the New Testament Doctrine of the Church." *Review and Expositor* 38 (January 1941):49-56.

"Deep in the Heart of Texas: Highland Park Methodist, Dallas—A Mighty Church in the Booming Southwest." *Christian Century* 69 (November 12, 1952):1312-18.

Dillistone, F. W. "How Is the Church Christ's Body?" *Theology Today* 2 (April 1945):56-68.

Easton, Burton S. "The Church in the New Testament." *Anglican Theological Review* 22 (July 1940):157-68.

Henry, Carl F. H. "The Perils of Ecumenicity." *Christianity Today* 1 (November 26, 1956):20-22.

———. "The Perils of Independence." *Christianity Today* 1 (November 12, 1956):20-23.

Hicks, R. Lansing. "Jesus and His Church." *Anglican Theological Review* 34 (January 1952):85-94.

Hitt, Russell T. "Church Merger: Threat or Hope?" *Eternity* 12 (February 1961):7-9, 26-28.

Hodge, Charles. "The Unity of the Church." *Eternity* 9 (June 1958):21-28.

"Homage and Courtesy." *Christianity Today* 5 (December 19, 1960):247.

Kennedy, Gerald. "The Church and Unity." *Christian Century* 78 (February 8, 1961):170-72.

Ladd, George E. "The Rapture Question: Walvoord's New Book Supporting Pretribulationism Reviewed by Fuller Seminary Professor." *Eternity* 8 (May 1957):8, 45-48.

———. "A Review of *The Greatness of the Kingdom* by Alva J. McClain." *Christianity Today* 4 (October 12, 1959):38-41.

Leitch, Addison H. "Review of Current Religious Thought." *Christianity Today* 5 (January 16, 1961):340.

Littel, Franklin H. "The Pope's Ecumenical Council." *Christian Century* 76 (February 25, 1959):224-25.

Lowell, C. Stanley. "What Is the Church's Real Task?" *Christianity Today* 5 (March 13, 1961):515-16.

McClain, Alva J. "The Greatness of the Kingdom." *Bibliotheca Sacra* 112 (1955):304-10.

———. Review of *Life in the Son,* by Robert Shank. *Grace Journal* 1 (fall 1960):34-36.

"Merger." *Christian Herald* 84 (February 1961):6.

Metzger, Bruce M. "Paul's Vision of the Church: A Study of the Ephesian Letters." *Theology Today* 6 (April 1949):49-63.

Michaels, J. Ramsey. "A Book Review of *The Gospel of the Kingdom* by George Eldon Ladd." *The Westminster Theological Journal* 23:47-50.

Newbigin, Lesslie. "The Scandal of Our Apartness." *Eternity* 12 (February 1961):13-16.

"New Delhi Marks Ecumenical Milestone." *Christianity Today* 6 (November 10, 1961):146-47.

"News." *Christianity Today* 5 (December 19, 1960):245.

Norborg, Christopher. "Restore the Christian Fellowship." *Theology Today* 4 (October 1947):332-45.

Ockenga, Harold John. "Resurgent Evangelical Leadership." *Christianity Today* 5 (October 10, 1960):11-15.

Oke, C. Clare. "My Testimony." *The Expository Times* 37 (July 1926):476-78.

Pache, Rene. "A Biblical Unity." *Bibliotheca Sacra* 108 (July 1951):300-309.

Petersen, William J. "Young Life and the Church." *Eternity* 14 (April 1961):12-14, 34-37.

Pickering, Ernest. "Editorially Speaking." *Voice* 5 (May 1957).

———. "Interdenominationalism." *Central Conservative Baptist Quarterly* 2 (Fall 1959):29-33.

Roth, Robert P. "Existentialism and Historic Christian Faith." *Christianity Today* 5 (March 27, 1961):3-5.

Ryrie, Charles C. "The Necessity of Dispensationalism." *Bibliotheca Sacra* 114 (July 1957):243-54.

Sasse, Hermann. "Facing New Delhi: Crisis of the Ecumenical Movement." *Christianity Today* 5 (April 10, 1961):579-82.

Seitz, Oscar J. F. "Upon This Rock: A Critical Re-examination of Matthew 16:17-19." *Journal of Biblical Literature* 69 (December 1950):329-40.

Skydsgaard, K. E. "Kingdom of God and Church." *Scottish Journal of Theology* 4 (December 1951):383-97.

Smedes, Lewis B. "The Essence of the Church." *Christianity Today* 4 (October 26, 1959):49-51.

"Symposium: The Body Christ Heads." *Christianity Today* 1 (August 19, 1957):3-13.

Taylor, Theophilus Mills. "Kingdom, Family, Temple, and Body." *Interpretation* 12 (1958):174-93.

Thomas, W. H. Griffith. "The Doctrine of the Church in the Epistle to the Ephesians." *The Expositor,* 7th series, 2 (1906):318-39.

Torrance, T. F. "The Israel of God." *Interpretation* 10 (July 1956):305-22.

Walvoord, John F. "The Nature of the Church." *Bibliotheca Sacra* 116 (October-December 1959):291-302.

———. "The Trend Toward a Superchurch." *Moody Monthly* 62 (September 1961):16-18, 61-63.

———. "What's Right About Fundamentalism." *Eternity* 8 (June 1957):6-7, 34-35.

Whitaker, G. H. "Studies in Texts—The Building and the Body." *Theology: A Journal of Historic Christianity* 13 (1926):335-36.

Williamson, William B. "The Doctrine of the Church." *Christianity Today* (December 8, 1961):235-37.

"Wisconsin Lutherans Break With Missouri Synod." *Christianity Today* 5 (August 28, 1961):989.

Young, Edward J. "Where Are We Going?" *The Presbyterian Guardian* 28 (May 26, 1959):154.

V. GRAMMARS, CONCORDANCES, AND LEXICONS

Abbott-Smith, G. *A Manual Greek Lexicon of the New Testament.* Edinburgh: T. & T. Clark, 1950.

Arndt, William F. and Gingrich, F. Wilbur. *A Greek-English Lexicon of the New Testament and Other Early Christian Literature.* Chicago: U. of Chicago, 1957.

Brown, Francis; Driver, S. R.; and Briggs, Charles A. *A Hebrew and English Lexicon of the Old Testament.* Based on the lexicon of William Gesenius as translated by Edward Robinson. Oxford: Clarendon, 1952.

Chamberlain, William Douglas. *An Exegetical Grammar of the Greek New Testament.* New York: Macmillan, 1952.

Cremer, Hermann. *Biblico-Theological Lexicon of New Testament Greek.* Translated by William Urwich. Edinburgh: T. & T. Clark, 1883.

Dana, H. E. and Mantey, Julius R. *A Manual Grammar of the Greek New Testament.* New York: Macmillan, 1950.

Hatch, Edwin and Redpath, Henry A. *A Concordance to the Septuagint and the Other Greek Versions of the Old Testament.* 2 vols. Oxford: Clarendon, 1897.

Liddell, Henry George and Scott, Robert. *A Greek-English Lexicon.* 9th ed. Oxford: Clarendon, 1953.

Lisowsky, Gerhard. *Konkordanz zum Hebraischen Alten Testament.* Stuttgart: Privileg. Wurtt Bibelanstalt, 1958.

Moulton, James Hope. *A Grammar of New Testament Greek.* 2 vols. Edinburgh: T. & T. Clark, 1906.

Moulton, W. F. and Geden, A. S. *A Concordance to the Greek Testament.* Edinburgh: T. & T. Clark, 1950.

Perrin, Porter Gale. *Writer's Guide and Index to English.* Chicago: Scott, Foresman, 1942.

Robertson, A. T. *A Grammar of the Greek New Testament in the Light of Historical Research.* Nashville: Broadman, 1934.

Smyth, Herbert Weir. *Greek Grammar.* Cambridge: Harvard U., 1956.

Thayer, Joseph Henry. *A Greek-English Lexicon of the New Testament.* 2nd ed. Edinburgh: T. & T. Clark, 1892.

Tregelles, Samuel Prideaux, trans. *Gesenius' Hebrew and Chaldee Lexicon to the Old Testament Scriptures.* Grand Rapids: Eerdmans, 1954.

VI. Dictionaries and Encyclopedias

Brandon, Owen R. "Body." In *Baker's Dictionary of Theology,* edited by Everett F. Harrison, pp. 101-2. Grand Rapids: Baker, 1960.

Cross, Frank Leslie. *The Oxford Dictionary of the Christian Church.* New York: Oxford U., 1957.

Dosker, Henry E. "Pentecost." In *The International Standard Bible Encyclopaedia,* 5 vols., edited by James Orr, 4:2318-19. Grand Rapids: Eerdmans, 1955.

Edwards, D. Miall. "Mystery." In *The International Standard Bible Encyclopaedia,* 5 vols., edited by James Orr, 3:2104-6. Grand Rapids: Eerdmans, 1955.

Forrester, E. J. "Church Government." In *The International Standard Bible Encyclopaedia,* 5 vols., edited by James Orr, 1: 653-55. Grand Rapids: Eerdmans, 1955.

Harrison, Everett F. "Rock." In *Baker's Dictionary of Theology,* edited by Everett F. Harrison, p. 463. Grand Rapids: Baker, 1960.

Hastings, James. *Dictionary of Christ and the Gospels.* 2 vols. New York: Scribner's, 1907.

———, ed. *Dictionary of the Bible.* Revised by Frederick C. Grant and H. H. Rowley. New York: Scribner's, 1963.

Ladd, George Eldon. "Kingdom of God." In *Baker's Dictionary of Theology,* edited by Everett F. Harrison, pp. 309-14. Grand Rapids: Baker, 1960.

Lambert, J. C. "Church." In *The International Standard Bible Encyclopaedia,* 5 vols., edited by James Orr, 1:650-53. Grand Rapids: Eerdmans, 1955.

LaVere, Christian Rudolph. "The Doctrine of the Church." In *Twentieth Century Encyclopedia of Religious Knowledge,* 2 vols, edited by Lafferts A. Loetscher, 1:254-55. Grand Rapids: Baker, 1955.

Maclean, A. J. "Marriage." In *Dictionary of the Apostolic Church,* edited by James Hastings, 2:11-17. Edinburgh: T. & T. Clark, 1926.

Moorehead, William G. "Priest." In *The International Standard Bible Encyclopaedia,* 5 vols., edited by James Orr, 4:2439-41. Grand Rapids: Eerdmans, 1955.

Orr, James. "Kingdom of God, of Heaven." In *A Dictionary of the Bible,* edited by James Hastings, 2:844-56. Edinburgh: T. & T Clark, 1901.

Plummer, Alfred. "Bride." In *A Dictionary of the Bible,* edited by James Hastings, 1:326-27. Edinburgh: T. & T. Clark, 1898.

———. "Bridegroom." In *A Dictionary of the Bible,* edited by James Hastings, 1:327. Edinburgh: T. & T. Clark, 1898.

Robinson, William Childs. "Church." In *Baker's Dictionary of Theology,* edited by Everett F. Harrison, pp. 123-26. Grand Rapids: Baker, 1960.

Selbie, J. A. "Corner-stone." In *A Dictionary of the Bible,* edited by James Hastings, 1:499. Edinburgh: T. & T. Clark, 1898.

Simpson, J. G. "Church." Revised by Frederick Clifton Grant. In *Dictionary of the Bible,* edited by James Hastings, revised by Frederick C. Grant and H. H. Rowley, pp. 160-62. New York: Scribner's, 1963.

Unger, Merrill F. *Unger's Bible Dictionary.* 3rd ed. Chicago: Moody, 1960.

Vine, W. E. *An Expository Dictionary of New Testament Words.* 4 vols. London: Oliphants, 1953.

Webster's New International Dictionary of the English Language. 2nd ed. Springfield, Mass.: Merriam, 1960.

VII. Unpublished Materials

Ackerly, Morton Ellwood. "The Theocracy, New Testament Ideal for the Visible Church." Master's thesis, Dallas Theol. Sem., 1939.

Anderson, Carl Ernest. "The Church Displayed in Ephesians." Master's thesis, Dallas Theol. Sem., 1938.

Anderson, Stanley Edwin: "Ecumenicity in the Light of the New Testament." Doctor's dissertation, Northern Bapt. Theol. Sem., 1947.

Baker, Charles F. "A Study in Relationships, Jew-Gentile-Church." Master's thesis, Dallas Theol. Sem., 1933.

Baker, Robert A. "An Introduction to the Study of the Development of Ecclesiology." Doctor's thesis, Southwestern Bapt. Theol. Sem., 1944.

Beckman, David L. "In Christ." Doctor's dissertation, Dallas Theol. Sem., 1956.

Bense, Walter F. "Christ's Ekklesia." Term paper for class in biblical theology, Western Conserv. Bapt. Sem., 1957.

Boehmer, John E. "The Unity of the Church in Acts." Master's thesis, Dallas Theol. Sem., 1945.

Bowman, Hoyle Eugene. "The Doctrine of the Church in the North American Baptist Association." Master's thesis, Dallas Theol. Sem., 1960.

Burnett, Argua Allen. "The Church, the Body of Christ." Master's thesis, Dallas Theol. Sem., 1944.

Cheshire, Ray L. "The Relationship of the Church to the Theocratic Kingdom." Master's thesis, Dallas Theol. Sem., 1960.

Dollar, George W. "The Life and Works of the Reverend Samuel Willard." Doctor's dissertation, Boston U. Grad. School, 1960.

Ellisen, Stanley A. "The Doctrine of the Church." Term paper for class in biblical theology, Western Conserv. Bapt. Sem., 1957.

Fuller, Daniel P. "The Hermeneutics of Dispensationalism." Doctor's dissertation, Northern Bapt. Theol. Sem., 1957.

Goddard, John Howard. "The Contribution of John Nelson Darby to Soteriology, Ecclesiology, and Eschatology." Doctor's dissertation, Dallas Theol. Sem., 1948.

Grubb, Luther L. "The Genius of Church Extension." W. H. Griffith Thomas Memorial Lectureship, Dallas Theol. Sem., November 7-10, 1961. Mimeographed.

Hepp, John, Jr. "The Kingdom: Its New Testament Meaning and Relation to the Church." Master's thesis, Dallas Theol. Sem., 1956.

Hofer, Johnny J. "The Mystery of Jew and Gentile in One Body the Church." Master's thesis, Dallas Theol. Sem., 1955.

Johnson, S. Lewis. Class lecture notes on First Corinthians, Dallas Theol. Sem., 1954.

———. Class lecture notes on Revelation, Dallas Theol. Sem., 1956.

McClain, Alva J. "The Church." Class lecture notes, Grace Theol. Sem., 1960.

McClenny, L. P. "The Mystery Age." Master's thesis, Dallas Theol. Sem., 1955.

Mencer, Fred J. "The Church and the Churches." Master's thesis, Dallas Theol. Sem., 1956.

Nash, Charles Ashworth. Class lecture notes on Acts, Dallas Theol. Sem., 1954.

Odman, Ralph Byron. "The Spiritual Body of Christ." Master's thesis, Dallas Theol. Sem., 1945.

Pentecost, J. Dwight. Class lecture notes on Ephesians, Dallas Theol. Sem., Spring 1957.

———. Class lecture notes on Romans, Dallas Theol. Sem., 1957.

Peters, G. W. "Major Theological Tenets of Sixteenth Century Anabaptist-Mennonitism." Bachelor of Divinity thesis, St. Andrews College, Saskatoon, Sask., 1955.

Rowe, Harley Edward. "The Kingdom in Matthew." Master's thesis, Dallas Theol. Sem., 1955.

Sanford, Carlisle J. "The Concept of *Ekklesia* in Matthew." Master's thesis, Dallas Theol. Sem., 1959.

Saucy, Robert Lloyd. "The Doctrine of the Church as a Seed of Abraham." Master's thesis, Dallas Theol. Sem., 1958.

———. "The Relationship of Dispensationalism to the Eternal Purpose of God." Doctor's dissertation, Dallas Theol. Sem., 1961.

Shive, Vernon L. "The Ecclesiology of Matthew Sixteen." Master's thesis, Dallas Theol. Sem., 1954.

Strauss, Richard L. "The Body of Christ in Ephesians." Master's thesis, Dallas Theol. Sem., 1958.

Toussaint, Stanley Dale. "The Argument of Matthew." Doctor's dissertation, Dallas Theol. Sem., 1957.

Via, Dan Otto, Jr. "The Doctrine of the Church in the Gospel of Matthew." Doctor's thesis, Grad. School of Arts and Sciences of Duke U., 1955.

Wade, Henry G. "The Church and Its Relationship With Other Churches and Institutions." Term paper for class in biblical theology, Western Conserv. Bapt. Sem., 1957.

SCRIPTURE INDEX

INDEX OF PERSONS

H

I

J

K

L

M

N

SUBJECT INDEX

N

O

P

R